teach yourself QuarkXPress 4 IN 14 DAYS

Kate Binder

Hayden Books

President
Richard K. Swadley

Publisher
John Pierce

Managing Editor
Lisa Wilson

Director of Marketing
Kelli S. Spencer

Product Marketing Manager
Kim Margolius

Acquisitions Editor
Rachel Byers

Development Editors
Brian-Kent Proffitt
Beth Millett

Production Editor
Kevin Laseau

Copy Editor
Erik Dafforn

Technical Editor
Joe Millay

Technical Edit Coordinator
Lorraine E. Schaffer

Publishing Coordinator
Karen Williams

Marketing Coordinator
Linda Beckwith

Cover Designer
Sandra Schroeder

Book Designer
Sandra Schroeder

Manufacturing Coordinator
Brook Farling

Production Team Supervisor
Brad Chinn

Production Team
Carol Bowers
Betsy Deeter
Tim Osborn
Carl Pierce

Indexer
Chris Barrick

Teach Yourself QuarkXPress 4 in 14 Days

Library of Congress Catalog Number: 96-72169
ISBN: 1-56830-411-0

Printed in the United States of America 1 2 3 4 5 6 7 8 9 0

Warning and Disclaimer

This book is sold as is, without warranty of any kind, either express or implied. While every precaution has been taken in the preparation of this book, the authors and Hayden Books assume no responsibility for errors or omissions. Neither is any liability assumed for damages resulting from the use of the information or instructions contained herein. It is further stated that the publisher and authors are not responsible for any damage or loss to your data or your equipment that results directly or indirectly from your use of this book.

Dedication

This book is dedicated to the best writer I know—my husband, novelist-to-be Don Fluckinger, who makes *me* possible.

About the Author

Kate Binder, owner of Ursa Editorial Design, is a writer and production artist from Massachusetts' North Shore. Co-author of *Photoshop 4 Complete* and a contributor to other titles such as *Illustrator 7 Complete*, Kate also inflicts her writing on readers of *DTP Journal*, where she covers topics ranging from digital cameras to proper kerning. Desktop production, technical and copyediting, and training are the other things with which Kate fills her working days (and nights). Her three favorite things (this month, anyway) are the word "dongle," Ohio hog roasts, and her Power Mac. Email UrsaDesign@aol.com, or check out the Ursa Editorial Design Web site at `http://members.aol.com/ursadesign`.

Acknowledgments

Thanks to former employers Patricia Gregg and Bob Russell, who put up with my nonsense long enough to make sure I learned QuarkXPress and learned it well. Even more thanks are due to editors Rachel Byers and Beth Millett, who taught me how to do this author thing and made sure I had a book to author.

Trademark Acknowledgments

Hayden Books

The staff of Hayden Books is committed to bringing you the best computer books. What our readers think of Hayden is important to our ability to serve our customers. If you have any comments, no matter how great or how small, we'd appreciate your taking the time to send us a note.

You can reach Hayden Books at the following:

Hayden Books
201 West 103rd Street
Indianapolis, IN 46290
317-581-3833

Internet: hayden@hayden.com

Visit the Hayden Books web site at `http://www.hayden.com`

About This Book

Certain conventions are used throughout this book. Keyboard shortcuts for Macintosh and Windows computers are designated by the Macintosh shortcut in parentheses, followed by the Windows shortcut in brackets: (Command-D)[Control-D].

Selecting commands from menus is indicated with the name of the menu, an arrow, and then the command: File➡Save.

Contents at a Glance

Contents

XPress Basics

- Using pages and spreads
- Using the pasteboard
- Using the floating palettes
- Viewing documents
- Navigating in documents
- Using rulers and guides
- Setting preferences

The key to becoming fluent in any software application is understanding the logic of the program, so that you have a reasonable idea of what you can expect the software to be able to do. With QuarkXPress, the first thing to realize is what restrictions and capabilities are imposed on the program by virtue of the software category it occupies: page layout software. Although it handles text, it's not a word processor and can't do word processor things like mail merges. And although it handles graphics, it's not a paint or draw program and can't create complex graphic images. What you can do with XPress's tools and commands is create document layouts that bring together sophisticated graphic and type treatments. In this chapter, you learn about the basic concepts that underlie QuarkXPress, along with how to set its preferences for the way you want to work.

Learning QuarkXPress's Visual Landscape

Each generation of technology has to build on what came before. QuarkXPress shows its allegiance to this principle by placing its users in a familiar print production environment that mirrors a paste-up studio. Open a QuarkXPress document, and you'll see **pages** lying on a **pasteboard**, with unneeded bits of type scattered off to the side on the pasteboard.

Non-printing **guides** are the electronic equivalent of guidelines drawn in non-repro blue ink.

But you can draw the parallels for yourself. The point is that although QuarkXPress may be able to do things you couldn't do with conventional paste-up, it works essentially the same way.

Note

As with almost all desktop computer applications these days, each QuarkXPress document occupies a separate window, with scroll bars along the bottom and right sides of the window so you can view different parts of the document. When you open a document, QuarkXPress restores the size and position of its window to the way they were the last time you worked with that file.

Pages and Spreads

The most basic concept in XPress's world is the page—all documents are made up of one or more pages, which can face each other to create spreads. It doesn't matter what you place on them—the pages are the final product, and only items placed on pages will be included when you print a document.

Before you can create a new document in XPress (see Day 2, "Creating, Opening, and Saving Documents"), you have to specify a page size. All pages in a QuarkXPress document must be the same size, and they must all be rectangular—although you can have your printer or bindery trim or fold them any way you like once they're output. Pages can be oriented in **landscape** (wide) or **portrait** (tall) mode, but all the pages in a document must have the same orientation.

Each page in XPress is bordered by a black line indicating the edge of the page and has a drop shadow behind it to help set it apart from the pasteboard surrounding it. You can't change the color of the page's "paper"; it and the pasteboard are always white (see Figure 1.1).

The Pasteboard

The pasteboard fulfills the same function as your work surface (whether it's a paste-up table or a desk) does in real life—a place to put your work and the stuff you're adding to and removing from it. In this case, that work consists of pages and the elements you're putting on the pages. You can leave as much stuff as you like lying around on the pasteboard, and unless it touches a page it'll never show up in a printout (see Figure 1.2). Because they're saved with the document, though, items on the pasteboard will make your files bigger, so delete items you're never going to need again.

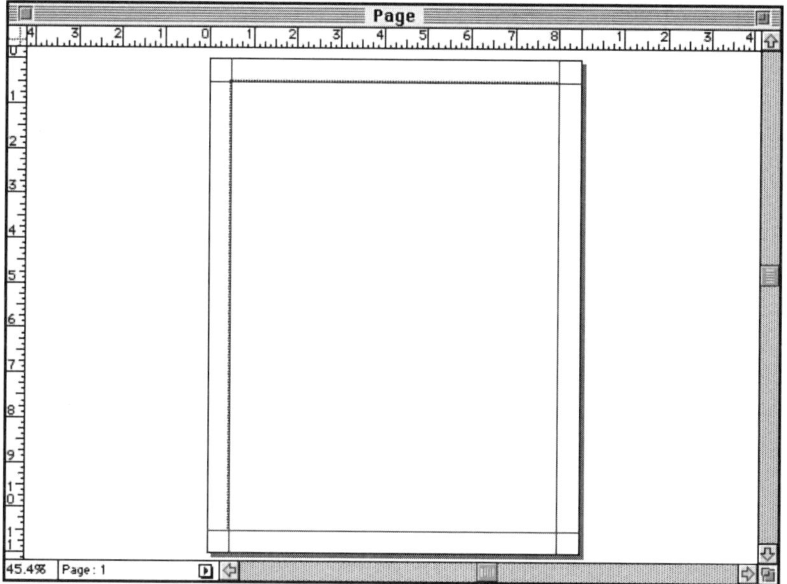

Figure 1.1

The almighty page—the basic unit of all QuarkXPress documents.

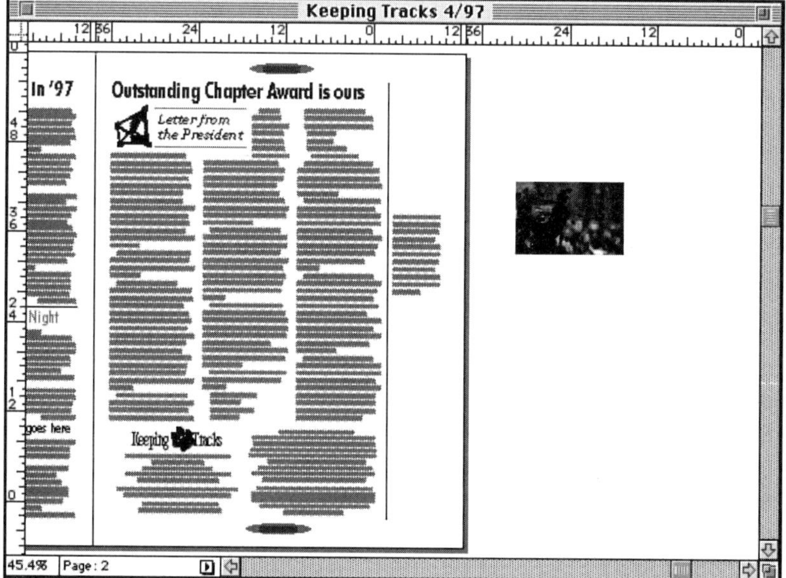

Figure 1.2

The photo to the right of the page won't be included when this document is printed, but it will remain on the pasteboard.

Note

PageMaker users are used to using the pasteboard, too, but they get only one for all their pages—anything on the pasteboard shows up next to every page in a document. In QuarkXPress, the pasteboard is as big as your document—it's like a magically expanding table that can hold all your pages at once, whereas PageMaker's pasteboard is like a small table that can hold only one or two pages at a time. If you drag an item onto the pasteboard next to page 2 of a document, you won't see that item anywhere except next to page 2.

Why would you place items on the pasteboard instead of directly on the page? Here are a few thoughts:

- You're not sure yet where an item will go or if you'll want it on the page at all.
- You need an overflow box to hold text that won't fit on its assigned page.
- You aren't using an element in this version of the document, but you'll need it again later.
- You're considering several alternative elements for a page—different photos or logos, for example.
- You want to leave a note for the next person who will use the file.

You can set the width of the pasteboard; see "Customizing QuarkXPress with Preferences," later in this chapter.

Document Elements

QuarkXPress is known for its box-based interface; it used to be that every element other than a line had to be inside a box. In version 4.0, you can place text along a line, but with this single exception, design elements, whether text or graphics, must still be placed within boxes. **Text boxes** contain text, and **picture boxes** contain **imported** graphics. **Empty boxes** don't contain other objects, but they can be used as graphic elements with colored **fills** and **borders** or to mask other elements. Figure 1.3 shows one of each kind of box.

Although you can't place text in a picture box, or vice versa, you can change a box's type; each kind of box can be converted into either of the other kinds. Once created, boxes can be moved, resized, deleted, assigned borders and colors, and set to print or not to print, as you require.

For more about creating and using boxes and other document elements, see Day 3, "Creating Text and Graphic Elements."

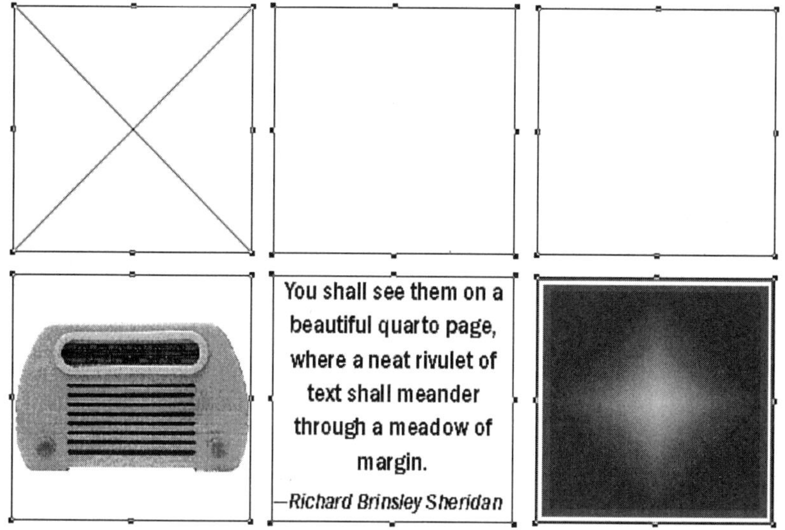

Figure 1.3

From left to right, a picture box, a text box, and an empty box. When it's empty, the picture box can always be identified by the "X" through it, whereas the text and empty boxes look the same. In the bottom row are the same boxes, filled with a picture, text, and a colored fill, respectively.

Using the Palettes

One of the first programs to introduce floating palettes, QuarkXPress has nine of them: Tools, Measurements, Document Layout, Styles, Colors, Lists, Profile Information, Trap Information, and Index. Some of these palettes, such as the Styles palette, duplicate menu commands, whereas others provide functions not accessible any other way, such as the Index and Lists palettes.

XPress remembers which palettes were showing and where they were placed when you quit the program and returns the palettes to that configuration the next time you start it up. You can show and hide palettes by using the Show/Hide commands in the View menu or their keyboard equivalents; you can also click the close box at the top-left corner of a palette to hide the palette, just as you'd close a window.

The Tool Palette

The Tool palette (press F8) initially shows 14 tools, but it contains variations on some of these tools in side menus (see Figure 1.4). To choose a tool, click its icon in the Tool palette; the tools and their uses (from top to bottom) are as follows:

- **Item**: Select, move, copy, and paste boxes and other elements.
- **Content**: Select, move, copy, and paste the contents of text and picture boxes.

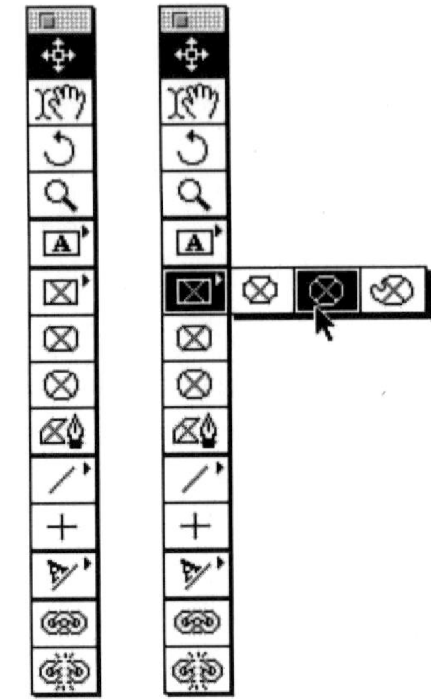

Figure 1.4

The Tool palette starts out with a set of default tools (left), but other tools are accessible via pop-up side menus (indicated by triangles next to tool icons). Here you can see the variations of the Picture Box tool.

Note

The Item and Content tools share a lot of the same functions, so it takes some practice to know which to use in a given situation. The key is to remember their names: the Item tool is for selecting and moving items as a whole, including their contents, whereas the Content tool is for adjusting what's inside boxes, such as selecting text and repositioning imported graphics within their boxes.

- **Rotation**: Rotate boxes and other elements.
- **Zoom**: Change the view percentage.
- **Text Box** (Rectangle, Rounded-Corner, Concave-Corner, Beveled-Corner, Oval, Bézier, Freehand Bézier): Create text boxes.
- **Picture Box** (Rectangle, Concave-Corner, Beveled-Corner, Freehand Bézier): Create picture boxes.
- **Rounded-Corner Picture Box**: Create rounded-corner picture boxes.
- **Oval Picture Box**: Create oval picture boxes.
- **Bézier Picture Box**: Create freeform picture boxes.
- **Line** (Line, Bézier Line, Freehand Bézier Line): Create straight or curved lines at any angle.
- **Orthogonal Line**: Create vertical or horizontal straight lines.

- **Line Text-Path** (Orthogonal, Bézier, Freehand Bézier): Create paths that can hold text.
- **Linking**: Link text boxes.
- **Unlinking**: Unlink text boxes.

Tip

Press (Command-Tab)[Control-Tab] to choose the next tool, or (Command-Shift-Tab)[Control-Shift-Tab] to choose the previous tool.

To choose one of the "extra" tools, click and hold down the mouse button on one of the tools with an arrow next to it; a "menu" of additional tools appears, and you can scroll across it and stop on the tool you want to use. That tool takes the original tool's place in the Tool palette. To add a tool to the palette without removing its "parent" tool, (Command-click)[Control-click] to select a tool (the palette grows to hold the additional tools). (Command-click)[Control-click] again to remove the tool from the palette. The Tool palette remains configured the same from session to session, retaining whatever changes you make to it.

Tip

The **Grabber Hand** is a hidden tool; all the tools except the Zoom tool turn into a grabber hand when you hold down the (Option)[Alt] key. Click and drag with the Grabber Hand to move around a page or document (see Figure 1.5).

The Measurements Palette

The Measurements palette contains controls for changing the size and position of boxes and adjusting their content, whether type or graphics. Its controls, in the form of numerical entry fields, pop-up menus, and buttons, change depending on the type of object that's currently selected and the tool used to select it (see Figure 1.6). Press F9 to show or hide the Measurements palette, and (Command-Option-M)[Control-Alt-M] to select the first field (the X coordinate of the selected object with respect to the page's zero point). If the selected object is a text box or text path, press Shift-F9 to jump directly to the font field on the Measurements palette. In any field, make sure the current value is selected, type the new value (or font name, and press (Return)[Enter] to change the value or font.

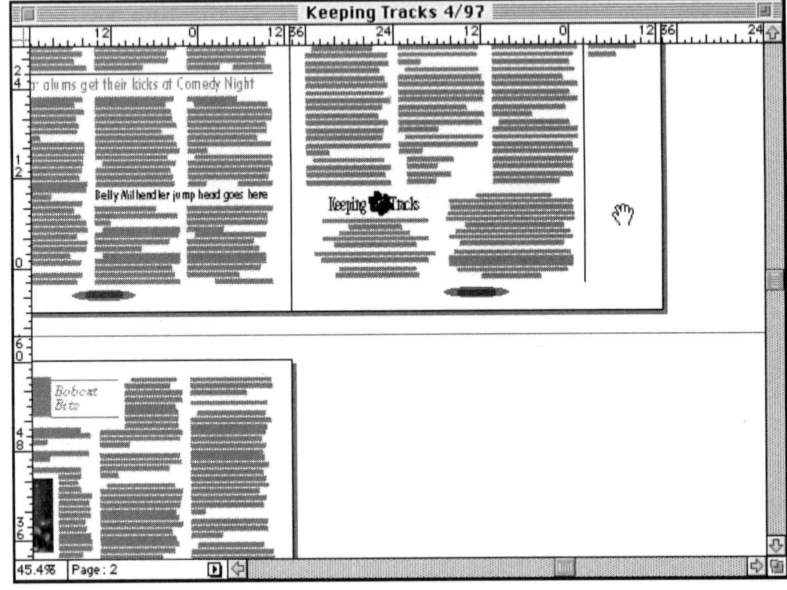

Figure 1.5

With the Grabber Hand, you can move pages around on the screen just as though you were moving them with your own hand.

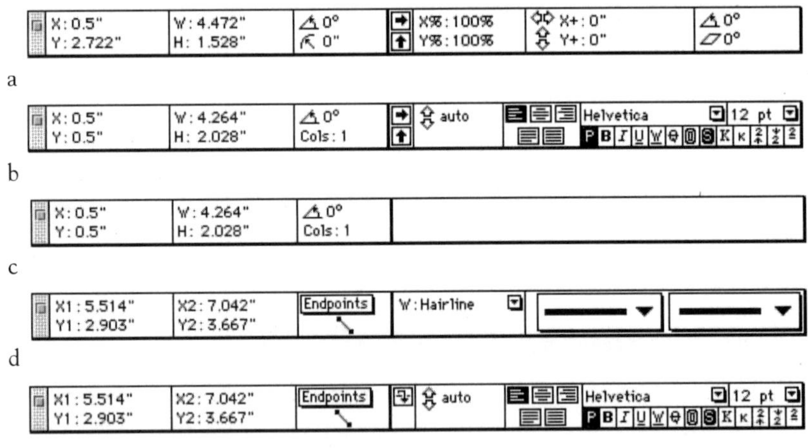

Figure 1.6

The Measurements palette changes as different items are selected. (a) picture box selected; (b) text box selected with Content tool; (c) text box selected with Item tool; (d) text path selected with Item tool; and (e) text path selected with Content tool.

See Day 4, "Importing and Editing Text," and Day 5, "Formatting Text and Using Style Sheets" for more information on using the Measurements palette.

The Document Layout Palette

The Document Layout palette (press (F10)[F4]) shows a **thumbnail** representation of your entire document, with an icon for each document page and each master page. You can add **document pages** and **master pages**, change page numbering, move pages around, and apply master pages using the Document Layout palette (see Figure 1.7). Most of the time, though, this palette is incredibly handy for moving around a document (by double-clicking on a page icon) and viewing the pages' relationships to each other.

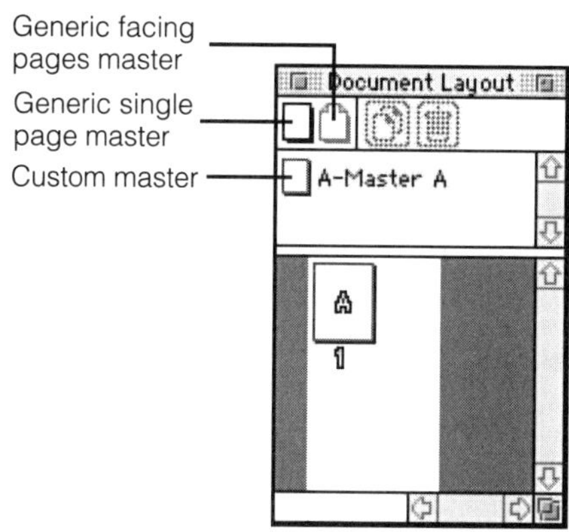

Figure 1.7

The Document Layout palette in its simplest possible form, displaying a single-sided document with one page and one master page.

See Day 8, "Creating and Using Master Pages," for more about manipulating document pages using the Document Layout palette; see "Viewing and Navigating Within Documents," later this chapter, to learn how to move around a document using the Document Layout palette.

The Style Sheets Palette

The Style Sheets palette (press F11) contains a list of the paragraph and character **style sheets** in a document, which are collections of (respectively) paragraph and character attributes that can be applied to text (see Figure 1.8). Clicking a character style name in the Style Sheets palette applies that style to any text that's currently selected, while clicking on a paragraph style name applies that style to the entire paragraph the **text cursor** is currently in. The palette's styles are grayed out if there's no text box or text path selected.

See Day 5, "Formatting Text and Using Style Sheets," for more information on using the Styles palette to create and apply style sheets.

The Colors Palette

The Colors palette displays the colors defined for use in a document; using the Colors palette, you can apply colors to lines, object borders, text, **imported graphics**, and the interior of picture and text boxes (see Figure 1.9).

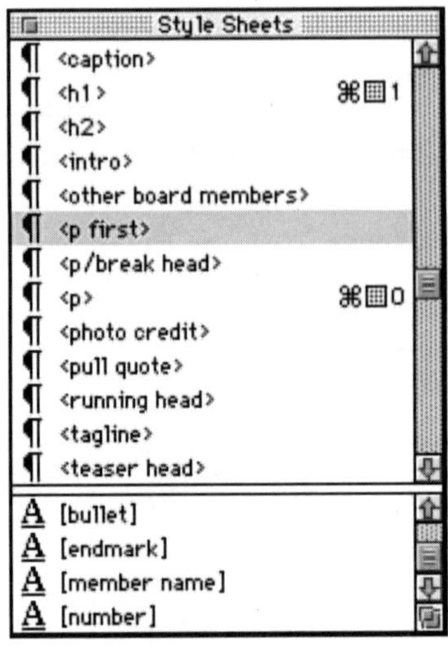

Figure 1.8

The Style Sheets palette shows the document's style sheets and their associated keyboard shortcuts.

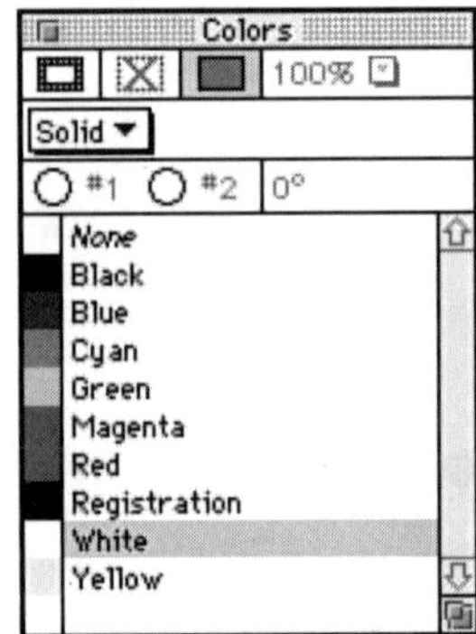

Figure 1.9

The three buttons at the top of the Colors palette determine what part of an element will take on the color selected: the border, the contents (for pictures) or text (for text), or the interior of the box itself.

The Colors palette always shows the four **process ink colors** (cyan, magenta, yellow, and black) and white; by default, it shows red, green, and blue as well, but these colors can be deleted from a document. A "None" color can be applied to box interiors, but not to contents, for example, text or imported graphics. See Day 9, "Using Color," for more information on using the Colors palette.

The Lists Palette

The Lists palette shows the lists defined for use in a document, such as tables of contents and lists of figures. Lists are compiled based on the style sheets used in a document; for example, a list of figures might include the text of all paragraphs in the document that use "Figure number" and "Figure caption" style sheets. The list shown in Figure 1.10 is built from the "Chapter number" and "Chapter title" style sheets in a book about cats.

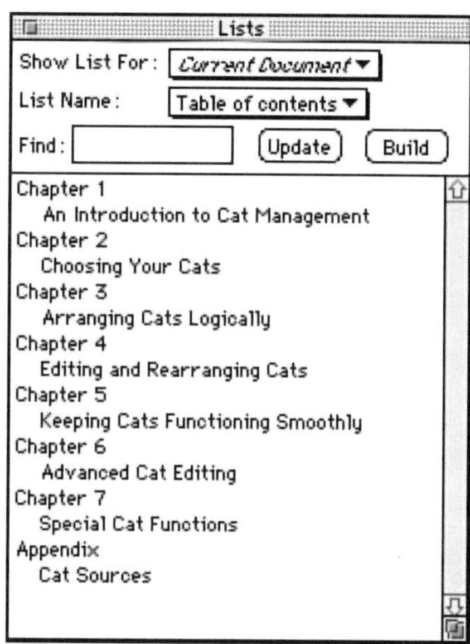

Figure 1.10

This Lists palette displays the "Table of contents" list for a book.

You can display the contents of a list by choosing a list from the List Name pop-up menu, and you can see each list entry in the document window by double-clicking on it in the Lists palette. The Build and Update buttons are used to generate the actual text of the lists.

See Day 10, "Managing Long Documents," for more information about defining and generating lists.

The Trap Information Palette

Trapping refers to slight alterations in the shape of overlapping colored objects so that any misregistration in printing plates won't cause the paper color to show through where it shouldn't. The Trap Information palette (see Figure 1.11) displays information about how a selected object will be trapped, including how large the trap, or overlap, will be, what colors the overlapping objects use, and whether the trapping value of the selected object is taken from the document-wide Trapping preferences or is a value entered by the user specifically for that object.

See Day 12, "Printing," for more information on using trapping.

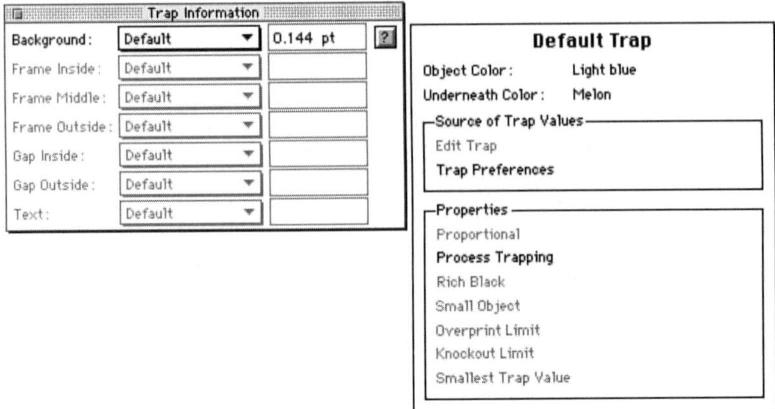

Figure 1.11

Clicking the question mark icon on the Trap Information palette brings up the additional information shown on the right.

The Profile Information Palette

The Profile Information palette shows what **device profile** has been assigned to an imported picture (see Figure 1.12). The device profile provides information about the scanner, digital camera, or other device that originated the image, so that XPress's **color management** software can try to ensure that the color onscreen and in the printed output of the document matches the original image. The palette also enables you to turn off color correction for individual images.

Profile Information
Picture Type: Color
File Type: TIFF
Color Space: RGB
Profile: Apple 13" RGB Standard
☒ Color Correction

Figure 1.12

The Profile Information palette shows the color management device profile assigned to imported images.

See Day 9 for more information on color management.

The Index Palette

The Index palette lists the **index markers** that have been placed in a document's text and enables you to control how each marker will be used in the index—what its indent level will be, how it will be formatted, and how its page number should be calculated (see Figure 1.13). You can also use the Index palette to find index markers in the text.

See Day 10 for more information about creating indexes.

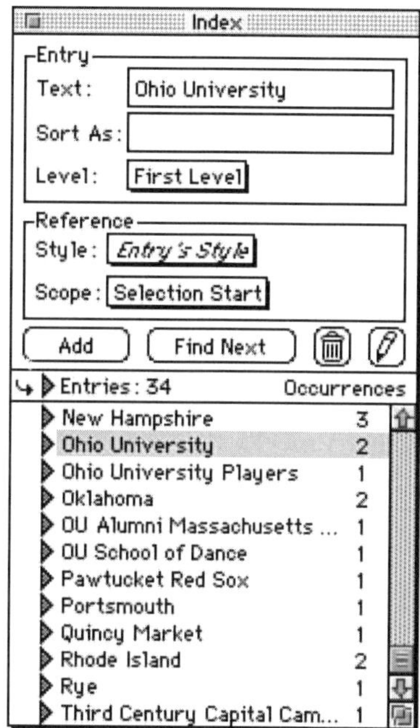

Figure 1.13

The text of each index marker inserted in the text is listed in the Index palette.

Viewing and Navigating Within Documents

If most of your XPress documents are one-page flyers or business-card layouts, it may seem silly to spend so much time talking about navigating documents. But as documents grow (to hundreds of pages in some cases) and become more complex, you'll need to know the best ways to move around from page to page. XPress also offers several kinds of visual guides to help in placing objects.

Viewing Documents at Different Sizes

You can view documents at any percentage between 10% and 800%. Zooming out to lower percentages lets you see more of a page or multiple pages at one time, depending on the page size and the size of your monitor; zooming in to higher percentages lets you see individual elements at larger sizes. There are several ways to zoom in and out of a document.

- Press (Command-Option-V)[Control-Alt-V] or double-click in the View Percentage field in the lower-left corner of the document window, then type a new view percentage and press (Return)[Enter] (see Figure 1.14).

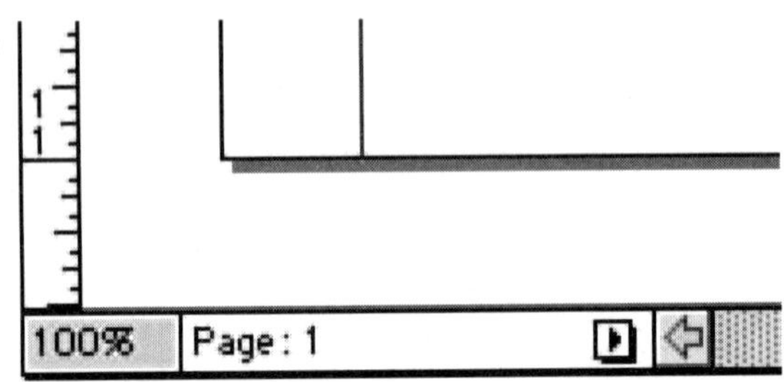

Figure 1.14

Type a different percentage in the View Percentage field to zoom in or zoom out.

- Click with the Zoom tool, which looks like a magnifying glass with a plus sign on the lens, to zoom in; (Option-click)[right-click] to zoom out (the plus sign changes to a minus sign). You can specify the amount that the view percentage changes with each click in the preferences (see "Document Preferences," later this chapter).
- Again using the Zoom tool, click and drag to fill the document window with a specific portion of the document (this is how you end up with strange view percentages like 314.7%).

Tip

Temporarily switch to the Zoom tool while any other tool is active by holding down the Control key (Mac OS users) or holding down the Shift key and clicking with the right mouse button (Windows users) to zoom in. Add (Option)[Control] to that combination to zoom out.

- Choose one of the following commands from the View menu: Fit in Window ((Command-0)[Control-0]), 50%, 75%, Actual Size ((Command-1)[Control-1]), 200%, or Thumbnails (Shift-F6).

Tip

Hold down (Option)[Control] as you choose View➡Fit in Window to adjust the view so that the entire width of the pasteboard fits in the window, rather than just the width of the pages or spreads. This will enable you to see all the elements that are on the pasteboard.

Note

Thumbnails view is a special view equivalent to 12%; the difference is that you can only select entire pages, rather than individual objects, in Thumbnails view. Use it for rearranging pages in a document and for dragging pages from one document to another—just click a page, or shift-click a range of pages, and drag (see Figure 1.15).

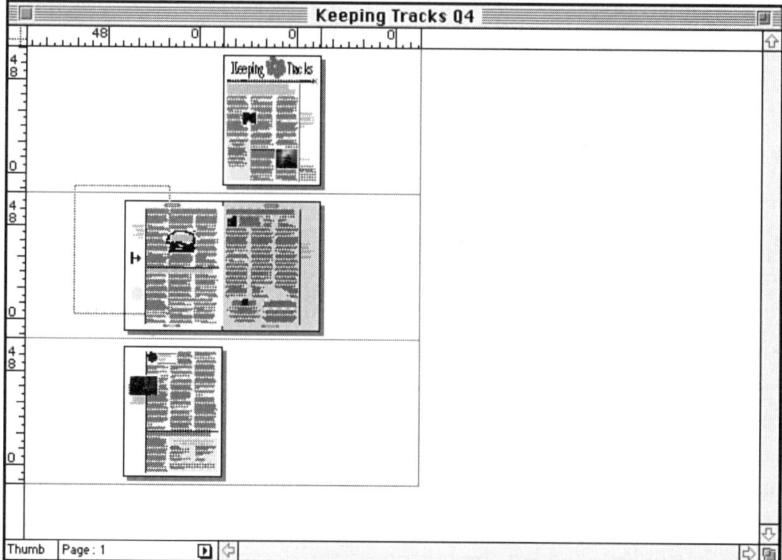

Figure 1.15

In Thumbnails view you can move document pages by dragging them just as you can in the Document Layout palette.

Moving Around a Document

The more pages your documents have, the more important it becomes to know how to get to any given page when you need to. You can move around your document in several ways; some (such as the Go to command) work best with long documents and others (such as the window scroll bars) work best with short documents.

- Choose Page➡Go or press (Command-J)[Control-J] and enter a page number to view a specific page (see Figure 1.16).

Figure 1.16

The Go to Page dialog box.

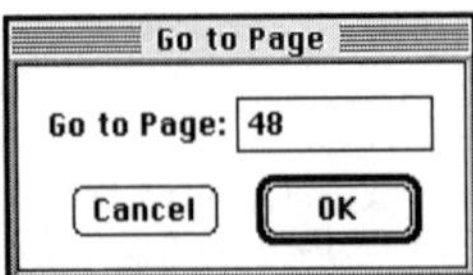

Tip

If you can't remember the page number you want, but you know it's the fifth page in the document (for example, when the document is a book chapter that starts on page 57 rather than page 1), enter +5 in the Go to Page dialog box. This works with printing, too—enter +5 in the From and To fields of the Print dialog box to print only the fifth page of the document, no matter what its actual page number is.

- To move back and forth between the master pages and the document pages, choose Page➡View Masters or Page➡View Document.
- The Document Layout palette is designed to give you a view of your entire document (see Figure 1.17). Move to a particular document or master page by double-clicking on its icon in the palette.
- Use the document window's scroll bars to move around a document; click the arrows to move a specified distance (see "Application Preferences," later this chapter for how to adjust the Scroll Speed), or click in the gray area of the scroll bars to jump one screen at a time. Or be a traditionalist and move the slider box in the scroll bars.
- Double-click in the Page field at the bottom of the document window, type in a new page number, and press (Return)[Enter] (see Figure 1.18).
- Click the small triangle in the Page field at the bottom of the document window to display an iconic menu of master and document pages in the document. Slide the mouse until the page you want to go to is highlighted, then let go of the mouse button (see Figure 1.19).
- If you have an extended keyboard, you can use the Home and End keys to view the beginning and end of a document, respectively. The Page Up and Page Down keys move you up and down one screen at a time, but holding down the (Command)[Control] key as you press Page Up or Page Down moves you to the previous or next page in the document, and holding down (Option)[Alt] with Page Up or Page Down moves you to the page directly above or below the one you're on—so if you're on a left-hand page, you move to the previous or next left-hand page.

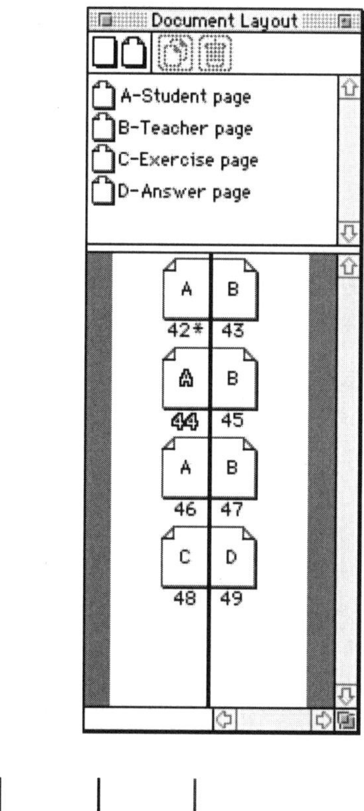

Figure 1.17

The Document Layout palette shows all master and document pages; the master page letter and page number are in outline style for the current page (in this case, 44).

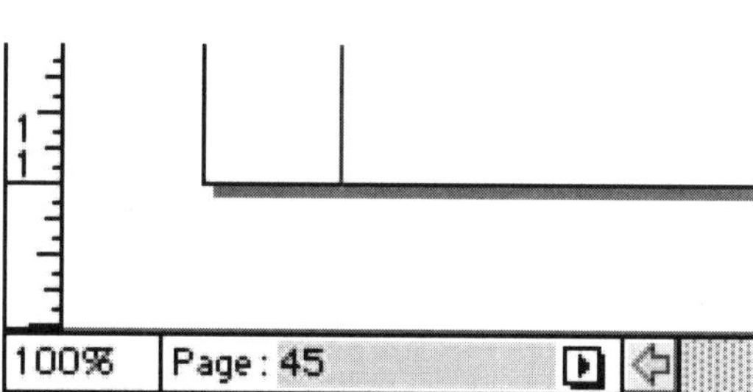

Figure 1.18

Select the current page number in the Page field and type another page number to jump to a different page.

Using Rulers and Guides

XPress users have always appreciated the level of precision the software enables in everything from kerning to object placement on the page. **Rulers** and guides help in placing objects, and they can be made visible and hidden as necessary.

Rulers

The rulers along the top and left edges of document windows can help you estimate the size of objects as you create and edit them (see Figure 1.20). They can use one of several units of measurement (such as inches or picas) or be hidden to give you more viewable area within a document window; press (Command-R)[Control-R] to toggle between showing and hiding the rulers. See "Document Preferences," later this chapter, for how to change the units used by the rulers.

Figure 1.19

If you're constitutionally opposed to the Document Layout palette, try the Page pop-up menu for navigating your documents.

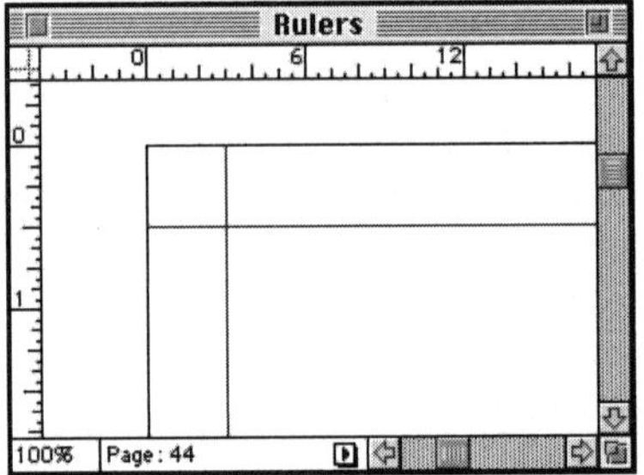

Figure 1.20

The rulers are marked in the units specified in the preferences; this document's rulers show inches down and picas across.

Ruler Guides

Ruler guides act as an extension of the rulers, letting you align more than one object in a specific position on the page. To place a horizontal ruler guide on the page, click on the top ruler and pull the mouse down; use the left-hand ruler for vertical guides. If the Measurements palette is visible, the position of the guide is displayed there; the position of the guide is also marked by a gray line—really an extension of the guide—on the opposite ruler to the one from which the guide originated. So if you pull down a horizontal guide from the horizontal ruler, it will move up and down on the page, and a gray tick-mark will move up and down on the vertical ruler at the side of the page.

Guides can be placed either on the page alone or on the pasteboard (in which case they'll extend across the entire pasteboard and both pages of a spread). Which type of guide you place is determined by where your mouse is when you stop dragging the guide and let go of it; if you're over the page, the guide will be a page guide, and if you're over the pasteboard, the guide will be placed on the pasteboard (see Figure 1.21). To move a guide, just click and drag. You might have trouble with this sometimes if you're clicking over an object; the solution is to click somewhere else along the guide.

Figure 1.21

The upper guide was placed on the page, whereas the lower one was dragged onto the pasteboard.

Guides can be hidden without removing them from a document (choose View➡Show/Hide Guides or press F7), so you can get a better idea of what the layout looks like, and you can pick the colors you prefer for guides in preferences (see "Document Preferences," later this chapter). Turning on Snap to Guides (choose View➡Snap to Guides or press Shift-F7) forces objects to align perfectly with a guide as soon as they get within a user-specified distance of it (see "Document Preferences," later this chapter).

Note

Margin guides, defined by the margin measurements you enter when you create a document, are similar to ruler guides but can't be moved with the mouse. To change margins, choose File➡Document Setup.

Baseline Grid

The **baseline grid** is a set of horizontal guides a specified distance apart that's intended to help you maintain consistent vertical spacing among text elements; press (Option-F7)[Control-F7] to show and hide the baseline grid (see Figure 1.22). The Snap to Grid feature works the same way as the Snap to Guides feature, using the same preferences setting for how close your cursor must be before it snaps to the guide. If the baseline grid is visible, Snap to Grid is automatically on; turn it off by hiding the grid.

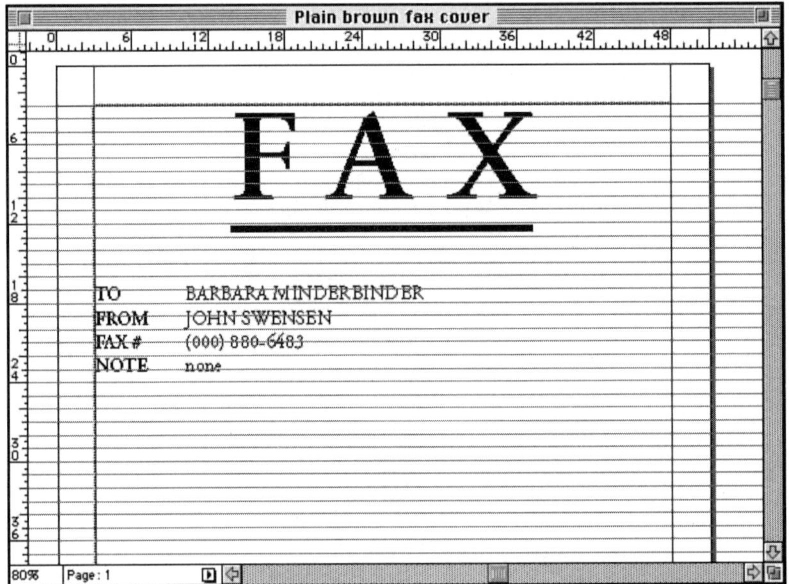

Figure 1.22

The baseline grid.

You can also choose a color for the baseline grid and specify at what vertical point on the page it starts (see "Document Preferences," later this chapter).

Note

Unfortunately, QuarkXPress doesn't have a built-in way to create multiple evenly spaced vertical guides, but you can use third-party XTensions such as Guide Master, GridLock II, and Scitex Grids & Guides to accomplish this. See Day 13, "XTending XPress's Capabilities," for more information on these and other XTensions.

Switching Documents

View➥Windows lets you stack or tile documents and move from one document window to another; Mac users can also access the commands in this submenu by Shift-clicking the title bar of the active document window (see Figure 1.23). If you can see another document window, the quickest way to get to it is just to click on it.

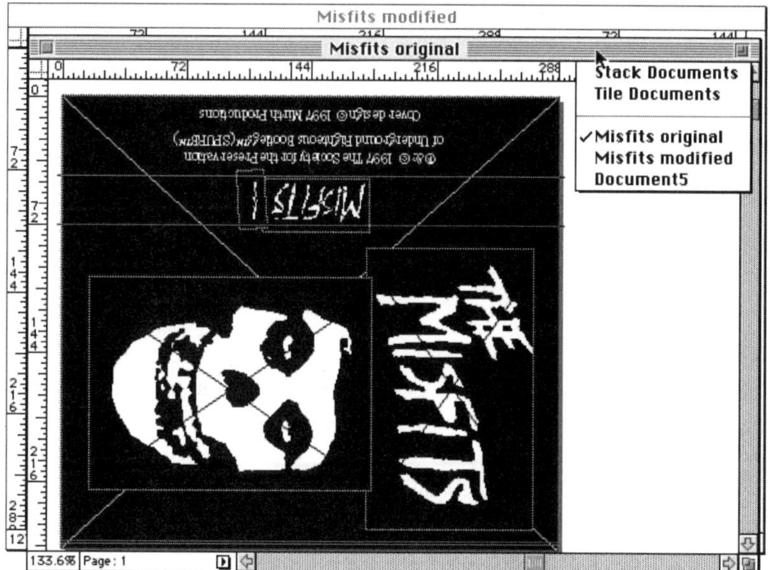

Figure 1.23

Mac users can also use the View➥Windows commands by Shift-clicking the active window's title bar.

Windows users can cycle through all open documents one at a time by pressing Control-F4.

Redraw

Your computer has to redraw the screen every time you change an element in a QuarkXPress document. Sometimes the screen isn't redrawn correctly due to minor bugs in either the system software or QuarkXPress; in this case, you can force XPress to redraw the screen.

- Press (Command-Option-.)[Shift-Escape] to force a redraw.
- Press Escape to stop a redraw.

You can continue working while the screen redraws, a familiar capability to Photoshop users.

Customizing QuarkXPress with Preferences

QuarkXPress divides its **preferences** into several sections, based on whether they control features of the application itself, the documents you create, or XTensions. As soon as you start to become comfortable with what XPress looks like and what you can do with it, you should close all open documents and set all the preferences as you like them; then each new document will open with those preferences already assigned to it.

Application Preferences

To set preferences that affect how XPress works, choose Edit➡Preferences➡Application, or press (Command-Option-Shift-Y)[Control-Alt-Shift-Y]. Within Application Preferences, several groups of settings are indicated by tabs in the dialog box.

Display Preferences

Click on the Display tab to change preferences relating to how documents look on the screen (see Figure 1.24).

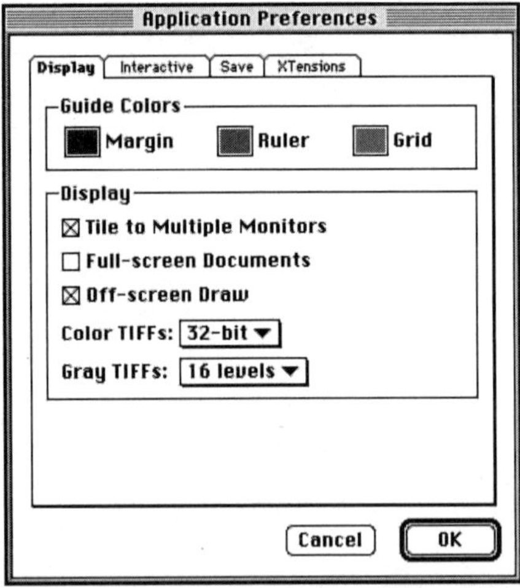

Figure 1.24

The Display tab of the Application Preferences dialog box.

- Specify colors for the various guides (Margin, Ruler, and Grid) by clicking the color swatches and using the **Color Picker** to choose new colors. The default colors are bright blue for margin guides, green for ruler guides, and pink for the baseline grid.

- In Application Preferences, "tiling" refers to resizing document windows so that they're all the same size and placed next to each other, without overlapping. If you're using more than one monitor, check Tile to Multiple Monitors to enable QuarkXPress to use both screens when it tiles open documents.

Tip

Most people who use more than one monitor prefer to move all the palettes to the smaller screen and use the larger screen to display the document itself. That way the palettes can be displayed all the time without covering up any of the document window. If you want to work this way, leave Tile to Multiple Monitors unchecked to keep XPress from placing documents on the second monitor when it tiles.

- Check Full-screen Documents to display document windows using almost the entire screen, rather than the somewhat smaller window XPress usually uses.
- Check Off-screen Draw to force XPress to redraw the entire screen at once, rather than a portion at a time.
- Choose a **color depth** for the screen preview of color TIFFs: 8-bit, 16-bit, or 32-bit. The higher the color depth, the closer to the actual picture the preview will look, but the longer XPress will take to redraw the screen any time it has to show color TIFFs. Generally, stick to 8-bit previews unless you really need screen previews to look like the original images, such as if you'll be showing a layout to a client onscreen. This setting doesn't affect the actual image, only the way it's shown onscreen.
- You have the same choice for **grayscale TIFF** previews; choose either 16 levels or 256 levels from the Gray TIFFs pop-up menu. Again, the lower the settings, the faster the screen redraw.

Interactive Preferences

Click on the Interactive tab to set preferences affecting how QuarkXPress deals with your commands to it (see Figure 1.25).

- Several settings affect how fast you can scroll around a document. First, adjust the Speed slider between Fast and Slow to set how far the window "jumps" each time you click on an arrow in the window's scroll bars. Then click Speed Scroll off or on—generally on—to temporarily "greek" (display as gray boxes) pictures and blends as you scroll. Turn on Live Scroll to update the document as you scroll rather than only when you've finished scrolling.

Figure 1.25

The Interactive tab of the Application preferences.

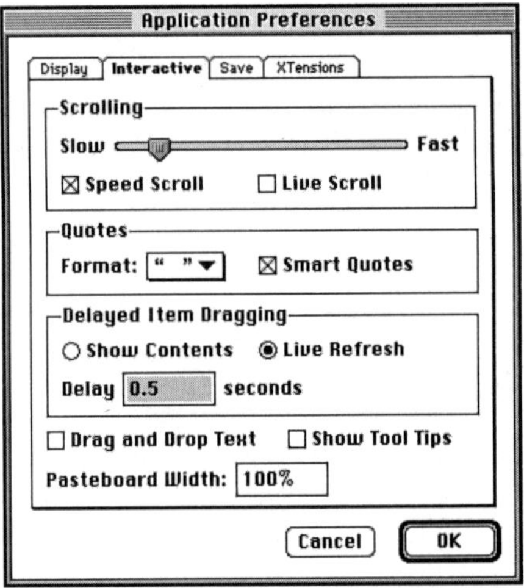

Tip

You can turn Live Scroll off and on temporarily by pressing (Option)[Alt] as you scroll to toggle to the opposite of the preferences setting for the duration of that scrolling operation.

- Check **Smart Quotes** on to automatically insert typographer's quotation marks and apostrophes when you type straight ones, then choose a format for the quotation marks from the Format pop-up menu. The different formats are used in different countries, so choose the format that's most common in your country.

Tip

Hold down the Control key as you type quotation marks and apostrophes to insert straight ones even if Smart Quotes is on. (Windows users, use Control for apostrophes and Control-Alt for quotation marks.)

- With the Delayed Item Dragging settings, you can see a more accurate screen image as you drag objects. Click Show Contents to display the contents, either text or a picture, of a box as you drag it, and click Live Refresh to update the other objects on the screen (with respect to text flow, primarily) as you drag an object. These features are activated by clicking on an object and waiting for a few seconds before you start dragging it; you can specify how long that wait must be to activate the features by entering a value between .1 and 5 (in seconds) in the Delay field.

- Just as you do in a word processor, you can drag and drop text in QuarkXPress. Click Drag and Drop Text on to enable this feature, then cut-and-paste by selecting, clicking the selection, and dragging, and copy-and-paste by selecting, clicking the selection, and Shift-dragging.

Tip

Even if Drag and Drop Text is turned off in your preferences, Mac users can use the feature by Command-Control-dragging to cut and Command-Control-Shift-dragging to copy text.

- Click Show Tool Tips on to display the names of tools or palette icons when your cursor hovers over them for a second.
- Set your preferred Pasteboard Width as a percentage of the page width in the document. If, for example, Pasteboard Width is set at 100%, the pasteboard in a letter-size document will be 8 1/2" wide on either side of a page or spread. No matter how low you set the Pasteboard Width, though, the minimum size of the pasteboard is .5" on either side; the maximum size of the pasteboard plus the document page or spread is 48". You can't specify the vertical size of the pasteboard; it's always .5".

Tip

Markzware's freeware Mac XTension Pasteboard XT lets you set both the height and width of the pasteboard as percentages; as with XPress's own preference setting, neither the height or the width of the pasteboard plus the document page or spread can total more than 48". You can download the XTension at `http://www.markzware.com`.

This XTension caused all kinds of havoc in its early days because after you'd saved a document while Pasteboard XT was installed—even if you weren't using its pasteboard-extending features—someone who didn't have that XTension installed couldn't open the document. That's no longer a problem with more recent versions of the software.

Saving Preferences

Click the Save tab to change settings affecting how documents are saved (see Figure 1.26).

Figure 1.26

The Save tab of the Application Preferences dialog box.

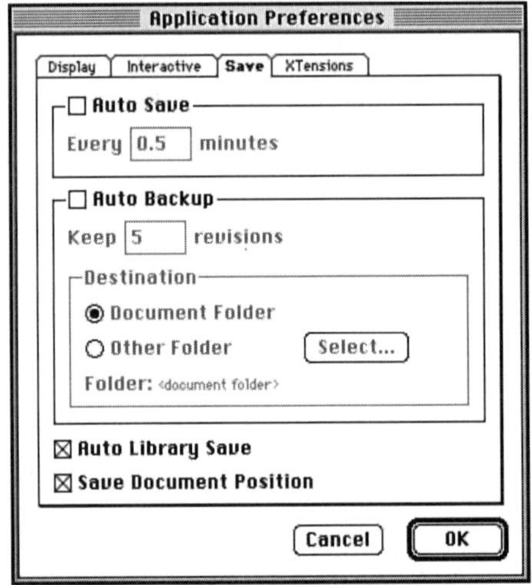

- Because we don't always remember to save as often as we should (and realizing that you didn't save after the power goes off can be very traumatic), XPress can automatically save open documents at specified intervals between .25 minutes and 10,000 minutes. Auto Save creates a temporary file and saves the changes there, rather than overwriting the original file. When you reopen a document after a crash or power failure, you get the choice of reverting to the **Auto Saved** version or the last version you saved manually (using File➥Save). Saving often can slow you down because you can't work while XPress is actually saving a file to disk, but it's usually worth it! Try an interval of 5 minutes, and adjust it up or down depending on how much you hate redoing your work and how often you crash.

Note

Macintosh Auto Save files have ".AutoSave" tacked on to the end, whereas Windows Auto Save files use a file extension of ".ASV."

- Once you've got that saving thing down, the next step is backing up files. Check Auto Backup to have a specified number of revisions (between 1 and 100) stored in a folder of your choice; choosing Document (Folder)[Directory] stores the backup versions in the same folder or directory as the original document, while clicking Other (Folder)[Directory] leads you to a dialog where you can specify another folder or directory. Each time you save, the previous version is renamed with a number tacked onto the end of the filename and moved to the specified folder or directory. When the specified number of backups has been reached, XPress starts deleting the oldest backup files.

  How many backups you keep depends on how often you find yourself wishing you could go back in time to *before* you made a change. Most users don't use this feature at all, but if you're really safety-conscious it can be helpful. Note that XPress saves the 100 (or whatever number) most recent revisions of all the files you're working on, not 100 of each. The backup files are regular XPress files and can be opened, renamed, and deleted just like any other files.
- Check Auto **Library** Save to save changes to a library every time you add an entry to it. Keeping this setting on ensures that your libraries will be saved intact.
- Check Save Document Position if you want the document window to have the same size and position the next time you open the document. Turning this preference on keeps document windows from opening at full-screen size unless they were that size when you closed the document, even if Full-screen Documents is checked in Display Preferences.

XTensions Manager Preferences

Click on the **XTensions** tab to adjust settings for the XTensions Manager, which determines which XTensions load each time you start up QuarkXPress (see Figure 1.27).

- The only decision you need to make on this tab is when you want the XTensions Manager displayed automatically (Show XTensions Manager at startup); choose Always, When XTensions folder changes, or When Error loading XTensions occurs. You probably don't want to see the XTensions Manager every time you run XPress, so pick one of the other choices depending on how much of a control freak you are.

Document Preferences

To set preferences that affect XPress documents, choose Edit➡Preferences➡Document, or press (Command-Y)[Control-Y]. Within Document Preferences, several groups of settings are indicated by tabs in the dialog box.

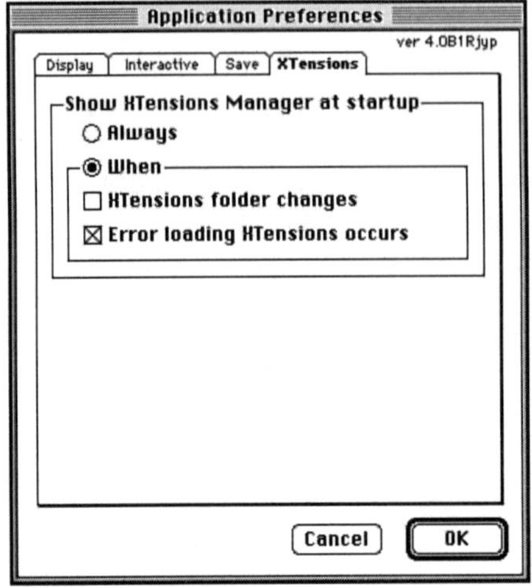

Figure 1.27

The XTensions tab of the Application Preferences dialog box.

General Preferences

Click on the General tab to change preferences controlling several different aspects of each document (see Figure 1.28).

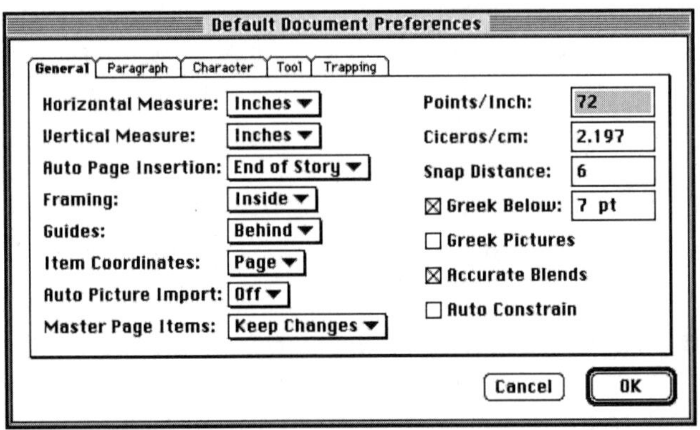

Figure 1.28

The General tab of the Default Document Preferences dialog box.

- Choose measurement units for the horizontal ruler from the Horizontal Measure pop-up menu; you can use Inches, Inches Decimal, Picas, Points, Millimeters, Centimeters, Ciceros, and Agates. Inches display on the ruler with tick marks every eighth of an inch, whereas Inches Decimal puts a tick mark every tenth of an inch.
- Choose a corresponding unit from the Vertical Measure pop-up menu; the choices are the same as for Horizontal Measure. The horizontal and vertical units don't have to be the same, but unless you're designing a newspaper (in

which case you might want picas across and inches down) you'll probably want them to be the same.

Note

The units you choose for horizontal and vertical rulers are also used in the Measurements palette, the Modify dialog box, and other places where measurements are shown. You can use different units in these places by typing in a number and the unit rather than just the number.

- Turn Auto Page Insertion off or on; turn it off if your document must be a certain number of pages and turn it on (by choosing a location for inserted pages) if you want pages inserted to hold overflow text from the pages in your document. By default, Auto Page Insertion is on, with new pages added at the end of the overflowing story; you can also choose to have pages added at the end of the section containing the overflowing text or at the end of the document.
- Choose an option for the position of box borders (or frames) from the Framing pop-up menu; Inside places the borders of all subsequently created boxes inside the dimensions of the box, whereas Outside places borders outside the box (see Figure 1.29). Use Inside if you want the box's total size, including the border, to equal the measurements shown for it; use Outside if you want the measurements to represent the empty space inside the box—in other words, the size of the box not including the border. This preference option doesn't affect whether individual boxes have borders, just where the borders will be placed if you do add one to a box.

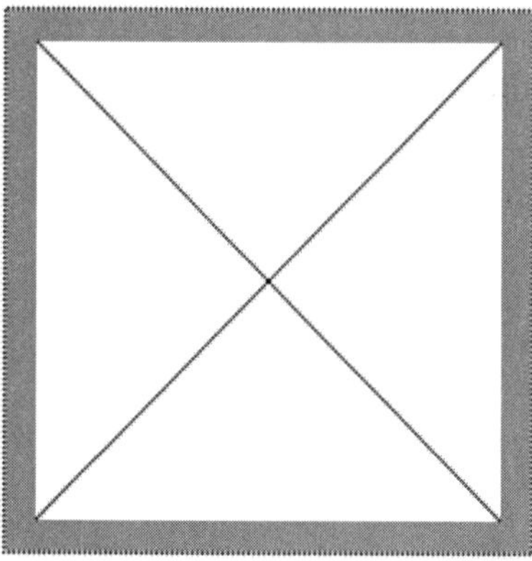

Figure 1.29

The border of the left-hand box uses inside framing, whereas the right-hand box's border is outside the box—the apparent size of the box will change if the width of the border is altered.

- From the Guides pop-up menu, choose Behind or In front to determine whether objects can hide guides (Behind). Most people use In front, because there's no point in having guides if you can't see them. If guides start to get in the way of your view, you can hide them by pressing F7; press it again to turn them back on. For some bizarre reason, the default is Behind.
- Choose how the **X and Y coordinates** of objects are determined from the Item Coordinates pop-up menu, either Page or Spread. In the former case, the horizontal ruler starts over again in the middle of each spread, whereas in the latter case it extends across both pages.
- To have imported pictures automatically updated each time you open an XPress document, set Auto Picture Import to On. If you'd like to confirm the operation before the pictures are updated, choose On (verify) to have XPress present the Picture Usage dialog when you open a document whose pictures have been modified. Then you can choose which pictures to update. If you'd rather update your pictures when you feel like it (or when you know it needs to be done), choose Off.
- The Master Page Items pop-up menu determines how XPress handles master items (items placed on a document page by virtue of being on a master page) that you've modified when you reapply a master page. If you choose Keep Changes, modified master items will stay on the page; if you choose Delete Changes, they'll be deleted.
- Because traditional typesetting used slightly more than 72 points to the inch, while electronic typesetting has standardized on exactly 72 points to the inch, XPress includes a Points/Inch field where you can enter your own preferred value for the number of points in an inch. For the sake of compatibility with every other desktop publishing application, it's best to stick with the default 72.
- The same situation exists with the number of ciceros in a centimeter; here, the default for the Ciceros/cm field is 2.1967.
- Guides aren't just visual helpers; they can actually pull your mouse cursor toward them to ensure precision. You can specify how close to a guide the cursor must be to activate this "gravitational" effect in the Snap Distance field, where the default is 6 points.
- To speed redraw further, you can have XPress replace small text with gray bars by entering a point size in the Greek Below field. All text smaller than this point size at 100% view will be **greeked**. At other view percentages, the size limit for greeking is determined by dividing the preferences point size by the view percentage, so if the setting is 7 points (the default), at 200% everything smaller than 3.5 points will be greeked.

- Greeking pictures is much simpler—turn it on and pictures will be replaced in their boxes by a gray fill. When you select a picture, it's "ungreeked" as long as it's selected.
- If your monitor is set to show only **8-bit color** (256 colors), checking Accurate Blends provides better (but slower) onscreen representation of color blends. Monitors set to display **16-bit** or **24-bit color** aren't affected by this setting—they always display accurate blends.
- Auto **Constrain** is a carryover from QuarkXPress's early days. If this setting is turned on (the default is off), and you draw a box inside another box, the new box will literally be inside the first box—it can't be moved outside or made larger than its "parent" unless you choose Item➡Unconstrain to manually unconstrain it. Most people don't use Auto Constrain—it causes more problems than it solves.

Paragraph Preferences

Click on the Paragraph tab to change settings affecting paragraph attributes of the text in your documents (see Figure 1.30).

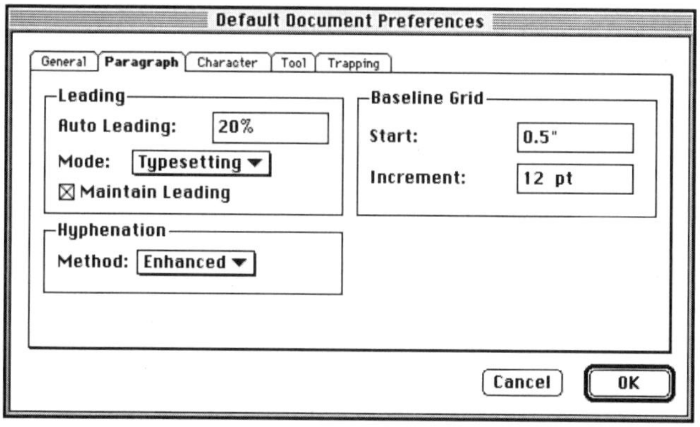

Figure 1.30

The Paragraph tab of the Default Document Preferences dialog box.

- In the **Leading** section, first specify a value for Auto Leading; this determines how much leading is applied to text using auto leading rather than a specific amount of leading. The default is 20%, meaning that 10-point type will usually be leaded at 12 points when using auto leading ("usually," because XPress assigns more leading to some fonts). You can also use a numerical value such as 6 points, which would normally result in that same 10-point type being leaded at 16 points. Then choose a leading Mode: Typesetting or Word Processing. The former measures leading upward from baseline to baseline, whereas the latter measures it downward from ascent (the top of the tallest character) to ascent. Typesetting is the default. Then click Maintain Leading off or on; this affects how text is placed when an object interrupts a text flow with a runaround. If Maintain Leading is off, the first line of text below the object will touch the bottom of the object, whereas if it's on, the first line will be moved down to place its baseline an even number of leading units below the line of text immediately preceding the obstructing object (see Figure 1.31).

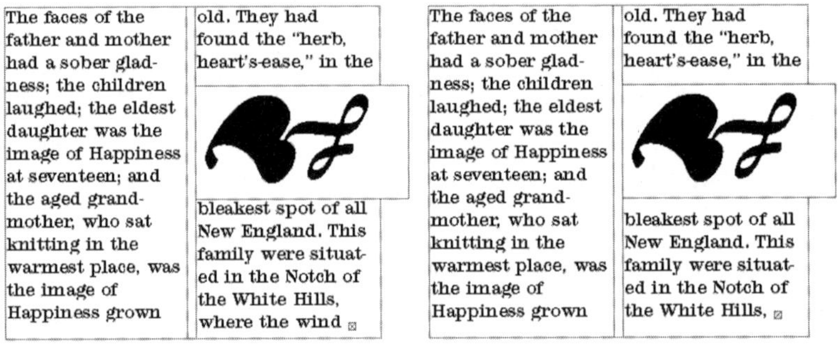

The faces of the father and mother had a sober gladness; the children laughed; the eldest daughter was the image of Happiness at seventeen; and the aged grandmother, who sat knitting in the warmest place, was the image of Happiness grown
old. They had found the "herb, heart's-ease," in the
bleakest spot of all New England. This family were situated in the Notch of the White Hills, where the wind
The faces of the father and mother had a sober gladness; the children laughed; the eldest daughter was the image of Happiness at seventeen; and the aged grandmother, who sat knitting in the warmest place, was the image of Happiness grown
old. They had found the "herb, heart's-ease," in the
bleakest spot of all New England. This family were situated in the Notch of the White Hills,

Figure 1.31

On the left, Maintain Leading is off; on the right, it's on.

- Choose from the Hyphenation pop-up menu (Standard, Enhanced, Expanded) to determine how XPress calculates hyphenation points in words. Standard uses the algorithm XPress used in its first versions; Enhanced uses a better algorithm introduced in version 3.1; and Expanded uses a dictionary and an algorithm, for the best possible hyphenation. The only time it's better to use Standard or Enhanced is when working with older documents that you don't want to reflow. (See Day 6, "Fine-tuning Type.")
- The Baseline Grid settings determine how far from the top of the page the grid starts (Start) and how far apart the lines on the grid are placed (Increment).

Character Preferences

Click on the Character tab to make settings affecting typography in your documents (see Figure 1.32).

- First, choose a size and offset (equivalent to a baseline shift) for **superscript** characters. The default settings are Offset 33%, VScale 100%, and HScale 100%, which will move superscripts up 33% of their point size from the baseline, while leaving them the same size as surrounding text. It's more common to use about 65% for the VScale and HScale values, which will shrink superscripts to 65% of their nominal **point size** (10-point superscript characters will be the same size as 6.5-point characters in the same font).

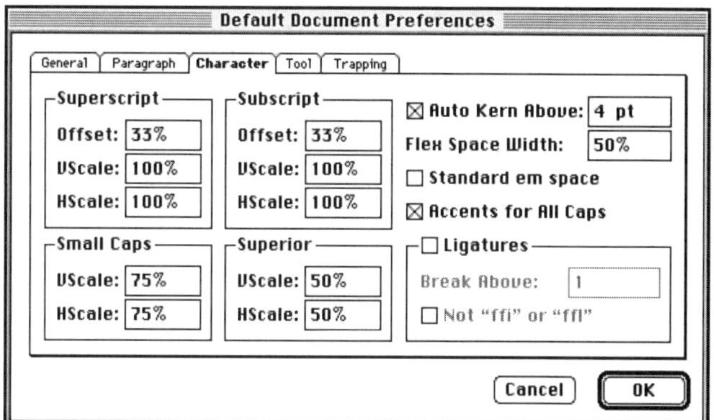

Figure 1.32

The Character tab of the Default Document Preferences dialog box.

- Make the same settings in the **Subscript** area, only you'll probably want to use a slightly smaller value for Offset—about 20%—to keep subscripts from bumping into the ascenders of characters on the line below.
- You can also specify the size of **small caps** document-wide; all small caps in a document will be sized based on this percentage, no matter what typeface they are in. Although this isn't ideal, because small caps by definition are the same height as lowercase letters and so should vary in size from typeface to typeface, at least Quark gives you the choice. The default setting of 75% is usually about right.

Note

For true, properly designed small caps, choose a typeface that comes with a special small caps font rather than using XPress's small caps feature. Use XPress's small caps only when you don't have the small caps font for a typeface (or you can't afford it) or if one doesn't exist.

- The **Superior** character style is used when typesetters want to reduce the size of a character and raise it so it top-aligns with the capital letters in the text; characters you might want to do this to include asterisks and daggers, trademark and copyright symbols, and other text (not numeric) characters. You can specify the scaling of superior characters in the VScale and HScale fields, with the default being 50%.
- Specify a value in the Auto **Kern** Above field to determine how large type must be before XPress uses the built-in kerning values in the font to automatically kern it for optimum visual spacing. (See Day 6.)

- Set a value for the **Flex Space** Width; you can type a flex space by pressing (Option-Shift-space)[Control-Alt-5]. (See Day 6.) The size of a flex space is expressed as a percentage of an en space, and the default is 50%, about the size of a standard space.
- Check Standard **em space** off or on; when it's on, an em space (created by typing two **en spaces**) will be as wide as the point size of the text, and when it's off, an em space will be as wide as two zeroes in the font in question. (See Day 6.)
- Turn on Accents for All Caps to allow accents and other diacritical marks to be placed above capital letters created via the All Caps style (as opposed to actually typing capital letters). (See Day 6.)
- Turn on **Ligatures** to substitute ligature characters for letter combinations such as "fi" and "fl," and enter a kerning/tracking value above which ligatures will be broken back into their component characters (this ensures that widely tracked type won't have two characters "glued" together as a ligature, ruining the letterspacing effect). Check Not "ffi" or "ffl" if you want to skip using ligatures in these combinations; some typefaces contain three-letter ligatures and others don't so this setting makes sure that those letter combinations will be set consistently in different fonts. (See Day 6.)

Note

Windows fonts don't typically contain ligature characters, so Windows users don't have the option of using ligatures. Ligatures in Mac OS XPress documents will be converted back to regular letters if the documents are opened on a Windows system.

Tool Preferences

Click the Tool tab to set the preferences for XPress's tools. You can set preferences for one tool at a time or for multiple tools. If you select more than one tool, you can only change preferences that the tools have in common. First, click the tool (or Shift-click on multiple tools) for which you want to set preferences (see Figure 1.33).

- Click the Modify button to display the Modify dialog box (see Figure 1.34). Any changes you make in this dialog will become the default settings for objects you create with the selected tool or tools. If you want all new text boxes to have a **text inset** of 6 points, for example, select all the text box tools, click Modify, and enter p6 in the Text Inset field. Some fields aren't available, such as Width and Height, because these values naturally vary from object to object.

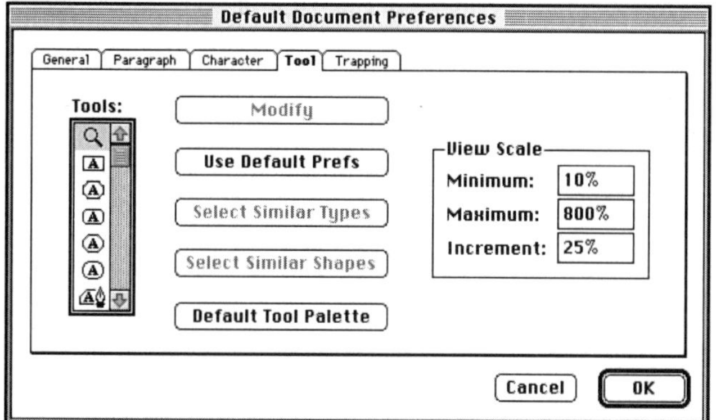

Figure 1.33

The Tool tab of the Document preferences.

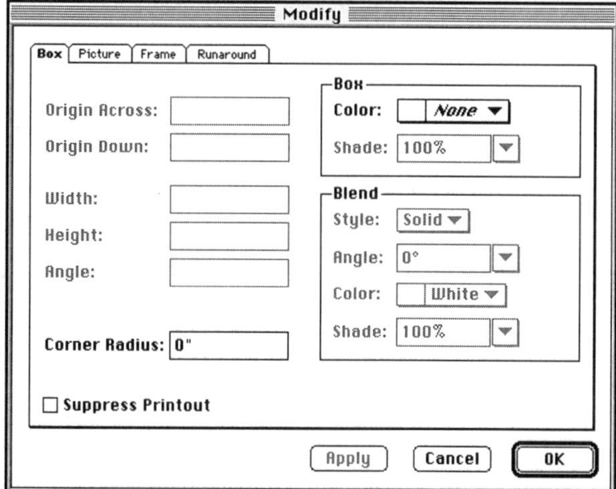

Figure 1.34

The Modify dialog box is different for different object creation tools; this version appears when you're modifying preferences for a picture box tool.

- Click Use Default Prefs to return the preferences for the selected tool or tools to the factory defaults.
- Click Select Similar Types to select tools with similar functions to the one selected (such as all the picture box tools), then click Modify to make changes that will apply to all the selected tools.
- Click Select Similar Shapes to select tools with similar shapes to the one selected, such as both the Rounded-Corner Text Box tool and the Rounded-Corner Picture Box tool, then click Modify to make changes that will apply to all the selected tools.
- Click Default Tool Palette to return the Tool palette to its default setting (as described in "The Tool Palette," earlier in this chapter).

- The Zoom tool doesn't create objects, so you can't click the Modify or Select Similar buttons when it's selected; its only preferences are set in the View Scale area at the right of the Tool Preferences tab. Enter percentages for the Minimum and Maximum view percentages (10% and 800% are as high and as low as you can go) and the Increment—the amount the view percentage changes when you click in a window with the Zoom tool (the default is 25%).

There are no preferences for the Rotate, Linking, and Unlinking tools.

Trapping Preferences

Click the Trapping tab to change settings affecting how overlapping colored objects in your documents are trapped. See Day 12 for information on how trapping works and when to change the default settings (see Figure 1.35).

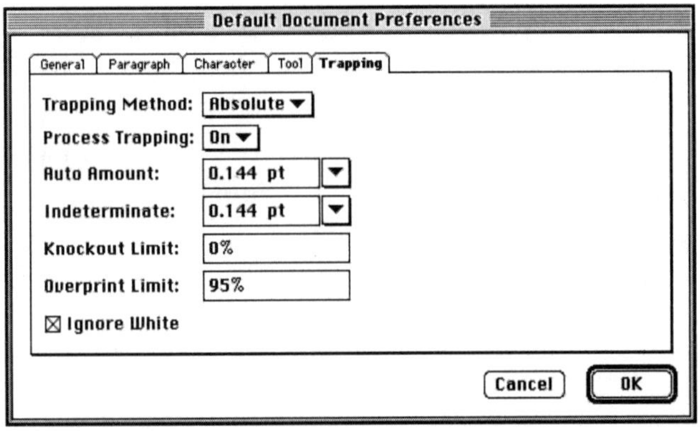

Figure 1.35

The Trapping tab of the Document preferences.

- First, choose a Trapping Method: Absolute, Proportional, or Knockout All. Absolute applies the trapping values in the Auto Amount and Indeterminate fields to all objects, regardless of their color. Proportional varies the amount of trap depending on the difference in brightness between the two colors. **Knockout** All turns off trapping entirely. The default is Absolute.
- Set Process Trapping to On or Off. When it's on, XPress calculates trapping for each process color plate independently; when it's off, XPress traps each object the same amount on all color plates containing that object. The default is on.
- Enter a value in the Auto Amount field to determine how much trap is applied to objects when Absolute trapping is being used. The default is .144 points.
- Enter a value in the Indeterminate field to determine how much trap is applied to objects that are in front of multi-colored backgrounds (meaning that XPress can't figure out how to trap the objects itself because there are too many

different colors involved.) Or choose Overprint from the pop-up menu to make all objects in front of indeterminate backgrounds overprint the backgrounds. The default is .144 points.

- Enter a value in the Knockout Limit field to determine how much difference there must be in the brightness values of two colors for the background to be knocked out behind the foreground object. The default is 0%, meaning that all background colors will be knocked out; higher percentages would keep lighter colors, like pale yellow, from knocking out—instead, darker objects would overprint the light backgrounds.
- Enter a value in the **Overprint** Limit field to determine whether colors containing percentages of black will overprint their backgrounds. Objects containing less black than the percentage specified will knock out their backgrounds instead of overprinting them. The default is 95%.
- Check Ignore White (the default is on) to specify that the trap for a foreground object in front of a background containing both white and another color will ignore the white.

Color Management Preferences

Color management software is intended to improve the predictability of color on-screen and in printed documents. Once activated, QuarkXPress's color management features operate in the background, requiring little attention as you work on your documents. Most of the work involved in using color management comes in making the preference settings, so that's covered in Day 9.

Index Preferences

The Index preferences control how index markers are shown in your document and what punctuation is used in generated indexes (see Figure 1.36).

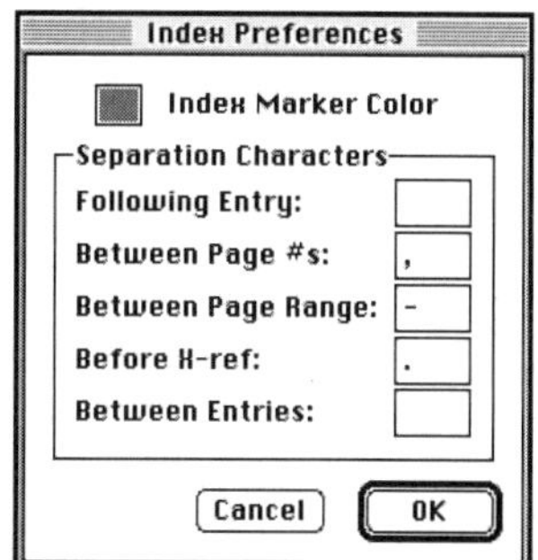

Figure 1.36

The Index Preferences dialog box.

1. Choose an Index Marker Color by clicking the color swatch and using the Color Picker to specify another color.
2. Choose **Separation Characters** to be used in the index entries when the index is generated.
    - The character in the Following Entry field is placed after the index entry, before the page numbers. The default is a space.
    - The character in the Between Page #s field is placed between multiple page numbers in the entry. The default is a comma.
    - The character in the Between Page Range field is used between page numbers in a range; this should be an en dash, which is the default.
    - The character in the Before X-ref field is placed between the index entry text and a cross-reference to another entry; the default is a period.
    - The character in the Between Entries field is placed between index entries; the default is a carriage return.

See Day 10 for more information on creating an index.

XTension-Specific Preferences

Some XTensions have their own preferences dialogs, so they add extra commands to the Edit➡Preferences submenu. These will vary depending on which XTensions you have installed, and you'll need to consult the XTension documentation for instructions on setting these preferences.

Summary

In this chapter you've toured QuarkXPress's visual landscape: its document window, tools, and floating palettes. Becoming familiar with these elements of the program is essential to learning it completely—you have to know what you're looking at before you can use it. For traditional graphic artists, XPress looks a lot like their familiar workspace—pages on a pasteboard, with tools neatly arranged on the side. The different drawing tools are analogous to the artist's triangles and French curves. At some point, though, it's time to drop the analogies and become thoroughly electronic.

Setting preferences before starting work can save a lot of time in the long run. If, for example, your text boxes should always be white, with a 0.5-point black border and a 6-point runaround, you can specify those attributes with no document open so that every text box you create from then on is just that way. Other preferences are more vital, such as the Trapping preferences; if your documents are to trap properly, these need to be set correctly. Fortunately, most printers and service bureaus prefer to make trapping settings themselves.

Creating, Opening, and Saving Documents

- Creating documents
- Adding pages
- Moving pages
- Opening documents
- Saving documents
- Creating templates
- Auto saving and making backups
- Saving pages as EPS files

Although the New, Open, and Save commands in QuarkXPress work just like those in most Mac OS and Windows programs, there are a few quirks that you need to be aware of as you create and work with documents in XPress. In this chapter you learn about the pitfalls of creating new documents, saving them, and working with documents created by other people. You also learn how to have your work saved automatically and have backup files created as you go, to make sure you never lose your work due to a system crash or other disaster.

Beginning a Document

Word processors and page layout programs share many functions. When you create a new document, though, you see one of the major differences between these two types of software programs—word processors open with a new, untitled document, whereas page layout programs require you to specify some information about that document before you begin working on it. When you create a QuarkXPress document, you first have to make a few decisions about what you're planning to do with this document and what you want its underlying structure to be. You can always change your mind later, but you have to make some choices now, or XPress can't create the document.

1. Press (Command-N)[Control-N], or choose New from the File menu to create a new document. The New command has a submenu that contains three options: Document, Library, and **Book**. If you don't make a choice in the New submenu, XPress assumes that you're creating a document rather than a library or book. Therefore, you can ignore this submenu unless you want to make a library or book.

Tip

If you *do* want to make a library, the keyboard shortcut for the New Library command is (Command-Option-N)[Control-Alt-N].

2. You're now looking at the New Document dialog box (see Figure 2.1), where you make the basic settings for your document. The first decision you need to make is to determine the dimensions of the pages in the document—as large as 48 inches square, or as small as one inch square. Choose a standard page size from the pop-up menu, such as US Letter (8 1/2" × 11"), or enter a custom page size by typing dimensions in the Width and Height fields.

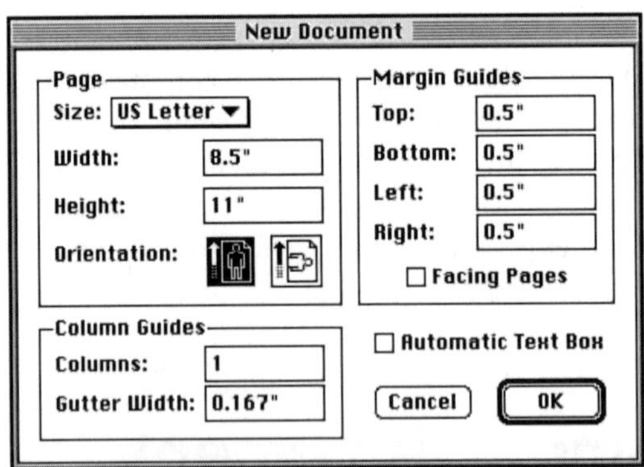

Figure 2.1

The New Document dialog box.

Tip

In the New Document dialog box, as with all QuarkXPress dialog boxes, you can ask XPress to convert measurement units and do math for you. You can enter sizes in whatever units you prefer—inches, millimeters, picas, even didots—and you don't even have to use the same units for both dimensions. Even better, if you don't know the exact dimensions of your document, but only that it should be twice as big as an 8 1/2" × 11" sheet, you can enter math equations and XPress will solve them, converting, say, 2*8.5 inches into 17 inches. The math symbols the program understands are + (plus), – (minus), * (times), and / (divided by).

3. Now decide whether the document should have **facing pages**. If you'll need to distinguish between left and right pages, you should click the Facing Pages box. Most books, magazines, and other documents that have different elements on the left and right pages need to use facing pages, whereas simpler documents such as flyers don't need to have facing pages.

   The result of clicking Facing Pages is that each page in your document is tagged as a right or left page, and the document's master pages can take the form of spreads or single pages. In the master spread in Figure 2.2, for example, the placement of the **running head** and **folio** (page number) is different on the left and right pages, as well as on the margins.

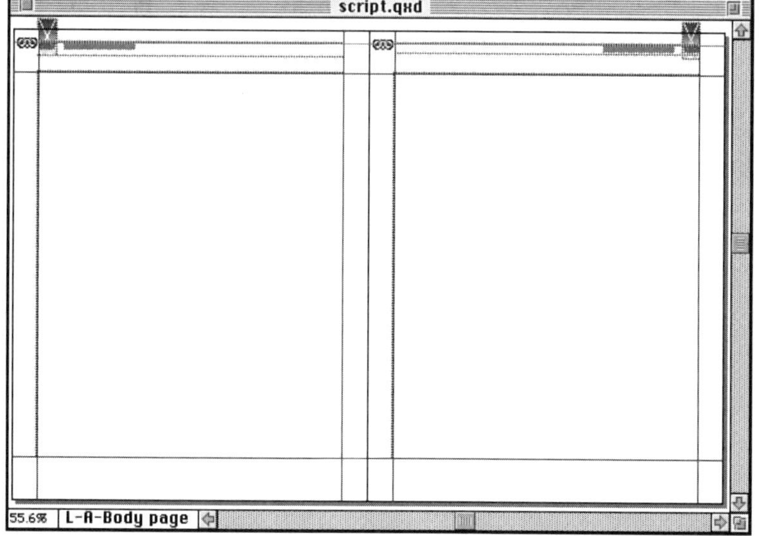

Figure 2.2

Documents that use Facing Pages can have master spreads, instead of single master pages.

Note

In book publishing, right pages are called **recto** pages and left pages are called **verso** pages.

4. The next step is to define the document's margins. If Facing Pages is checked, you'll see fields for Top, Bottom, Inside, and Outside margins. Otherwise, Inside and Outside will be replaced by Left and Right. The **inside** and **outside margins** refer to, respectively, the side margins closer to the middle of each spread and the side margins further from the middle of each spread. Therefore, the inside margin is on the right on a left page and on the left on a right page (see Figure 2.3).

   These margin settings place non-movable guides around the edges of the document—the default color for the margin guides is blue. They won't keep you from placing page elements anywhere on the page or pasteboard—they exist only as visual placement guides.
5. If your document contains a text box in the same position on every page, click **Automatic Text Box** to add a text box to the master page or pages. The size of the text box is determined by the margins you set in Step 4, and it is automatically linked. This means that the corresponding text boxes on the pages using this master page are linked, each to the next.

   It's usually not worth it to use Automatic Text Box if you're creating a document that will have different sizes and shapes of text boxes on each page; although you can change the automatic text boxes on document pages, you might as well just draw a new one on each page. See Day 8 for more information on creating, editing, and using master pages, and Day 3, "Creating Text and Graphic Elements," for more information on text boxes.
6. Finally, indicate the number of columns the document should use—one or more, up to a maximum of 30—and the gutter space that should be placed between the columns, ranging from 3 points (.0417 inches) to 24 picas (4 inches). Unfortunately, you can't have columns without a **gutter** between them, and you can't have asymmetrical columns. If your design includes columns of varying widths, you'll have to use separate, linked text boxes.

   Column guides are placed on the first master page in the same color used for the margin guides (bright blue by default). The automatic text box on those pages is also divided into the appropriate number of columns. To change the column guides, see the section "Changing Document Settings," later in this chapter.
7. Click OK to create the document.

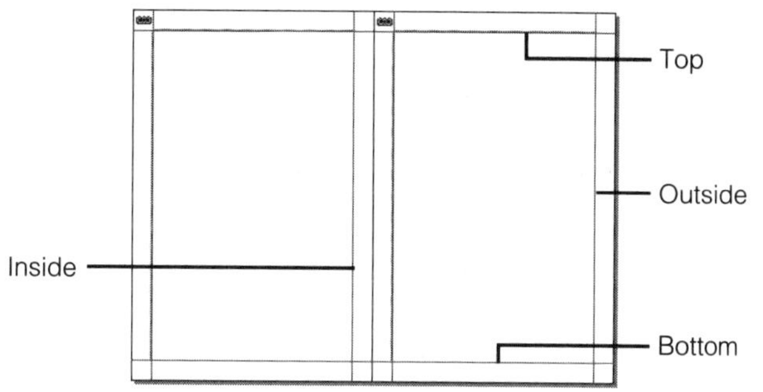

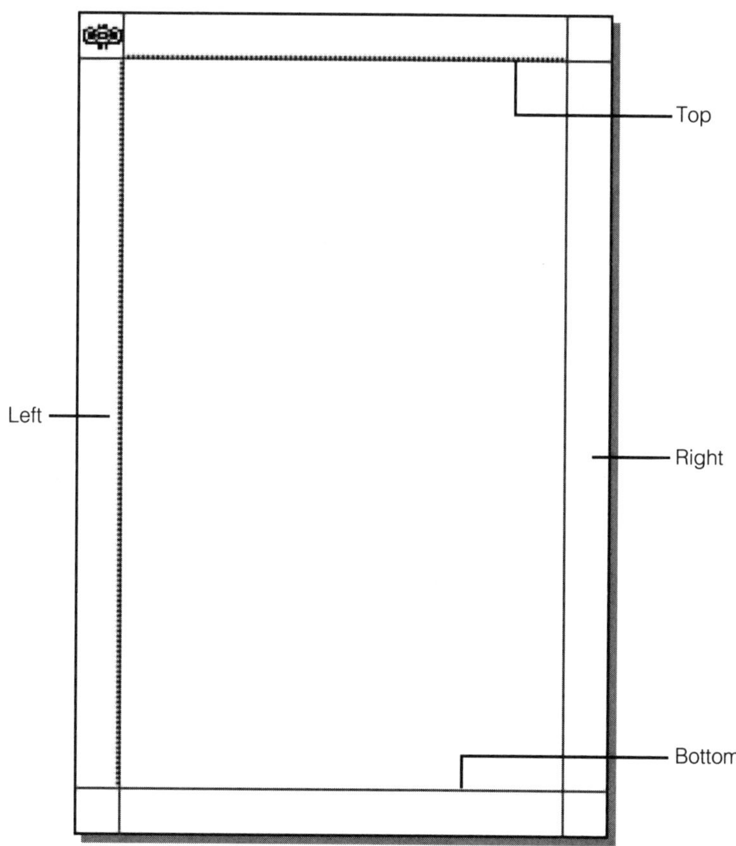

Figure 2.3

Facing pages use inside and outside margins rather than left and right margins.

Having made all these settings, you're now faced with an empty QuarkXPress document. The first page in the document has automatically been assigned the first master page, named "A-Master A," but now you can apply a generic master page to it or create more custom master pages and apply one of those.

Changing Document Settings

Sometimes, as you create a new document, you realize that you don't know yet how you want to set the options in the New Document dialog box. Maybe the design isn't completely formed in your mind, or maybe you know what the document will look like, but you're not sure yet how you'll execute it. Fortunately, you can change your mind about any of these settings using the Document Setup and Master Guides dialog boxes after the document is created:

- **Page size:** Choose Document Setup from the File menu (Command-Option-Shift-P)[Control-Alt-Shift-P] (see Figure 2.4). In the Document Setup dialog box, enter the new dimensions of the page. If the new size is smaller than the original size and, therefore, causes elements existing on the document's pages to extend outside the pasteboard area, XPress won't enable the change. You have to move or delete the problem items before you can change the page size. Margin and column guides move to the locations they would be if you had created the document at this size in the first place.

Figure 2.4

The Document Setup dialog box.

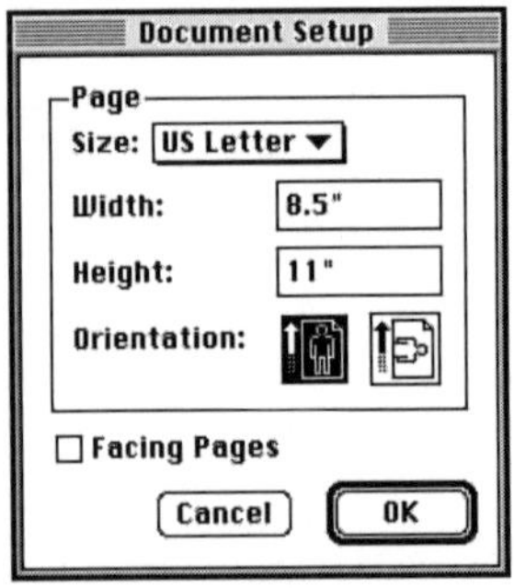

- **Facing Pages:** Choose Document Setup from the File menu and check on or off Facing Pages.

  If you're turning Facing Pages off, you'll first have to change all master pages to single pages instead of spreads by applying the "Blank Single" master to them. To do so, drag the "Blank Single" master (found at the top left corner of the Document Layout palette) on top of each custom master page icon in the

Document Layout palette. Doing so deletes any elements you've added to the custom master pages; you can save those elements via copy and paste if you still need them.

If you're turning Facing Pages on, you'll notice that the custom master pages and document pages don't change to facing pages after you click OK. You need to create new facing page master pages and apply them to the document pages. See Day 9 for more information on altering master pages.

- **Margin Guides:** View the master page you want to modify and choose Master Guides from the Page menu (see Figure 2.5). Enter new values for the margins. If you're using an automatic text box on this master page and you haven't changed the size or position of the text box, it will be resized to fit in the new margins.

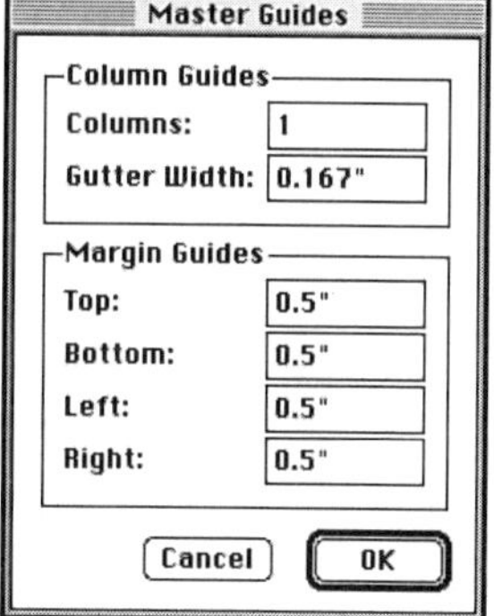

Figure 2.5

The Master Guides dialog box.

- **Column Guides:** Switch to viewing the master page you want to modify, and choose Master Guides from the Page menu. Enter new values for the number of columns and the gutter width. If you haven't changed the size or position of an automatic text box on this master page, its columns and gutters change to match the new guides.

Note

You can't change the margin and column guides for the **generic master pages** at the top of the Document Layout palette—these masters always use the values you entered when you originally created the document. For more information on master pages, see Day 8.

Adding Pages

Few QuarkXPress documents stay one-page files for long, so QuarkXPress has several methods for adding pages. Using the Document Layout palette enables you to see exactly where you're inserting pages, whereas using Page➡Insert enables you to add more than one page and decide whether that page's text box should be linked to the existing text chain. If you're using automatically linked text boxes on master pages, document pages are added automatically as your text expands.

Adding Pages Manually

To add one page at a time, use the Document Layout palette—press (F10)[F4] to bring it up if it's not visible. In the palette, scroll to the place where you want to add a page, and drag a master page icon to that position in the palette. A small arrow indicates where the page is inserted, depending on how you position it—to the right or left of an existing page or above or below it (see Figure 2.6).

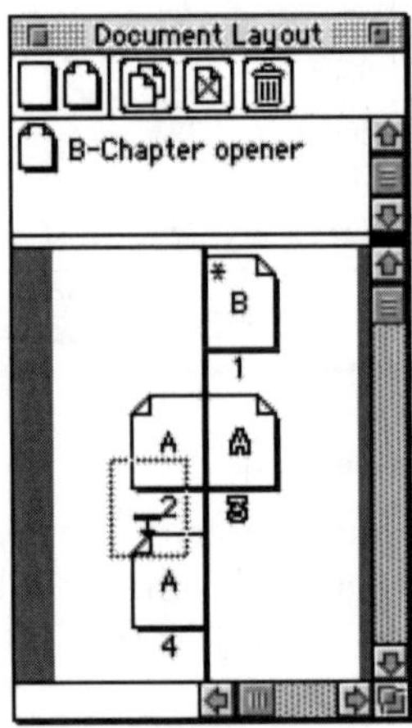

Figure 2.6

When you insert a new page via the Document Layout palette, a shadow outline of the page shows where it is added.

To add more than one page, use the Insert command:

1. If you want to link text boxes on the new pages to an existing set of linked boxes, choose the Content tool and click in the text to which you want the new pages to link. You don't have to add the new pages in this position in the document—in Step 4, you'll be able to choose where the pages are added.
2. Choose Page➡Insert to bring up the Insert Pages dialog (see Figure 2.7).
3. Enter the number of pages. You can use this command to add only one page, but it's usually easier to do that with the Document Layout palette.

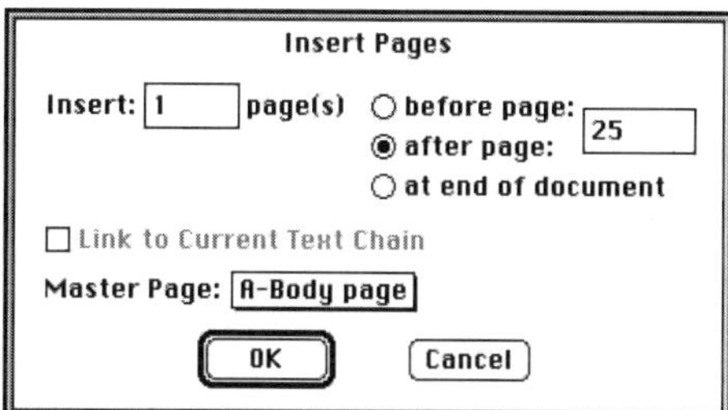

Figure 2.7

The Insert Pages dialog box.

4. Specify where you want the new pages to be added—before a certain page, after a certain page, or at the end of the document.
5. If you want the automatic text boxes on the new pages to be added to the current text chain, click Link to Current Text Chain. If you didn't select a text box with the Content tool in Step 1, this option is grayed.

   No matter where in the document you're adding the pages, they'll be linked to the *end* of the text chain. To link them to the pages before them—so that the text isn't out of order—choose the Linking tool while holding down the (Option)[Alt] key, click the text box on the page before the new pages, then click the text box on each of the new pages in order. Using the (Option)[Alt] key keeps the Linking tool active as you link multiple text boxes; otherwise it reverts to the Item or Content tool after the first link is made.
6. Choose a master page to apply to the new pages. You can't choose more than one, and you can't choose none—every page in a QuarkXPress document has to have a master page, even if it's only the generic master.
7. Click OK to add the pages or Cancel to keep your document as it is.

Adding Pages Automatically

If you're using automatically linked text boxes on master pages, it's like having invisible gremlins adding pages whenever you need them (and sometimes when you don't) without bothering to ask first. This can be good or bad, depending...

First of all, it's important to understand how and when XPress adds pages automatically. It goes like this: If the text in the current text chain becomes too long to fit in the boxes included in that chain, and the last box in the chain is an automatic text box, new pages are added after the last page in the chain, and the text flows automatically onto them. The new pages are linked to the text chain in question.

That's if you're using the default preferences. Choose Edit➡Preferences➡ Document and click the General tab to change where XPress adds pages. Your choices are End of

Story, End of Section, or End of Document (or Off, in which case pages are not added automatically).

Note

An automatic text box is a text box on a document page that corresponds to an automatically linked text box on the master page applied to that document page.

How many new pages will be added? Enough to hold all the text currently existing in that text chain. And what kind of pages? They'll have the same master page as the former last page in the text chain. That's the program's best guess as to the master page you'll want to apply to those new pages; sometimes it's right and sometimes it's not.

If it's not, you can simply change the master page for those document pages. Unfortunately, you can change only one master page at a time, so if you anticipate that a many pages will be added automatically, it's a good idea to make sure that the last page in the text chain uses the master page that you want to use for added pages.

When XPress adds new pages that you don't want, you need to find another way to deal with the extra text that caused the creation of the new pages. There are two possible solutions:

- First, you might have extra returns or spaces at the end of your text that you don't see; the answer is simply to delete them.
- On the other hand, if the text is overflowing, you'll probably need to change your design or edit the text to accommodate it. In this case, you can make a text box off to the side of your pages, on the pasteboard, to hold the overflow until you've dealt with it; this box should be linked to the last page that you actually want in the document (see Figure 2.8).

After the extra text on the new pages is eliminated, you can delete those pages and they won't come back.

Moving Pages

No matter how pages are inserted in a document—automatically or manually—if you don't want them where they're added, moving them is simple. You have two choices of method: the Document Layout palette or the Move command.

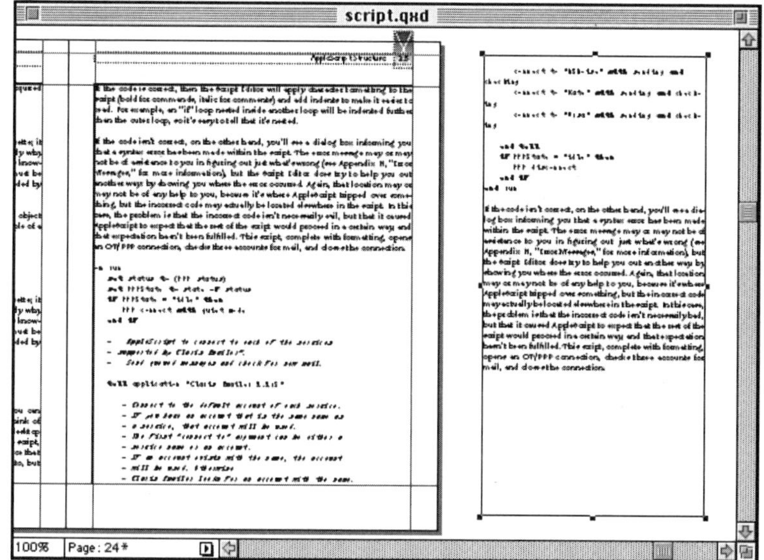

Figure 2.8

An extra text box off to the side of a page can be used to hold overflow text and keep XPress from adding new pages.

To move multiple pages via the Document Layout palette, click the first page you want to move, Shift-click the last page you want to move, and drag all the selected pages to their new location (see Figure 2.9).

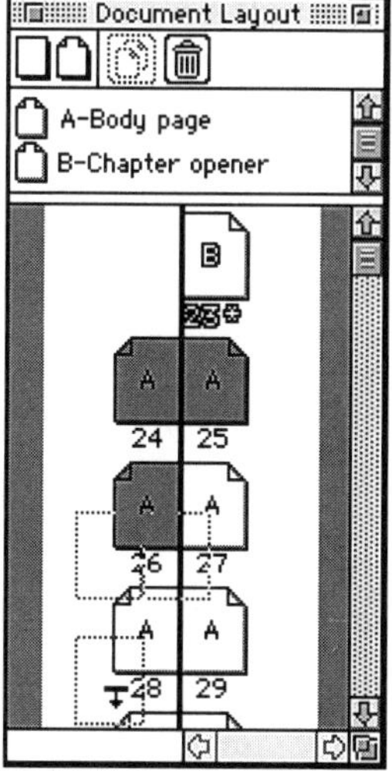

Figure 2.9

The icons of the selected pages are shaded to show which pages are being moved.

To bypass the Document Layout palette, choose Page➡Move to bring up the Move Pages dialog box, and then enter the pages you want to move and the location you want to move them to (see Figure 2.10). Moving pages doesn't affect text box links at all—in other words, the text boxes are still linked in their new location.

Move Pages
Move page(s): 23 thru: 25
before page:
after page:
to end of document
OK
Cancel

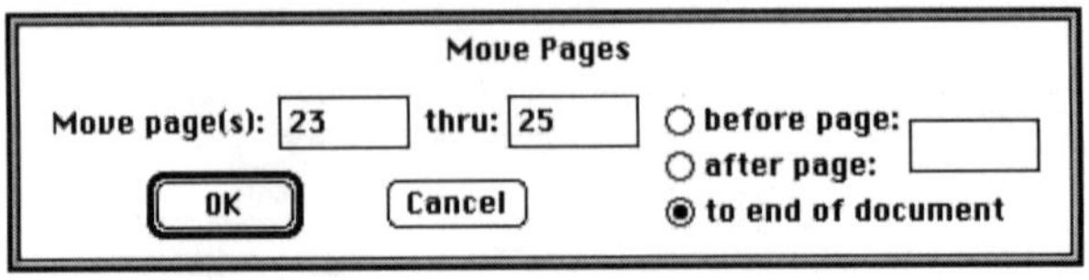

Figure 2.10

The Move dialog box.

Opening Documents

Opening a document should be simple, right? You double-click its icon, or choose its name in the Open dialog box, and the document reveals itself in all its glory on your screen. Unfortunately, sometimes QuarkXPress runs into circumstances that prevent it from opening a document right away. These circumstances are discussed next.

Reconciling Different Preferences

Sometimes when you open an XPress document, you'll see a dialog box that tells you that some of the settings in the document don't match those in QuarkXPress's preferences (see Figure 2.11). What this means is that one of three things is different: custom kerning or **tracking** values, hyphenation exceptions, or custom frames. These actually have nothing to do with any changes you make to XPress's preferences, and they may be different because you changed them after you created the document in question or because the document wasn't created using the current copy of the program.

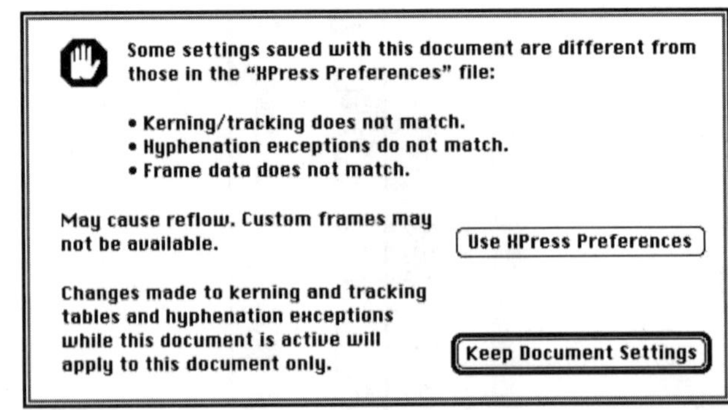
Some settings saved with this document are different from those in the "XPress Preferences" file:
• Kerning/tracking does not match.
• Hyphenation exceptions do not match.
• Frame data does not match.
May cause reflow. Custom frames may not be available.
Use XPress Preferences
Changes made to kerning and tracking tables and hyphenation exceptions while this document is active will apply to this document only.
Keep Document Settings

Figure 2.11

This dialog box tells you that some settings in the document being opened don't match those in the copy of QuarkXPress you're using.

In this alert dialog box, you have two choices; you can use the settings associated with the current copy of XPress, or you can use the old settings:

- If you want to maintain text breaks and box borders as they currently exist in the document, click Keep Document Settings. This choice is the default, meaning that this is what happens if you press (Return)[Enter]. As the dialog box informs you, any changes you make to **hyphenation** exceptions, tracking tables, and kerning tables while the document is open affect only this document. See Day 6 for more information on hyphenation exceptions, kerning, and tracking.
- If you're trying to standardize a set of documents so that their kerning, tracking, hyphenation exceptions, and custom frames all match, click Use XPress Preferences. Don't ever, ever do this with someone else's document that you don't want to change. Bypassing the document's preferences can cause text to reflow, a potentially expensive problem.

Dealing with Missing XTensions

Handy as XTensions are, they can cause problems if they're not installed on every system on which the document is opened. This is primarily the case with XTensions that enable documents to have attributes they couldn't otherwise have. A few examples:

- Cool Blends creates radial and other unusual types of gradients in text and graphics boxes, so if you try to open a document with one of these blends without having Cool Blends installed, you won't have any luck (see Figure 2.12). By the way, Cool Blends is free and can be downloaded from Quark's Web site (`http://www.quark.com`).

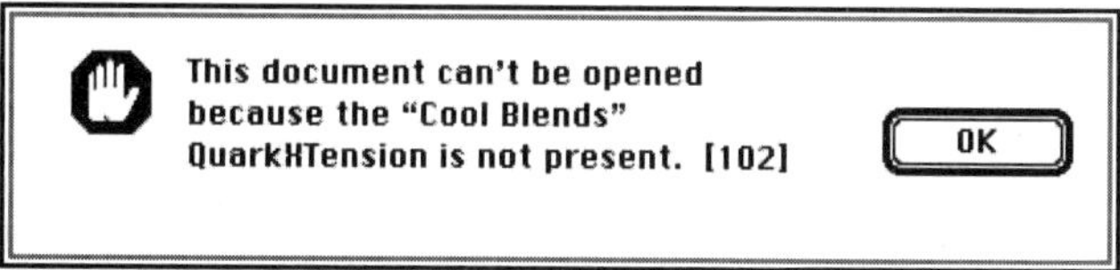

Figure 2.12

This dialog box results from trying to open a document containing Cool Blends effects without having the XTension installed.

- PasteBoard XT is a notorious XTension created by MarkzWare that enables you to change the vertical size of the pasteboard surrounding the pages in your documents. Unfortunately, if you've done this using earlier versions of PasteBoard XT, you won't be able to open those documents unless you have PasteBoard XT installed—or have one of the XTensions created in response to this terrible plague, such as PasteBoard XTerminator (Mac) or PasteBoard Killer (KILLPB.xxt, Windows). Many users think PasteBoard XT is more like a virus than a helpful utility, especially because you can already change the width of the pasteboard in the preferences (just not the height).

- If a QuarkXPress document contains math equations created with the PowerMath XTension, you can open the document without having PowerMath installed, but you can't see the equations. You see empty boxes that print as blanks. You don't get a warning when you open the document.

The answer to the missing XTension problem is almost always to obtain the XTension in question. You won't always know what's missing—sometimes you just can't open the document—so your best bet is to contact the person who created the file and find out what XTensions were installed at the time.

Dealing with Missing Fonts

If you try to open a document that uses fonts you don't have installed, you are faced with a dialog box listing the missing fonts and asking you what fonts, if any, you want to substitute. You can cancel the operation and install the fonts, you can open the document anyway, or you can tell XPress what fonts you want to substitute (see Figure 2.13).

Figure 2.13

Opening a document without the necessary fonts results in this alert.

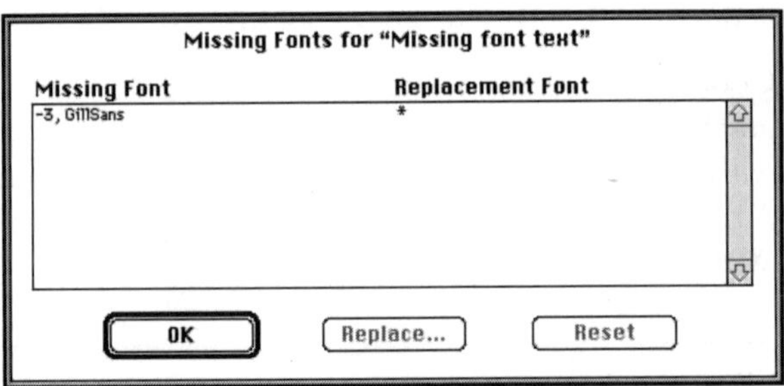

If you open a document without the correct fonts and without replacing those missing fonts, QuarkXPress displays the text in one of your system fonts. You can edit the text and even save the document without losing the original font assignment—meaning that if you later open the document with the correct fonts installed, all the text will appear in the original font.

If there's no chance that you'll later be able to install the missing fonts, you have the option of replacing the fonts with others that you do have installed. Click the name of the missing font, and then click the Replace button to bring up a dialog box with a font pop-up menu (see Figure 2.14). Choose the font you want, and then click OK twice to open the document.

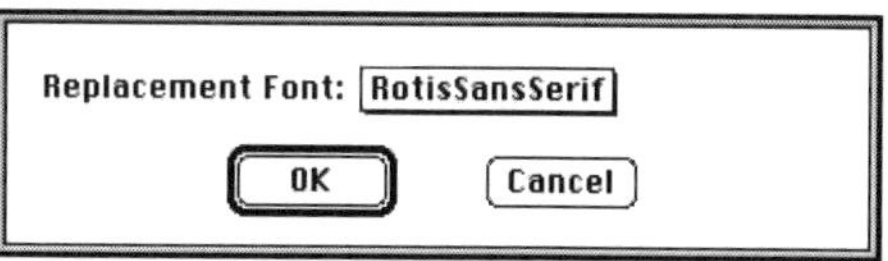

Figure 2.14

You can choose a font to replace any missing fonts in the document you're opening.

Why Can't I Open This Document?

If you can't open a document and you've eliminated the possibility that you are missing XTensions, here are a few other potential stumbling blocks:

- *You're using an earlier version of QuarkXPress.* There's often nothing you can do about this other than upgrade to the new version. If, however, you're using XPress 3.3 and the document is in 4.0, you can have a 4.0 user resave the document in 3.3 format. You'll be able to open it, but some 4.0-specific features such as index markers may be lost.
- *XPress can't identify the file as one of its own.* This is generally due to an incorrect filename extension (Windows) or incorrect file type and creator attributes (Mac), and it usually happens only when you try to open the file by double-clicking its icon (see Figure 2.15). Try opening the file by choosing File➡Open from XPress.

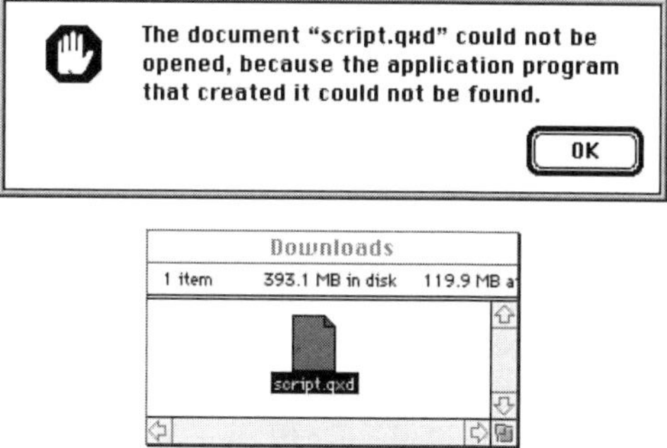

Figure 2.15

This Mac file lost its "identity" as an XPress document when it was transferred over the Internet, so double-clicking doesn't open it.

- *The file isn't an XPress document.* Unlike, say, Photoshop, XPress can't open documents created by any other program. Word processing files and graphics files need to be imported into a QuarkXPress file, rather than opened—and there's no reliable way of opening a PageMaker document in QuarkXPress.
- *The file is corrupted.* Or perhaps one of your fonts is corrupted. To find out if this is the case, try uninstalling all fonts except one basic system font and opening

the document. If you don't have any problems opening it this way, one of your fonts is corrupted. Use a font utility such as Adobe Type Manager Deluxe to find the corrupted font and delete it.

Sometimes the screen preview for an imported graphic becomes corrupted. The tip-off to this problem is that you can open the document, but QuarkXPress quits when you move to a particular page.

You can try to locate the problem graphic with this technique. First, expand the Document Layout palette to cover the entire screen, and then choose File➡Open and hold down (Command) as you double-click the name of the file or click Open. Then press (Command-Y) to open the General Preferences dialog and click the Greek Pictures option on. Now you can close the Document Layout palette and scroll through the document because all the imported graphics are greeked. Click each imported graphic in turn; when you get to the corrupted one, XPress will quit. Now you know the evil graphic, so you can get rid of it. When you've restarted QuarkXPress, expand the Document Layout palette to cover the screen again and choose Utilities➡Usage then click the Pictures tab. Click the name of the problem graphic and then click the Show button; switch to the Content tool, and press the Delete key to delete the graphic. Now you should be able to move around the file at will, even with Greek Pictures turned off.

MarkzTools is an XTension from MarkzWare that repairs and opens some corrupted documents. See Appendix B for more information on MarkzWare.

Saving Documents

Any time you're working with a file that would take more than a minute to re-create, you should save early and often. XPress offers both a Save command and a Save As command; there's no difference, except that Save As is used normally to create a copy of a document with a different name. The two commands even use the same dialog box (see Figure 2.16); it's just that you only see a dialog box with the Save command the first time you use it. Your only choices are whether you want to save the file as a document or a template (see "Creating a Template," which follows) and what name you want to assign the file.

Tip

When you decide to abandon the changes you've made to a document and go back to the last version you saved, use XPress's File➡Revert to Saved command. If there's an Auto Save version of the file that's more recent than the last manually saved version, XPress offers you the option of using either the manually saved or the Auto Save version.

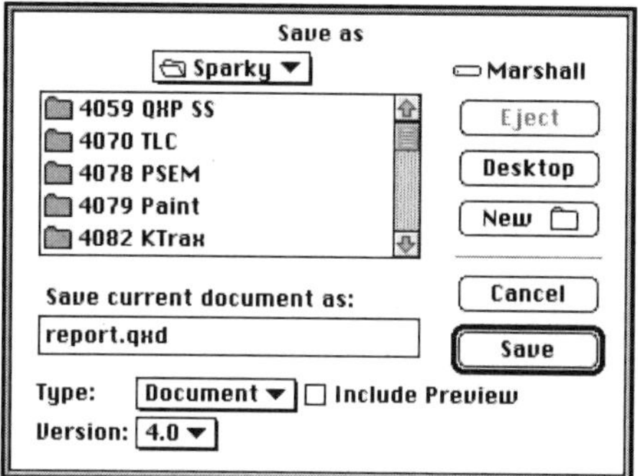

Figure 2.16

The Save (and Save As) dialog box.

QuarkXPress enables you to name your documents anything you want, so there are no required naming conventions.

In the Windows version of XPress, the QXD (for documents) and QXT (for templates) extensions are automatically tacked on to the end of each filename when you assign it, but you don't have to use these extensions. If you're not using them, though, make sure you choose Show All from the file type pop-up menu in the Open dialog box, or you won't be able to see them.

If you close a document without saving it first, XPress asks whether you want to save it. Mac users have the option of quickly closing all open documents by Option-clicking the close box of the foreground window.

Creating a Template

A QuarkXPress **template** is simply a document that you can't open (see Figure 2.17). That probably doesn't sound like a good idea, but it is. If you try to open a template, what you'll actually get is a new untitled document that looks exactly like the template. You might make a template from your letterhead design, for example, so that you can simply open the template and start typing. All the styles, master pages, and other elements you choose are automatically at your disposal.

Figure 2.17

Icons for documents (left) and templates (right) are different.

To create a template, first set up the document the way you want it, with any styles, master pages, and other elements you want to include. Then choose File➡Save As, provide the new file a name (preferably ending with .QXT if you're working in Windows), choose Template from the file type menu, and click Save.

From this moment on, the document is a template—if you make any changes and then save, you'll get the Save As dialog and be asked to create a new document with a new name. Save changes to the template by choosing Template from the file type menu again and typing the template name (XPress asks whether you want to replace the old file with the new one—you should click OK).

Tip

Windows users can quickly turn a document into a template by simply changing the filename extension from QXD to QXT.

Tip

Mac users have the option of adding a preview to the template that will be visible in the Open dialog box if the Preview box is clicked; you'll be able to see a low-res color image of the template's first page (see Figure 2.18).

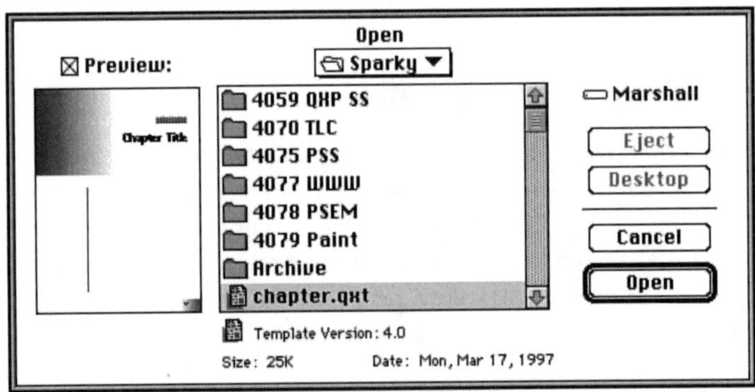

Figure 2.18

The preview window in the Open dialog box shows the first page and page size of XPress templates.

Auto Saving and Making Backup Files

Two items in the General Preferences enable you to automate saving and backing up your files. If Auto Save is clicked, XPress saves at specified intervals, and if Auto Backup is clicked, XPress makes a backup copy of your document each time you save so that you can go back to as many as 100 previous versions. You can also specify the location for these backup files. See "Customizing QuarkXPress with Preferences" in Day 1, "XPress Basics," for more information on setting this preference.

Saving Pages as EPS Files

Saving a page as an EPS file is a handy way to turn a single page from a QuarkXPress document into a graphic that can be imported and opened in other applications, or shared with people who don't have QuarkXPress. It's easy enough to do:

1. Choose File➡Save Page as EPS, or press (Command-Option-Shift-S) [Control-Alt-Shift-S] to bring up the Save Page as EPS dialog box (see Figure 2.19).

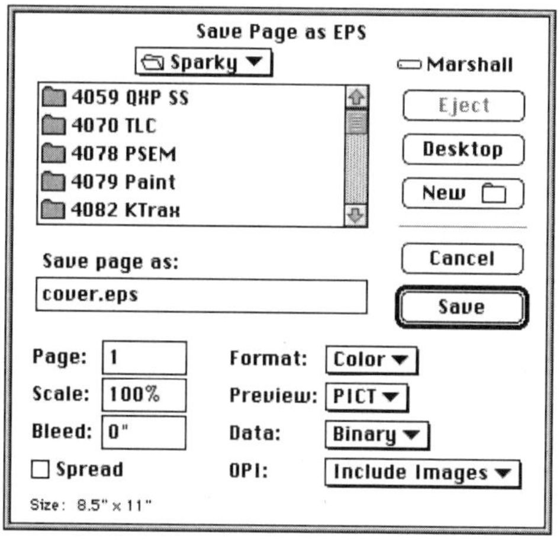

Figure 2.19

The Save Page as EPS dialog box.

2. Navigate to the location where you want to save the EPS file and assign it a name.
3. Enter the number of the page you want to save—unfortunately, you can't save more than one page or spread to EPS format at a time.
4. Enter a scaling percentage between 10 and 100 percent. The size of the resulting scaled page is displayed below the Scale entry field.
5. Enter the amount of bleed you want to include in the EPS file—the amount of area outside the boundaries of the page itself that should be included.
6. Click Spread to save facing pages in one EPS file.
7. Choose a format, depending on what platform the resulting EPS file will be used on. The choices are as follows:
   - **Color:** Use this option for color documents.

- **B&W:** Use this option for black-and-white documents.
- **DCS:** Use this option to create a color-separated set of EPS files in DCS (Desktop Color Separation) format. Using DCS format will speed up printing a color file because the output device doesn't have to create color separations.
- **DCS 2.0:** Use this option to take advantage of the newer DCS 2.0 format's capability to save more than four plates, enabling you to include plates for spot colors.

8. Choose a preview option: PICT, TIFF, or None. Use PICT if the EPS file is destined for use on a Mac OS system and TIFF if it's headed for a Windows system.
9. Choose an encoding option from the Data pop-up menu: ASCII, Binary, or Clean 8-bit. Use Binary unless you experience printing problems with the resulting EPS files; some networks and applications prefer ASCII encoding. The printed results are the same, but ASCII-encoded files take much longer to print.
10. Just as when you're printing a file, you have the option when creating an EPS file to include imported graphics or not include them. The OPI (Open Prepress Interface) options are Include Images (embeds the imported graphics in the EPS file), Omit TIFF, and Omit TIFF & EPS. The latter two don't embed TIFF files, and the final option also doesn't embed EPS files. Instead of embedding the imported graphics, these two options include information for the destination application (such as PageMaker or Illustrator) on where to find the TIFF and/or EPS files.
11. Click Save to save the EPS file.

Being able to create EPS files from QuarkXPress pages comes in handy whenever you need to include an image of an XPress file within another file (see Figure 2.20). A book publishing house's annual catalog, for example, might include EPS images of the books' covers, or a poster advertising the latest issue of a new magazine might include an EPS image of that issue's cover.

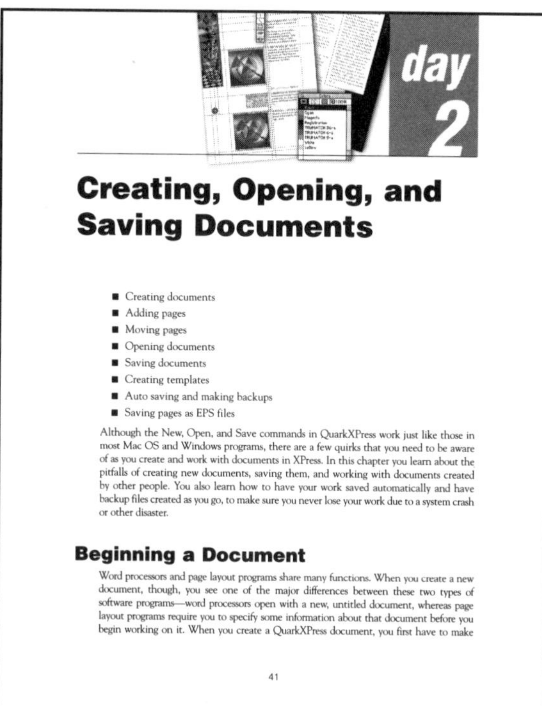

Creating, Opening, and Saving Documents

- Creating documents
- Adding pages
- Moving pages
- Opening documents
- Saving documents
- Creating templates
- Auto saving and making backups
- Saving pages as EPS files

Although the New, Open, and Save commands in QuarkXPress work just like those in most Mac OS and Windows programs, there are a few quirks that you need to be aware of as you create and work with documents in XPress. In this chapter you learn about the pitfalls of creating new documents, saving them, and working with documents created by other people. You also learn how to have your work saved automatically and have backup files created as you go, to make sure you never lose your work due to a system crash or other disaster.

Beginning a Document

Word processors and page layout programs share many functions. When you create a new document, though, you see one of the major differences between these two types of software programs—word processors open with a new, untitled document, whereas page layout programs require you to specify some information about that document before you begin working on it. When you create a QuarkXPress document, you first have to make

41

Figure 2.20

The first page of this chapter, saved as an EPS file.

Summary

In this chapter you learned the basics of working with QuarkXPress files—creating, saving, and opening them, as well as making them into template files that can be used as the basis for many similar files. You can also save individual pages of XPress files as EPS files to use as artwork or share with people who don't use QuarkXPress. This is the first step toward creating artwork from an XPress page, like a book cover that you want to feature on your web site.

Saving and backing up are made easier by QuarkXPress. If you're the type who never remembers to save until *after* the power goes off, you'll want to use these two features. The automatic backup feature is also useful when you're experimenting with different designs because you can go back to an earlier version of the file you're working on.

Creating Text and Graphic Elements

- Creating and modifying objects
- Moving objects
- Combining shapes
- Converting type to boxes
- Editing Bézier shapes
- Changing an object's fill and border
- Grouping and constraining objects
- Running text around objects
- Layering objects
- Embedding objects in text
- Locking and unlocking objects

QuarkXPress recognizes three basic types of objects: boxes, lines, and text paths, with boxes and lines divided into several subcategories. If you've read the "The Tool Palette" section in Day 1, "XPress Basics," you probably already have a good idea of what kinds of objects you can create in XPress, since you use different tools to make different objects. Throughout this chapter, we'll work on creating a poster advertising a new album from a mythical blues band, creating and editing all different kinds of elements in the process.

Creating Objects

This project incorporates all the basic kinds of elements (boxes, with various contents, and lines, both with text along them and without). You can change an object's content type by selecting it and choosing Item➡Content, and then picking an option from the submenu: Picture, Text, or None. This lets you convert picture boxes to text boxes, or text paths to regular lines, but not boxes to lines or vice versa (see "Changing an Object's Size and Shape" later in this chapter, to change an object's shape type).

1. Press (Command-N)[Control-N] to create a new file with the settings shown in Figure 3.1. The project is a 24" by 26" (vertical, or portrait, orientation) poster with no margins; because it's a poster, it doesn't need to use facing pages or automatic text boxes.

Figure 3.1

The blank poster file.

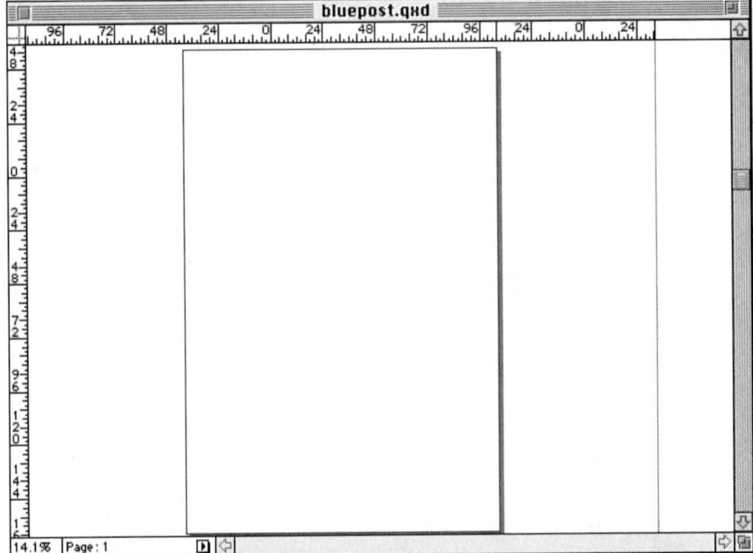

Note

This project uses the Thin Thin Slim (in the Snyder folder on the CD) and Octavian (in the Scriptorium folder on the CD) font, so make sure they're installed in your system before you start.

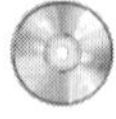

2. Save the new document on your hard drive with any name you like. The version shown is named bluespst.qxd.
3. Choose Edit➡Colors (Shift-F12) and click Append to import colors from another document. In the Append Colors dialog box (see Figure 3.2), choose lessons/chap3/bluescol.qxd on the CD that came with this book and click Open.

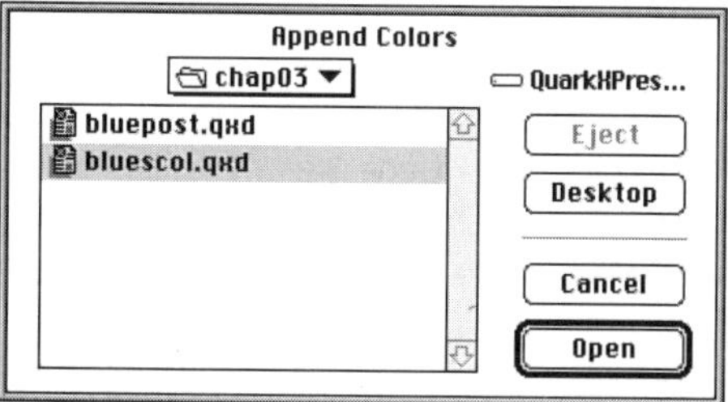

Figure 3.2

The Append Colors dialog.

4. The next dialog lets you pick which colors you want to add to your document. You can click on individual colors, then click the right arrow button to add them to the list of colors to be appended, or you can click the Include All button to add the entire list of colors (see Figure 3.3). In this case, you'll need all the new colors from bluescol.qxd to complete the exercise, so click Include All, then OK; back in the Colors dialog, click Save to finish adding the new colors.

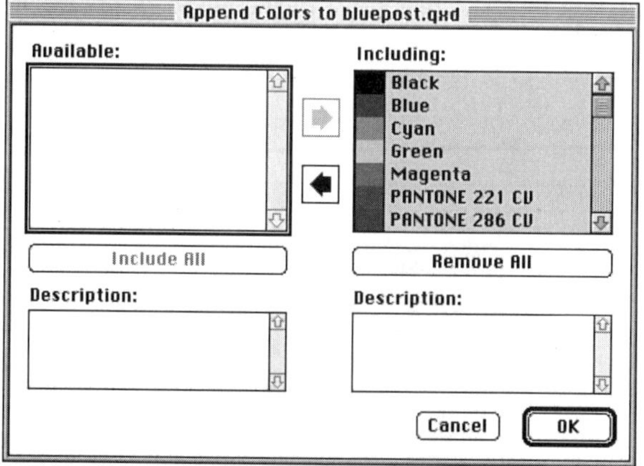

Figure 3.3

Choose the colors you want to add to your document, then click OK.

5. First create a background for the poster. Choose the picture or text box tool—it doesn't matter which—and draw a box covering the entire page. In an actual project, this box would need to extend outside the edges of the page (bleed) in case the printer didn't trim the poster exactly right, but since this project won't really be printed, you can use the blue margin guides to make the box exactly the size of the page.

> **Tip**
>
> To make a text or picture box, click where you want one of the box's corners to be, and then drag diagonally across to where the opposite corner should be. You can start with any corner, although most people instinctively start with the upper left corner and drag down and to the right. Once the box is drawn, you can change its size and proportions by dragging any of its corner points.

6. Since this box won't contain any text or pictures, you can convert it to an empty box by choosing Item➡Content➡None. There are two reasons to do this; first, you won't be able to accidentally type in it or paste a picture into it, and second, it will make the file size slightly smaller, since XPress doesn't have to keep track of what it contains or doesn't contain.
7. With the empty box still selected, press F12 to show the Colors palette if it's not visible. Click the background icon in the palette and choose Linear Blend from the pop-up menu. Then click the #1 radio button and click PANTONE 286 CV to make a dark blue the first color in the blend. Click the #2 button and click black to make black the second color. At this point, the box contains a blend, but it's from left to right. Double-click the 0 in the angle area of the Colors palette and change the angle to 90° (see Figure 3.4).

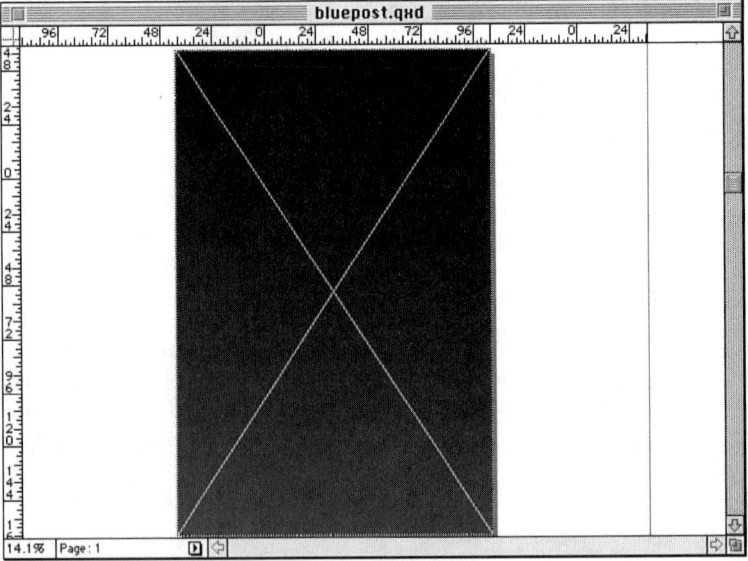

Figure 3.4

The poster with a blue and black background.

Note

The blue color used here is a Pantone **spot color**, meaning that it will be printed with a blue ink rather than created from a combination of process inks (cyan, magenta, yellow, and black).

8. Now add the name of the album. Choose the Text Box tool and draw a text box running from the top margin guide to the bottom one, starting about 1" in from the left margin guide and about 9" wide. Type **Born in the Land of Blues** in the box.

Tip

If your preferences aren't set to use inches, you can either change the preferences (see Day 1) or just type inch measurements in the Measurements palette's fields and let XPress do the conversion to whatever units it's currently using. For example, if you're using picas, double-click in the X coordinate field of the Measurements palette, type **1"**, and press (Return)[Enter]. The measurement in the palette changes to 6p.

9. With the text box still selected, press F9 to view the Measurements palette if it's not visible, then press (Command-A)[Control-A] to select all the text in the box. Click the small triangle next to the font name to view a pop-up menu of fonts and choose Thin Thin Slim. Then double-click in the font size field next to the font name, type **558** and press (Return)[Enter]. This changes the name of the album to 558-point Thin Thin Slim.
10. Click the text color icon in the Colors palette, then click White to make the text white so it'll show up against the dark background (see Figure 3.5).
11. The poster has two photos—one of the band and one taken from the cover of the album. Each needs a picture box to be imported into. First, choose the Rectangular Picture Box tool and draw a picture box from the top margin of the poster to the bottom, about 10" wide and 12" from the left edge of the page.
12. If you need to, switch to the Content tool. Then press (Command-E)[Control-E] to bring up the Get Picture dialog (see Figure 3.6). Choose lessons/chap3/river.tif on the CD that came with this book and click Open to import the picture into the box.

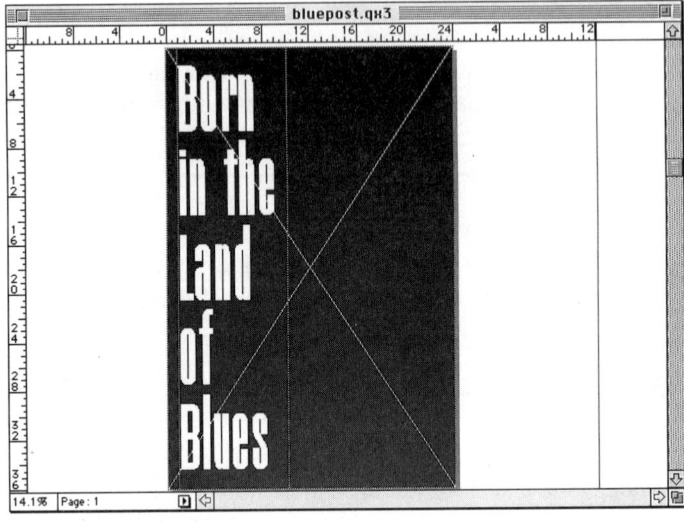

Figure 3.5

The name of the album in 558-point white Thin Thin Slim.

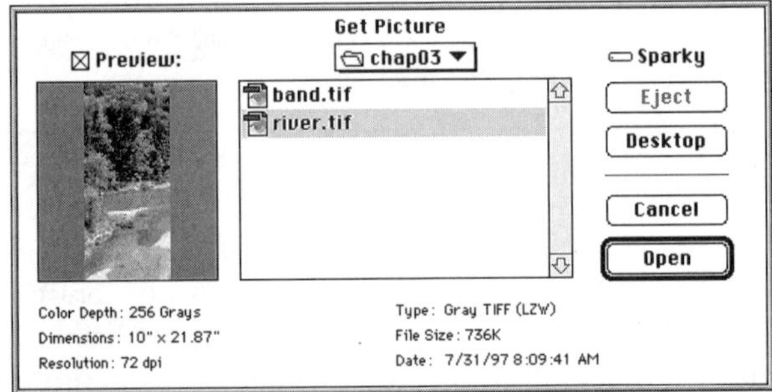

Figure 3.6

The Get Picture dialog box.

13. The photo doesn't fit the box perfectly—it's too small and its proportions aren't quite right (see Figure 3.7). Resize it to exactly fill the box by pressing (Command-Shift-F)[Control-Shift-F]. This alters the proportions of the image, so don't use this shortcut on any image that's supposed to look realistic.

Warning

When you're creating the final version of a project—the file that will actually be printed—it's usually not a good idea to resize photos in QuarkXPress, especially by enlarging them. This reduces the effective resolution of the image and may result in "jaggies," as well as taking more time to print out. And in the final stages of production, when you're paying for film output rather than just laser proofs, time is money.

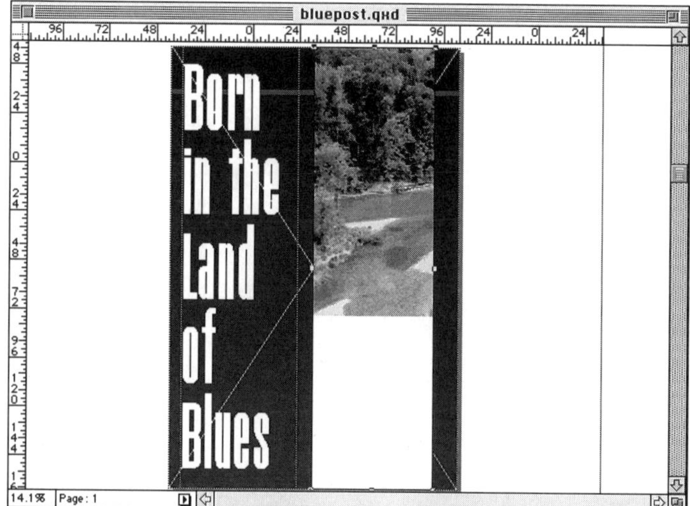

Figure 3.7

The river photo is the wrong size and proportions for its box.

14. The photo needs some color to jazz it up, and since it's grayscale rather than color, you can substitute your own color choices for the black and white that make up the image. With the Content tool still active, click the image icon on the Colors palette and click PANTONE 286 CV in the list of colors (see Figure 3.8). This changes the black portions of the image to PANTONE 286 CV.
15. To change the white portions of the image, click the background icon and click Black in the color list. See Figure 3.9 for the results.

Note

TIFF, PICT, and JPEG images can be colored this way; other image file formats don't allow it.

16. A bit of explanatory text would go well about now. Click and hold the Text Path tool to bring up a side menu of variations on the Text Path tool. Move the cursor over the Freehand Bézier Text Path tool to choose it (see Figure 3.10).
17. Carefully draw a curved text path near the bottom of the poster, from the album title almost to the right edge of the page (see Figure 3.11). The Freehand Bézier Text Path tool is easy to use—just click and drag—but it produces perfect Bézier curves. You can adjust the curve by choosing Item➡Edit➡Shape, clicking a point, and moving its Bézier handles.

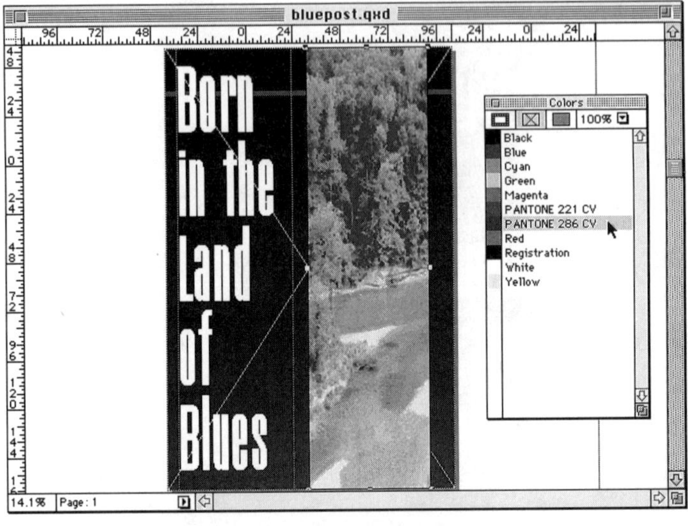

Figure 3.8

Clicking the image (middle) icon and then a color name in the Colors palette applies the color to the imported picture in the selected box.

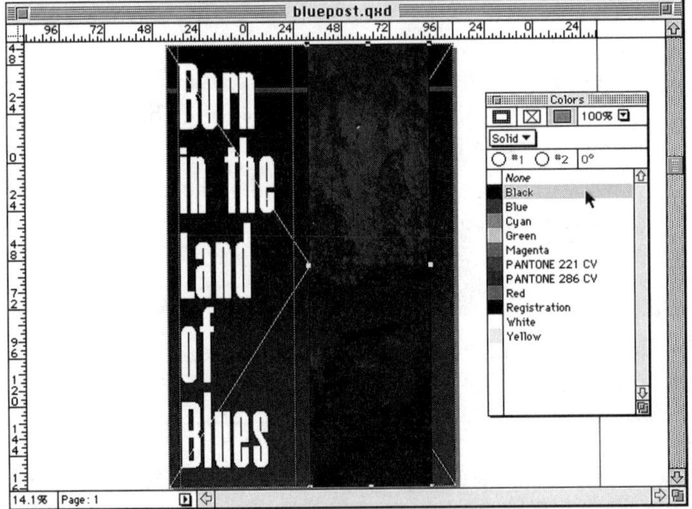

Figure 3.9

Click the background (right) icon in the Colors palette to apply the specified color to the box itself.

Note

Just as a box can be a picture box, a text box, or an empty box, a text path is really just a line with text fastened to it. You can convert a text path to a regular line by choosing Item➡Content➡None, which will also delete all the text along the line.

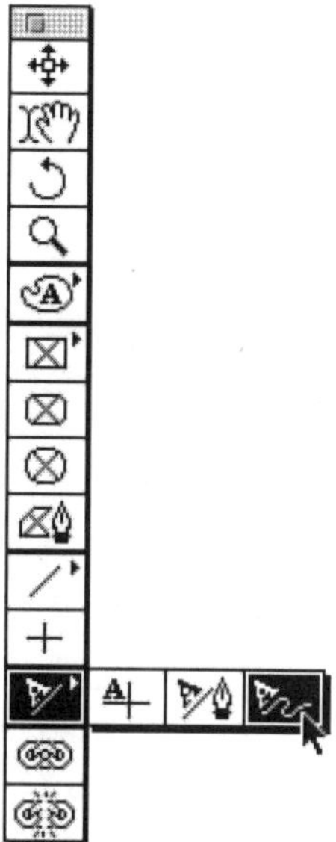

Figure 3.10

The Freehand Bézier Text Path tool.

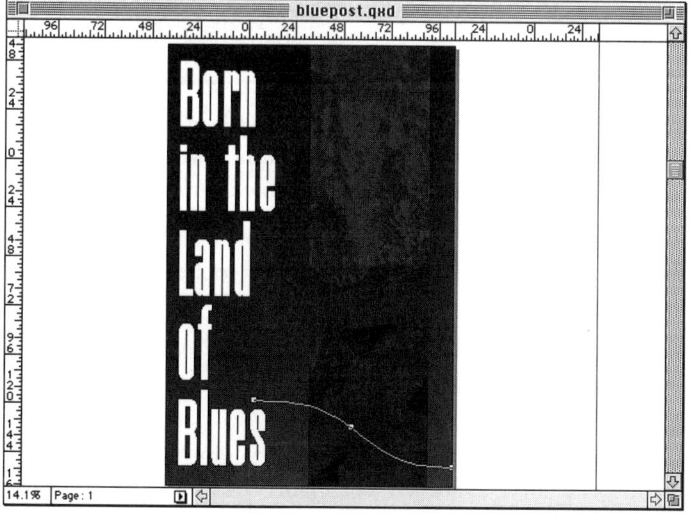

Figure 3.11

The Freehand Bézier version of the Text Path tool produces smoothly curved text paths.

18. The cursor reverts to the Content tool when you let up on the mouse button at the end of the text path, and you can start entering text right away. Type **a new album from blue river** along the text path.
19. Press (Command-A)[Control-A] to select all the text along the path, then click the text color icon in the Colors palette and make this text white as well.

20. In the Measurements palette, choose Octavian for the font and enter 65 for the point size. Click the small "K" icon (not the large one) on the Measurements palette to make the type small caps rather than lowercase, then double-click in the tracking field and enter a new value of 5 (see Figure 3.12).

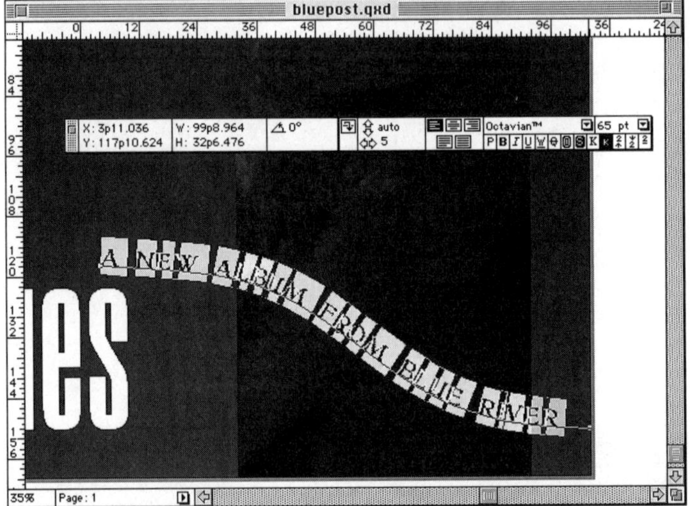

Figure 3.12

The style buttons on the Measurements palette let you apply local formatting to selected text.

21. For the second photo, a shot of the band, choose the Bézier box tool and draw a curved box with lines similar to that of the text path. If you're not familiar with Bézier curves, here's a step-by-step rundown on how to make this box:
    - Click once where you want the upper-left corner to be.
    - Hold down the Shift key and click again a few inches below that (see Figure 3.13). This makes a straight vertical line.
    - Click again to the right, where the middle of the box's lower edge will be, and drag the cursor slightly down and to the right to make a curved line (see Figure 3.14).
    - Click at the lower-right corner of the box, dragging slightly up and to the right, to alter the curve as shown (see Figure 3.15).
    - Holding down the Shift key again, click at the upper-right corner of the box (see Figure 3.16). The right-hand side of the box is all blown out of shape, but you'll fix that when the box is done.

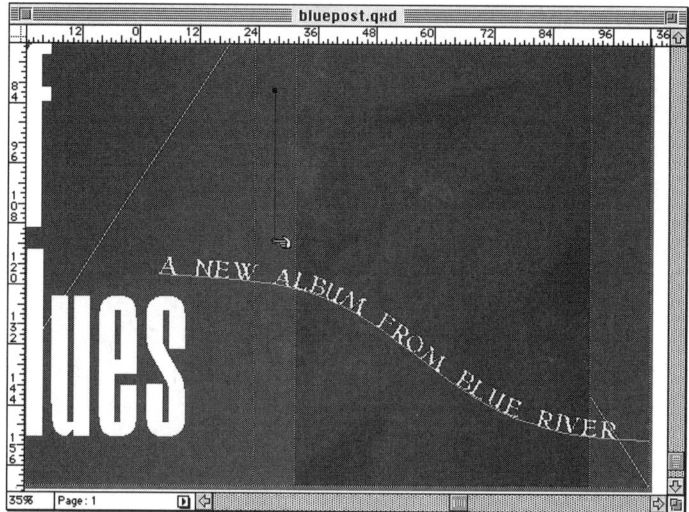

Figure 3.13

The first side of the Bézier box.

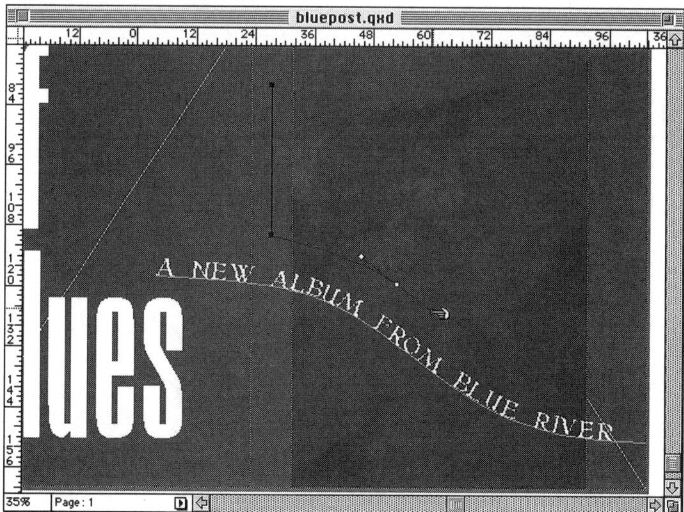

Figure 3.14

Beginning the second side of the box.

- Click at the midpoint of the box's top side, and drag down and to the left to curve the line (see Figure 3.17).

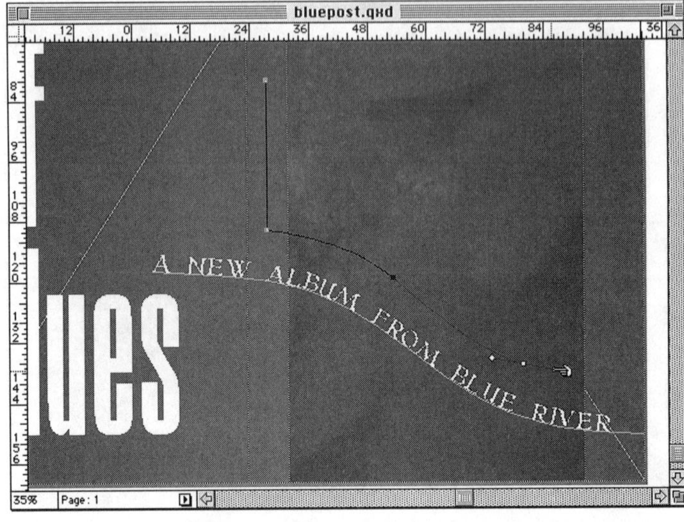

Figure 3.15

Completing the curve that makes up the bottom of the box.

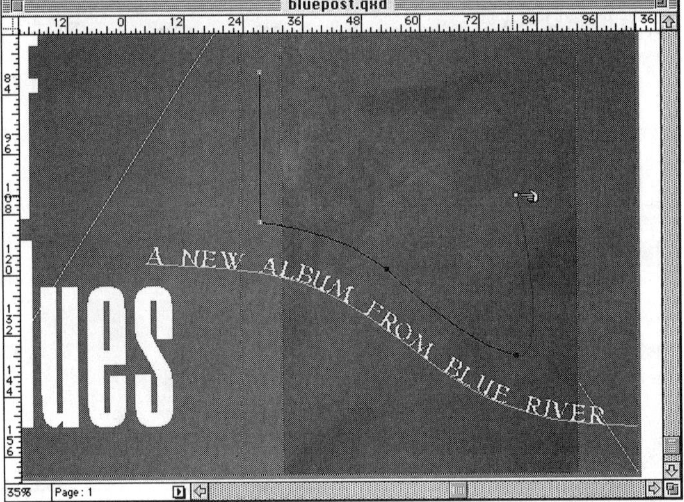

Figure 3.16

The right side of the box is misshapen, but that can be corrected later.

- Back where you started, move the cursor over the first point until it shows a rounded-corner square to indicate that clicking will close the box, then click (see Figure 3.18).

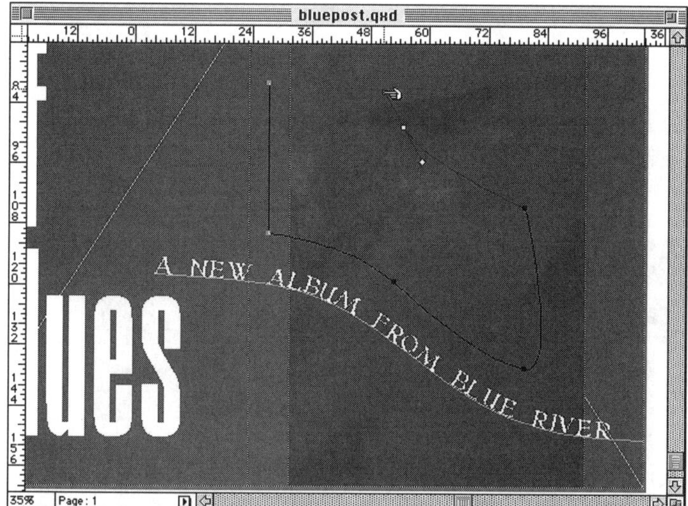

Figure 3.17

Halfway through the fourth side of the box.

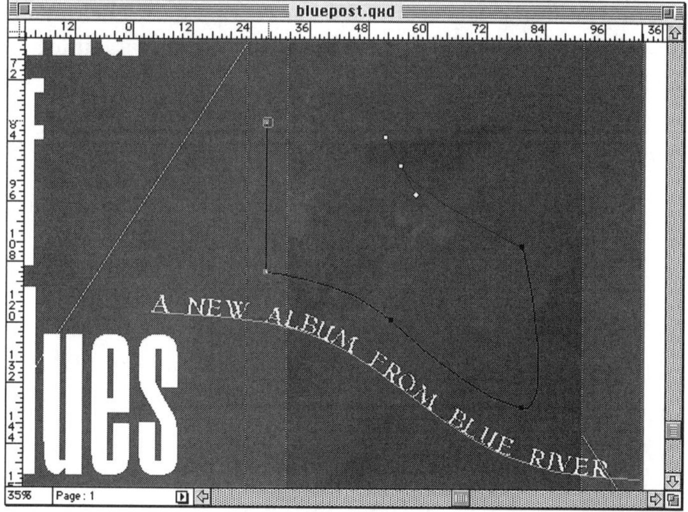

Figure 3.18

The rounded-corner square cursor indicates that clicking will close the box.

- Now choose Item➡Edit➡Shape (Shift-F4) so that you can adjust the points, and click the lower-right corner of the box to select that point. Turn it into a corner point by clicking the corner point icon in the Measurements palette (see Figure 3.19), then hold down the Shift key as you drag the outer curve handle straight up. This gives the box a corner rather than a curve and makes the right edge of the box straight.

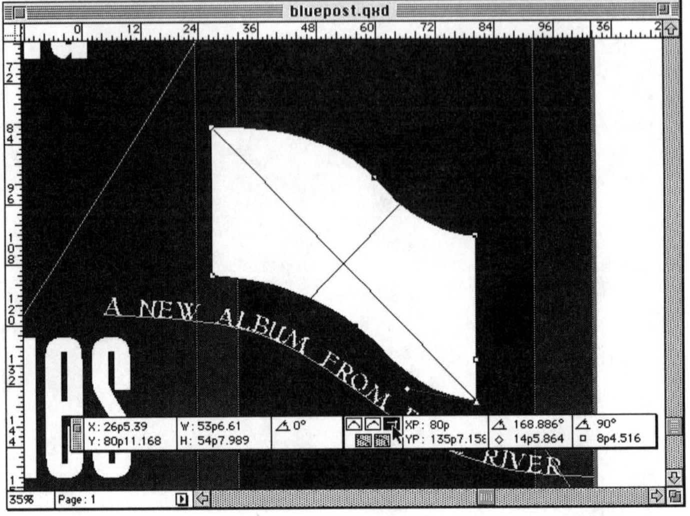

Figure 3.19

The point's type can be changed on the Measurements palette.

Adjust the box to your liking as you adjusted the text path, by clicking points and moving their handles or clicking between points and moving line segments. The idea is that the box will follow the lines of the text path, but it doesn't have to be perfect. It should either match very closely, or be pretty far off, rather than matching along part of its length and not along the rest (see Figure 3.20).

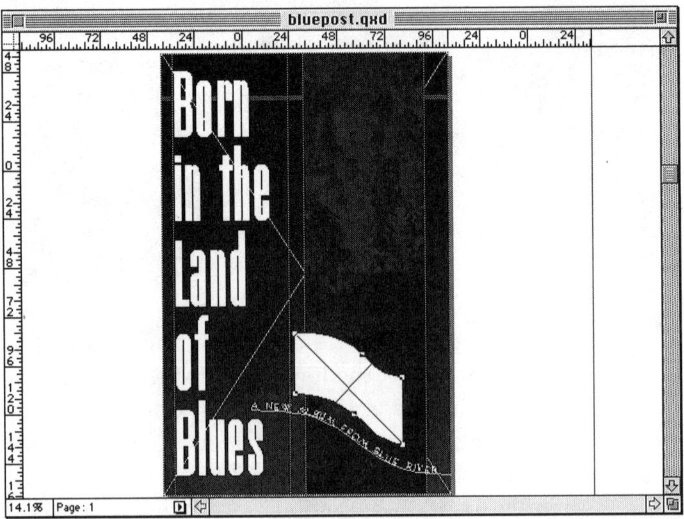

Figure 3.20

The Bézier box loosely follows the curve of the text path.

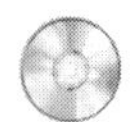

22. Switch back to the Content tool and import the second photo from the CD-ROM (choose File➡Get Picture or press (Command-E)[Control-E]); the file is lessons/chap03/band.tif.
23. This photo needs be reduced to fit in the box (if your box matches the one shown here), but altering its proportions will distort the band members' faces. To get an idea of what reduction percentage will work, press (Command-Shift-F) [Control-Shift-F] and look at the percentages in the Measurements palette (see Figure 3.21).

    The percentages will probably be different—my picture was reduced to 71.5 percent horizontally and 73.4 percent vertically—so to bring it back to the correct proportions, double-click in each of those two percentages and change them both to be slightly more than the larger percentage (I changed them to 80 percent). Move the photo around in the box (with the Content tool) until you can see everyone's face (see Figure 3.22).

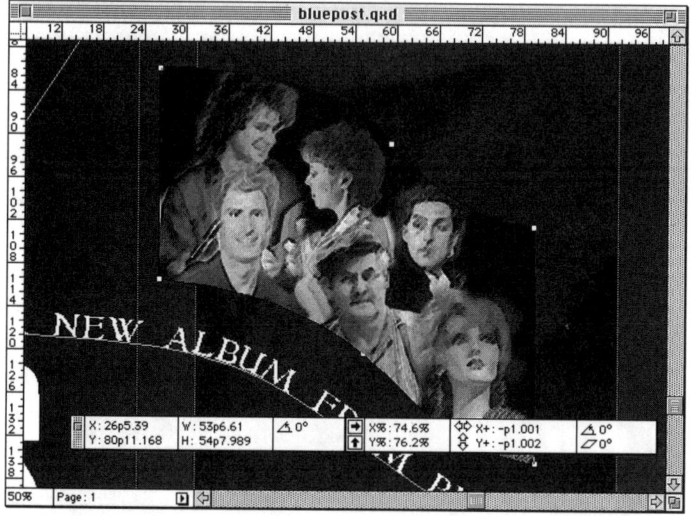

Figure 3.21

The percentages indicate how much the picture was resized in each direction to fit the box.

24. Press (Command-B)[Control-B] to bring up the Frame tab of the Modify dialog box, where you can choose a color, size, and style for the box's border. Choose PANTONE 221 CV from the Color pop-up menu and enter 12 in the width field. Leave the other options as they are.

25. As a finishing touch, choose the Orthogonal Line tool, which draws only horizontal and vertical lines, and draw a line from the left edge to the right edge of the page through the word "Born." On the Colors palette, click PANTONE 221 CV to make the rule dark red, then double-click in the rule width field of the Measurements palette, type 24, and press (Return)[Enter] to make the rule 24 points wide (see Figure 3.23).

Figure 3.22

Clicking a picture box with the Content tool lets you move the box's picture around, rather than the box itself.

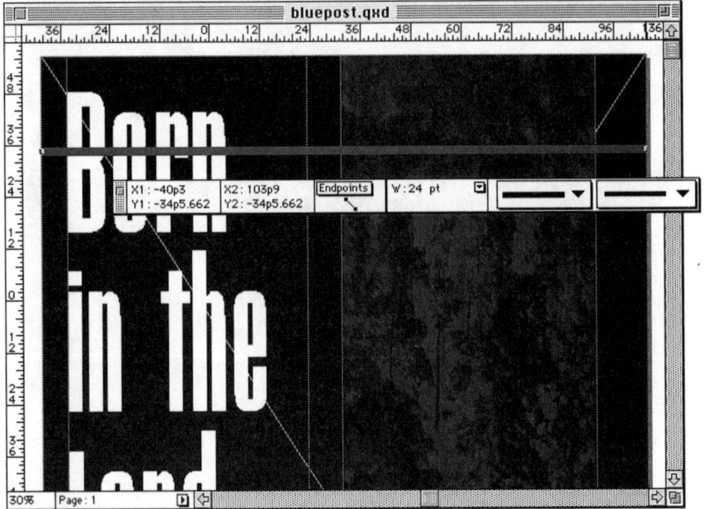

Figure 3.23

Adjusting the size of the rule in the Measurements palette.

Note

When you're working with rules, you don't have to click an icon on the Colors palette before choosing a color, because the only thing you can change is the color of the rule itself.

26. Switch to the Item tool and Shift-click to select both the text box containing the album title and the river picture. Choose Item➡Bring to Front, so that the rule falls behind these two objects but in front of the background (see Figure 3.24).

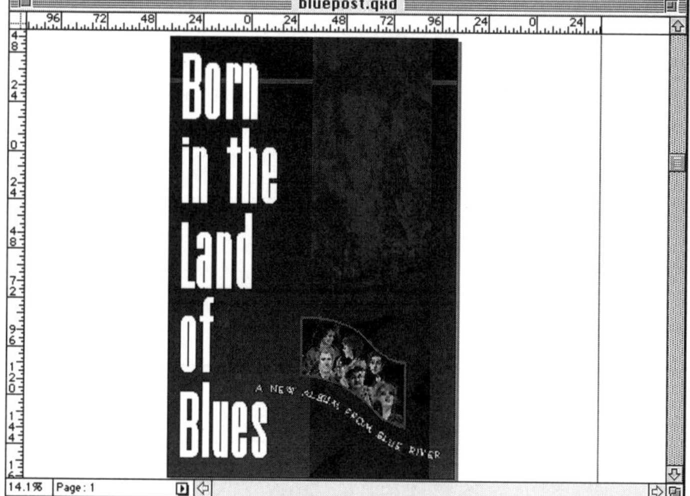

Figure 3.24

The rule falls behind the album title text box and the river picture box.

Note

It may seem obvious, but just in case: To delete an object, click it with the Item tool (not the Content tool) and press (Delete)[Backspace]. Mac users have more fun in this case—they also have the option of pressing Command-Option-Shift-K while either the Item or Content tool is active. Don't ask what happens—just try it.

This poster is just a "comp"—meaning that it's not suitable for final reproduction, but it's fine for presenting a design concept. Once a final design has been decided on, you'd need to go back and create high-resolution, exact-size versions of the two imported images and extend the background, dark red rule, and river photo to bleed off the edges of the page.

Modifying Objects

Once you've created an object, depending on what it is, you can modify it in several different ways, from just moving it around the page to changing its shape radically and even altering its object type.

The Modify dialog box (choose Item➡Modify or press (Command-M)[Control-M]) contains controls for every attribute of each kind of object, with the controls grouped into different tabs—view different groups of controls by clicking on the tab name at the top of the dialog box (see Figure 3.25).

The tabs you'll see in the Modify dialog box change depending on the object you have selected. For example, if a line is selected, the first tab is Line, but if a box is selected, the first tab is Box. These two contain similar controls, but they're slightly different because the attributes of lines and boxes are different—for one thing, lines don't have color fills. Many of these controls are also available in the Measurements and Colors palettes (see Figure 3.26). You can use the palettes or the dialog box, whichever is easier for you.

Tip

The quickest way to get to the Modify dialog box if the Item tool is active is to double-click on the object. Windows users can right-click and choose Modify from the contextual menu.

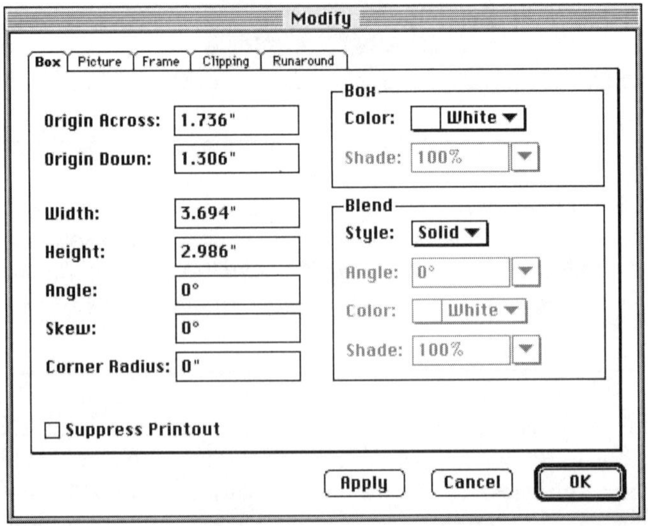

Figure 3.25

The Modify dialog box shows these tabs when a picture box with an imported picture is selected.

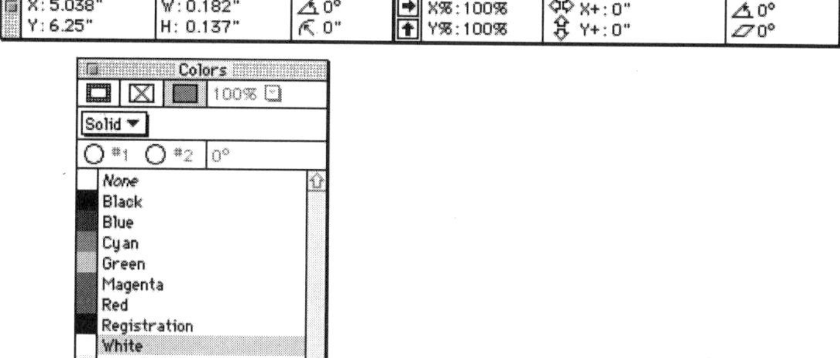

Figure 3.26

The Measurements and Colors palettes let you bypass the Modify dialog box to adjust most object settings.

Tip

You can see the results of your changes without leaving the Modify dialog box by clicking the Apply button.

Moving Objects

The most obvious modification you can make to an object is to move it using the Item tool. While it's often easiest to move objects around with the mouse, you can also move an object by typing in the exact position you want it to occupy in either the Measurements palette (the X and Y coordinates) or the Box or Line tab of the Modify dialog box. Origin Across and Down are the same as the X and Y coordinates; they reflect the position of the object with respect to the zeroes marked on the rulers, in whatever units the rulers are currently set to use.

Tip

It can be hard to figure out when to use the Item tool and when to use the Content tool. The rule is to use the Item tool to modify an item itself (to move it or delete it, for example) and the Content tool to modify the item's contents (add text or scale an imported graphic). To switch between the two quickly, use the Content tool and hold down the (Command)[Control] key to temporarily switch to the Item tool.

Changing an Object's Size and Shape

The size of most objects in QuarkXPress can be changed by clicking the object with either the Item or the Content tool, then dragging one of the object's handles. Straight lines have a handle at each end; rectangular boxes have a handle at each corner and one in the middle of each side. Irregular shapes may have more or fewer handles, depending on how many sides and how many curves they have (see Figure 3.27).

Both the Item and Content tools will work for resizing objects, unless you're working with one object in a **group** (see "Grouping and Constraining Objects" later in this chapter). In that case, using the Item tool will select the entire group; you'll need to use the Content tool to select just one item.

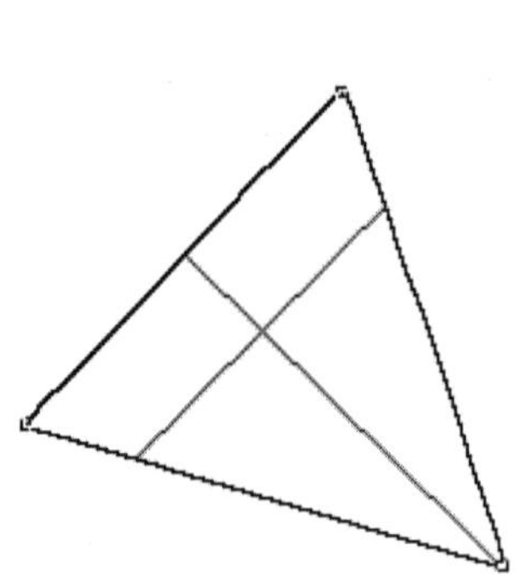

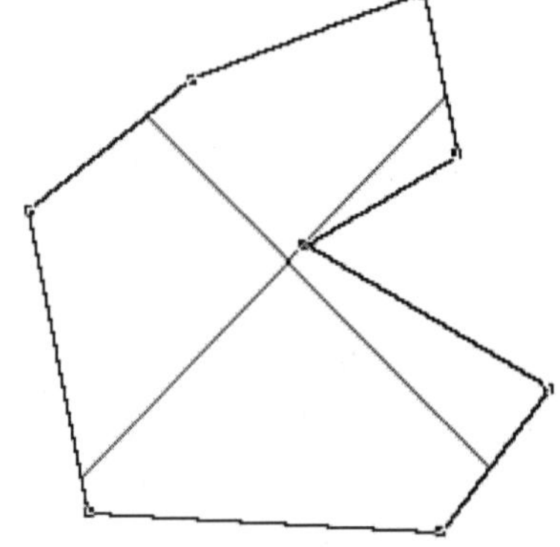

Figure 3.27

The simple triangle at left has only three handles, one for each vertex, while the more complicated irregular shape at right has eight handles.

Tip

Hold down the Shift key as you drag an object's handles to make it a perfect square or circle; hold down (Shift-Option)[Shift-Alt] as you drag to maintain its original proportions while resizing it.

You can also adjust the size of objects by changing the width and height measurements in the Box/Line tab of the Modify dialog box or in the Measurements palette. In both places, you can enter these measurements in whatever units you prefer (inches, picas, millimeters), and XPress will do the conversion to the current measurement system. You can also add, subtract, multiply, or divide in these fields. Say you want to make a box one pica wider, and its current width is six picas; place the cursor after the "6p" in either the Modify dialog or the Measurements palette and type "+1p," then press (Return)[Enter] (see Figure 3.28).

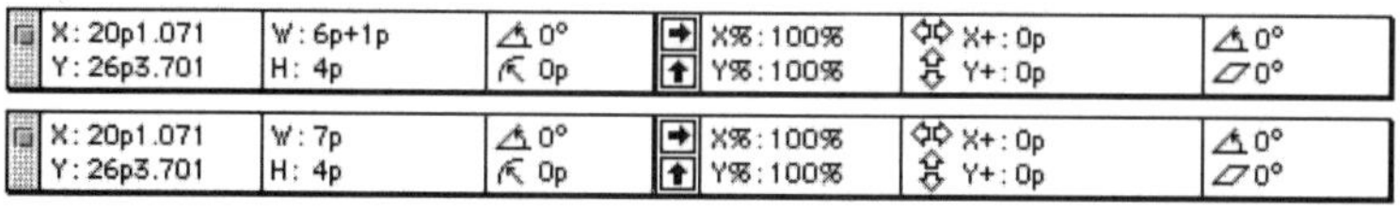

Figure 3.28

XPress does math—top, what you entered in the width field, and bottom, the resulting measurement.

The Measurements palette can display the position and length of a line four different ways. Choose one of four options from the pop-up menu to determine which is used (see Figure 3.29).

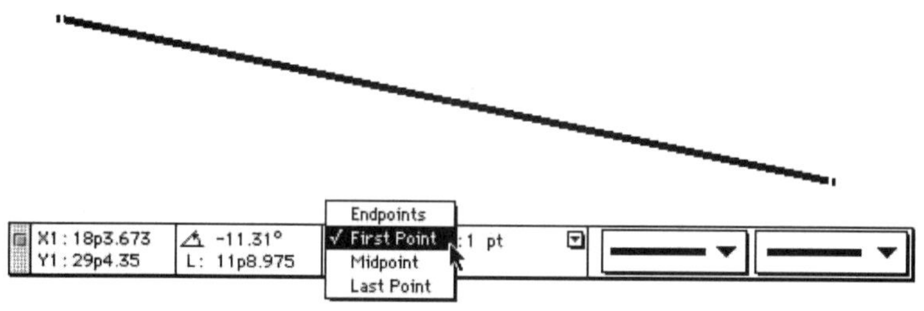

Figure 3.29

First Point is usually the most logical way to view a line's position and length.

- Endpoints display X and Y coordinates for both ends of the line (X1 and Y1, X2 and Y2).
- First Point displays X and Y coordinates for the first point created when you drew the line (X1 and Y1), as well as the line's angle and length.
- Midpoint displays X and Y coordinates for the middle of the line (XC and YC), as well as the line's angle and length.
- Last Point displays X and Y coordinates for the second point created when you drew the line (X2 and Y2), as well as the line's angle and length.

You can also change the width of a line on the Measurements palette, as well as its style and **endcaps** (arrowheads, for example).

Each object's shape is defined by the tool that was used to create it—create a text box with the Concave-Corner Text Box tool, and it will have concave corners. But, just as you can change a picture box to a text box and vice versa with the Item➡Content command, you can change the fundamental shape of an object by choosing Item➡Shape and picking a new shape from the submenu (see Figure 3.30).

In the case of the concave-corner text box, choosing the Bézier box shape from the submenu changes the box to a Bézier box with the same outline—only now you can edit the outline by moving individual points and adjusting each curve separately. As long as the text box remains a standard concave-corner box, you won't be able to change its shape, only its size and vertical/horizontal proportions.

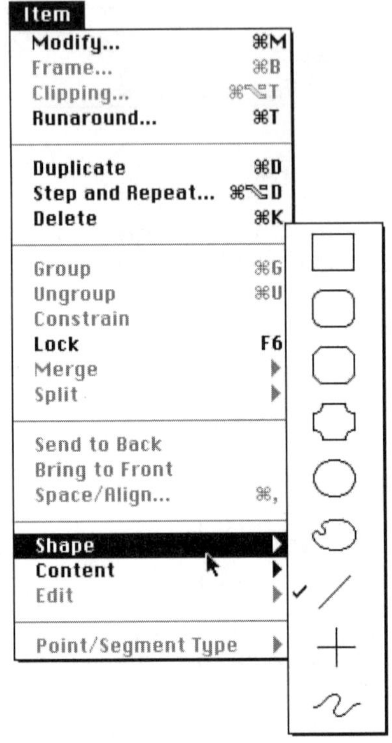

Figure 3.30

The shapes in the Shape submenu replicate the tool icons in the Tool palette—choosing one turns the selected object into the shape type of the matching tool in the Tool palette.

The Shape command is easy to follow when you're changing one kind of box to another kind of box, but it gets a bit hairier when you're changing boxes to lines and vice versa.

- Changing a line to a non-editable box results in an empty box the same width as the original line (see Figure 3.31).

Figure 3.31

Changing a 12-point wide, 4-pica long line to a rectangular box results in a 12-point wide, 4-pica deep box.

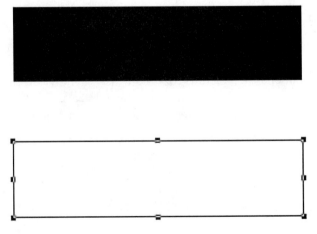

- Changing a line to a Bézier box results in a box shaped like the outline of the line—as long as the line is as wide as the box's border is and includes any arrowheads or dotted line effects (see Figure 3.32).

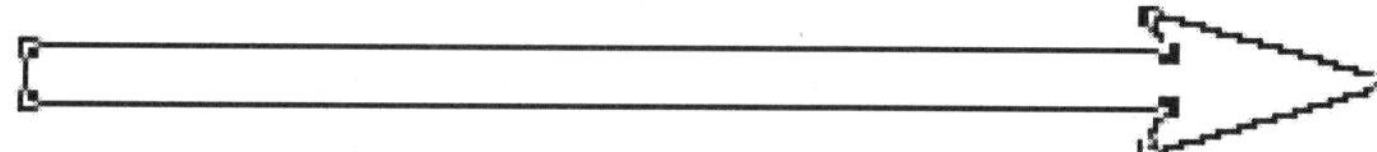

Figure 3.32

Changing a line to a Bézier box preserves arrowheads but not dotted line shapes.

Note

Don't try to change a very narrow line, such as a **hairline** rule, to a Bézier box—the resulting box will be so narrow that you won't be able to see all the points, and it will be no fun at all to edit into something you can use.

- Changing a box to a non-editable line results in a straight line running diagonally from the upper-left corner of the box to the lower-right corner (see Figure 3.33).
- Changing a box to a Bézier line results in an open-ended Bézier path with the same shape as the original box (see Figure 3.34).

Another "quick change" for a box is to adjust its **corner radius** to give it curved corners (see Figure 3.35). Change this setting in the Box tab of the Modify dialog box or in the Measurements palette to round off the box's corners by entering a measurement between 0 and the equivalent of 2". The higher the number, the further from the actual corner point the rounding extends. The radius measurement actually refers to the radius of an imaginary circle tucked into the corner of the box—the box's curved corners follow the outline of the circle.

There are two ways to rotate objects—freehand, using the Rotate tool, or in precise increments, by specifying a rotation angle.

- Rotate objects freehand by choosing the Rotate tool from the Tool palette, clicking in the document window, and moving the mouse in a circle around the point where you clicked. Any selected objects will rotate around that point (see Figure 3.36). The closer you click to the selected objects, the closer they'll stay to their original position as they rotate. Hold down the Shift key to restrict the rotation to 45° increments.

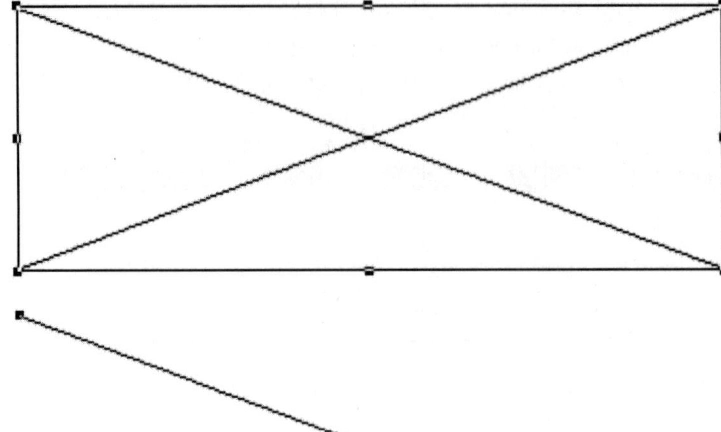

Figure 3.33

Changing a box to a line gives you a diagonal line.

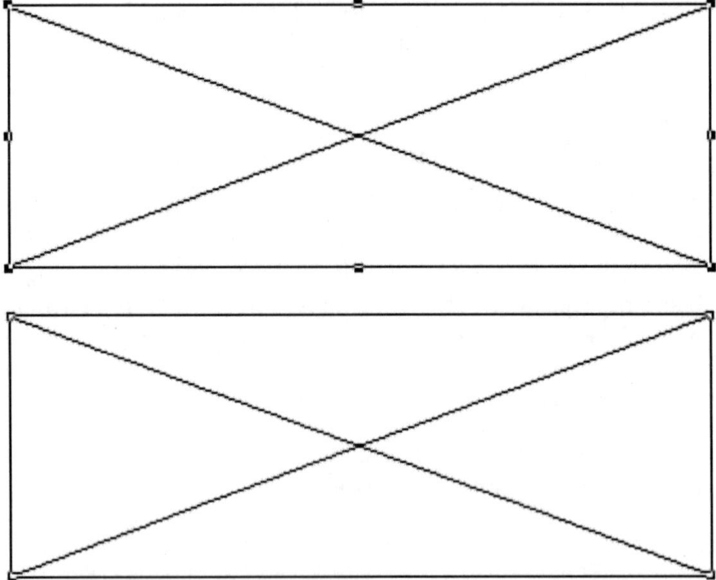

Figure 3.34

Changing a box to a Bézier line gives you a line with the same shape as the original box.

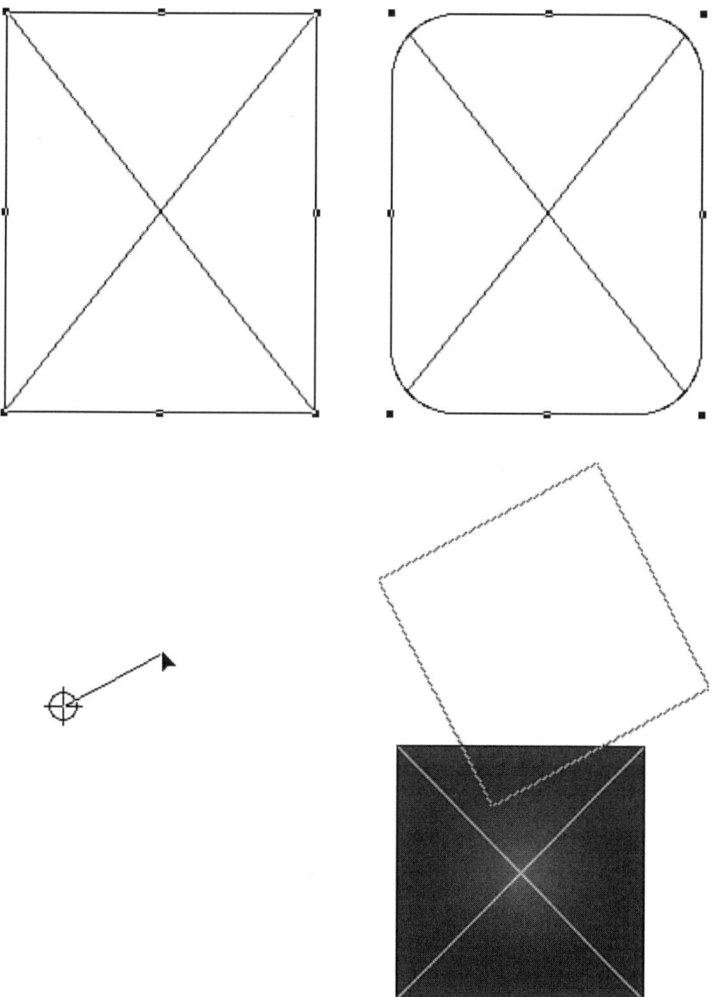

Figure 3.35

Left, the original box with a corner radius of 0p (the default), and right the same box with a corner radius of 3p.

Figure 3.36

Objects rotate around the point where you click the Rotation tool.

- Adjust an object's angle in the Box tab of the Modify dialog box or in the Measurements palette, and enter a number of degrees (either positive or negative) to rotate the object. Positive values rotate the object to the left (counter-clockwise), while negative ones rotate the object to the right (clockwise).

Related to rotating is **skewing**. You'll find it in the Box tab of the Modify dialog box, where you can enter a number of degrees between -75 and 75 to tilt an object to the left or right (see Figure 3.37). Any contents of the object will be skewed as well, but you can unskew an imported picture by entering the opposite amount of skewing in the Picture Skew field on the Picture tab of the Modify dialog box or in the Picture Skew field at the right end of the Measurements palette.

Figure 3.37

A box skewed by 45°.

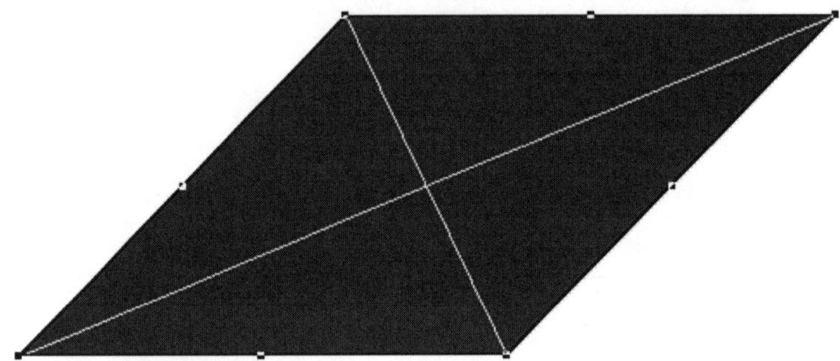

Combining Shapes

Any time more than one object is selected, the Merge command is available. Choose one of the options in the Item➡Merge submenu to combine the selected objects into one object. The color, border width, and content type of the resulting object depends on the content type of the bottom object (see "Layering Objects" later in this chapter to learn how objects are "stacked"). If the bottom object is a picture box, the resulting object is a Bézier picture box; if the bottom object is a text box or a text path, the resulting object is a Bézier text box. Of course, you can change the object's content type (see "Changing an Object's Size and Shape" earlier in this chapter).

The Merge command can work several different ways, depending on which option you choose from the submenu (see Figure 3.38).

- Intersection creates a shape from the area where the selected objects overlap the bottom object.
- Union combines all the objects' shapes to create the new object.
- Difference deletes all areas of the objects except any area of the bottom object that isn't overlapped by any other selected object.
- Reverse Difference creates a Union shape and then deletes the area occupied by the bottom object.
- Exclusive Or makes a Union shape but then deletes any overlapping areas, placing two points at any corner where two objects overlapped.

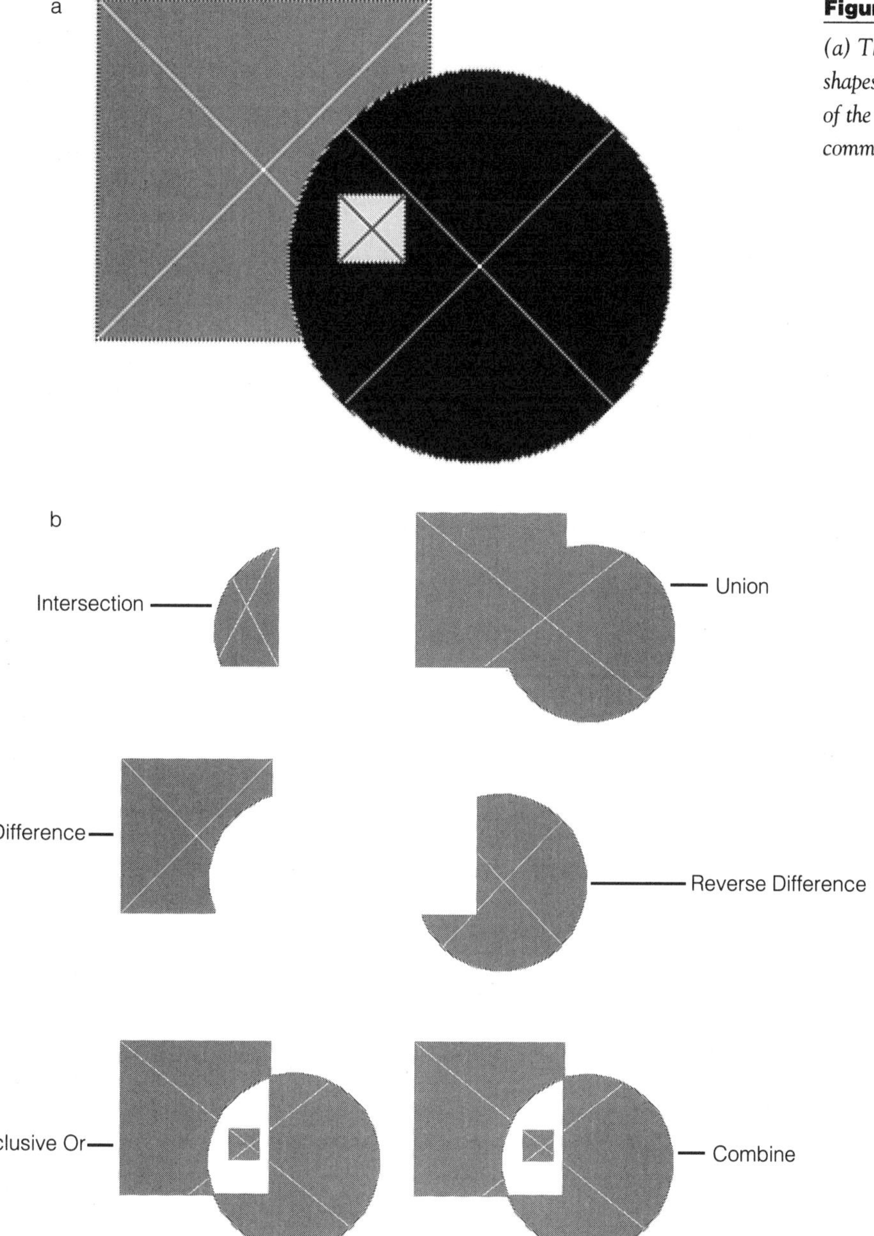

Figure 3.38

(a) The three original shapes, and (b) the results of the various Merge commands.

- Combine does the same thing as Exclusive Or but only creates one point at intersections.
- Join Endpoints creates a Bézier line (instead of a box) from two lines, or text paths are selected when an endpoint of one line or path overlaps or is close to an endpoint of the other line or path (see Figure 3.39). The allowable distance is determined by the Snap Distance in the General tab of the Document Preferences.

Figure 3.39

Join Endpoints turns two Bézier lines into one.

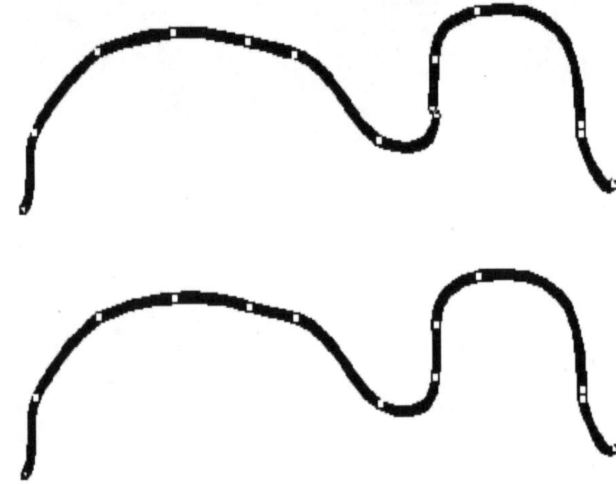

Merged objects don't have to overlap; the boxes created by the Merge commands are considered **complex boxes**, because they can include sections that don't touch each other. When you import a picture or apply a color to a complex box, the picture or color will be visible in all the sections of the box, just as parts of the same view are visible from different windows in the same wall (see Figure 3.40).

The opposite of the Merge command is the Split command (choose Item➡Split and choose Outside Path or All Paths). This breaks up a merged object into multiple objects; Outside Path separates objects that don't touch, while All Paths separates all objects in a complex box (see Figure 3.41).

Converting Type to Boxes

A particularly handy special effect in QuarkXPress 4.0 is the ability to convert text to boxes, which can be empty boxes, text boxes, or picture boxes. The possibilities are myriad: You can import stock texture photos into the boxes, give them gradient fills, edit the character shapes—the same things you could do with any box.

Figure 3.40

All the component boxes of a complex box show the same imported picture.

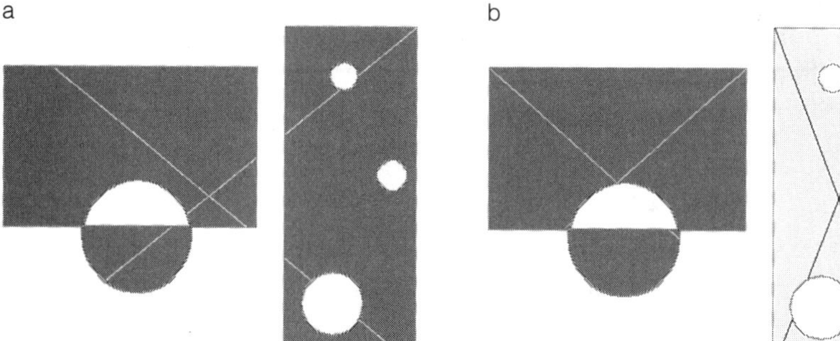

Figure 3.41

(a) Applying Split➡Outside Path to this shape results in two boxes; (b) applying Split➡All Paths results in six boxes.

Like merged boxes, the shapes created in converting text to boxes are complex boxes, which means that a picture imported into one box will show through all the boxes (assuming the picture is large enough) and that the shapes can be broken down into their components by splitting them.

To convert text to boxes, create a text box or text path and enter some text. Select the text you want to convert, apply the point size and font you want (you can't change the font after you convert it to a box), and choose Style➡Text to Box (see Figure 3.42). What you end up with is a single complex picture box.

Figure 3.42

100-point Goudy Sans converted to a box and then filled with a gradient.

To move or edit the component letters, choose Item➡Split➡Outside Paths, which gives you a box for each letter; Item➡Split➡All Paths breaks up the letters from each other and also breaks down the letters into their components. To turn the box into a text or empty box, choose one of the two options from the Item➡Content submenu.

Editing Bézier Shapes

The whole point of Bézier shapes, which are new to QuarkXPress 4.0, is that you can edit them infinitely. Any point in a Bézier shape can be moved by clicking and dragging, and any curve can be altered by dragging it or adjusting its handles. Two conditions must be fulfilled before you can do any of this, however:

- The object you want to edit must be a Bézier box or line. If it's not, choose Item➡Shape and pick one of the Bézier shape types.
- There must be a checkmark next to Shape in the Item➡Edit submenu (press (Shift-F4)[F10] to toggle this setting off and on). You can tell if an item's shape is currently editable by its **selection handles** (see Figure 3.43). This is a document-wide setting—either all objects are editable or none are.

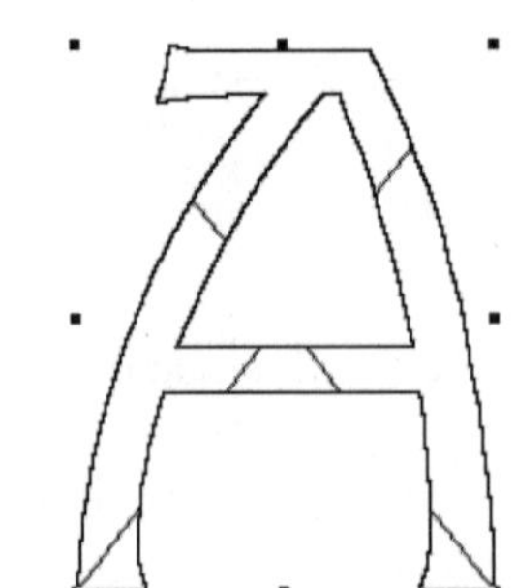

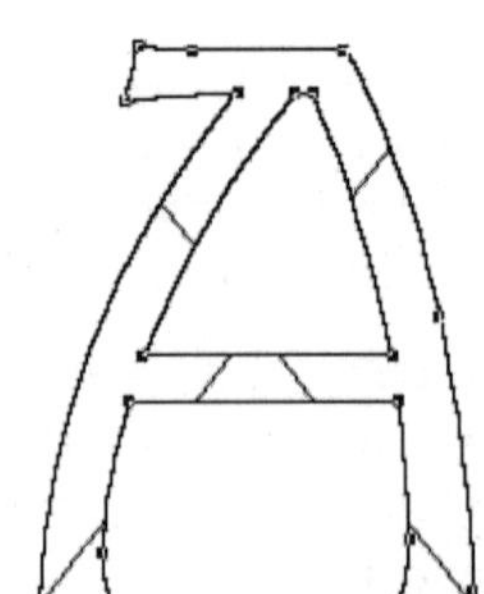

Figure 3.43

(a) If an object's selection handles are large and follow the "bounding box" of the shape, the item's shape is not editable; (b) if the handles are smaller and appear along the box's edges, the shape is editable.

Part of editing a Bézier shape is adding and deleting points that you can then adjust as needed. To add and delete points, make sure Item➡Edit➡Shape is turned on, then choose the Item tool and hold down the (Option)[Alt] key as you click the path. Clicking where there are no points adds a point, while clicking on an existing point deletes it, and the cursor changes to reflect what will happen if you click at any given point (see Figure 3.44).

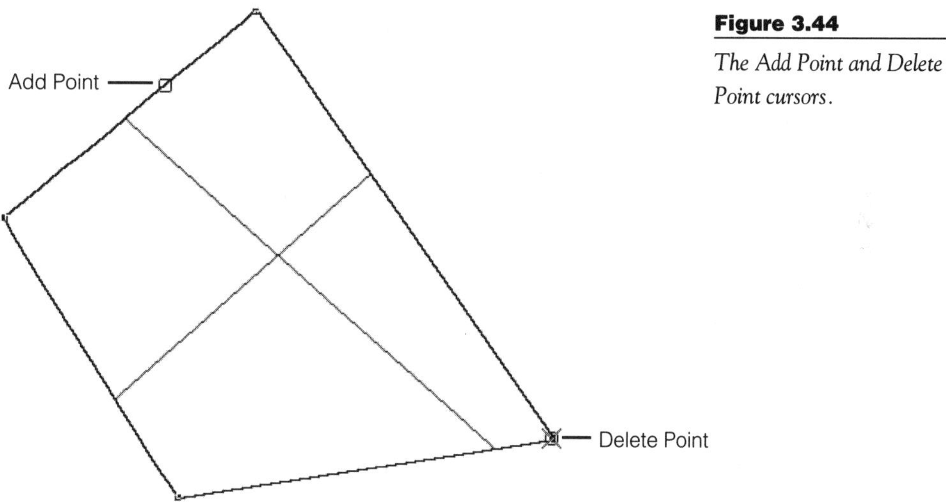

Figure 3.44

The Add Point and Delete Point cursors.

The other key to editing Bézier shapes is recognizing and changing the different types of point and segment that control the shape. By default, each point on a new Bézier shape is a **smooth point**, whose handles must stay 180° from each other, making the resulting curve smooth. A **symmetrical point** is similar to a smooth point, except that its handles must also remain the same length so that the curve looks exactly the same on either side of the point. Finally, a **corner point** allows its handles to move completely independently of each other (see Figure 3.45). You can change a point's type by clicking the point (shift-click to select more than one point) and then clicking the appropriate button on the Measurements palette (see Figure 3.46).

The line segments between points have different types, too: curved and straight. *Straight segments* are those created by clicking to create a point, without dragging; *curved segments* are created by dragging to create a point, which is the first chance you get to adjust the point's handles (see Figure 3.47). Click a segment between two points and then click the straight segment or curved segment button on the Measurements palette to change the segment's type (see Figure 3.48). Straight segments can't be curved by dragging; dragging them moves the segment and the two points on its ends.

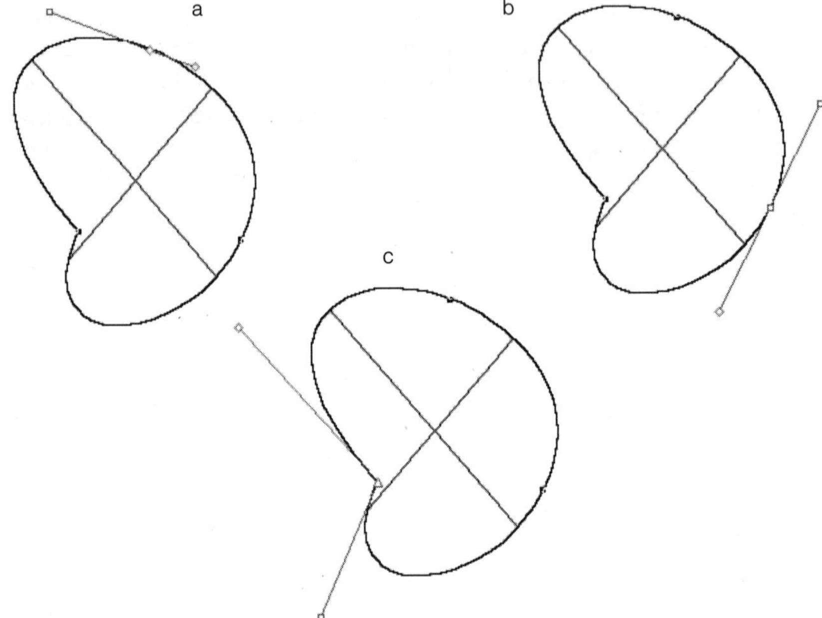

Figure 3.45

(a) Smooth, (b) Symmetrical, and (c) Corner points.

Smooth point button
Symmetrical point button
Corner point button
Straight segment button
Curved segment button

Figure 3.46

These five buttons appear on the Measurements palette when a point or segment on a Bézier shape is selected.

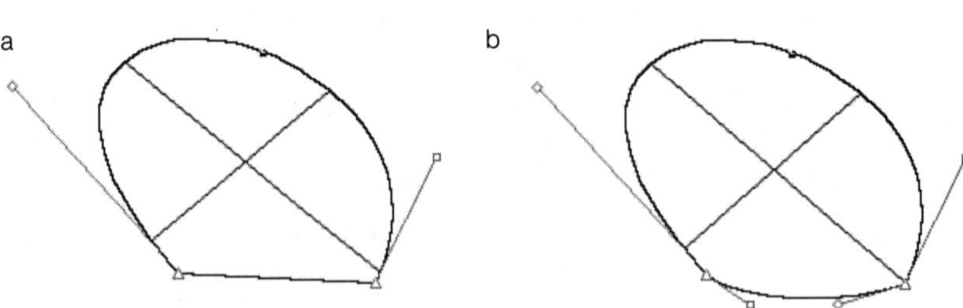

Figure 3.47

(a) The points on either end of a straight segment don't have curve handles, while (b) those marking a curved segment do have handles.

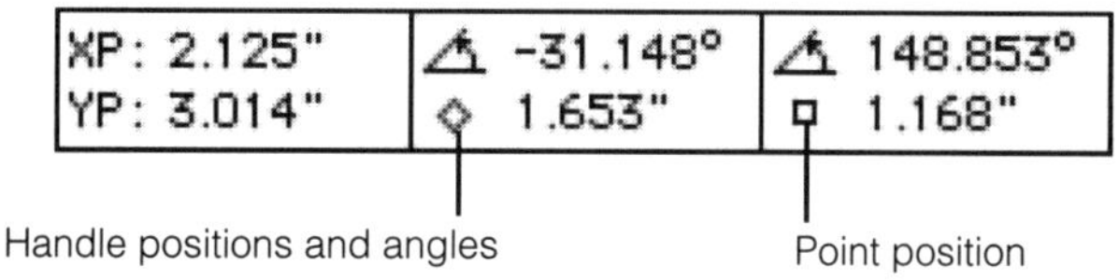

XP: 2.125" YP: 3.014" | -31.148° 1.653" | 148.853° 1.168"

Handle positions and angles — Point position

Figure 3.48

These three sections on the Measurements palette show the position of the selected point and the position and angles of the two curve handles attached to that point.

Tip

Select all points in a Bézier object by double-clicking any point; triple-click if the object is a complex object with more than one path.

When you're editing a Bézier shape, the Measurements palette also gives coordinates for individual points on the shape, as well as the angles and lengths of the two curve handles associated with each point. You can tell which handle the angle and length measurements correspond with by looking at the handles closely—one is a square and one is a diamond, and these small icons are repeated in the Measurements palette next to the corresponding measurements.

Changing an Object's Fill and Border

Any box can have a border and a colored fill, no matter what kind of box it is, and these attributes can be edited in both the Modify dialog box and in the palettes. You can set a box's background color and shade percentage in the Box tab of the Modify dialog box or in the Colors palette (click the third icon at the top of the palette and choose a color from the list—see Figure 3.49).

A background doesn't have to be a solid color; XPress can use two colors and **blend** them with several kinds of gradient. The Blend area of the Modify dialog box's Box tab lets you choose a blend style and angle, as well as a blend color and shade. With an angle of 0°, the main color of the box will be on the left, graduating to the blend color on the right.

Blends can also be applied in the Colors palette by choosing a blend type from the pop-up menu. When a box has a blend, the Colors palette displays two radio buttons, marked #1 and #2, to let you choose the two colors for the blend, with the original **background color** being #1 and the **blend color** being #2 (see Figure 3.50). The shade percentages for these two colors can be adjusted independently—they don't have to be the same.

Figure 3.49

Apply a background color to a picture box by clicking the background icon in the Colors palette and then choosing a color and a shade percentage.

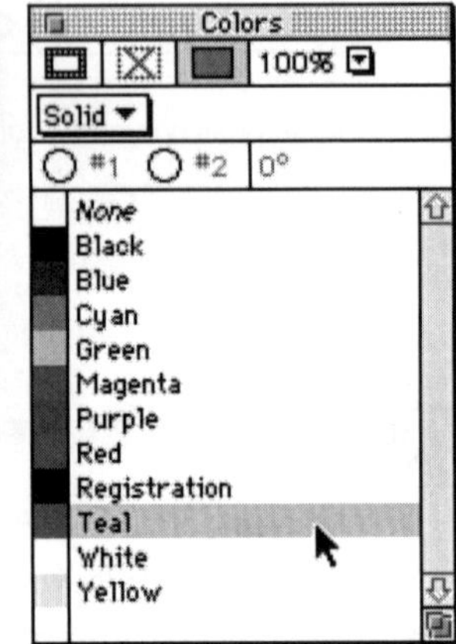

Figure 3.50

If a blend type is chosen in the Color palette's pop-up menu, radio buttons indicate color #1 (the box's background color) and color #2 (the blend color).

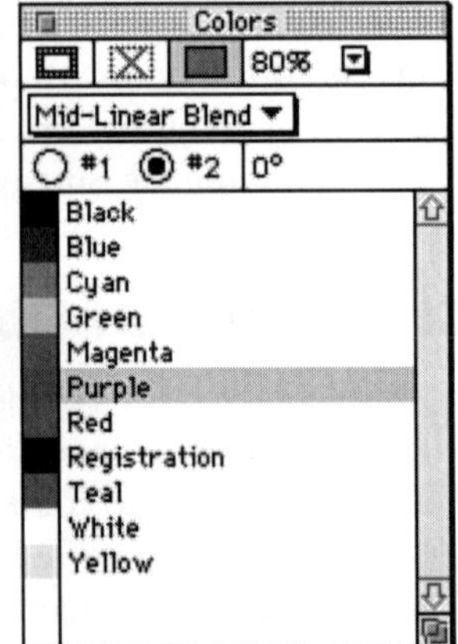

Note

By default, every box starts out with a background color of white and a border color of black. You can change these defaults by closing all documents and editing the Tool preferences for the box tools (see Day 1).

Lines don't have background colors, but they do have borders, just like boxes. To see a box's border, you first have to assign it a width. Unless you've adjusted your preferences to change the default border width, all boxes start out with a border width of zero. To assign a wider border to a box, press (Command-B)[Control-B] to bring up the Frame tab of the Modify dialog box (see Figure 3.51). Lines start out with a hairline width (the thinnest line any given printer can produce), and they can be changed via the Measurements palette or the Line tab of the Modify dialog box.

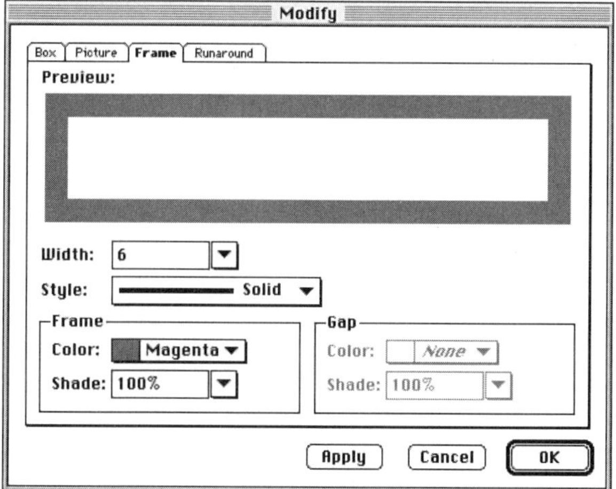

Figure 3.51

The Frame tab of the Modify dialog box.

The settings in the Frame tab include the border width, which can be between 0 and 864 points, the border style, the border color, and the border's gap color. There are 20 built-in border styles, some made up of multiple lines, and the gap color is the color that's shown between those lines. As with background colors, you can choose any shade (between 0 percent and 100 percent) for both the border color and the gap color.

The Dashes & Stripes dialog box for custom frames and lines works like the Styles dialog box, letting you create new custom dashed and striped line styles, delete them, edit them, and append them from other documents. To create or edit a dashed or striped line style:

1. Choose Edit➡Dashes & Stripes to bring up the Dashes & Stripes dialog box (see Figure 3.52).
2. Click the New button to display a submenu and choose one of two options: New Dash and New Stripe.
3. To create a new dashed line style, edit the settings in the Edit Dash dialog box (see Figure 3.53):

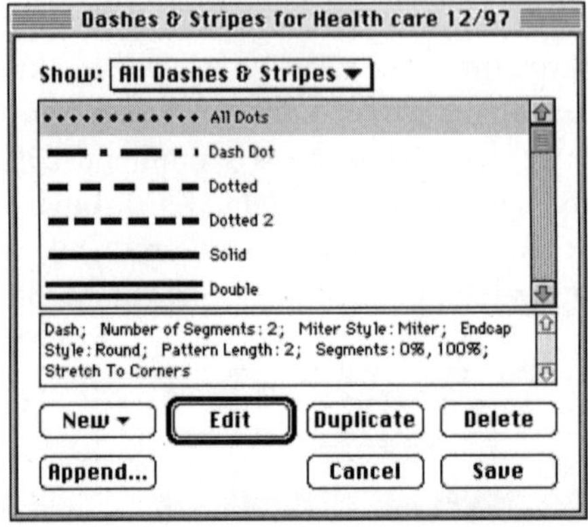

Figure 3.52

The Dashes & Stripes dialog box.

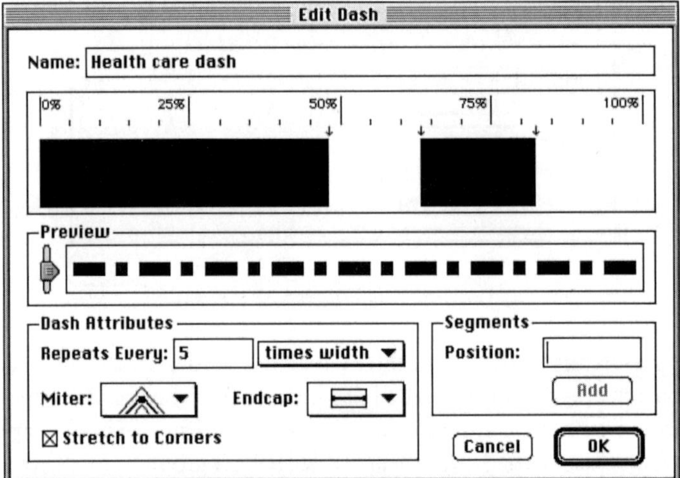

Figure 3.53

The Edit Dash dialog box.

- Enter a name for the style in the Name field.
- Click in the ruler area above the large black line to make a break in the line and drag the small arrow marking the end of each line segment to change the length of the dashes that make up the line.
- You can also add line segments, or dashes, by entering a percentage in the Position field of the Segments area and clicking the Add button.
- Enter a value between 0.1 and 50 in the Repeats Every field, and choose either "times width" or "points" from the pop-up menu next to the field. This determines how long the dashes will be relative to the width of the line. To determine the distance of a particular dash, first figure out how long the repeat is—either the number of points you entered or the width

of the line multiplied by the number in the Repeats Every field. Then multiply that measurement by the percentage shown on the ruler as the length of the dash.

For example, if a line is three points wide, repeats every five times the width of the line, and contains a dash that extends from the 25 percent mark on the ruler to the 75 percent mark, that dash will be 7.5 points long. Change the width of the line to one point, and the dash will only be 2.5 points long.

- Choose a Miter type from the pop-up menu; this determines what corners on a line with this style will look like.
- Choose an Endcap type from the pop-up menu. This determines what the ends of each dash in a line with this style will look like.
- Click Stretch to Corners on if you want the dashes to be adjusted slightly to fit evenly along any length line.
- See how the new line style will look by watching the Preview area as you change these settings.
- Click OK to create the style and return to the Dashes & Stripes dialog box or Cancel to return to the Dashes & Stripes dialog box without creating the new style.

4. To create a new striped line style, edit the settings in the Edit Stripe dialog box (see Figure 3.54). There are fewer Stripe settings than Dash settings.

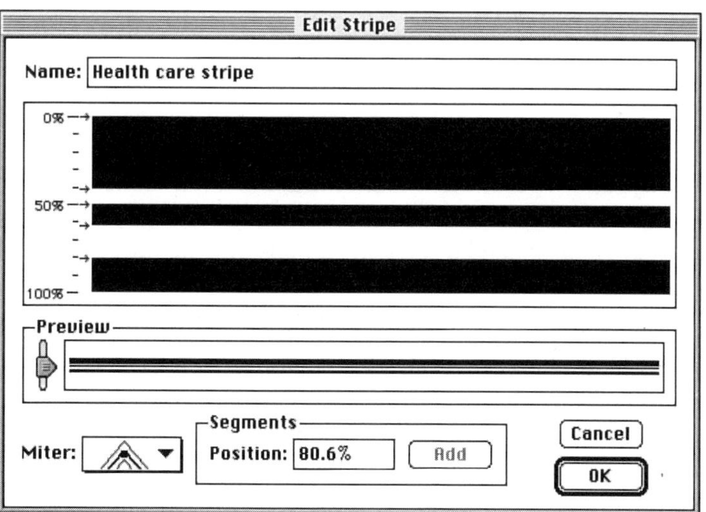

Figure 3.54

The Edit Stripe dialog box.

- Enter a name for the style in the Name field.
- Click in the ruler area to the left of the large black line to make a break in the line, and drag the small arrow marking the end of each line segment to change the width of the stripes that make up the line.
- You can also add stripes by entering a percentage in the Position field of the Segments area and clicking the Add button.
- Choose a Miter type from the pop-up menu; this determines what corners on a line with this style will look like.
- See how the new line style will look by watching the Preview area as you change these settings.
- Click OK to create the style and return to the Dashes & Stripes dialog box or Cancel to return to the Dashes & Stripes dialog without creating the new style.

5. Click the name of a style to view its attributes, then click Edit to change those attributes (or double-click the style name).
6. To remove a style, click its name, then click the Delete button.
7. To copy a style, click its name, then click the Duplicate button.
8. To append styles from another document, click the Append button and choose a document in the Append dialog box.
9. Once you're done modifying the line styles, click Save to save the changes you've made or Cancel to return to the document without changing the line styles.

Printing

Sometimes you don't want to include a particular object in the printout of a document. It may be a note to page layout personnel about how to work on the file; it might be an object that's crashing your printer (see Day 12, "Printing"). Whatever the reason, you can suppress the printout of a box and its contents by clicking Suppress Printout in the Box tab of the Modify dialog box, and you can suppress just an imported picture by clicking on Suppress Picture Printout in the Picture tab of the Modify dialog box.

Another way to see which pictures are suppressed and change their status is in the Pictures tab of the Usage dialog box (see Figure 3.55). Choose Utilities➡Usage to bring up the dialog box. A checkmark in the Print column of the list of pictures indicates that the picture will print; no checkmark means that it won't print. Click in the area to toggle back and forth between a checkmark and no checkmark, or choose Yes or No from the Print pop-up menu (click the small triangle to see the pop-up menu).

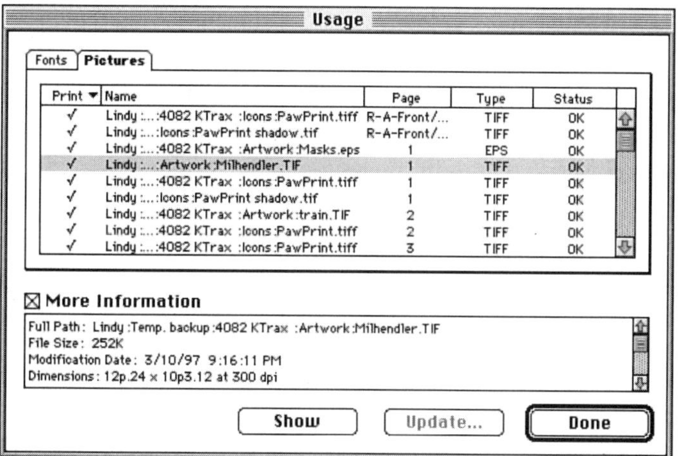

Figure 3.55

The Pictures tab of the Usage dialog box.

Adjusting an Object's Contents

The Modify dialog box also contains controls affecting an object's contents, whether text or a picture. Primarily, these controls allow you to adjust the position of text or an imported picture.

If a picture box is selected, the Modify dialog box contains a Picture tab with the following settings (see Figure 3.56):

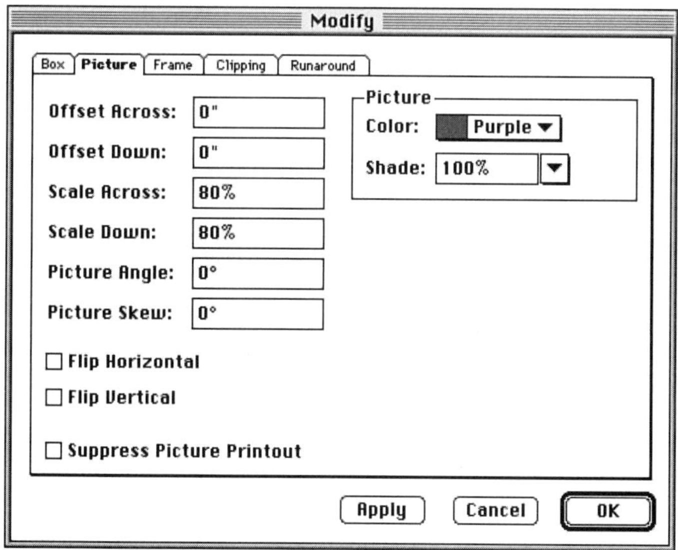

Figure 3.56

The Picture tab of the Modify dialog box.

- The Offset Across and Down fields here are the same as the picture position X and Y coordinates in the Measurements palette.
- The Scale Across and Down fields here are the same as the scaling X and Y percentages in the Measurements palette.
- Picture Angle and Skew are also in the Measurements palette; enter a number of degrees in the Angle field to rotate the picture within the box, and a number of degrees between -75 and 75 to tilt the picture within the box.
- Flip Horizontal and Vertical correspond to those mysterious arrows visible in the middle of the Measurements palette when a picture box is selected with the Content tool; as you'd expect, these functions flip the image horizontally or vertically, or both.
- The Picture area contains color and shade controls for the picture, the same ones accessible by clicking on the picture (center) icon on the Colors palette.
- Click Suppress Picture Printout to keep the picture from printing when you output the file; the box will still print, although it won't show unless it has a border or a background color other than white or None.

You can also control how much of a picture is visible by adjusting the picture's **clipping path** in the Clipping tab of the Modify dialog. See Day 7, "Importing and Editing Graphics," for more information.

If the selected object is a text box, the Picture tab in the Modify dialog box is replaced by a Text tab (see Figure 3.57). It has these controls:

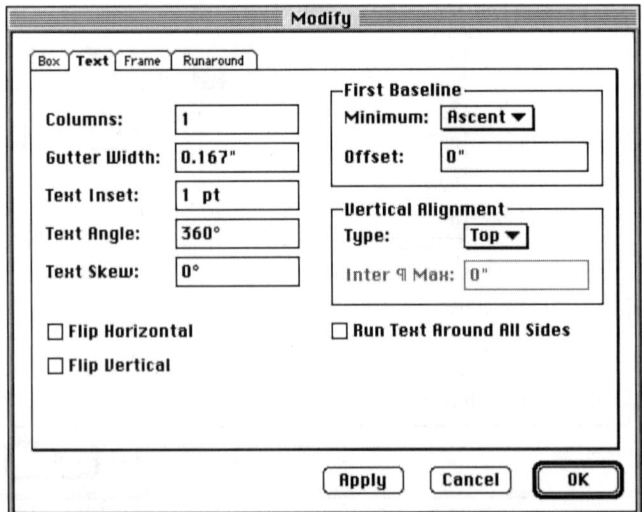

Figure 3.57

The Text tab of the Modify dialog box.

- Enter a number between 1 and 30 in the Columns field for the number of columns in the text box (see Figure 3.58).
- Enter a measurement between 0 and 288 points (4") in the Gutter Width field to determine the width of the gutters between the columns (see Figure 3.58).
- Enter a measurement between 0 and 288 points (4") in the Text Inset field to determine how much empty space will be left between the inside edge of the box and the text it contains (see Figure 3.58).

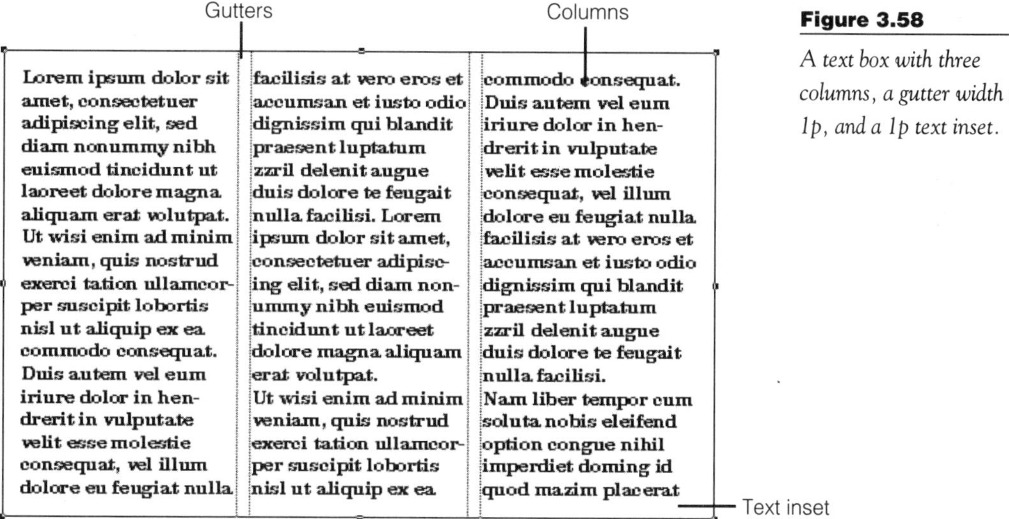

Figure 3.58

A text box with three columns, a gutter width of 1p, and a 1p text inset.

- Enter a positive or negative number of degrees between 0 and 360 to rotate the text within the box—a value of 90° gives you text that runs sideways, from bottom to top of the box, rather than from left to right across it.
- Enter a positive or negative number of degrees between 0 and 75 to determine how much the text will be skewed or tilted.
- Click Flip Horizontal, Flip Vertical, or both to flip the text within the box. You can still type when the text is flipped, but don't be surprised if it's hard to tell what you're typing.
- Choose an option from the Minimum pop-up menu in the First Baseline area. This determines the highest point within the box that the first text baseline can fall. Choose Cap Height to place the capital letters in the first line flush against the top of the box, and choose Cap + Accent to allow enough room for any accents above capital letters to be at the top of the box. Then choose Ascent to place the first line so that the **ascenders** (such as the vertical stroke of a lowercase "d"), which may be slightly taller than the uppercase letters, will just hit the top of the box (see Figure 3.59).

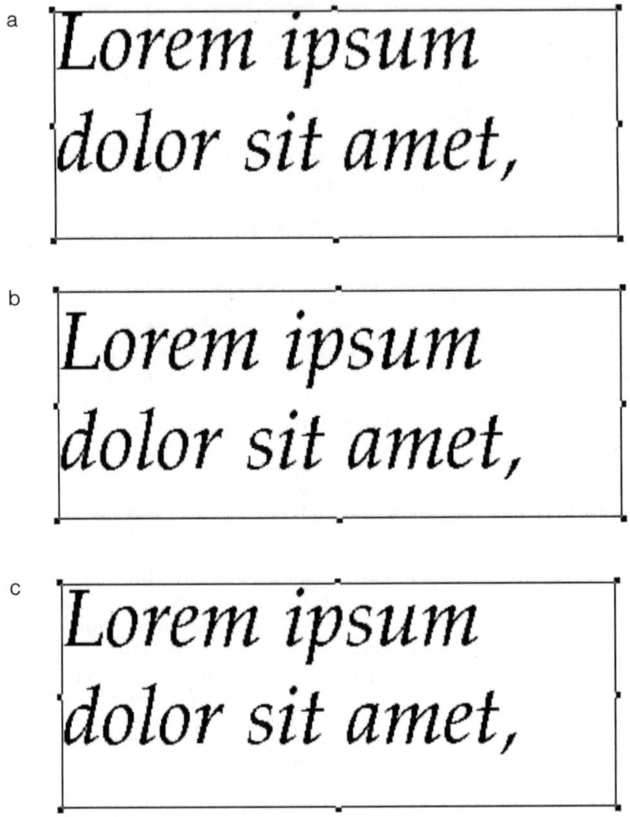

Figure 3.59

Three text boxes with different First Baseline settings: (a) Cap Height, (b) Cap + Accent, and (c) Ascent.

a

Lorem ipsum dolor sit amet,

b

Lorem ipsum dolor sit amet,

c

Lorem ipsum dolor sit amet,

- Alternatively, enter a measurement in the Offset field to place the first baseline at a specific vertical point within the box.
- Choose a vertical alignment option from the Type pop-up menu in the Vertical Alignment section: Top, Centered, Bottom, and Justified. These options place the text in the box at the top of the box (the default), in the vertical center, at the bottom, or spread out over the entire height of the box, respectively (see Figure 3.60). The extra space needed to vertically justify text is added between paragraphs, not between lines, unless leading is set to Auto.
- If you choose justified alignment in the Vertical Alignment Type menu, enter a measurement between 0 and 15" in the Inter-Paragraph Max field to determine the maximum amount of space XPress can add between paragraphs when vertically justifying text. If a text box can't be justified using this setting, XPress adds extra leading, not extra space between paragraphs.
- Click Run Text Around All Sides to allow text in the box to run on all sides of an object placed over it. See "Running Text Around Objects" later in this chapter, for more information.

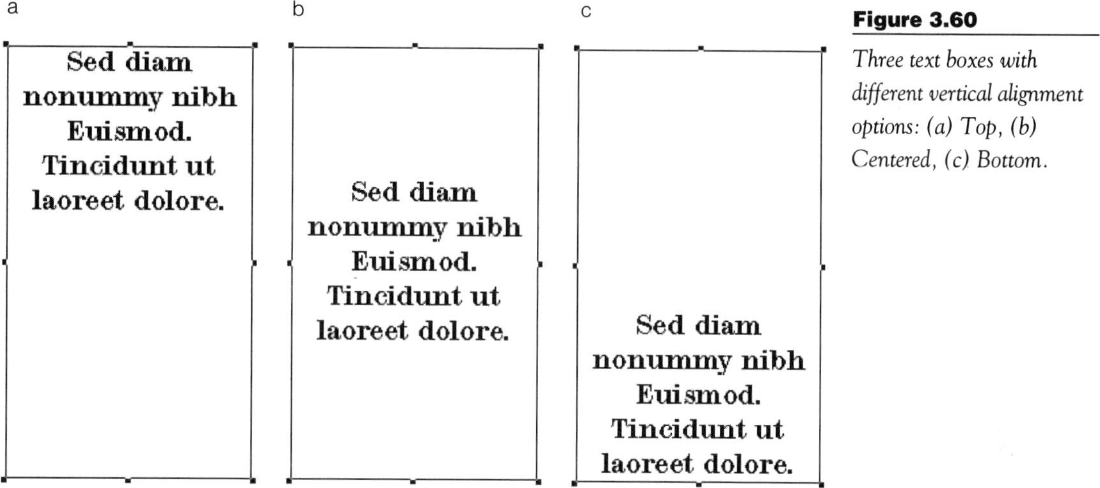

Figure 3.60

Three text boxes with different vertical alignment options: (a) Top, (b) Centered, (c) Bottom.

And if the selected object is a text path, there's a Text Path tab in the Modify dialog box, containing these options (see Figure 3.61):

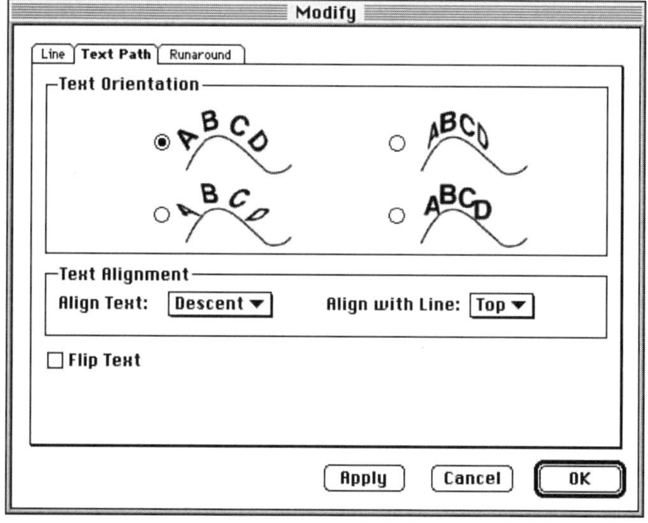

Figure 3.61

The Text Path tab of the Modify dialog box.

- Choose one of four options in the Text Orientation section to determine how the text is rotated or skewed to fit the path: rotated, but not skewed (upper left), rotated and skewed (upper right), skewed but not rotated (lower left), and neither rotated nor skewed (lower right). (See Figure 3.62.)

Figure 3.62

Four options for placing text along a text path: (a) rotated, (b) rotated and skewed, (c) skewed, and (d) not rotated or skewed.

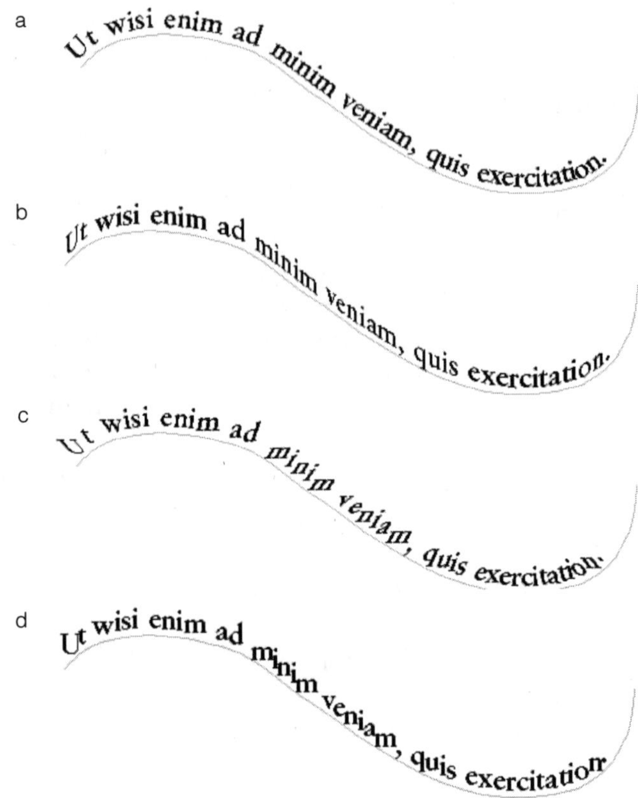

- In the Text Alignment section, choose an option from the Align Text pop-up menu to determine what part of the text follows the path: Ascent, Center, Baseline, or Descent (see Figure 3.63).
- Choose an option from the Align with Line menu to determine what part of the line the text sits on: Top, Center, or Bottom. This setting has no apparent effect unless the line is wider than a hairline—the wider the line, the more this setting makes a difference (see Figure 3.64).
- Click Flip Text to move the text to the other side of the line, starting from the opposite end (see Figure 3.65).

Figure 3.63

Four options for aligning text along a text path: (a) Ascent, (b) Center, (c) Baseline, and (d) Descent.

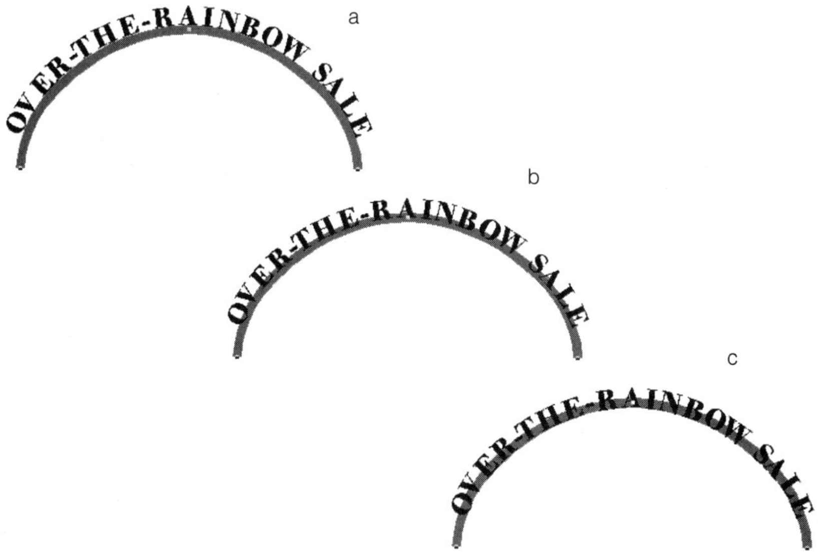

Figure 3.64

Three options for vertically aligning text along a text path: (a) Top, (b) Center, and (c) Bottom.

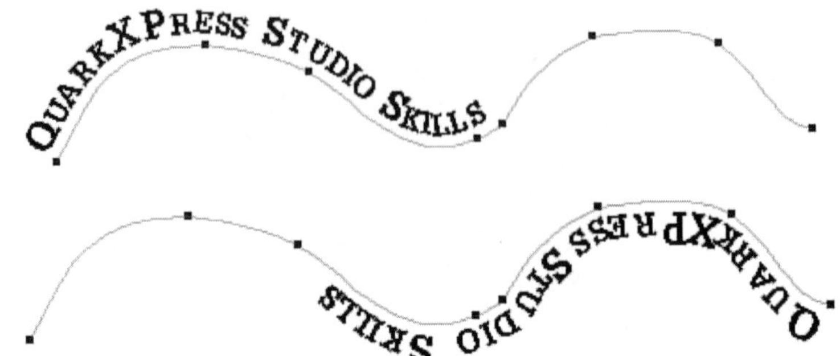

Figure 3.65

The Flip Text option moves the text 180° around the text path; (a) before and (b) after.

Changing Relationships Among Objects

Manipulating objects' relationships with each other is a key part of learning to use QuarkXPress efficiently—it's important to know how objects interact and how to change the way they interact. The commands to control these interactions are spread all over QuarkXPress, rather than consolidated in one palette or dialog box.

Grouping and Constraining Objects

If two or more objects are selected, moving one of the objects moves all of them, maintaining their positions with respect to each other. To gain this advantage without having to select all the objects you want to move each time, you can select multiple objects and group them by pressing (Command-G)[Control-G] or choosing Item➥Group. To select an entire group, click any of its members with the Item tool (see Figure 3.66). To select just one member of the group, click on that object with the Content tool. To reverse the grouping effect, select the group and press (Command-U)[Control-U] or choose Item➥Ungroup.

Tip

You can move one object in a group independently of the others by selecting it with the Content tool and then holding down (Command)[Control] as you move the object.

Constraining, a seldom-used holdover from earlier versions of QuarkXPress, is similar to grouping. When an object is constrained by another object, it is grouped with that object and bounded by the dimensions of that object so that it can't be moved outside the other object's area or sized to be larger than that object. Neither can the constraining object be resized so that it's too small to hold the object it contains. There are two ways to constrain objects.

Figure 3.66

When the group is selected, a dotted line indicates its boundaries.

- Turn on Auto Constrain in the General tab of the Document preferences (see Day 1). Then draw an object—a line, box, or text path—completely within the boundaries of an existing object. The new object will be constrained by the existing object.
- Select multiple objects, group them, and then choose Item➥Constrain to convert the regular group into a constrained group.

To convert a constrained group back into a regular group, choose Item➥Unconstrain. Other than the restrictions on moving and resizing objects in a constrained group with respect to each other, using constrained groups is just like using regular groups.

Note

Most XPress users agree that constraining objects is a useless feature. It's left over from a time when all boxes had "parent-child" relationships with other boxes around and within them—long ago in the early days of QuarkXPress.

Running Text Around Objects

When text overlaps another object, and that object is in front of the text box (see "Layering Objects" later in this chapter), one of two things can happen: The text can just keep on going, running right over the other object, or it can run around the object.

There are two settings that determine what happens in a given case: the overlapping object's runaround setting and whether Run Text Around All Sides is checked in the text box's Modify dialog. To determine how text runs around an object

1. Select the object that overlaps the text box and press (Command-T)[Control-T] to bring up the Runaround tab of the Modify dialog (see Figure 3.67).

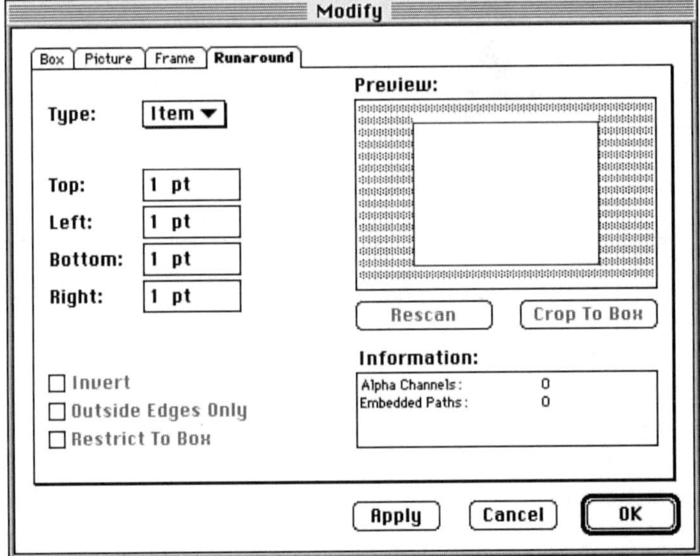

Figure 3.67

The Runaround tab of the Modify dialog box.

2. Choose a runaround type from the Type pop-up menu. If the object is a text box, you'll see these options:
   - None allows the text to run over the object. If you choose this option, no other settings are available.
   - Item forces the text to run around the object's borders. If you choose this option, you can specify Outset measurements between 0 and 288 points (4") for Top, Left, Bottom, and Right to determine how close the text can come to the borders (see Figure 3.68).

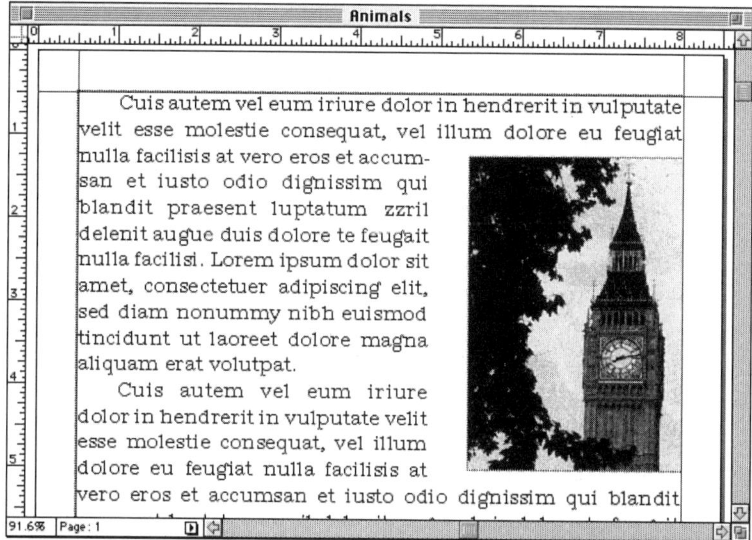

Figure 3.68

The picture box forces the text to run around it, using a 1p outset on the top and bottom and a 3p outset on the left and right.

If the object is a line or text path, you'll see None and Item, joined by Manual, which creates a runaround path like that created by the Item option, but lets you edit the path after it's created (see below).

If the object is a picture box with an imported image, you'll see None, Item, and the following choices:

- Picture Bounds runs the text around the entire picture, even if you can't see all of it in the picture box. As with Item, you can specify Outset measurements for all four sides of the picture.
- Embedded Path runs the text around the object based on a **clipping path** drawn in Photoshop, which can be any path the Photoshop user felt like creating. If you choose this option, you'll see a Path pop-up menu, which lets you choose from multiple paths in an image; an Outset field, where you can enter an amount that will be used all the way around the path; and a Tolerance area. In the Tolerance area, enter values for Noise (the smallest subpath that will be included in the runaround path) and Smoothness (how accurately the runaround must match the path).
- Alpha Channel creates a runaround based on an alpha, or mask, channel in a TIFF image. If you choose this option, you'll see an Alpha pop-up menu, where you can choose which channel to use; an Outset field; and a Tolerance area. In the Tolerance area, enter values for Noise, Smoothness, and Threshold (how much less than 100 percent black a pixel must be to fall inside the runaround path).

Note

Alpha channels are grayscale masks that contain black, white, and gray pixels; if you choose this option, the dark pixels in the image's mask will be overlapped by the text, and the lighter areas in the mask will force the text to run around them.

- Non-White Area runs the text around non-white areas of the image. If you choose this option, you'll see the same settings as for Alpha Channel, except for the Alpha menu. In this case, the Tolerance setting determines how much less than 100-percent white a pixel must be to fall inside the runaround path.
- Same As Clipping runs the text around based on a clipping path drawn for the object in QuarkXPress—a way of drawing a path to silhouette an image. See Day 7 for more information on clipping paths. If you choose this option, you'll see an Outset field and a Smoothness field.

As you change runaround settings, your changes are shown in the Preview area of the Runaround tab, with the path drawn in magenta and the theoretical overlapping text drawn as gray bars (see Figure 3.69).

3. Click Invert to reverse the effect of the runaround, running text inside the runaround path (see Figure 3.70). It's only available with the Embedded Path, Alpha Channel, and Non-White Areas options.
4. Click Outside Edges Only to run text only outside the boundaries of the image, leaving any open areas (such as the hole in a doughnut) empty.
5. Click Restrict to Box to force the runaround to take effect only within the boundaries of the picture box. The runaround path you've created stays the same, but it has no effect outside the box.
6. Click Rescan to redraw the preview of the run-around path using the current settings and working from the actual high-resolution image. Otherwise, the preview of the path is drawn using the low-resolution preview image you view onscreen; the high-resolution image isn't accessed until you click OK to apply the runaround settings. This button doesn't change the final result of the runaround settings; it just provides a more accurate preview in the Run-around tab.

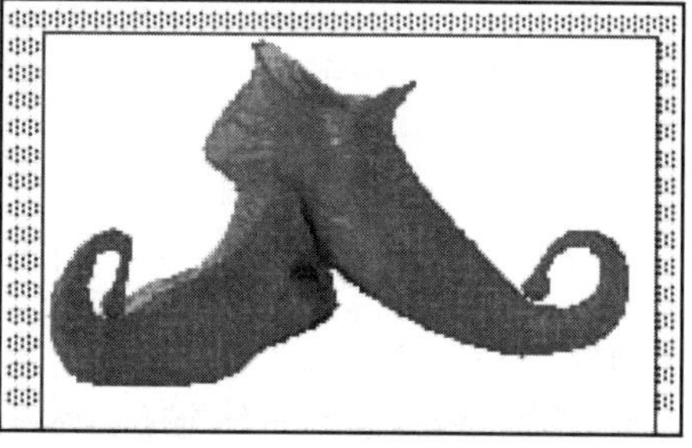

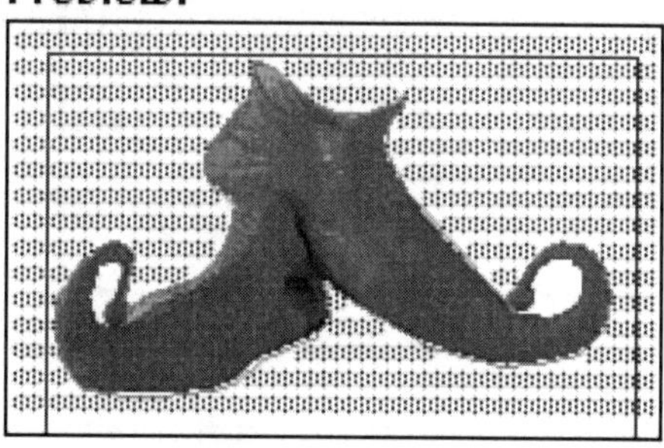

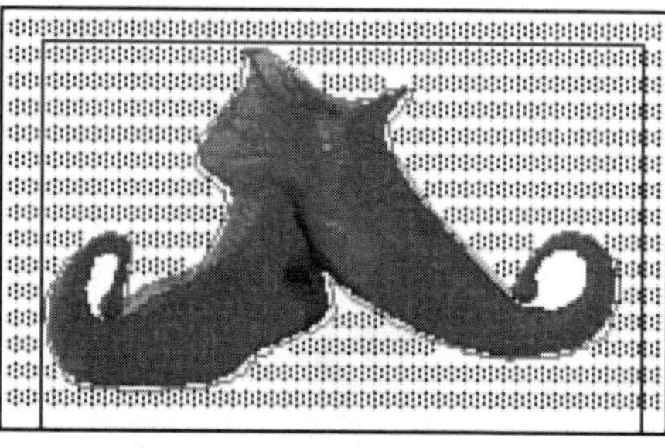

Figure 3.69

The Preview area of the Runaround tab for the (a) Item, (b) Embedded Path, and (c) Non-White Areas options.

7. Click Crop to Box to redraw the runaround path so that areas outside the picture box are eliminated.
8. Select the text box and press (Command-M)[Control-M] to bring up the Modify dialog box; click the Text tab and click Run Text Around All Sides to allow text to run to the left and right of the obstructing object. Leave this setting off to allow text to run only to one side of the object—it will flow to whichever side has more room (see Figure 3.71).

Figure 3.70

(a) Inverting the runaround forces the text to run inside the runaround path, (b) behind the photo.

a

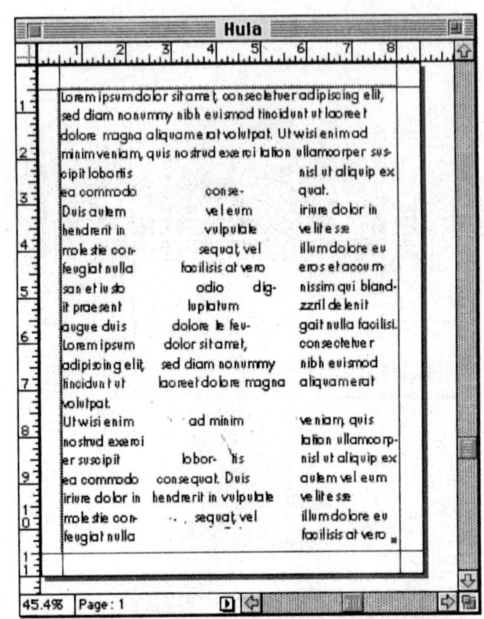

b

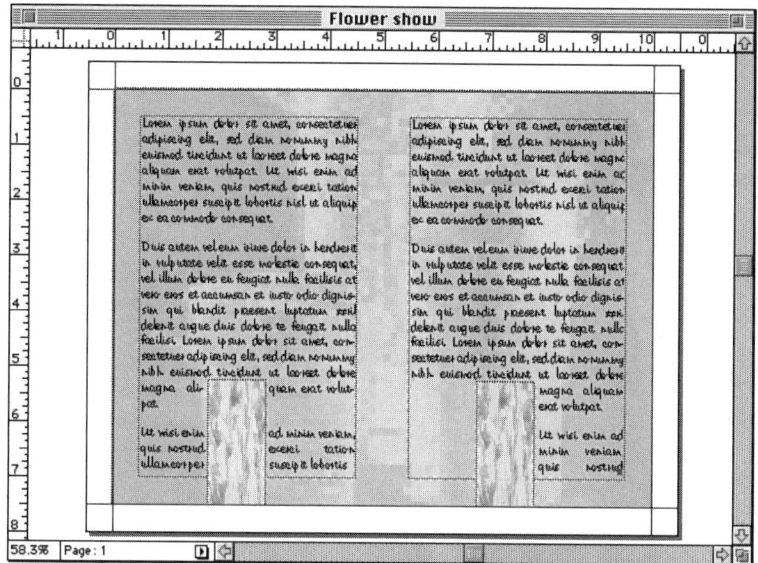

Figure 3.71

Left, the text flows on both sides of the picture; right, the text flows only on the right, because that side has more room between the picture and the edge of the text box.

9. Click OK or press (Return)[Enter] to apply the effects of the runaround and return to the document.

The Information area of the Runaround tab lists any alpha channels and embedded paths contained in the imported image.

Unless you use the Item runaround type, once you've created a runaround path, you can edit it just as you would a Bézier shape. Select the object and choose Item➡Edit➡Runaround (press (Option-F4)[Control-F10) to view the object's runaround path (see Figure 3.72). It'll be the same color as the baseline grid (see Day 1). Editing the path works just like editing a Bézier shape (see "Editing Bézier Shapes" earlier in this chapter). All the points are created as corner points, but you can change them to Smooth or Symmetrical points, move them, and adjust their curve handles.

Layering Objects

Although QuarkXPress doesn't have actual layer controls like Illustrator or Photoshop, its objects do have what's called a "stacking order" that's initially determined by the order in which they were created. If you create three objects, the first one is in the back, the last one is in the front, and the second one is in between. The stacking order doesn't matter for objects that don't overlap each other, but if they do, it affects both visibility and text runaround.

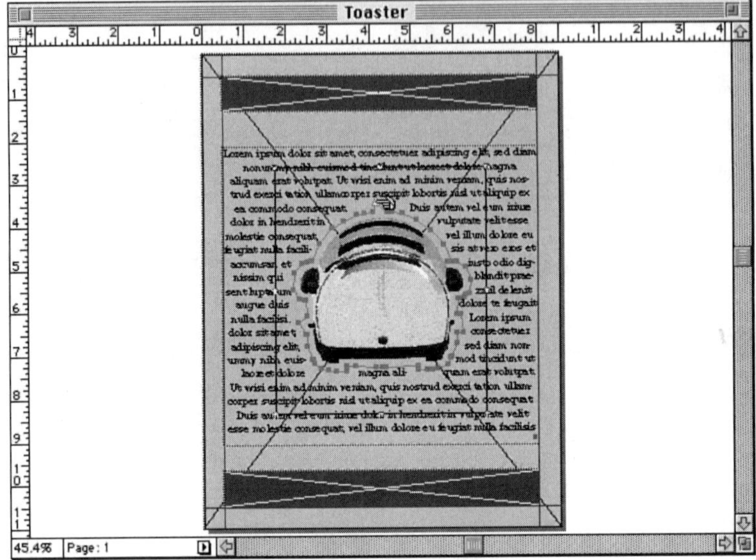

Figure 3.72

The runaround path for an object can be edited just like a Bézier path.

Obviously, if an object is in front of another object in the stacking order, and it's then moved so that it overlaps the other object, it will cover up part of that object, unless it's a box with no border and a background color of None. Less apparent are the effects of stacking order on text runaround, but they're just as important. To force text to run around itself, an object must be in front of the box containing the text.

To change the stacking order of objects, choose one of two commands from the Item menu:

- Send to Back (Shift-F5) places the object behind all other objects in the document.
- Bring to Front (F5) brings the object in front of all other objects in the document.

To move objects just one step at a time, instead of all the way back or forward, use (Option-F5)[Alt-F5] to move objects forward and (Option-Shift-F5)[Alt-Shift-F5] to move objects backward.

Tip

QX-Layers (Extensis, `http://www.extensis.com`) and Layer It! (Vision's Edge, `http://xtender.com/`) are two XTensions that let you work with real layers in QuarkXPress.

Embedding Objects in Text

Sometimes you need a box to flow with text, so that a picture, table, or other object can stay near its reference in the text. You can accomplish this by copying the object using the Item tool (using the Content tool copies the contents, not the box), clicking in the text where you want the object to be placed, and pasting it. You can paste in any box (not lines, though), no matter what its shape, and once it's pasted in, it's called an *inline box* (see Figure 3.73).

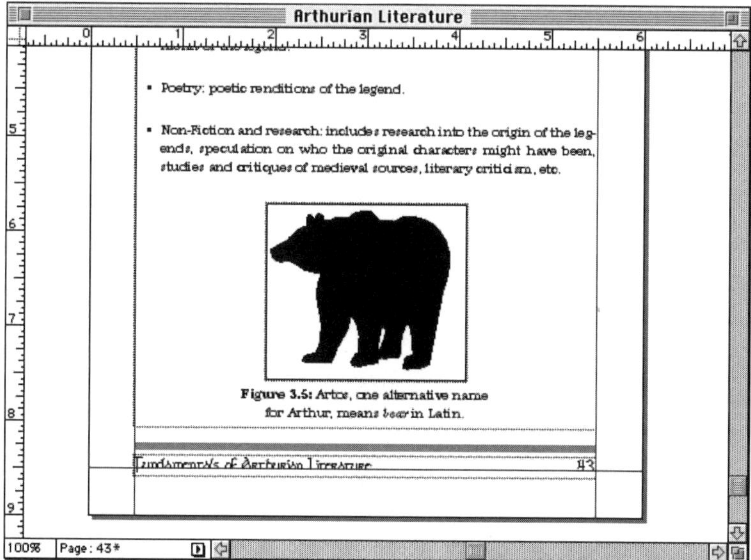

Figure 3.73

An inline picture box.

Tip

A paragraph that contains an inline box is one of the few places it's appropriate to use Auto leading. Generally, Auto leading is both aesthetically inappropriate and dangerous to use, since it varies with the size of the text—so if you insert a dingbat bullet in a larger point size than your body text, the leading of that paragraph will no longer be the same as that of other body paragraphs. However, Auto leading is the easiest way to let a line expand to hold an inline box no matter how you resize the box.

There are two ways to select an inline box: drag the text cursor over it as though it were a character in the text, or click directly on it with the Item tool. If you want to cut or copy it and paste it elsewhere in text, use either method. To cut or copy it and paste it as an independent object, rather than an inline one, click directly on it with the Item tool. You'll also need to click directly on it to access its settings on the Measurements palette.

The Measurements palette settings for an object change when it's inline; the X and Y coordinates are gone, and in their place are two buttons controlling how the box lines up with the surrounding text (see Figure 3.74). Click the Ascent button to "hang" the box from an invisible line along the text's ascenders and click the Baseline button to have the box "sit" along the text's baseline (see Figure 3.75). These settings can also be adjusted with radio buttons in the Box tab of the Modify dialog, as well as another setting—Offset, which is only available if you choose the Baseline option. Enter a value between -3p (-.5") and 69p (11.5") in the Offset field to control how far above or below the text's baseline the box's baseline will fall (this is similar to applying a baseline shift to the box).

Figure 3.74

The Measurements palette for an inline box shows the Ascent and Baseline buttons.

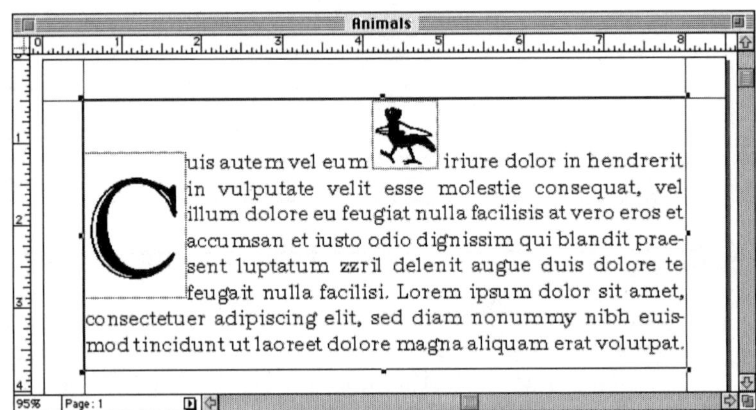

Figure 3.75

The inline text box uses the Ascent alignment option, while the inline picture box uses the Baseline alignment option.

Locking and Unlocking Objects

It's pretty easy to move or reshape an object accidentally—the more so as documents become more complex, with more different elements. XPress's Lock command (Item➡Lock or F6) prevents you from moving or reshaping an object with the Item or Content tool, although you can still change its **stacking order**, adjust its contents (whether text or graphics), change its color, or move or reshape it by changing its coordinates in the Measurements palette or Modify dialog box.

Locking is particularly useful for master page items, so that it's harder to change them on document pages. When you click on a locked object, or when the cursor is over a selection point on a locked item, it turns into a padlock to indicate that you can't move the point or the object (see Figure 3.76). To unlock an object, press F6 or choose Item➡Unlock.

Figure 3.76

The padlock cursor indicates that the selected item is locked.

Tip

When several objects are stacked on top of each other, it's sometimes hard to select the item you want, which may be at the bottom of the stack. In a situation like this, XPress's Locking command would be more useful if it worked like Illustrator's version, which doesn't let you select locked items. But there is a way around the problem: hold down (Command-Option-Shift)[Control-Alt-Shift] as you click repeatedly on the problem object. With each click, XPress selects a different object in that location—keep clicking until the one you want is selected.

Summary

Every QuarkXPress document is made up of a collection of elements: text boxes and paths, picture boxes, lines—all with different colors and other attributes. Arranging these elements with respect to the page and each other is what makes a design. Any object can be moved, resized, reshaped, moved up and down in the document's stacking order, locked, grouped with other objects, or even constrained by the size and position of other objects. Key to working with QuarkXPress elements are the two tools provided for manipulating elements once you've created them: the Item and the Content tool, for working with objects themselves and with their contents, respectively.

day 4

Importing and Editing Text

- Importing text
- Creating a text flow from page to page
- Editing text
- Exporting text
- Using XPress Tags

If design were only about graphics, you could do all your work in Photoshop or Illustrator (or FreeHand or Live Picture—I'm not arguing the relative merits here). Because text is involved in most designs, programs such as QuarkXPress are primarily designed to enable you to create text, import existing text created in word processing programs, and format text to fit the design of a particular document. In Day 3, "Creating Text and Graphic Elements," you created text boxes and modified their attributes. Now you will import text files into XPress documents and modify the formatting of the text itself.

Importing Text

To import text into an XPress document, you first have to create a text box, switch to the Content tool, and click the box with the Content tool if it's not already selected. Now that you have a box ready and waiting to receive text, you can use the Get Text command to import a text file into your document.

Assuming the default filters are installed in your copy of QuarkXPress, you can import text in the following formats:

- **WordPerfect documents** created in the Mac, Windows, or DOS versions of the word processor now owned by Corel.

- **Word documents** created in versions 3 through 6 of Microsoft's popular word processor. No special handling is necessary to import cross-platform Word files.
- **WriteNow documents**: This is a now-obsolete Mac word processor popular because of its low RAM requirements.
- **MacWrite II documents**: MacWrite was one of the original programs created for the Mac, along with MacPaint and MacDraw, but it lasted a lot longer. It's not widely used now.
- **ASCII text** (plain text with no formatting): Most word processors and many other programs, such as email programs, can save text in ASCII format.
- **XPress Tags** files (ASCII text files containing special formatting characters; see "Using XPress Tags," later in this chapter, for more information on this format).

Because each filter is a separate file, you can install just the filters you need (which will speed up XPress's startup time), and you can replace filters with updated versions as they're released. Quark releases new versions of specific filters as word processing applications are updated, usually making these updated filters available on the company's web site (`http://www.quark.com`).

Tip

When downloading a new or updated filter, make sure that the file you're downloading matches the version of QuarkXPress you have. If, for example, your copy of QuarkXPress is a 68K Mac version, a Power Mac version of an import filter won't work, even if your computer is a Power Mac.

Before you import text into QuarkXPress, you may need to do some prep work. If you're familiar with the features of your word processor, you may be able to save yourself a considerable amount of work in XPress by applying styles and local formatting in the word processor, as well as completing some quick search-and-replace commands.

If you want to work with documents in other word processor formats than the ones listed here, or if you want to convert one of those formats to Word or WordPerfect so you can import style sheets, you need to translate them to Word or WordPerfect (see the sidebar, "Whipping Text into a Format You Can Use").

Whipping Text into a Format You Can Use

Say you've got a nice ClarisWorks document, and you want to import it into your QuarkXPress layout. Not so fast—XPress doesn't speak ClarisWorks—only Word and WordPerfect. So the first thing to do is discover whether the document can be saved from ClarisWorks in either of those formats. Fortunately, the answer is yes—you can open the file in ClarisWorks and resave it as a Word file. You're all set.

The next possibility: Can another word processor (one you have access to) open the file and save it in a format you can use? After you start looking, it's amazing how many formats some of these programs can read and write.

If your word processor isn't quite so sophisticated, though, you'll need a translation program. On the Mac side, MacLink Plus (which is bundled with Mac OS 7.6) can translate to and from dozens of different text formats (as well as some graphics formats), including both Word and WordPerfect. Windows users can try Conversions Plus (from DataViz, the same company that makes MacLink Plus). Using a translation program doesn't always mean perfect results, so if you can, open the translated file in Word or WordPerfect and resave it before importing it.

For the purposes of this example, I'm assuming you're using Microsoft Word because XPress only imports Word and WordPerfect style sheets. The same basic techniques will work in WordPerfect, but the specific commands are different. Follow these steps:

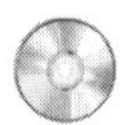

1. In Word, open lessons/chap4/manual.txt on the CD-ROM that accompanies this book. This is the text of a humorous manual for employers, written as a companion to an employee manual.
2. First, clean up the file. Choose Edit➡Replace to bring up the Replace dialog box (see Figure 4.1), and then search for and replace the following character combinations:

Search for	*Replace with*
two spaces (repeat until no changes are made)	one space
two paragraph returns (repeat until no changes are made)	one paragraph return
space followed by comma	comma
space followed by period	period
open quotation mark followed by space	open quotation mark
close quotation mark preceded by space	close quotation mark

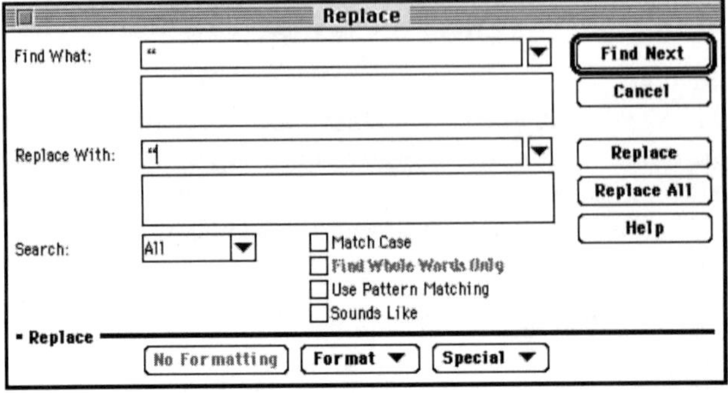

Figure 4.1

Microsoft Word's Replace dialog box.

3. Next, preserve local formatting by applying a style sheet to the entire document, using the same name as one of the style sheets that you use in the QuarkXPress document. Add a blank line to the beginning of the document. Select the whole blank paragraph (including the return character) by triple-clicking and remove all formatting—bold, italic, whatever, by pressing (Command-Shift-Z)[Control-Shift-Z].
4. Select the entire document (Command-A)[Control-A] and choose Format➡Style. Click the New button and type the name for the new style: "Text" (see Figure 4.2). Click OK to create the style, and then click Apply to apply it to the document. Now all the paragraphs in the document have the same style name as the basic paragraph style in the XPress document into which the text will be imported—this will save a lot of formatting time in XPress.

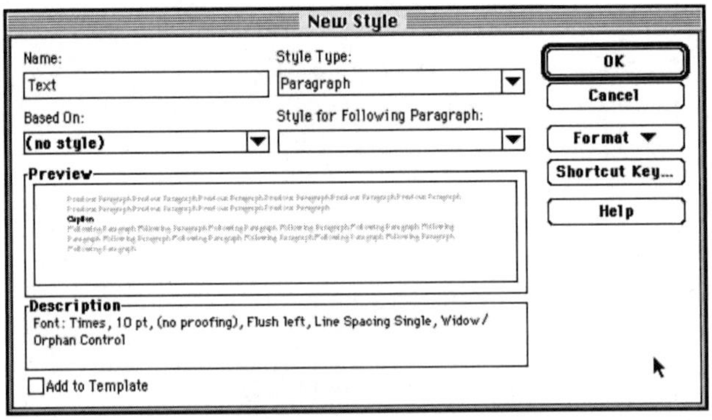

Figure 4.2

Creating the new "Text" style in Microsoft Word.

If you import the text without a style name that's already present in the XPress file, applying XPress styles to the paragraphs will override any locally applied bold, italic, or other formatting applied to the text in a word processor.

5. Triple-click in the first paragraph—the one you created—to select it and press (Delete)[Backspace].
6. Now you have the option of applying more style names. Here's where Word's search-and-replace features come in handy, because you can search for text patterns and "paste" styles into those paragraphs without changing the text.

   Click in the paragraph that begins with the number "1" and choose Format➡Style. Click the New button and type the name for another new style: "Section." Click OK to create the style, and then click Apply to apply it to the document (see Figure 4.3).

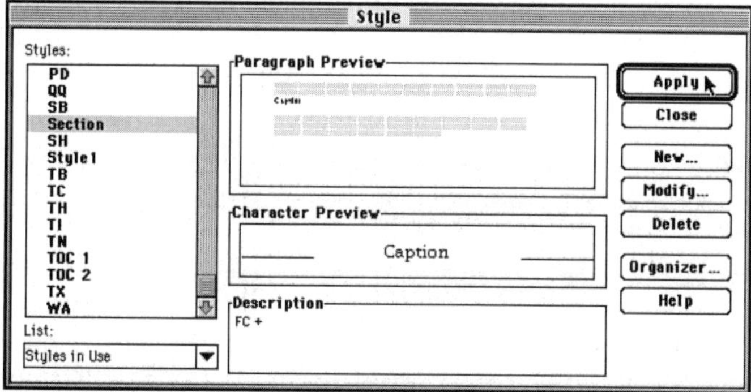

Figure 4.3

Applying the new "Section" style in Word.

7. Click in the next paragraph, which begins with "1.1," and choose Format➡Style. Click the New button and type the name for another new style: "Subsection." Click OK to create the style, and then click Apply to apply it to the document.
8. Choose Edit➡Replace and enter "^#.^t" in the Find field (not the quotation marks). Don't enter any text in the Replace field, but click and hold the Format button to bring up a pop-up menu and choose Style. From the list of styles, choose the Section style you just created, click OK, and then click Replace All. Doing so will find any occurrences of a number followed by a period and a tab character and will apply the Section style to those paragraphs without changing the text.
9. Still in the Replace dialog box, enter "^#.^#^t" in the Find field (not the quotation marks). Choose Style from the Format pop-up menu. From the list of styles, choose the Subsection style, click OK, and then click Replace All. Doing so will find any occurrences of a number followed by a period, another number, and a tab character and apply the Subsection style to those paragraphs without changing the text.

Note

With these styles, the formatting of the Word style doesn't matter—just the name. When you import the text into XPress, you can automatically apply the XPress styles, with the correct fonts and formatting, as long as the Word style names are the same.

10. Choose File➡Save As to save the file on your hard drive, giving it any name you like and changing the file's format to Word Document from Text Only. Using the Save As command prevents Word from doing a Fast Save, which would make the file unreadable by QuarkXPress, and it enables you to choose a format. If you save the file in Text Only format (ASCII), you can still import it into XPress, but the style names won't be included.

11. Switch to QuarkXPress and open lessons/chap4/manual.qxd on the CD-ROM that accompanies this book. This is the XPress file for the employer manual.

Note

The font families used in manual.qxd are Jennerik (in the Ingrimayne folder on the CD that came with this book) and Ad Lib (in the Title Wave folder on the CD), so you need to install these fonts before opening the file.

12. Press (F10)[F4] to view the Document Layout palette—you should see two pages, with the "A-Opening page" master applied to the first page in the document and the "B-Text page" master applied to the second (see Figure 4.4).
13. With the Content tool, click in a text box on either page; it doesn't matter which one because they are all linked. Text imported into empty linked boxes always starts in the first box, regardless of which box you clicked.
14. Choose File➡Get Text, click the name of the text file you saved in Step 7, and click "Include Styles" and "Convert Quotes." Click Open to import the text.

    XPress pauses a second to scan the text file's styles, and then presents you with a dialog box telling you that the Text style sheet used in the Word document already exists in the XPress document (see Figure 4.5).

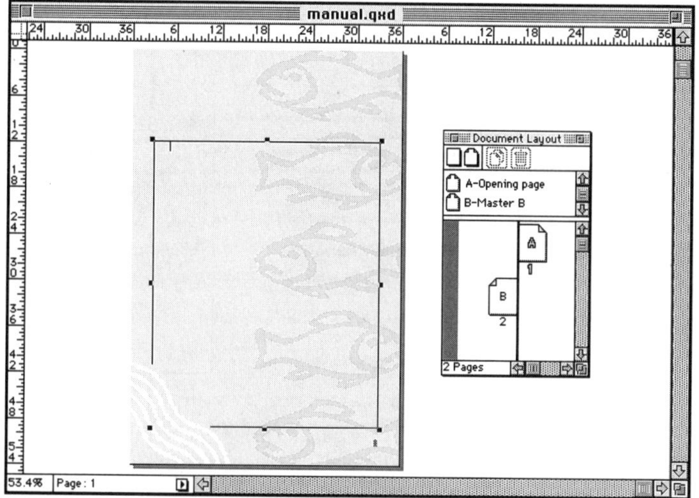

Figure 4.4

The empty manual.qxd document contains master pages and styles, but no text.

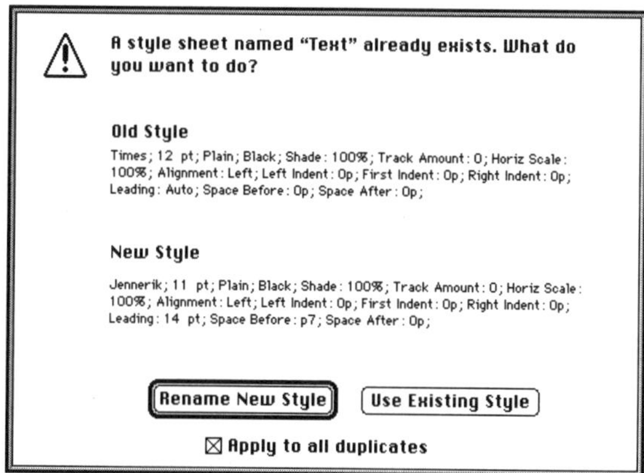

Figure 4.5

This dialog box details the styles in the Word document and the XPress document and asks which you want to use on the incoming text.

15. Click "Apply to all duplicates" and then click "Use Existing Style" to tell XPress to apply its own styles to the incoming text and not to bother you again with this dialog box. See Figure 4.6 for the results of applying the XPress styles to the imported text.
16. At this point, most of the document's formatting is done; an extra text page (using the "B-Text page" master) has even been added to hold the extra text. Only one paragraph style hasn't been applied, the one for the title. Click in the title paragraph ("Acme Corporation Manager Handbook") and apply the Title style to it by clicking Title in the Style Sheets palette (press F11 to bring up the Style Sheets palette if it's not visible).

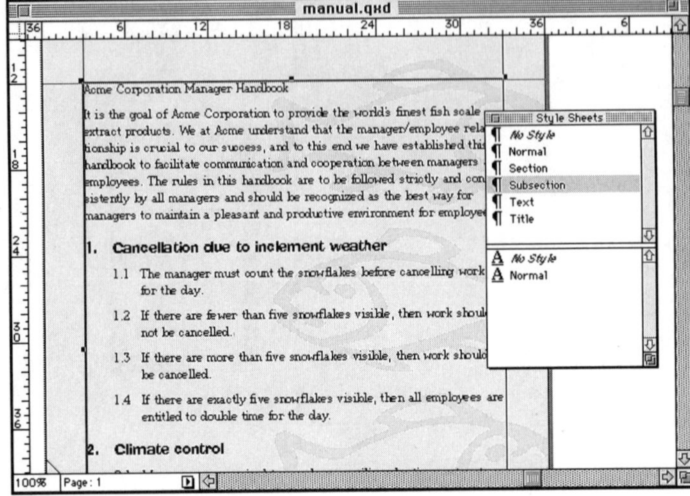

Figure 4.6

Enabling XPress to apply styles as you import text applies most of your formatting for you.

Tip

You can apply a style to each paragraph in your document within Word (or WordPerfect) and then import it into XPress fully formatted. But applying styles in Word isn't any faster than doing it in XPress, so it makes sense to apply only those styles for which you can use Word's search-and-replace features (along with the base text style to ensure that local formatting is maintained).

17. To finish the layout, you can format the numbers. Section numbers should be 14 points and blue (PANTONE 291). Subsection numbers should be bold. See Figure 4.7 for the final version of the manual.

Tip

QuarkXPress 4.0 supports character style sheets, which let you change character formatting with one click just as you can change the formatting of a paragraph by applying a paragraph style sheet. For more on using character styles, see Day 5, "Formatting Text and Using Style Sheets." These list entry numbers would be a good place to use character styles.

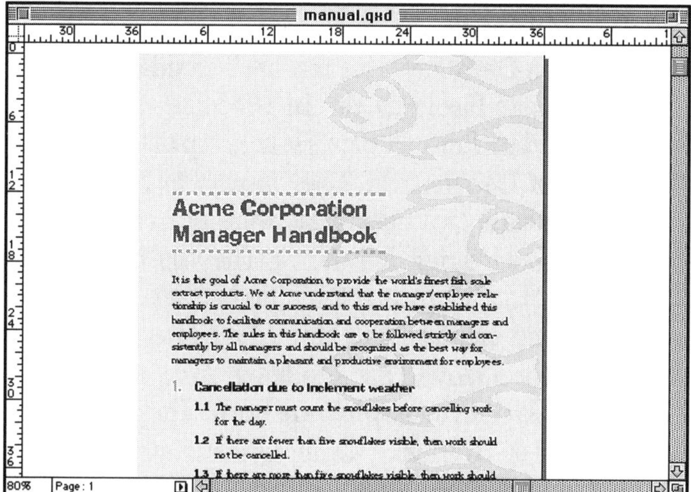

Figure 4.7

The Acme Corporation Manager Handbook should look like this when you are done.

Tip

The text in the XPress document isn't linked to the Word document you imported—in other words, if you make changes to the Word document, you have to reimport it and reapply the styles. You can save the text so that a writer or editor can make changes and reimport it with all your formatting intact by exporting it in XPress Tags format (see "Using XPress Tags," later in this chapter).

Linking Text Boxes

You can link text boxes for a text flow either before or after you import the text; if you import text into a box and then link the box to another box, any **overset text** will flow into the second box.

Note

A small red icon in the lower-right corner of the box appears when a text box contains overset text (see Figure 4.8).

Figure 4.8

The red "x-in-a-box" icon in the lower-right corner of this text box indicates that there's more text in the box than there's room to show.

> Mary Anna Weighant was born January 5,
> 1826 in Germany. Her mother's maiden
> name was Fleckenstein. In 1845 she was
> married to John George Hauck, a printer by
> trade at Georgetown. They moved to New
> York where two baby girls were born to
> them, both dying in infancy. They then
> moved to Cincinnati, Ohio, to better posi-
> tion, and another daughter, Mary, was born.
> They then moved back to New York, and
> Ferdinand and Joseph were born. They then
> moved to Sandusky, Ohio, where Kate,
> Lena and Fridolin were born; also a little
> girl who died when she was two years old.
> Then came the Civil war and John George
> enlisted as a Private in Company B, 181st
> Regiment Ohio Infantry, for which a cash ⊠

Here, you import text into a document and use several linked text boxes to place the text exactly where you want it on the page. By using linked boxes rather than entering the text into several separate boxes, you maintain the integrity of the text flow. There are several advantages to doing this:

- You can select all the text at the same time to change its format or copy it.
- You can export all the text into one text file with one operation, instead of having to export the contents of each text box separately.
- You can move through the entire document by using keyboard shortcuts to navigate the text (such as (Command-down arrow)[Control-down arrow] to move to the beginning of the next paragraph).

This particular document is a magazine ad for a new computer game, but the techniques used to import and flow the text work with any type of document.

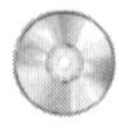

1. Open lessons/chap4/barbbest.qxd on the CD-ROM that accompanies this book.

Note

The font families used in barbbest.qxd are Caliph (in the Scriptorium folder on the CD) and Delphian Open Titling (in the Title Wave folder on the CD), so you need to install these fonts before opening the file.

2. Choose the Text Box tool and create a text box at the top of the page, flush with the left and right margin guides and about 1 inch (6 picas) deep (see Figure 4.9). In the Colors palette (press F12), make sure the box has a border and fill color of None.

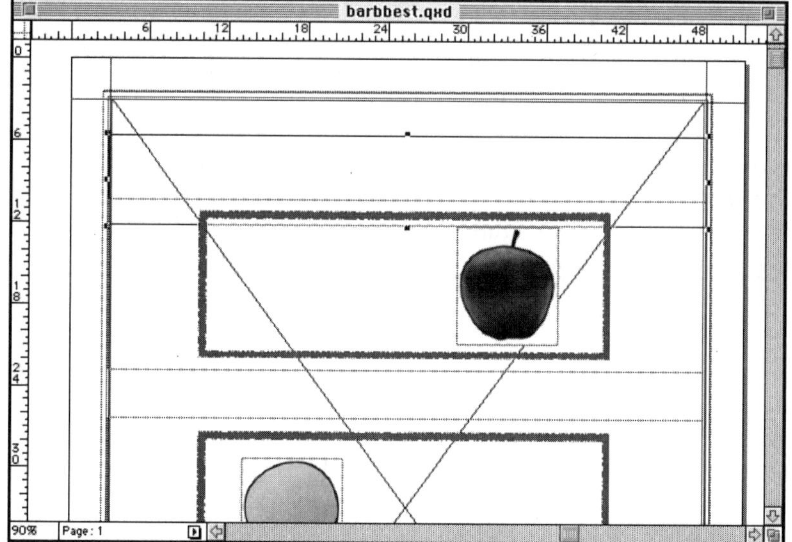

Figure 4.9

The first text box for the Barbara's Best ad.

3. Choose the Content tool and click in the new text box, and then choose Edit➡Get Text and import the applorng.xtg text file on the CD. This is an XPress Tags file, so click the Include Styles box in the Get Text dialog box to make sure that the XPress Tag formatting is applied as the text is imported.
4. The words "Why compare apples &" are visible in the text box, and the rest of the text is overset (see Figure 4.10). To make the remainder of the ad's text visible, you create several new text boxes in the following steps.

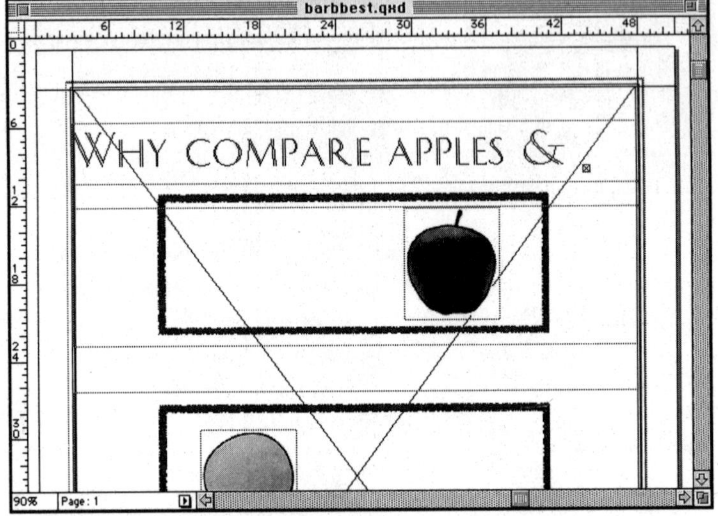

Figure 4.10

The "x-in-a-box" icon in the corner of the text box indicates that there's extra text in the box that can't be shown.

5. Hold down the (Option)[Alt] key and click the Text Box tool in the Tool palette. Ordinarily, you're automatically returned to the Item tool or the Content tool after creating a picture or text box, depending on which tool you were using before making the box. If you press the (Option)[Alt] key as you select a creation tool, though, you'll stay in that creation tool until you actively switch to another.
6. Draw four more boxes below the first one, as shown in Figure 4.11: one next to the apple image that is just big enough to hold the word "apple," one below it that stretches the width of the page, a third next to the orange image to hold the word "orange," and a fourth below that to hold the remainder of the text. Make sure that all four boxes have border and fill colors of None.
7. (Option-click)[Alt-click] the Linking tool to activate it.
8. Click each of the five text boxes you've created, in turn from top to bottom. As you click each box, its borders turn into an animated dotted line and a gray arrow connects it to the previous box in the text flow. After you've connected the five text boxes in the correct order, click the Content tool in the Tool palette to deactivate the Linking tool (otherwise you'll rearrange the linking order each time you click another text box).
9. You should see text in each of the top four text boxes (see Figure 4.12). If any of these four boxes doesn't contain any text, select it with the Content tool and pull the bottom of the box down until it's deep enough for the text to fit.

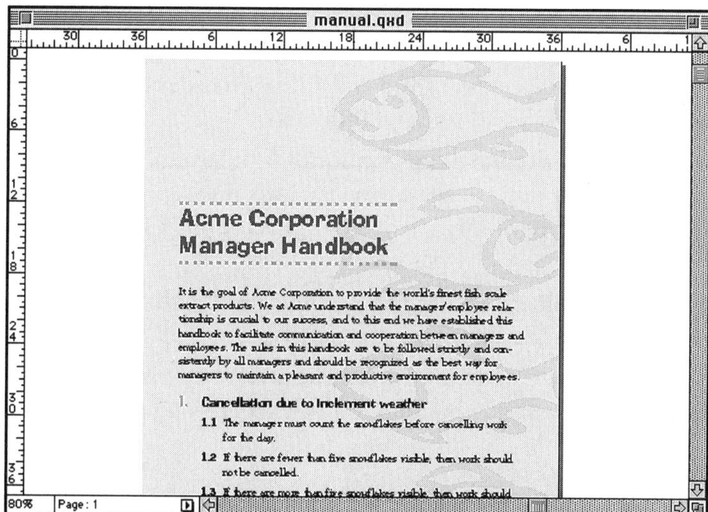

Figure 4.11

Five text boxes are needed to hold the text for the Barbara's Best ad.

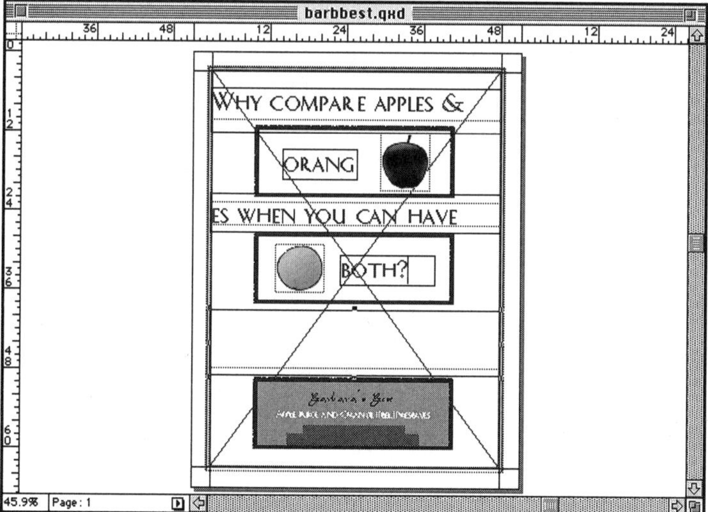

Figure 4.12

Although all five text boxes are linked, the text runs only into the first four.

10. To force text into specific boxes, you can use special keystrokes. Press Enter on the numeric keypad to force all the text after your cursor to the next column, and press Shift-Enter to force the following text to the next text box. If the text boxes in question are single-column, such as the ones in this document, the two key combinations have the same effect.

Position your cursor just before the word "apple" and press Enter; "apple" moves to the second text box. Do the same just before the & (ampersand) and the word "orange" to move them to the third and fourth boxes, respectively, and before the word "when" to bump it to the fifth box.

11. Now all the text is in the correct place, but it needs to be aligned properly. All the text is **center-aligned** now, so **left-align** "apples" (press (Shift-Command-L)[Shift-Control-L]) and **right-align** "oranges" (press (Shift-Command-R)[Shift-Control-R]).

    You can apply different alignments to the different lines of the text because pressing Enter breaks the text into separate paragraphs.

12. Insert a **soft return** (press (Shift-Return)[Shift-Enter]) before the word "can" to break the last section of text at a better point (see Figure 4.13 for the final version).

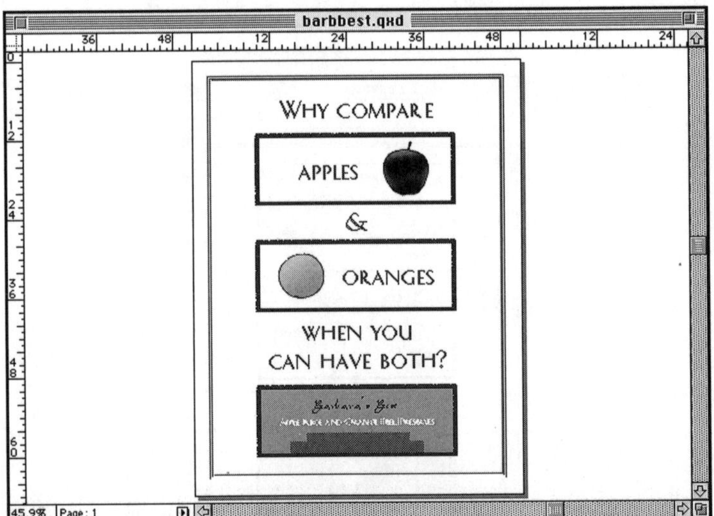

Figure 4.13

The final version of the Barbara's Best ad.

Editing Text

As with most software geared toward handling text, QuarkXPress has tools to let you search for and replace text and check your spelling. It also has standard cut, copy, and paste commands. There's also a selection of keyboard shortcuts you can use to make your way through a section of text, as follows:

Press...	*...to move to:*
(Command-up arrow)[Control-up arrow]	The beginning of the paragraph the cursor is in or to the beginning of the previous paragraph (if you're already at the beginning of a paragraph)
(Command-down arrow)[Control-down arrow]	The beginning of the next paragraph
(Command-left arrow)[Control-left arrow]	The beginning of the word the cursor is in or to the beginning of the previous word
(Command-right arrow)[Control-right arrow]	The beginning of the next word to the right
(Command-Option-up arrow)[Control-Alt-up arrow]	The beginning of the text flow
(Command-Option-down arrow)[Control-Alt-down arrow]	The end of the text flow
(Command-Option-left arrow)[Control-Alt-left arrow]	The beginning of the line
(Command-Option-right arrow)[Control-Alt-right arrow]	The end of the line

Add Shift to any of these keyboard shortcuts to select text as you move.

Tip

Switching back and forth between the keyboard and the mouse really slows you down, and no matter how much you like using your mouse, keyboard shortcuts are almost always faster. One of the marks of a power user in most software, including QuarkXPress, is knowing and using lots of keyboard shortcuts.

You can select ranges of text by clicking, too. Click at the beginning or end of a section of text, and then Shift-click at the other end of the range to select everything between clicks. Click more than once to select sections as follows:

- Twice (double-click) to select one word.
- Three times (triple-click) to select one line.
- Four times to select an entire paragraph, including the paragraph return at the end (if there is one).
- Five times to select the entire text flow (or click in the text flow and press (Command-A)[Control-A]).

Find/Change

The Find/Change command in QuarkXPress, as its name suggests, enables you to find text and then change its textual content, its formatting, or both at the same time. Most of the time, people tend to ignore the "change" part of that operation, especially when it comes to changing formatting, but Find/Change is a powerful tool for speeding up document formatting.

The Find dialog box enables you to search for text by its content, its style sheet, the font it's set in, its point size, or its style, and then change any of those aspects. Using these capabilities on both sides of the Find dialog box can help you accomplish global changes in a document very quickly. Here's a quick list of ways you might use Find/Change:

- Search for double spaces and change them to single spaces.
- Search for the incorrect spelling of someone's name and replace it with the correct spelling.
- Search for bullets in a text flow and change their paragraph style sheet to "Bulleted list."
- Search for bullets and change their text and font (or their character style sheet) to use dingbats (such as a Zapf Dingbats "n" to make a small square instead of a round bullet).
- Search for "+" signs and change them to a math font (such as Symbol).

Remember to save before you search and replace because Find/Change operations can't be undone. If you save and then change your mind, you can choose File➡Revert to Saved to return to the previous version of the document.

Warning

Replacing a paragraph return character with another paragraph return shouldn't change anything at all, but it does. The paragraph following the paragraph return will change to the same paragraph style sheet as the paragraph above it (the one with the return character at the end). So be careful!

To use Find/Change:

1. Choose Edit➡Find/Change (Command-F)[Control-F] to bring up the Find dialog box (see Figure 4.14). It's really a floating palette, such as the Tools, Style Sheets, and Colors palettes, so it will stay in front of the document window until you dismiss it.

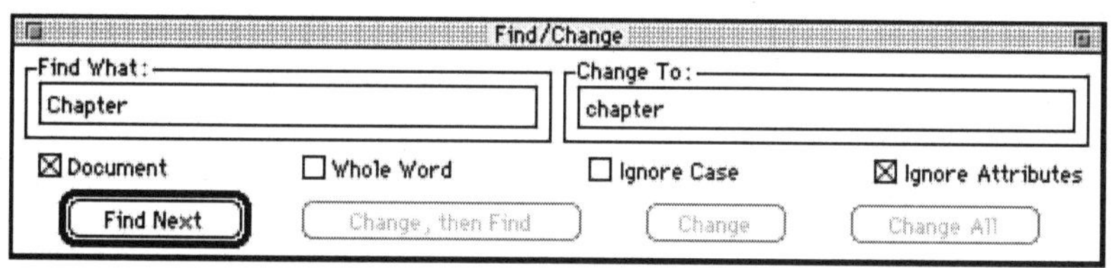

Figure 4.14

In the basic Find/Change dialog box (with Ignore Attributes clicked on), you can search for and replace text only.

2. Check Ignore Attributes if you want to search and replace text only, without regard to formatting. Click it off if you want to search for or replace some aspect of formatting (see Figure 4.15).

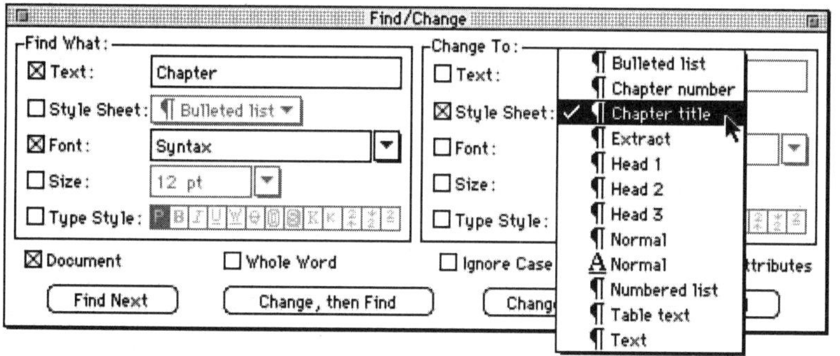

Figure 4.15

Clicking Ignore Attributes off lets you search for text formatting; here instances of "Chapter" in Syntax will be found and changed to the style sheet "Chapter title."

3. Enter the text, style sheet, font, point size, or style you want to search for—or a combination of any of these. Remember, you can search for just a style sheet, font, or other aspect without entering any text to search for, or you can search for text and specify formatting to find only occurrences of that text that are formatted a specific way.
4. On the Change side of the dialog box, choose the changes you want to make. Again, you can change aspects of the text such as its point size without changing the text itself.
5. Check Document to search the entire document; leave it unchecked to search only in the current text flow. If you leave it unchecked, choose the Content tool and click in the text flow you want to search.

Note

If you're on a master page, the Document checkbox will say "Masters" instead. Checking it will search all master pages, whereas leaving it unchecked will search only the current master page or spread. You can't search master and document pages at the same time.

6. Check Whole Word if you're searching for text and want to find only cases where that text has spaces, returns, or punctuation on both sides of it—in other words, if it's the whole word, not just part of a word. Using this option can help or hinder you. Suppose you want to change "her" throughout a document to "his." If Whole Word is checked, you'll find every occurrence of "her," and you won't find "fur*ther*"—which is good. But you also won't find "hers," which should also be changed to "his" in this case.
7. Click Ignore Case if you want to find all occurrences regardless of whether they're upper- or lowercase. If Ignore Case is checked, replacement text follows the capitalization patterns of the original text; for example, searching for "The" and replacing it with "this" results in "This" if Ignore Case is on. If it's off, "The" is replaced with "this," leaving you with a lowercase letter at the beginning of a sentence. You won't find any occurrences of "the," either, because XPress is matching the search string ("The") exactly with respect to case.
8. Click Find Next to find the next instance that appears after the position of the cursor in the text flow (if Document is not checked) or after the page you're viewing (if Document is checked). To find instances before that point, hold down the (Option)[Alt] key to turn the Find Next button into a Find First button, and then click it. Doing so will find the first instance of what you're searching for in either the text flow or the entire document, depending on whether Document is checked.

9. When XPress finds what you're searching for, it highlights the text on the screen and you can click Find Next to go on to the next occurrence of the search criteria, or click one of three buttons to make the change:
   - Change and then Find makes the change and then locates the next instance.
   - Change makes the change but doesn't continue searching.
   - Change All makes the change to all instances of the search criteria throughout the document or text flow, without pausing to ask you each time whether to make the change. Use Change All with great care—only if you're absolutely sure that the text or formatting change should be made in every case.
10. When you're done with the Find/Change dialog box, you can leave it open and simply click in the document window to keep working on your document. If you have a small monitor (or you're just allergic to screen clutter), you'll want to get rid of it by clicking in the close box at the (upper-left)[upper-right] corner of the palette.

Tip

If you keep the Find/Change dialog box open as you work, it won't register any new fonts or style sheets you add to the document, so they won't appear in the dialog box's pop-up menus. Close the dialog box and reopen it by pressing (Command-F)[Control-F] again to add new fonts and style sheets to the menus.

Wildcard Searches

Like Microsoft Word and other word processors, QuarkXPress can use wildcard characters in the Find/Change dialog box to search for special characters:

Any character	\?
Tab	\t
Paragraph return	\p
Soft return	\n
New column character	\c
New text box character	\h
Previous text box page number	\2

continues

Current text box page number	\3
Next text box page number	\4
Punctuation space	\.
Flex space	\f
Backslash	\\

You can also enter most of these characters by holding down (Command) [Control] as you press the keyboard shortcut for the character you want to search for; for example, enter a carriage return by pressing (Command-Return)[Control-Enter]. The only one of these characters that can't be entered in the Change To field is "\?" because XPress has no way of figuring out what the "any character" is that you would be changing the found text to.

The "any character" wildcard is literally used to search for any character. If, for example, you want to search for a name but weren't sure if the name was "Tim" or "Tom," you can enter "T\?m" in the Find field, and XPress will find all occurrences of Tim, Tom, Tam, Tum, or any other three-letter words that start with "T" and end with "m."

Spell-Checking Your Document

Although it's usually a good idea to spell-check text in its originating word processor, you need to check the spelling again after entering edits. And, of course, not all text originates in a word processor; documents such as display ads that aren't text-intensive may have all their text entered directly in QuarkXPress. To check the spelling in a document:

1. Save the document first, because you can't undo changes made during a spell-check.
2. Choose Utilities➡Check Spelling and choose one of the three options (Word, Story, or Document) from the submenu that appears to the side (see Figure 4.16). Word will check only the word the text cursor is currently in, and Story checks an entire text flow; both of these options are grayed if you don't have a text box currently selected with the Content tool. Document checks the entire document, and this option is always available.

Note

If you choose any of the spell-checking commands when your document doesn't contain any text, you'll hear an error beep and nothing will happen.

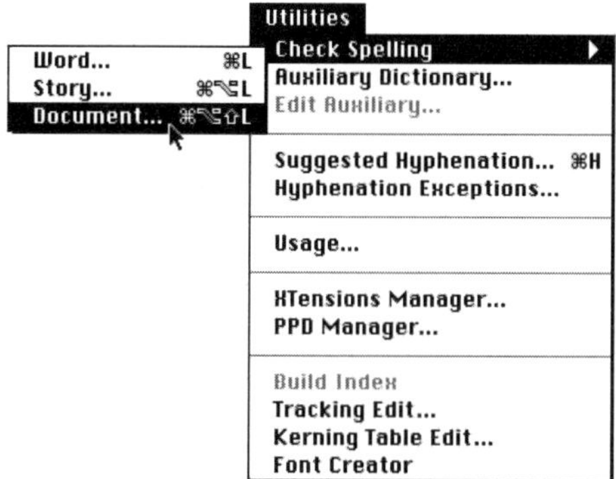

Figure 4.16

The Check Spelling menu command offers you three options.

3. The first thing you'll see after choosing one of the Check Spelling commands is a Word Count dialog box showing how many words are in your document or story, how many of them are unique (used only once), and how many XPress doesn't recognize (see Figure 4.17). Click OK to move on.

Figure 4.17

The Word Count dialog box.

Tip

There are two reasons the Word Count dialog box is useful. First, it's the only way to get a word count in XPress, so if you need to know how many words are in a document or story, this is the way to find out. Second, the number of words XPress doesn't recognize gives you an idea how long it's going to take to complete the spelling check.

4. Then the Check Story dialog box appears (see Figure 4.18), showing the first word that doesn't appear in XPress's dictionary (Suspect Word) and how many times that word appears in the document or story (Instances). Click Lookup to see correct spelling suggestions.
5. To change the word, either choose a suggested word from the list or type in your own correction, and then click Replace or press (Return)[Enter]. Click Add to add the word to an auxiliary dictionary (if one is open; see text that

follows list), or click Skip to move on to the next word without changing this one.

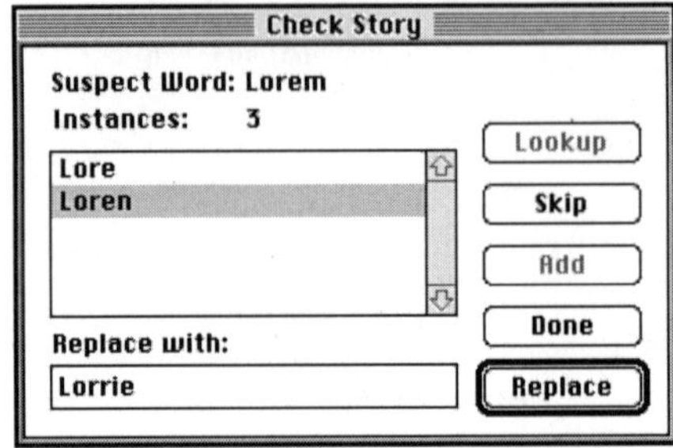

Figure 4.18

The Check Story dialog box.

6. When you've dealt with the last word, the dialog box simply goes away. You can stop checking at any time by clicking the Done button.

QuarkXPress uses its own dictionary to check the spelling in documents. You can supplement that dictionary by adding words to **auxiliary dictionaries** as you encounter them during spell-checking. You can have as many auxiliary dictionaries as you want (for example, one containing medical terms for medical textbooks, and another containing computer terms for an Internet magazine), but you can have only one auxiliary dictionary open at a time.

To use an auxiliary dictionary:

1. Choose Utilities➡Auxiliary Dictionary to bring up the Auxiliary Dictionary dialog box (see Figure 4.19). The name of the current auxiliary dictionary appears at the bottom of this dialog box—"none" if there isn't one open.

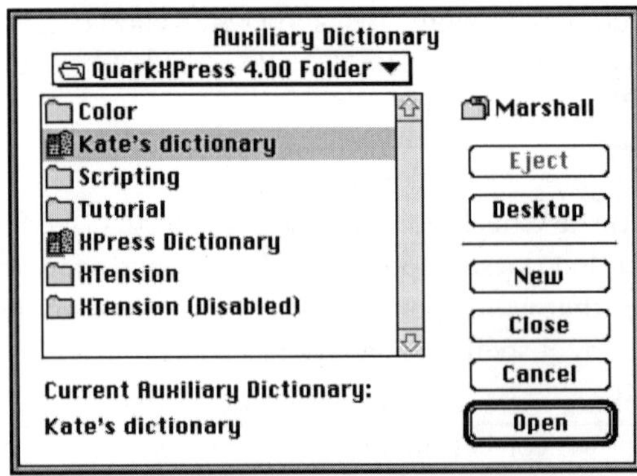

Figure 4.19

The Auxiliary Dictionary dialog box.

Tip

If you create or open an auxiliary dictionary when no documents are open, that dictionary will become your default; it'll be the auxiliary dictionary for any documents you create after that point. You can reverse this process by closing or changing the dictionary with no documents open.

2. To open an existing dictionary, navigate to the dictionary you want to use and click Open.
3. To make a new dictionary, click New to bring up a dialog box in which you can assign a name and a location to a new, empty auxiliary dictionary (see Figure 4.20).

Figure 4.20

This dialog box lets you create a new auxiliary dictionary for spell-checking.

4. To close an open dictionary, click Close. The dialog box disappears and you're returned to your document. To open a new dictionary, choose Edit➡Auxiliary Dictionary again.
5. To add words to, delete words from, or change words in an auxiliary dictionary, choose Utilities➡Edit Auxiliary (see Figure 4.21).

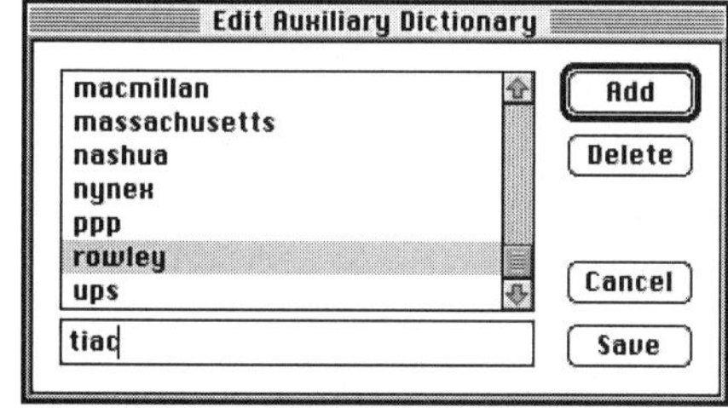

Figure 4.21

The Edit Auxiliary Dictionary dialog box.

6. To add a word, type it and click Add. To delete a word, click it and then click Delete. To change a word, delete it and then add the changed version. When you're done making changes, click Save to exit the Edit Auxiliary Dictionary dialog box.

Tip

When you're spell-checking, you can add all unknown words in the document by holding down (Shift-Option)[Shift-Alt] and clicking the Done button in the Check Story dialog box. This is a great way to quickly beef up a new auxiliary dictionary—just open a document that you know has a lot of words you want to add to the dictionary. You can also import the text of another user's auxiliary dictionary into an XPress document (just treat it as though it were a text file) and then add all those words using this technique.

Exporting Text

In addition to importing and editing text, XPress enables you to export text to one of several formats. This feature is useful when you want to supply text from an XPress document to another person, who will edit the text in a word processor or import it into a different page layout document (even one created in PageMaker!). The formats available for text export are a subset of the ones that XPress can import. To export text from XPress:

1. Choose the Content tool and click anywhere in the text flow that you want to export. You can export only one text flow at a time.
2. If you don't want to export all of the text in the flow, select the portion you do want to export by clicking at the beginning of the range and then Shift-clicking at the end of it.
3. Choose File➥Save Text or press (Command-Option-E)[Control-Alt-E] to bring up the Save Text dialog box (see Figure 4.22).
4. If you selected a range of text, click next to either Entire Story or Selected Text to indicate whether you want to export the entire text flow or just the part you selected. If no text is selected in the text flow, the Selected Text option is grayed.
5. Choose a format from the pop-up menu. These are the same formats XPress recognizes when importing text.

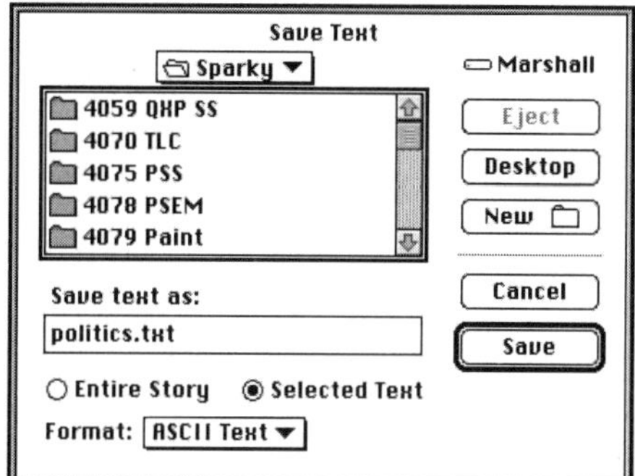

Figure 4.22

The Save Text dialog box.

6. Navigate to the location where you want to save the text and give the new file a name.
7. Click Save to create the new text file.

The text you've exported will look and act just like any text file created in the application you chose from the format menu, and you can open the file and edit it in that application. If you choose XPress Tags or ASCII text, the file is a plain text file that can be edited in any word processor. After your edits are complete, you can resave the file (be sure to save XPress Tags files in ASCII format) and reimport the text into QuarkXPress or pass it along to another person who needs the text.

Using XPress Tags

Being able to export and import text in XPress Tags format offers a powerful tool for manipulating XPress's text formatting. Word processor text files can be formatted with XPress Tags codes, resulting in as much or as little formatting as you want being applied instantly when the text is imported into a QuarkXPress document. Although styles and style sheets applied to text in word processor documents can be preserved as the file is imported into XPress, using that approach limits you to using Microsoft Word or Corel WordPerfect. Because XPress Tags files are ASCII text, they can be produced by any word processor or text editor. You can also

- Automate formatting using XPress Tags and macros.
- Change complex combinations of text and formatting via search-and-replace.
- Export formatted text from databases such as FileMaker Pro.
- Have writers and editors insert codes to save time on the layout end of production.
- Convert XPress text to HTML, SGML, MIF (used by FrameMaker), or other formatting languages using search-and-replace macros.

The best way to learn how XPress Tags work is to export the text of a formatted document to XPress Tags format and take a look at what coding is inserted to represent the formatting in the file:

1. Open lessons/chap4/xprstags.qxd on the CD-ROM that accompanies this book. This is a very ugly document, so don't look at it—it's just nonsense text with lots of different formatting so you can see a wide range of XPress Tags coding.

Note

The font families used in xprstags.qxd are Glytus, Ad Lib, and Symbol, so you need to install these fonts before opening the file.

2. Choose the Content tool from the Tool palette and click anywhere in the text box on the first page of the file.
3. Choose File➡Save Text to bring up the Save Text dialog box; choose XPress Tags from the Format pop-up menu and save the entire text flow to your hard drive, using any name you like.
4. Open the newly created text file in your favorite word processor and take a look (see Figure 4.23). Some of the coding won't mean very much to you, but much of it has an obvious purpose.

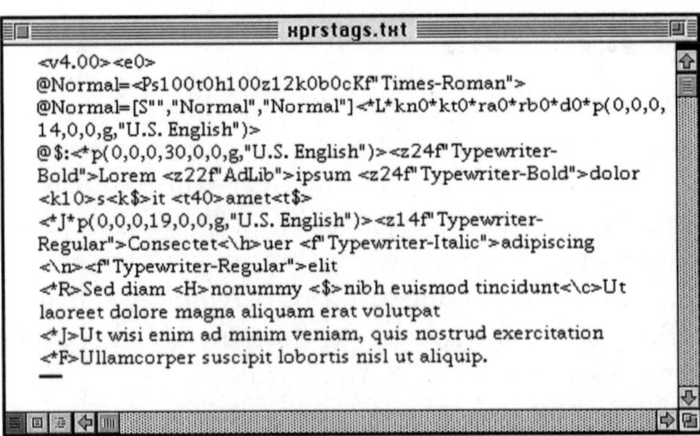
xprstags.txt

```
<v4.00><e0>
@Normal=<Ps100t0h100z12k0b0cKf"Times-Roman">
@Normal=[S"","Normal","Normal"]<*L*kn0*kt0*ra0*rb0*d0*p(0,0,0,
14,0,0,g,"U.S. English")>
@$:<*p(0,0,0,30,0,0,g,"U.S. English")><z24f"Typewriter-
Bold">Lorem <z22f"AdLib">ipsum <z24f"Typewriter-Bold">dolor
<k10>s<k$>it <t40>amet<t$>
<*J*p(0,0,0,19,0,0,g,"U.S. English")><z14f"Typewriter-
Regular">Consectet<\h>uer <f"Typewriter-Italic">adipiscing
<\n><f"Typewriter-Regular">elit
<*R>Sed diam <H>nonummy <$>nibh euismod tincidunt<\c>Ut
laoreet dolore magna aliquam erat volutpat
<*J>Ut wisi enim ad minim veniam, quis nostrud exercitation
<*F>Ullamcorper suscipit lobortis nisl ut aliquip.
```

Figure 4.23

The XPress Tags text file looks pretty messy at first glance.

5. The first line of the code gives information about the version of the XPress Tags filter used to create this file.

```
<v1.70><e0>
```

6. The next section of the file gives definitions for the style sheets used in the source XPress document. In this case, the second and third lines contain the definition of the only style sheet used: Normal. It uses the Standard H&Js, is left-justified, has no kerning or tracking, is 12-point Times Roman, and so on.

```
@Normal=[S"","Normal"]<*L*h"Standard"*kn0*kt0*ra0*rb0*d0*p(0,0,0,14,0,0,g,"U.S.
English")*t(0,0,"2  "):
Ps100t0h100z12k0b0c"Black"f"Times-Roman">
```

7. Then the actual text begins. First, the style sheet used by the text is provided (@Normal:). Then any local formatting is mentioned; here, the line started out as Normal style but was then changed to 24-point Glytus Bold on 30-point leading (<*p(0,0,0,30,0,0,g,"U.S. English")$z24f"Glytus-Bold">). The font changes to 22-point Ad Lib (<$z22f"AdLib">) before the word "ipsum" and then back to Glytus Bold after "ipsum" (<$z24f"Glytus-Bold">). There's 10 units of kerning between "dolor" and "s" (<$k10>), and 40 units of tracking applied to "amet" (<$t40> to begin it and <$t$> to end it).

```
@Normal:<*p(0,0,0,30,0,0,g,"U.S. English")$z24f"Glytus-Bold">Lorem
<$z22f"AdLib">ipsum <$z24f"Glytus-Bold">dolor <$k10>s<$k$>it
<$t40>amet<$t$>
```

8. The next line doesn't need a style sheet definition because it too uses Normal. Local formatting, though, shows up: This line has 14-point Glytus Bold on 19-point leading and is justified, rather than left-justified (<*J*p(0,0,0,19,0,0,g,"U.S. English")$z14f"Glytus-Regular">). There's a discretionary hyphen between "Consectet" and "uer" (<\h>) and "adipiscing" is Glytus Italic (<$f"Glytus-Italic">), with a soft return just after it before "elit" (<\n>).

```
<*J*p(0,0,0,19,0,0,g,"U.S. English")$z14f"Glytus-Regular">Consectet<\h>uer
<$f"Glytus-Italic">adipiscing <\n><$f"Glytus-Regular">elit
```

9. The third line of text is right-justified (<*R$>), with "nonummy" set in small caps (<H> to begin it and <$> to go back to regular caps and case). After "tincidunt," there's a new column character (<\c>), which bumps the rest of the line to the next page, where it's centered rather than right-justified (<*C$>).

```
<*R$>Sed diam <H>nonummy <$>nibh euismod tincidunt<\c><*C$>Ut laoreet
dolore magna aliquam erat volutpat
```

10. Back to justified text for the next line (<*J$>).

```
<*J$>Ut wisi enim ad minim veniam, quis nostrud exercitation
```

11. Finally, the only local formatting is that this line is force-justified (<*F$>).

```
<*F$>Ullamcorper suscipit lobortis nisl ut aliquip.
```

The point of all this is not that you should memorize the XPress Tags codes, but that the codes are pretty easy to recognize after you start looking. To figure out what the code is for any particular formatting you want to use, just apply that formatting to some text and then export the text as XPress Tags to see how the coding is done. So if you wanted to change, say, all the right-justified text in your document to force-justified (no, I can't think of a good reason for doing that, but I'm sure there is one), you could do it quickly by exporting to XPress Tags, searching for "<*R$>" in a word processor, and replacing it with "<*F$>."

Try making some changes in this XPress Tags file, and then reimporting the text into QuarkXPress. Some things you might want to try:

- Search for "AdLib" (notice that the font name doesn't have a space in the Tags file) and replace it with "Toxica" (or any other font you have installed).
- Search for "$z24" and replace it with "$z56."
- Search for "*p(0,0,0" and replace it with "*p(36,12,36."

One caveat: Be very careful with your changes. Add one incorrect character (or leave one out) and you'll get an error when you try to reimport the file. Fortunately, XPress imports as much of the file as it can, so you can see exactly where the error occurred and check out that spot in the XPress Tags file.

Summary

Although word processing functions may not be very glamorous, they're often necessary in QuarkXPress—think how tedious it would be to have to return to a word processor every time you wanted to do a search-and-replace operation. Although it doesn't have as many text editing features as word processors—no macros, fewer wildcard characters, and so on—XPress offers what's needed for working on text within a design, from a small display advertisement all the way up to thousand-page books (see Day 10, "Managing Long Documents"). If you do need to move text into another program, you can export it from XPress, and the formatting language XPress Tags enables you to analyze and change text formatting on a microscopic level.

Formatting Text and Using Style Sheets

- Formatting text with character attributes
- Formatting text with paragraph attributes
- Creating and applying style sheets
- Appending style sheets from other documents
- Managing style sheets

More than anything else, QuarkXPress is designed to format text, making use of the thousands of beautiful fonts on the market and adding to their impact with precise alignment and other formatting—**point size**, leading, spacing, **horizontal scaling**, and so on. There are two ways to apply text formatting: locally and using style sheets. Each method has its place, and most design projects use both—style sheets for consistent elements and local formatting for a word here or there within those elements. In this chapter, you'll apply local formatting to text in a two-page **display ad**, then create and apply style sheets for a book on programming.

Formatting Text Locally

Local formatting—which means applying each change directly to the text rather than creating and revising style sheets—is best used in three situations:

- When you're experimenting to create a design.
- When you're designing a layout that has very little text.
- When you're making a small change that is the exception rather than the rule.

If you're going to use a particular type style throughout a document, creating a style sheet saves time and ensures consistency. But in the situations mentioned previously, making a style sheet will take more time than it's worth.

Text formats come in two flavors: **character** and **paragraph**. Character attributes include font, point size, color, and style—attributes having to do with the individual letters; they're applied using the Character Attributes dialog box (Command-Shift-D)[Control-Shift-D]. Paragraph attributes include characteristics such as leading, **indentation**, and **alignment**, and they're applied using the Paragraph Attributes dialog box (Command-Shift-F)[Control-Shift-F].

This project is a tourism advertisement promoting New Orleans:

1. Open lessons/chap05/orleans.qxd on the CD-ROM that accompanies this book (see Figure 5.1). This is a two-page spread for a magazine advertisement; the images have already been placed on the page, so you need only to add and format the text.

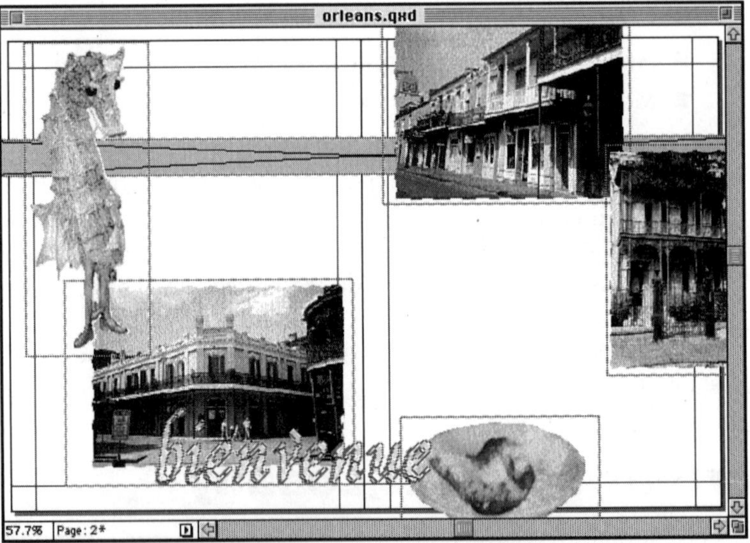

Figure 5.1

The New Orleans ad layout with its graphics but no text.

Note

This file uses FlyHigh and FansiPensleTwo (both in the Ingrimayne folder on the CD), so make sure those font families are installed in your system.

2. First, place the ad's headline on the first page. Draw a rectangular text box about 4.5 inches wide and 2 inches deep above the photo of the French Quarter and flush with the page's inside margin.
3. Switch to the Content tool and type "Welcome to New Orleans" in the box. The text is assigned the Normal style (see Figure 5.2).

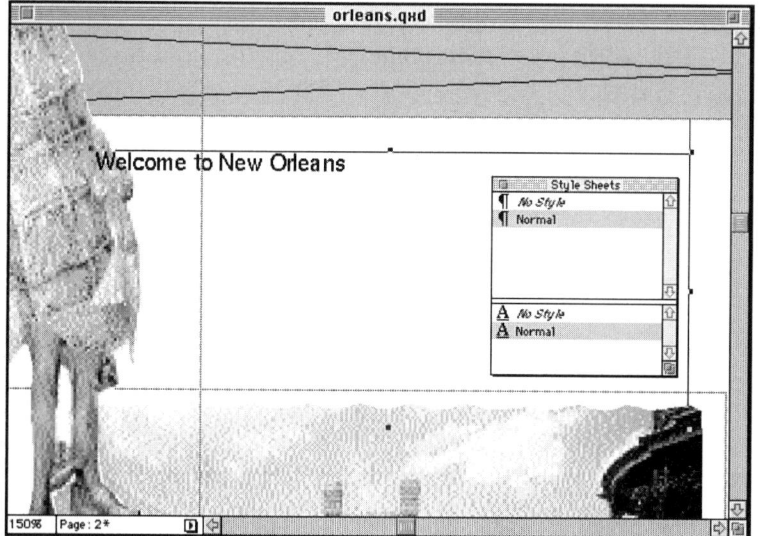

Figure 5.2

When you first enter text into a new box, it's assigned the Normal style sheet. You can change the definition of the Normal style sheet, but you can't get rid of it.

4. Press (Command-A)[Control-A] to select all the text, and then press (Command-Shift-D)[Control-Shift-D] to bring up the Character Attributes dialog box (see Figure 5.3).

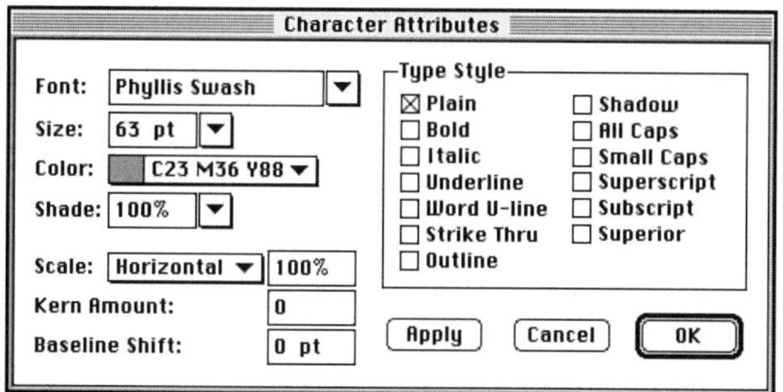

Figure 5.3

The Character Attributes dialog box.

5. This dialog box contains controls for all the character attributes that you can change.
   - Choose FansiPensleTwo from the Font pop-up menu, or start typing the name of the font in the entry field; as you type, XPress inserts the name of the first font in its list that matches the characters you've typed so far.
   - Double-click in the Size field and type 63 to make the type 63 points. You can also use the pop-up menu to choose a preset size: 7, 9, 10, 12, 14, 18, 24, 36, 48, 60, or 72 points. The point size can range from 2 to 720 points.
   - Choose C23 M36 Y88, a gold color, from the Color pop-up menu. This color was already defined in the file on the CD-ROM; if you were starting from scratch, you'd have to define this color before it would be available in the document (see Day 9, "Using Color").
   - Leave the Shade value at 100 percent to make the type 100 percent gold; a lower percentage would make the type lighter gold, and 0 percent of any color is the same is white.
   - Leave the Scale value at 100 percent; lower or higher values would compress or stretch the type vertically or horizontally, depending on whether Horizontal or Vertical is chosen in the Scaling pop-up menu. Scaling values can range from 25 percent to 400 percent.

Tip

Try to avoid using horizontal or vertical scaling as much as possible—it distorts the letterforms. If a design calls for narrow or wide type, try to find a true condensed or expanded typeface.

   - Leave the Track Amount set at 0; values can range from –500 to 500 and determine how much space is subtracted or added between each character in the type (see Day 6, "Fine-tuning Type").
   - Leave Baseline Shift set at 0; this value shifts the selected characters up or down, away from the baseline, as much as 189 points (negative values move the type down, positive ones move it up).
   - In the Type Style area, make sure only Plain is checked (see sidebar, "Don't Be Too Stylish").

Don't Be Too Stylish

Here's a word of advice about QuarkXPress's character attributes—such as bold, underline, and shadow: don't use them. All right, that's a little harsh. Here's a rundown of which ones you should use, which ones you shouldn't, and why.

- **Bold and italic:** To make sure that what you see onscreen is what you get when you send your files for imagesetter output, you should always use the specific fonts if they're available. In other words, use Times Bold, not Times with the bold attribute. On the other hand, creating a design goes a lot faster if you use the attributes. My practice is to use them and then change them to the correct fonts through Font Usage when a design is complete. Sometimes this reflows the text, so check over your document again after making the change.

Note

Some fonts, including FlyHigh (used in the New Orleans ad), require that you access their different variants by using the character attributes. The only way you can get FlyHigh Italic is by using FlyHigh with an italic attribute. You *can* tell the difference between this and a font that's not designed this way because the character shapes actually change when you apply the attributes. Watch closely in Step 13 to see this happen.

- **Underline and word underline:** There are very few typographically correct reasons to use underlining; words that are underlined on a typewriter are italic when you're doing real typesetting. When you do need underlining, the free Stars and Stripes XTension (available at `http://www.quark.com`) enables you to create custom underlines—double rules, for example, or rules at a specific distance from the text.
- **Strikethrough, outline, and shadow:** These are just not pretty. If you're going for a special effect that needs to look clunky, have fun, but these effects can be achieved much more attractively using XPress's drawing tools or another application such as Illustrator or Photoshop.
- **All caps and small caps:** Remember three considerations here. First, use all caps sparingly, not just for emphasis in running text—it's like shouting, as any Internet guru will tell you. Second, if the font you're using has an expert set with true small caps, use those instead of the XPress character

continues

attribute—they're actually shaped differently from the capital letters that are scaled down to make small caps in XPress. Third, if your font doesn't have a small caps set, use the XPress feature, but remember that you can change the small caps' size in the Character tab of the Document Preferences (see Day 1, "XPress Basics").

- **Superscript, subscript, and superior:** These are definitely the exception to the rule; for most fonts there's no other way to achieve these effects. As with small caps, however, superior numbers are sometimes included in expert font sets. If you can get them, use them—trust the type designer's judgment.

6. Click Apply to see the results of your changes without leaving the Character Attributes dialog box; if you're satisfied, click OK to return to the document.
7. Now it's time to edit the paragraph formatting; press (Command-Shift-F)[Control-Shift-F] to bring up the Paragraph Attributes dialog box (see Figure 5.4). The type should still be selected, but the next steps apply to the whole paragraph even if the text cursor is just sitting in the paragraph with no characters selected.

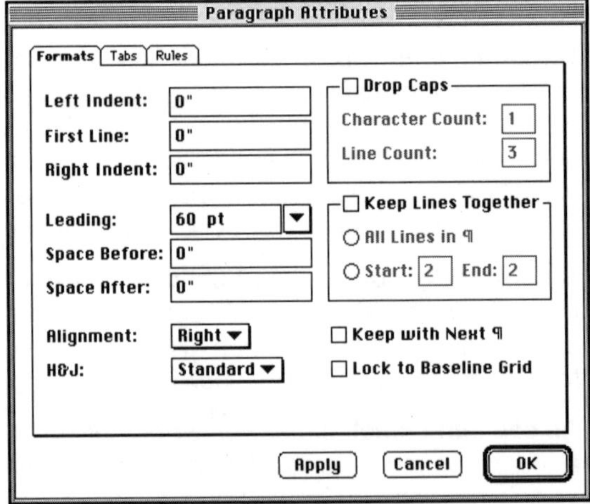

Figure 5.4

The Paragraph Attributes dialog box.

8. This dialog box contains controls for all the paragraph attributes.
   - Leave the Left Indent, First Line, and Right Indent set at 0; these values determine how much the left edge of the paragraph, its first line, and the right edge of the paragraph, respectively, are indented. The First Line

indent is "extra"—in other words, the first line starts at the Left Indent value plus the First Line value. These values are limited only by the width of the text box or column.

Tip

Enter a positive Left Indent and a negative First Line value to get a "hanging indent," in which the first line starts to the left of the rest of the paragraph (numbered and bulleted lists usually use hanging indents). The first line can't be indented past the side of the text box (or past the box's Text Inset value, if you're using one).

- Change the Leading value to 60 points; leading can range from –1080 to 1080, but you can't actually lead two lines of text tight enough so that they overlap, so there usually isn't a difference between, say, –500 and –400 leading.
- Keep the Space Before and Space After values at 0. These values add extra space between paragraphs, either above each paragraph or below; the amount of extra space can range from 0 to as much as 15 inches (90p).
- Choose Right from the Alignment pop-up menu; the choices are Left, Centered, Right, Justified, and Forced. Left-justified type lines up at the left side of the text box; right-justified type lines up at the right side; and centered type is, of course, centered in the box. Justified type is subtly spaced out so that it lines up with both sides of the text box, except for the last line of each paragraph, and the Forced setting justifies even the last line.
- Leave the H&J (hyphenation and justification) setting at Standard (see Day 6 for information on creating and using different H&J settings).
- Leave Drop Caps unchecked. If Drop Caps is checked, Quark enlarges the first character or characters of the paragraph and moves it down so that its top aligns with the top of the rest of the first line. The Character Count box lets you specify how many characters are included, and the Line Count determines the size of the drop cap relative to the other lines in the paragraph. A Line Count setting of 3, the default, base-aligns the drop cap with the third line of the paragraph and enlarges it to the height of three regular-sized lines.

- Check Keep Lines Together and then click All Lines in Paragraph. This keeps the two lines of this paragraph from being split up; if there isn't room for the entire paragraph in the text box, the whole paragraph will be overset or bumped to the next box in the series until this box is made larger. The alternative to All Lines in Paragraph is to set Start and End values to specify how many lines at the beginning and end of the paragraph must be kept together. This is useful for making sure that you don't end up with one line of a paragraph on a page by itself, with the rest flowing to the next or previous page.
- Leave Keep with Next Paragraph off. This setting keeps a paragraph from being separated from the paragraph that follows it; it's useful for keeping headings with the text they describe.
- Leave Lock to Baseline Grid off. This setting forces the first line of the paragraph to sit on the nearest baseline grid guide (see Day 1 for how to set the spacing of the baseline grid in the Document Preferences).

9. Click Apply to see the results of your changes without leaving the Paragraph Attributes dialog box; if you're satisfied, click OK to return to the document. The left page of the spread should look like Figure 5.5.

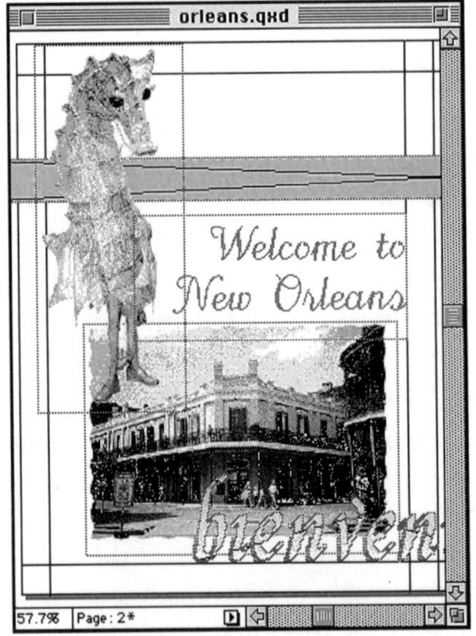

Figure 5.5

The formatted headline completes the left page of the spread.

10. The second copy block goes at the left side of the right page. Draw a rectangular text box about 4.1 inches wide and 4 inches deep above the plate of beignets

(these wonderful pastries are reason enough in themselves to visit New Orleans).

11. Switch to the Content tool if it's not active, and then press (Command-E)[Control-E] to bring up the Get Text dialog box and choose lessons/chap5/orleans.txt on the CD-ROM that accompanies this book. Click Convert Quotes, but don't click Include Style Sheets; then click Open to import the text file into the text box.

12. Press (Command-M)[Control-M] to bring up the Modify dialog box, and click the Text tab. Set the Vertical Alignment of the text box to Centered, and click OK to apply the change. The text is centered vertically in the box instead of starting at the top.
13. This time, use the Measurements palette (F9) to adjust some of the text's attributes (see Figure 5.6). Select all of the text (Command-A)[Control-A] and choose FlyHigh from the Measurements palette's font menu, then choose the italic attribute by clicking the small "I" button. Double-click in the palette's point size field, type 16, and press (Return)[Enter] to apply the change to the text.

Figure 5.6

Several paragraph and character attributes can be edited using the Measurements palette's leading, tracking/kerning, alignment, font, size, and style controls.

14. With the text still selected, double-click in the Measurements palette's leading field, type 20, and press (Return)[Enter] to apply the change to the text.
15. Keeping all the text selected, choose Style➡Horizontal/Vertical Scale, which brings up the Character Attributes dialog box with the Horizontal Scale field already selected, type 88, and press (Return)[Enter]. This scales the text to 88 percent of its normal width—technically a typographical no-no, but a common practice all the same.
16. The fastest way to adjust the paragraphs' alignment is to click the text cursor in each paragraph and use a keyboard shortcut. Click in the first paragraph and press (Command-Shift-L)[Control-Shift-L] to make it left-justified; click in the second paragraph and press (Command-Shift-C)[Control-Shift-C] to center the paragraph; click in the third paragraph and press (Command-Shift-R)

[Control-Shift-R] to right-justify it; and click in the last paragraph and press (Command-Shift-J)[Control-Shift-J] to make it justified. You can also change the **justification** of a paragraph in the Paragraph Attributes dialog box or by clicking the five justification icons in the Measurements palette (see Figure 5.7).

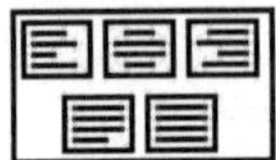

Figure 5.7

Clicking one of these five buttons changes the alignment of any selected paragraphs.

17. Click anywhere in the second paragraph and drag the cursor down to select the remainder of the second paragraph and the beginning of the third paragraph, and then press (Command-Shift-F)[Control-Shift-F] to bring up the Paragraph Attributes dialog box. Double-click in the Space Before field, type .15, and press (Return)[Enter] to apply the changes. The change is made to both paragraphs, even though they're not completely selected, because it's a paragraph-level attribute.

Tip

You can move from field to field within a dialog box and in the Measurements palette by pressing Tab to move to the next field or Shift-Tab to move to the preceding field.

18. Click in the fourth paragraph and press (Command-Shift-F)[Control-Shift-F] to bring up the Paragraph Attributes dialog box again. Double-click in the Space Before field, type .25, and press (Return)[Enter] to apply the changes. Because this is a paragraph-level attribute, no text in the paragraph has to be selected to make this change—the cursor just has to be within the paragraph.
19. To change the text in the fourth paragraph to a different style, quadruple-click (four quick clicks) in the paragraph to select the entire paragraph. Click the "I" button on the Measurements palette to remove the italic attribute from the text. That completes the formatting in this text block (see Figure 5.8).
20. One last text block is needed to finish the ad. Draw a rectangular text box flush with the right and bottom margins of the page, about 2.5 inches wide and 2 inches deep.

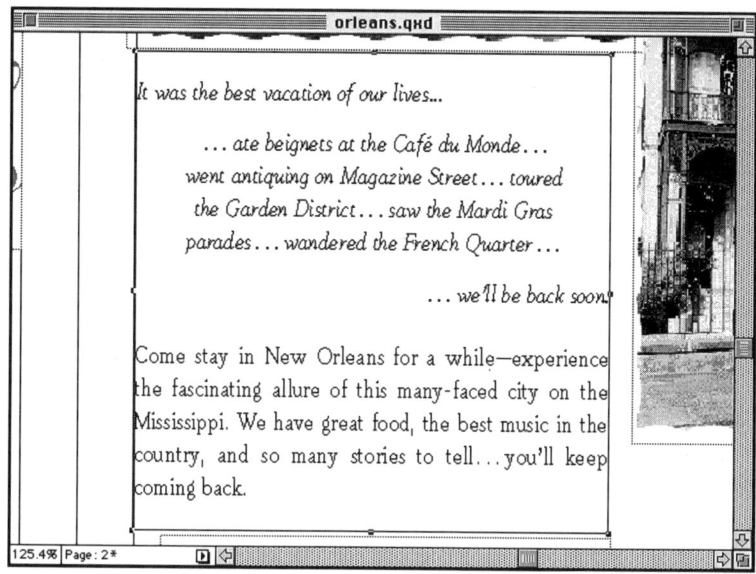

Figure 5.8

The main text of the ad is complete.

21. The Content tool should be active as soon as you finish drawing the box because it was the last tool active before you switched to the Rectangular Text Box tool, so you can start typing immediately. Enter the following text: "Call now for your free New Orleans vacation kit! 1-800-555-1212."

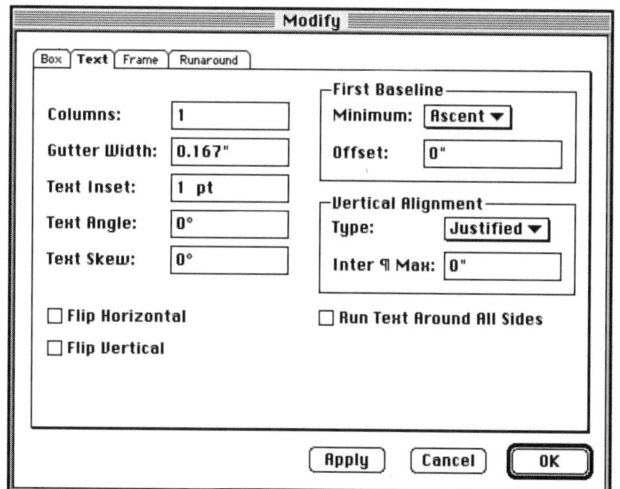

Figure 5.9

The Text tab of the Modify dialog box.

22. Press (Return)[Enter] after “now,” “free,” “Orleans,” and “kit!” to break the text into shorter lines.
23. Select all by pressing (Command-A)[Control-A], choose FlyHigh from the font menu on the Measurements palette, and click the “B” button on the palette to make the text bold. Then click the right-justify button or press (Command-Shift-R)[Control-Shift-R] to right-justify the text. Make sure the leading field on the Measurements palette says Auto.
24. Press (Command-M)[Control-M] to bring up the Modify dialog box, and click the Text tab (see Figure 5.9). Set the Vertical Alignment of the text box to Justified, and click OK to apply the change.
25. Place the cursor at the beginning of the text, before the word “Call,” and press (Command-Shift-down arrow)[Control-Shift-down arrow] four times to select all but the last line of text, and then double-click in the point size field of the Measurements palette, type 16, and press (Return)[Enter] to apply the changes.
26. Triple-click in the phone number line to select the whole line, and then try using a keyboard shortcut to change the text’s point size to 19. Hold down (Command-Shift-Option)[Control-Shift-Alt] as you press the right angle bracket key (>) to increase the point size of the type one point at a time, and hold down the same modifier keys as you press the left angle bracket key (<) to decrease the point size one point at a time. If you leave out the (Option)[Alt] key, the size of the type increases or decreases to the next preset size; the sizes are 7, 9, 10, 12, 14, 18, 24, 36, 48, 60, 72, 96, 120, 144, 168, and 192 points (these are similar to the choices in the point size menu).

Note

Although you can’t make text any larger than 192 points or smaller than 7 points using (Command-Shift)[Control-Shift] and the angle bracket keys, you can make type as small as 2 points or as large as 720 points using any other method.

27. Again, select all the text in the box and press F12 to show the Colors palette if it’s not visible (see Figure 5.10). Click the text icon at the top of the Colors palette (the middle icon) and click C18 M42 K10 in the list of colors to change the type to a lavender. See Figure 5.11 for the final layout (with guides hidden—press F7 to toggle guides).

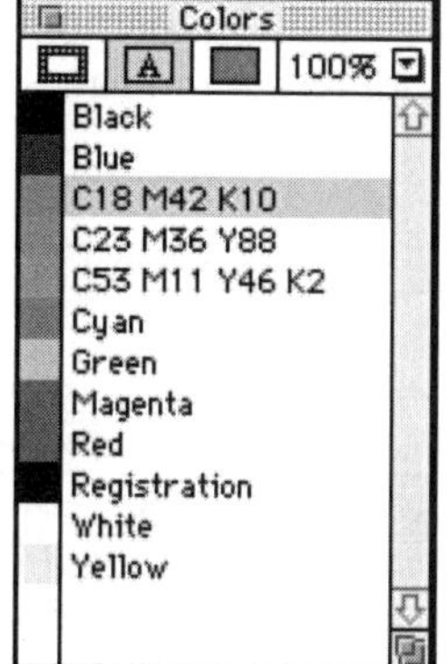

Figure 5.10

When a text box is active, click the middle icon in the Colors palette to change the color of selected text.

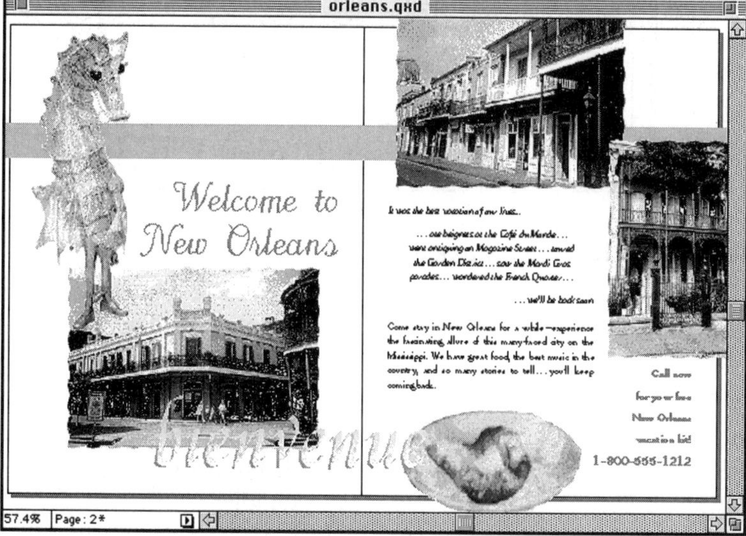

Figure 5.11

The final New Orleans ad.

One of the nicest things about QuarkXPress is that the program provides so many ways to make changes to text attributes. Use whichever methods are most comfortable for you—most people use a combination of all these methods—but do make an effort to learn the keyboard shortcuts as you go because they're the fastest.

Rules and Tabs

Two paragraph attributes that have separate tabs in the Paragraph Attributes dialog box are Rules and Tabs. The Rules tab lets you place rules (lines) above and below a paragraph; to add rules to a paragraph, follow these steps:

1. Press (Command-Shift-N)[Control-Shift-N] to bring up the Rules tab of the Paragraph Attributes dialog box, or press (Command-Shift-P)[Control-Shift-P] and click the Rules tab (see Figure 5.12).

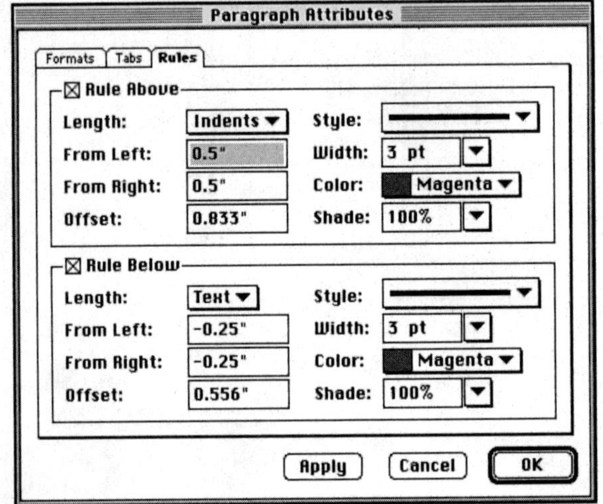

Figure 5.12

The Rules tab of the Paragraph Attributes dialog box.

2. Click Rule Above or Rule Below to make the options active.
3. From the Length menu, choose Indents or Text; the former creates rules that are as wide as the left and right indents of the paragraph will allow, whereas the latter creates rules that are exactly as wide as the text in the adjacent line of the paragraph (the first line for Rule Above, the last line for Rule Below).
4. If you want to adjust the rule's length further, you can enter values in the From Left and From Right fields; these values will be added to the existing values created by your choice in the Length menu. For example:
   - A Length setting of Indents and From Left/Right settings of .5 inches creates a rule that's 1 inch narrower than the text (see Figure 5.13).
   - A Length setting of Text and From Left/Right settings of -.25 inches creates a rule that's .5 inches wider than the text area, because the From Left/Right settings are negative (see Figure 5.13).
5. Enter a percentage or a measurement (in inches, picas, or one of the other measurement systems XPress can use) in the Offset field to determine how far from the text's cap height (for Rule Above) or baseline (for Rule Below) the rule will fall. Entering a percentage allows the rule offset to change automatically if you change the size of the text.

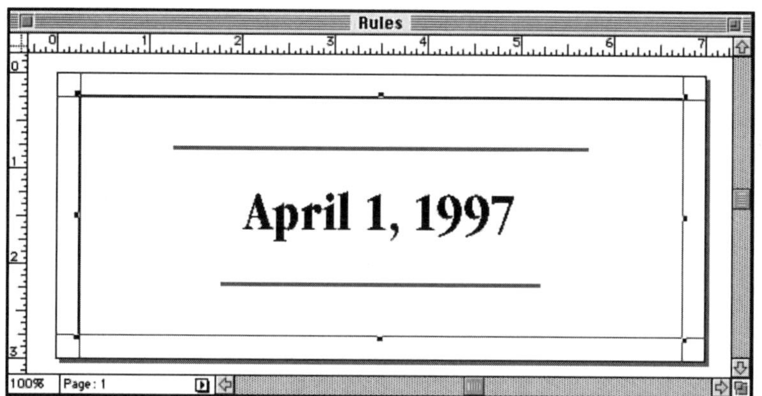

Figure 5.13

The rule above this paragraph has a Length setting of Indents and From Left/Right settings of .5 inches, whereas the one below has a Length setting of Text and From Left/Right settings of -.25 inches.

6. Choose a rule style from the Style menu; the choices here are the same as for the Line tools, including custom borders you create using the Dashes & Stripes dialog box (see Day 3, "Creating Text and Graphic Elements").
7. Enter a width in the Width field, or choose one of the preset values from the pop-up menu (**Hairline**, 1, 2, 4, 6, 8, and 12 points).
8. Choose a color from the Color menu, and enter a shade in the Shade field (or choose a preset value).
9. Click Apply to see the results of your changes without leaving the Paragraph Attributes dialog box; if you're satisfied, click OK to return to the document.

A paragraph can have rules both above and below it, and you can even adjust the offset so that a rule goes through the text itself. A Rule Above adjusted this way will fall behind the text; this is a handy technique for creating headlines that consist of text on a bar of another color (see Figure 5.14).

The Tabs tab of the Paragraph Attributes dialog box lets you set tab stops to determine where the cursor will be placed with each tab character you insert in a line of text. If you don't set tab stops, XPress adds .5 inches (3p) of space for each tab character inserted; many people just insert multiple tab characters to move text to the desired position. It's a good idea to use tab stops instead so you can specify the exact position of each tab.

1. Press (Command-Shift-T)[Control-Shift-T] to bring up the Tabs tab of the Paragraph Attributes dialog box, or press (Command-Shift-P)[Control-Shift-P] and click the Tabs tab (see Figure 5.15).
2. As the Tabs dialog box appears, a ruler appears at the top of the text box or window (if the top of the text box isn't visible) that shows any tab stops already set. The ruler also indicates the positions of the left, right, and first line indents

with small triangles (see Figure 5.16). You can reposition the indents by dragging the triangles; drag the right triangle to change the right indent, drag the top half of the left triangle to change the first line indent; and drag the bottom half of the left triangle to change the left indent.

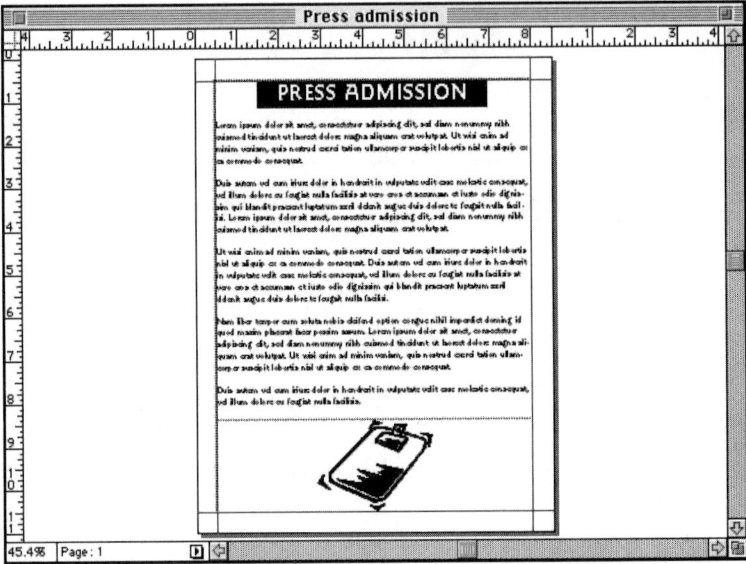

Figure 5.14

The heading is white text with a rule above; the offset is 1p and the width is 45 points.

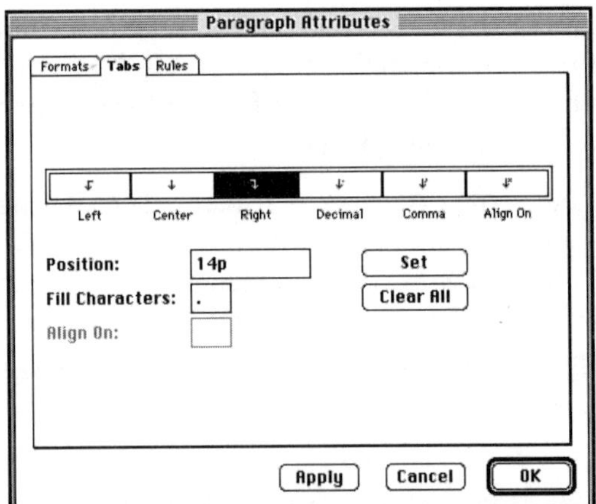

Figure 5.15

The Tabs tab of the Paragraph Attributes dialog box.

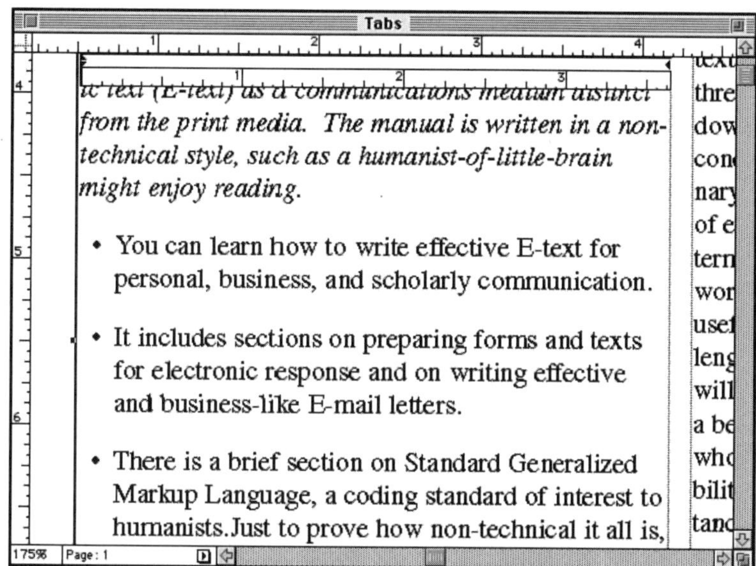

Figure 5.16

The tab ruler also shows the left, right, and first line paragraph indents; move the triangles to change the indents.

3. To place a tab stop, click a type of tab in the Tabs dialog box and either type in a position in the Position field then click Set, or click the tab ruler to position the tab stop. There are six kinds of tabs (see Figure 5.17):
   - Left tabs align the beginning of the following text at the tab stop position.
   - Right tabs align the end of the following text at the tab stop position.
   - Center tabs align the center of the following text at the tab stop position.
   - Decimal tabs align the next period character after the tab character at the tab stop position.
   - Comma tabs align the next comma character after the tab character at the tab stop position.
   - Align On tabs let you specify a character to be positioned at the tab stop position. Enter the alignment character in the Align On field.

   You can have thousands of tab stops in each paragraph.
4. To add a **tab leader** to a tab stop, click the tab in the ruler (indicated by a small arrow that matches the one shown for that type of tab in the Tabs dialog box) then enter one or two leader characters in the Fill Characters field. Leader characters appear in the space created by the tab character (see Figure 5.18). The most common leader character is a period; to space the periods a bit further apart, enter a period and a space.

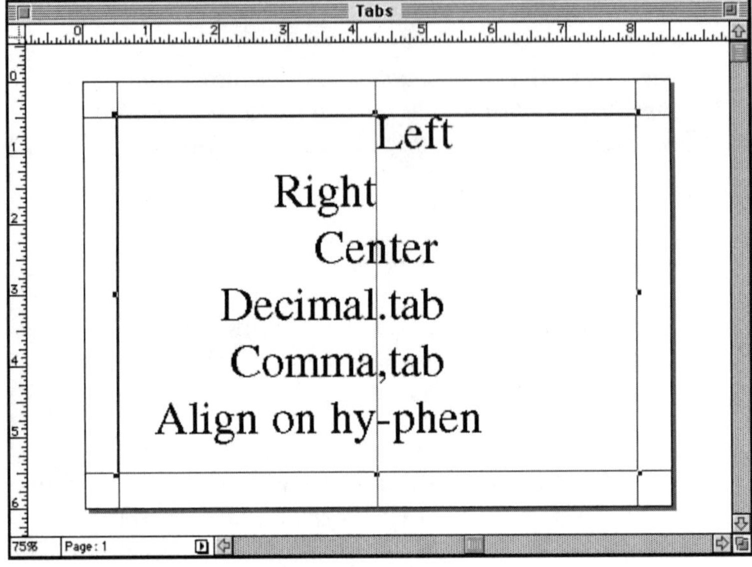

Figure 5.17

Each of these six lines begins with a tab character and has a tab stop set at the position of the vertical guide.

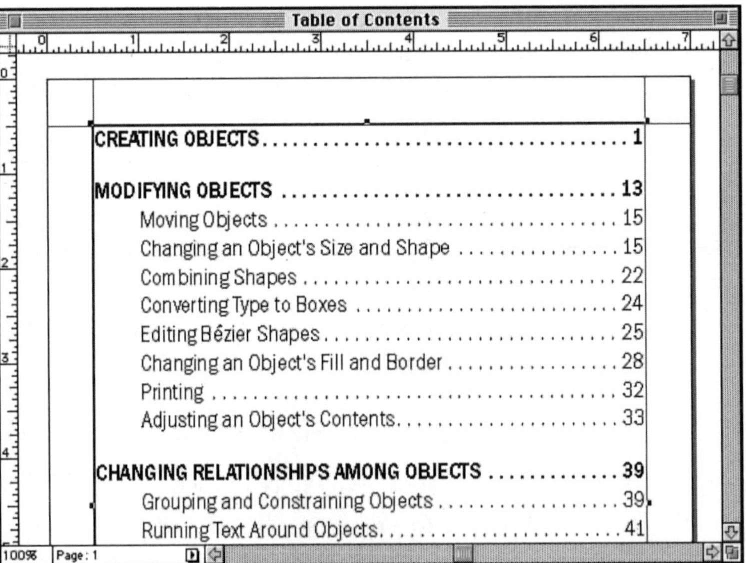

Figure 5.18

Dot leaders are often used in tables of contents; the periods appear in the space occupied by the tab character.

5. To clear all the tab stops, click the Clear All button.
6. To move a tab stop, click its arrow and drag the arrow along the ruler; to delete it, drag the arrow entirely off the ruler.

7. Click Apply to see the results of your changes without leaving the Paragraph Attributes dialog box; if you're satisfied, click OK to return to the document.

Creating and Using Style Sheets

Style sheets provide a way to instantly change all the character and paragraph attributes with the click of a mouse or a user-specified keyboard shortcut. Although they take time to set up at the beginning of a job, using them can cut production time to a fraction of what it would be if each paragraph in a document were formatted locally. Each document can contain thousands of style sheets, and you can even create styles based on other styles, so that the "child" styles change when their "parent" styles are modified.

It's a good idea to use consistent style sheet names throughout a document and from job to job; if you always use "bullet" for bulleted list style sheets, for example, you'll always be able to find the bulleted list style in the Style Sheets palette without trying to remember what you named it for this particular job. Keyboard shortcuts can make applying styles even quicker, and those should be consistent, too.

Note

This book's projects use a variety of different style names to show various naming conventions that might work in different situations.

In this example, you create the style sheets necessary to format a chapter from a book about programming in AppleScript, and then apply them to the text to format the chapter.

1. Open lessons/chap05/script.qxd on the CD-ROM that accompanies this book (see Figure 5.19). This file contains the first two pages of the chapter, without the text.

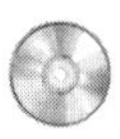

Note

This file uses Andrew Andreas, JetJane Mono (both in the Ingrimayne folder on the CD-ROM), and Patrician (in the Scriptorium folder on the CD-ROM), so make sure those font families are installed in your system.

2. Click the Content tool in the Toolbox palette, and then click in the top text box on the first page of the file.

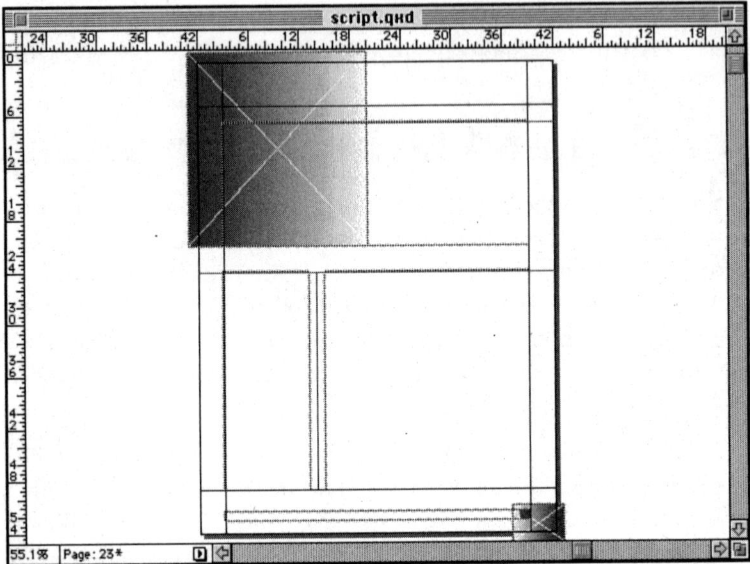

Figure 5.19

The first page of the chapter file.

This page uses a master page called "B-Chapter opener," which contains the running footer at the bottom of the page as well as extra text boxes for the chapter number and title and the chapter objectives. The document's body pages use a master page called "A-Body page."

3. Choose File➡Get Text or press (Command-E)[Control-E]. In the Get Text dialog box, click Include Style Sheets and click lessons/chap05/script.xtg on the CD-ROM that accompanies this book. This XPress Tags file contains the text of the chapter; click Open to import it. More pages are added to hold all the text, using the same master page as the last page that already existed, A-Body page.
4. If the Style Sheets palette isn't visible, press F12 to show it (see Figure 5.20).
5. Press Shift-F11 or choose Edit➡Style Sheets to bring up the Style Sheets dialog box (see Figure 5.21). This dialog box works just like the Dashes & Stripes dialog box (see Day 3, "Creating Text and Graphic Elements"). A window shows all the paragraph and character style sheets, and buttons let you create new style sheets, duplicate or edit existing ones, delete them, append styles from other documents, and, of course, cancel or save your changes.
6. From the Show menu, choose Paragraph Style Sheets to view only the paragraph style sheets. At this point, the document contains only one paragraph style sheet: Normal, which you can't delete.

Figure 5.20

The Style Sheets palette always shows the Normal style.

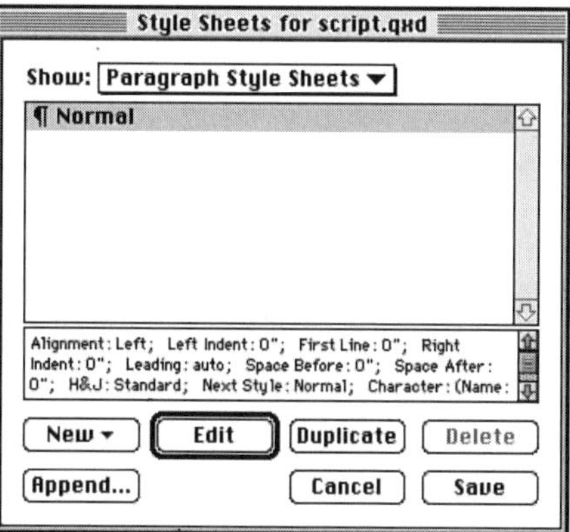

Figure 5.21

The Style Sheets dialog box.

7. Click the New button and hold down for a second to see a menu of choices: New Paragraph style and New Character style; choose New Paragraph style.
8. The Edit Paragraph Style Sheet dialog box has four tabs, three of which are going to look very familiar—Formats, Tabs, and Rules (see Figure 5.22). These are identical to the tabs in the Paragraph Attributes dialog box.
9. First, create a paragraph style sheet for the body text. In the Name field at the top of the General tab in the dialog box, type the word Body, then click each tab in turn to specify the style's paragraph attributes (some attributes don't need to be changed from their defaults).
   - **Formats:** Change the leading to 14 points, and change the space before to 14 points. Choose Justified from the Alignment menu, and click Keep Lines Together (Start: 2, End: 2).
   - **Tabs:** This style has no tab stops.
   - **Rules:** This style has no rules.

Figure 5.22

The Edit Paragraph Style Sheet dialog box.

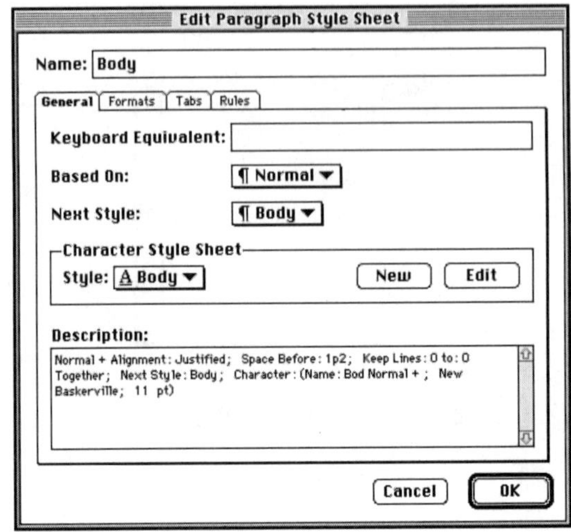

To specify the character attributes, click New in the Character Attributes area of the General Tab to bring up the Edit Character Style Sheet dialog box (see Figure 5.23). In the Name field, type Body, then specify the character attributes:

- **Font:** Choose Patrician.
- **Size:** Enter 11.

Leave all the other attributes set at their defaults.

Figure 5.23

The Edit Character Style Sheet dialog box.

Edit Character Style Sheet
Name: Body
Keyboard Equivalent:
Based On: A *No Style*
Font: Patrician
Size: 11 pt
Color: Black
Shade: 100%
Scale: Horizontal 100%
Track Amount: 0
Baseline Shift: 0 pt
Type Style
☒ Plain ☐ Shadow
☐ Bold ☐ All Caps
☐ Italic ☐ Small Caps
☐ Underline ☐ Superscript
☐ Word U-line ☐ Subscript
☐ Strike Thru ☐ Superior
☐ Outline
Cancel
OK

Tip

You don't have to create a character style sheet to specify character attributes in a paragraph style sheet, but it's a good idea to do so if you're likely to have several paragraph styles that use the same character style. In the case of a body text style, you're likely to have bulleted and numbered list styles that will use the same character style, among others.

10. Now create a paragraph style sheet for the chapter number. In the Name field at the top of the dialog box, type Chapter number, then specify the style's paragraph attributes.
    - Formats: Change the leading to 36 points, choose Right from the Alignment menu, and click both Keep Lines Together (All Lines in Paragraph) and Keep with Next Paragraph.

Tip

In general, use Keep with Next Paragraph and Keep Lines Together (All Lines in Paragraph) for headings, and Keep Lines Together (Start: 2, End: 2) for other text. Depending on how picky you are, you can increase the number of lines at the Start and End of each paragraph that must be kept together.

    - Tabs: This style has no tab stops.
    - Rules: Click Rule Below. Enter p3 in the Offset field and 2 in the Width field, and choose PANTONE 247 CV from the Color menu. Choose Text from the Length menu.

    Click Edit in the Character Attributes area of the General tab and specify the character attributes:

    - Font: Choose AndrewAndreas XB.
    - Size: Enter 16.
    - Tracking: Enter 30.
    - Style: Click All Caps.

    Leave all the other attributes set at their defaults.

11. Create a paragraph style sheet for the chapter title. In the Name field at the top of the dialog box, type "Chapter title," then specify the style's paragraph attributes.

- Formats: Change the leading to 24 points, choose Right from the Alignment menu, and enter 3p in the Space Before field. Click Keep Lines Together (All Lines in Paragraph).
- Tabs: This style has no tab stops.
- Rules: This style has no rules.

Click Edit in the Character Attributes area of the General tab and specify the character attributes:

- Font: Choose AndrewAndreas XB.
- Size: Enter 36.

Leave all the other attributes set at their defaults.

12. Create a paragraph style sheet for the first-level headings. In the Name field at the top of the dialog box, type Head1, then specify the style's paragraph attributes.
    - Formats: Change the leading to 36 points, choose Left from the Alignment menu, and enter 1p1 in the Space Before field. Click Keep Lines Together (All Lines in Paragraph) and on Keep With Next Paragraph.
    - Tabs: This style has no tab stops.
    - Rules: Click Rule Above. Enter 1p6 in the Offset field and 4 in the Width field, and choose PANTONE 247 CV from the Color menu. Choose Text from the Length menu.

    Click Edit in the Character Attributes area of the General tab and specify the character attributes:

    - Font: Choose AndrewAndreas XB.
    - Size: Enter 20.
    - Tracking: Enter 20.
    - Style: Click All Caps.

    Leave all the other attributes set at their defaults.
13. Create a paragraph style sheet for the second-level headings. In the Name field at the top of the dialog box, type Head2, then specify the style's attributes.
    - Formats: Change the Left Indent to 1p and the leading to 16 points, choose Left from the Alignment menu, and enter 1p2 in the Space Before field. Click Keep Lines Together (All Lines in Paragraph) and Keep with Next Paragraph.
    - Tabs: This style has no tab stops.

- Rules: Click Rule Above. Make the Offset 0p (not 0 percent) and change the indents to –1p (From Left) and 35p4 (From Right). Make the Width 8, and choose PANTONE 247 CV from the Color menu. Choose Indents from the Length menu.

These rule settings will make an 8-point rule that's 8 points long—a square—and flush with the left margin, whereas the Left Indent setting in the Formats tab will indent the text 1p to make room for the square.

Click Edit in the Character Attributes area of the General tab and specify the character attributes:

- Font: Choose AndrewAndreas XB.
- Size: Enter 16.
- Tracking: Enter 20.

Leave all the other attributes set at their defaults.

14. Create a variation on the Head2 style sheet for second-level heads that appear on the first page of the chapter. Because the text box is narrower on the chapter opener page, the From Right setting for the rule that makes the 8-point box needs to be changed. In the General tab, choose Head2 from the Based On menu, and enter Head2 first page in the Name field at the top of the dialog box, and then specify the style's attributes.

    - Formats: Don't change these settings.
    - Tabs: Don't change these settings.
    - Rules: Change the From Right setting to 23p4.

    Leave all the other attributes as they are; they'll be the same as the attributes in the Head2 style. If any of the attributes shared by Head2 and Head2 first page are changed in the Head2 definition, they'll also be changed in Head2 first page.

15. Create a paragraph style sheet for the chapter objectives section. In the Name field at the top of the dialog box, type Chapter objectives, then specify the style's attributes.

    - **Formats:** Change the leading to 14 points, choose Right from the Alignment menu, and enter 1p2 in the Space Before field. Click Keep Lines Together (Start: 2, End: 2).
    - **Tabs:** This style has no tab stops.
    - **Rules:** This style has no rules.

Click Edit in the Character Attributes area of the General tab and specify the character attributes:

- Font: Choose AndrewAndreas.
- Size: Enter 11.

Leave all the other attributes set at their defaults.

16. Create a paragraph style sheet for the chapter objectives heading. In the Name field at the top of the dialog box, type Chapter objectives head, then specify the style's attributes.
    - **Formats:** Change the leading to 21 points, choose Right from the Alignment menu, and click both Keep Lines Together (All Lines in Paragraph) and Keep with Next Paragraph. Make the Space Before value 90p—that will force the chapter objectives head to move to the top of the next text box in the flow, because that much space isn't available in any text box in this design.
    - **Tabs:** This style has no tab stops.
    - **Rules:** This style has no rules.

    Click Edit in the Character Attributes area of the General tab and specify the character attributes:

    - Font: Choose AndrewAndreas.
    - Size: Enter 18.
    - Color: Choose PANTONE 247 CV from the Color menu.
    - Style: Choose Bold.

    Leave all the other attributes set at their defaults.

17. Create a paragraph style sheet for the AppleScript code sections. In the Name field at the top of the dialog box, type Code, then specify the style's attributes.
    - Formats: Change the leading to 14 points and click Keep Lines Together (All Lines in Paragraph).
    - Tabs: This style has no tab stops.
    - Rules: This style has no rules.

    Click Edit in the Character Attributes area of the General tab and specify the character attributes:

    - Font: Choose JetJane Mono.
    - Size: Enter 10.

    Leave all the other attributes set at their defaults.

Note

Computer programming handbooks usually use a monospaced font such as Courier, Letter Gothic, or Monaco for sections of code.

18. Create a variation on the Code style sheet for the first line of each code section that will add space above it. In the General tab, choose Code from the Based On menu, enter Code first in the Name field at the top of the dialog box, and then specify the style's attributes.
    - **Formats:** Change Space Before to 1p2 and click Keep with Next Paragraph.
    - **Tabs:** Don't change these settings.
    - **Rules:** Don't change these settings.

    Leave the other attributes as they are; they should be the same as the attributes in the Code style.
19. In the Style Sheets dialog box, click Save to save the new style sheets and return to the document. The new paragraph and character style sheets now appear in the Style Sheets palette (see Figure 5.24).

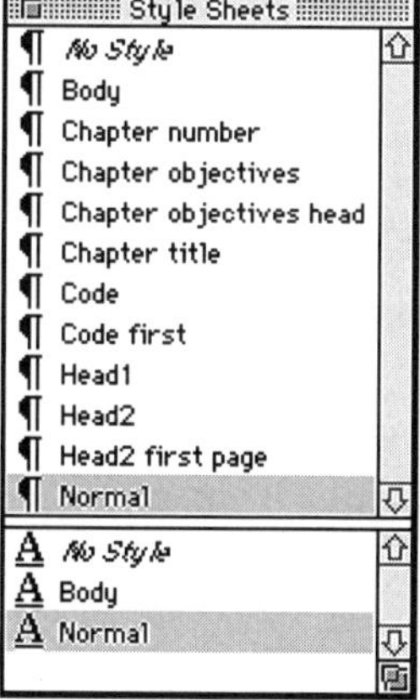

Figure 5.24

The Style Sheets palette now shows all the style sheets you created.

20. Now apply the style sheets to the text in the chapter. Because most of the paragraphs will use the Body style, select all (Command-A)[Control-A] and click Body in the Style Sheets palette to apply the style sheet to all the text (see Figure 5.25).

Figure 5.25

The chapter's first page with the Body style applied to all the text.

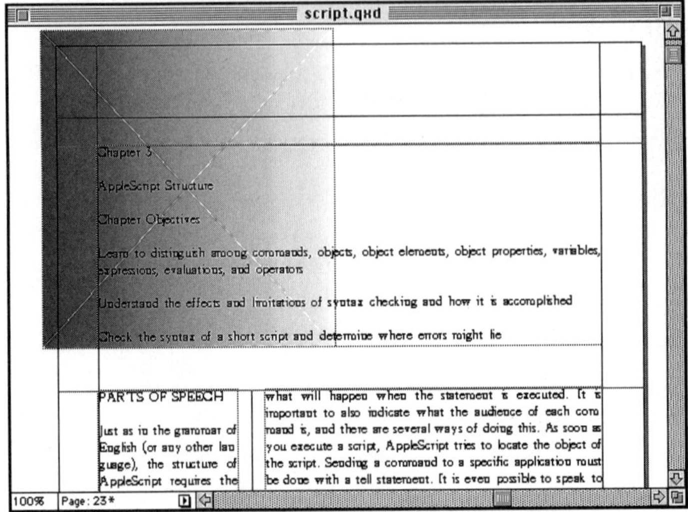

21. Apply the styles to the rest of the text by clicking in each paragraph and then clicking the name of the style sheet.

   - Apply Chapter number to the first paragraph, "Chapter 3."
   - Apply Chapter title to the second paragraph, "AppleScript Structure."
   - Apply Chapter objective head to the third paragraph, "Chapter Objectives."
   - Apply Chapter objective to the following three paragraphs.
   - Apply Head1 to the next paragraph, "Parts of Speech."
   - Apply Code first to the next paragraph and Code to the three following paragraphs.
   - Apply Head2 to the following headings in the rest of the chapter: "Commands," "Objects," "Comments," "Operators," and "Variables."
   - Apply Head 1 to the last heading in the chapter, "Syntax Checking."
   - Apply Code first to the first line of the code section that ends the chapter, "on run."
   - Apply Code to the rest of the code section.

   Figure 5.26 shows the first page of the chapter after all the style sheets are applied.

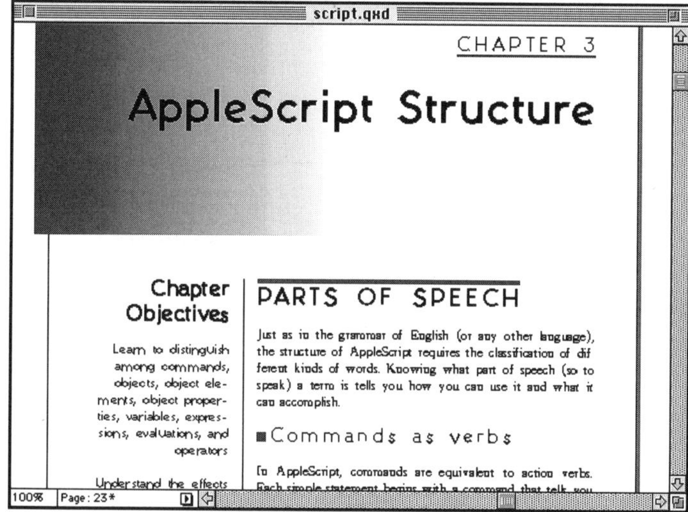

Figure 5.26

The formatted chapter.

As you can see, after the styles are set up, formatting the chapter goes very quickly. It can go even faster if you specify keyboard shortcuts in the General tab of the Edit Paragraph Style Sheet dialog box; just click in the Keyboard Equivalent field and press the keys you want to use for the shortcut.

Tip

Modifier keys (Command, Control, Option, Alt, and Shift) combined with the keypad number keys make great keyboard shortcuts for style sheets, because you're unlikely to use these key combinations at any other time.

You can also apply both character and paragraph style sheets by choosing the style sheet from the Style➡Paragraph Style Sheet or Style➡Character Style Sheet submenus. Applying a character style sheet changes the character attributes of the text but not the paragraph attributes.

If styles that you want to use are already set up in another document, you don't have to re-create them; you can append styles from other documents, choosing to have those styles override the ones already used in your document or not.

1. Choose Edit➡Style Sheets or press Shift-F11 and click Append. In the Append Style Sheets dialog box (see Figure 5.27), choose the file from which you want to append style sheets and click Open.

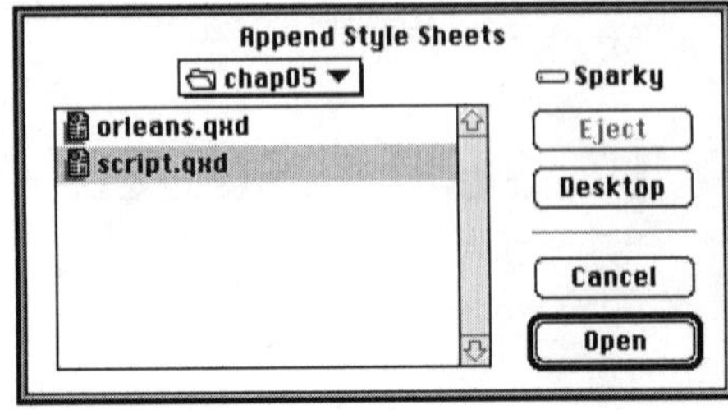

Figure 5.27

The Append Style Sheets dialog box.

2. The next dialog box lets you pick which styles you want to add to your document. You can click individual styles, and then click the right arrow button to add them to the list of colors to be appended, or you can click the Include All button to add the entire list of styles (see Figure 5.28). After you're done choosing styles, click OK to return to the Style Sheets dialog box, and click Save to finish adding the new styles.

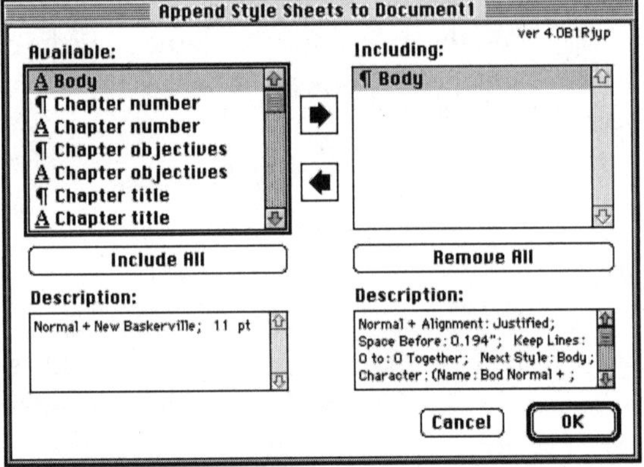

Figure 5.28

Choose the styles you want to add to your document, and then click OK.

3. A dialog box warns you that along with the paragraph and character style sheets you're importing will come any additional character styles, colors, H&Js, and custom borders (dashes and stripes) used in those style sheets (see Figure 5.29). Click OK to continue appending and Cancel to stop.
4. If any of the styles, colors, borders, or H&Js you append already exists in your document, you'll see a dialog box informing you of that fact (see Figure 5.30). The Existing and New fields describe the item as it's defined in each document; Existing is the item in the document in which you're currently working and New is the item in the document from which you're appending.
   - Click Rename to assign a new name to the new item (see Figure 5.31).

The appended style sheets and lists will include all embedded style sheets, H&Js, colors, and dashes & stripes. OK to append?
Cancel
OK

Figure 5.29

QuarkXPress automatically brings needed character style sheets, colors, custom borders, and H&J settings with appended style sheets.

Append Conflict

Color "Black" is already in use. How would you like to resolve the conflict?

Rename | Auto-Rename | Use New | Use Existing

Repeat For All Conflicts

Existing:

Separated color; Cyan: 0%; Magenta: 0%; Yellow: 0%; Black: 100%

New:

Separated color; Red: 0%; Green: 0%; Blue: 0%

Cancel

Figure 5.30

The Append Conflict dialog box.

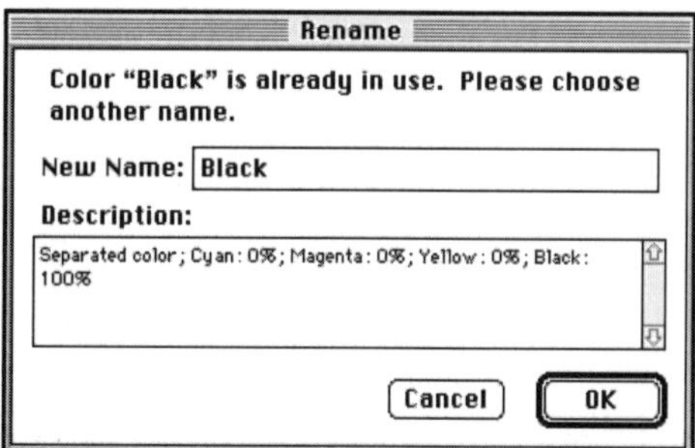
Rename
Color "Black" is already in use. Please choose another name.
New Name: Black
Description:
Separated color; Cyan: 0%; Magenta: 0%; Yellow: 0%; Black: 100%
Cancel
OK

Figure 5.31

This dialog box lets you assign a new name to an appended style sheet with the same name as an existing style sheet.

- Click Auto-Rename to have QuarkXPress assign a new name to the new item (it adds an asterisk to the beginning of the original name).
- Click Use New to change the item's definition to match its definition in the document from which you're appending.
- Click Use Existing to keep the item's definition as it is in the document from which you're appending.
- Click Repeat For All Conflicts to make your choice of the previous buttons apply to all conflicts XPress encounters.
- Click Cancel to go back to the Append Style Sheets dialog box.

Summary

One of the hallmarks of professional work is its consistency—not foolish consistency, but a reasonable use of the rules that design has developed to aid in communicating information to a reader. If, for example, you've used italics to indicate a book title in one place within a design, your reader will appreciate it if italics are used for that purpose throughout—even if she doesn't consciously notice it. It's easy to succumb to temptation and start using local formatting even when a style sheet would make sense, but the time invested in creating a style sheet results in both time saved and in improved consistency. QuarkXPress's style sheets features enable you to create style sheets easily (by basing them on existing type or existing style sheets) and apply them even more easily (with built-in, customizable keyboard shortcuts).

Fine-tuning Type

- Controlling automatic hyphenation
- Using special hyphenation characters
- Tracking and kerning type manually
- Controlling automatic tracking and kerning
- Using special space characters
- Using special punctuation
- Using ligatures
- Creating fractions

One of the best-kept secrets in desktop publishing is that there's more to text design than importing a text file into a page layout program and flowing it from page to page. Typography is a centuries-old craft refined through the years by type designers who created beautiful typefaces and typesetters who learned to set those typefaces in a way that would communicate both their beauty and the meaning of the material in the text.

Bound by modern time constraints, designers are forced to strike a balance between the typographic ideal—hand-cutting and positioning every letter to best showcase it—and the lowest common denominator—that poor, naked text file that's just imported into QuarkXPress and left there. That balance comes through careful use of XPress's typographic tools, which include:

- **Hyphenation** and **justification** controls
- Multiple **kerning** and **tracking** methods
- Special characters

In this chapter you'll work with an existing document to refine its typography using these controls, and you'll create a new design that takes advantage of kerning, tracking, and **baseline shift** to put type exactly where you want it.

Customizing Hyphenation and Justification

At first glance, hyphenation and justification may seem like pretty simple issues—hyphenate or don't hyphenate? Left-justified, right-justified, full-justified, force-justified, or centered text? But QuarkXPress's H&J controls let you determine exactly how lines are broken and words are spaced within a document's text—something that has an enormous effect on how a design looks.

In justification, the software adds and removes space along each line of a section of text to fill the specified line width. If you specify center-, left-, or right-justified text, then words that don't fit on a line are simply bumped to the next line, leaving short lines. But the Justification settings in QuarkXPress are still important—they enable you to specify how the program spaces words and characters within words, even though the spacing will be exactly the same throughout a section of text.

The other method QuarkXPress can use to fit text into its allotted column width is inserting hyphens between syllables in words that fall at the ends of lines, which is accomplished using an algorithm, or set of rules for how hyphenation should work. You can specify your choice of hyphenation algorithms: Standard, Enhanced (introduced with version 3.2), and (if you have them installed) third-party algorithms. See "Customizing QuarkXPress with Preferences" in Chapter 1 for more information on setting this preference.

Note

QuarkXPress Passport is a multilingual version of QuarkXPress that includes hyphenation algorithms and spelling dictionaries for several languages. Since hyphenation rules are different for each language, it's a good idea to upgrade to this version of XPress if you're publishing documents in more than one language.

Making Exceptions to Hyphenation Rules

Particularly in English, there are lots of exceptions to every rule, including those governing hyphenation. Fortunately, XPress lets you instruct it on exceptions that you want it to make to its hyphenation algorithm by using the Hyphenation Exceptions command.

1. Choose Utilities➡Hyphenation Exceptions to bring up the Hyphenation Exceptions dialog (see Figure 6.1).

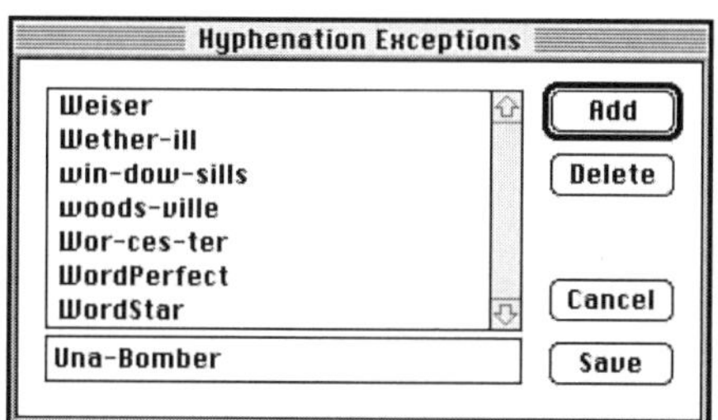

Figure 6.1

The Hyphenation Exceptions dialog box lets you specify when QuarkXPress should break its own hyphenation rules.

2. In the entry field at the bottom of the dialog box, type a word for which you want to specify hyphenation, inserting hyphens at the points at which you prefer that QuarkXPress break the word.
3. To add the word to the Hyphenation Exceptions, click the Add button or press Return.
4. To specify that a particular word should never be hyphenated, type it in the entry field with no hyphens.
5. To alter the specified hyphenation for a word, click the word and then click the Delete button and retype the word the way you want it; to remove a word from the Hyphenation Exceptions, click it and then click the Delete button.
6. You can enter as many exceptions as you want. When you're done, press the Save button to exit the Hyphenation Exceptions dialog box.

The next section covers XPress's H&J settings, which provide the software with more general guidelines for how it should hyphenate text in your documents, as well as guidelines for how you want it to justify text.

Editing the Standard H&J Settings

Each document created in QuarkXPress contains a set of H&J settings, a combination of numbers that govern spacing around and between words as well as hyphenation. This default set, called Standard, can be edited, and new sets can be created, named, and used in different circumstances. Although custom H&J settings can be deleted from a document, you can never delete the Standard H&J settings.

H&J settings are applied on a paragraph basis; in other words, you can't have different hyphenation settings for different words or lines in the same paragraph. You choose H&J setting in Format dialog box, either locally (for individual paragraphs) or within style sheets. All text starts out with the Standard setting applied.

The more text a document contains, the more important its H&J settings are. This is particularly true for books, which tend to be text-intensive. Chapter 5 showed how to format a chapter in a computer trade book using paragraph and character style sheets; now we'll use the same chapter for practice in creating custom H&J settings.

1. Open lessons/chap6/script.qxd on the CD-ROM that accompanies this book (see Figure 6.2).

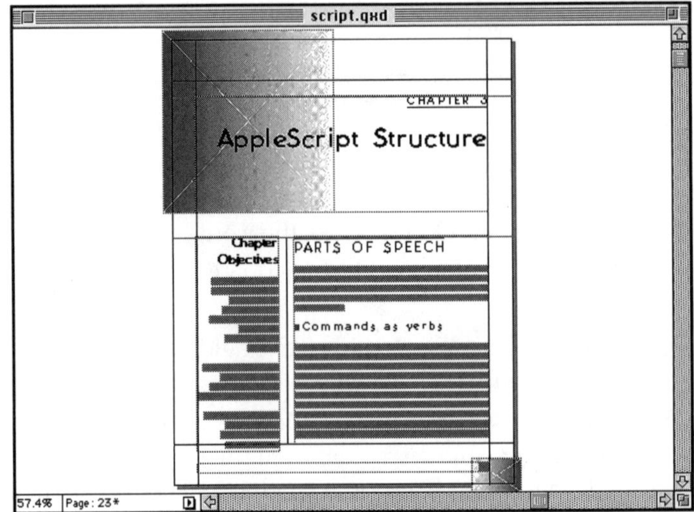

Figure 6.2

"AppleScript Structure" is Chapter 3 of a trade paperback about scripting with Apple's proprietary scripting language.

Note

This file uses AndrewAndreas, JetJane Mono (both in the Ingrimayne folder on the CD), and Patrician (in the Scriptorium folder on the CD), so make sure those font families are installed in your system.

2. Take a look at the text for places where the hyphenation and justification could be improved. The paragraph style sheets in script.qxd use the Standard hyphenation settings; while the Standard settings are marginally acceptable, using them can result in several problems.
   - Hyphenated words in titles or bylines
   - Two-letter hyphenation, such as "togeth-er," a definite no-no in book composition
   - Hyphenation of short words
   - More than two hyphens ending successive lines, another taboo

- Too much space between words within a line
- Too much space between characters within words

Because of the long line length, there are relatively few hyphenation problems in script.qxd, but the spacing could definitely be improved. In the next several steps, you'll change the H&J settings to accomplish this.

3. Choose Edit➡H&Js or press (Command-Option-H)[Control-Shift-F11] to open the H&Js dialog box (see Figure 6.3).

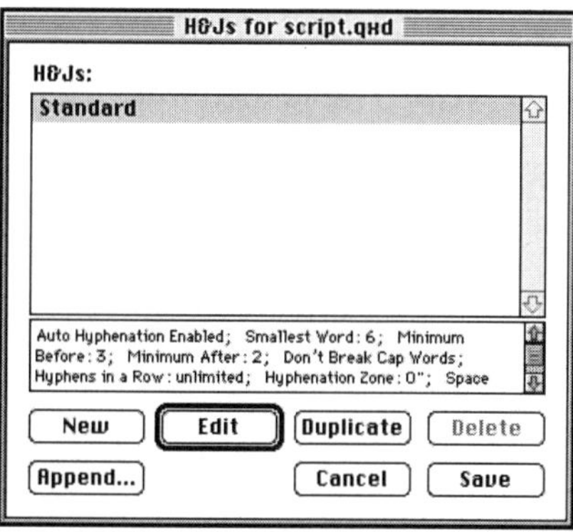

Figure 6.3

The H&Js dialog box lets you create and manipulate groups of hyphenation and justification settings.

4. Click Standard and then click the Edit button (or press Return) to bring up the Edit Hyphenation & Justification dialog box (see Figure 6.4).

Edit Hyphenation & Justification
Name: Standard
☒ Auto Hyphenation
Smallest Word: 6
Minimum Before: 3
Minimum After: 2
☐ Break Capitalized Words
Hyphens in a Row: unlimited
Hyphenation Zone: 0"
Justification Method
Min. Opt. Max.
Space: 85% 110% 250%
Char: 0% 0% 4%
Flush Zone: 0"
☒ Single Word Justify
Cancel
OK

Figure 6.4

Change settings in the Edit Hyphenation & Justification dialog box to affect how QuarkXPress spaces words and letters within words.

5. In the hyphenation section, the left-hand side of the dialog box, make the following settings:
   - Check the Auto Hyphenation box to turn on hyphenation.
   - Set the Smallest Word value to 7. This means that a word must be at least seven letters long before QuarkXPress will hyphenate it.

- Set the Minimum Before value to 3, to avoid two-letter hyphenation. QuarkXPress won't insert any automatic hyphens before the third letter of a word, so the shortest partial word you'll find at the end of a line will have three letters.
- Set the Minimum After value to three; this does the same thing as the Minimum Before value, only at the ends of words, so there won't be any partial words at the beginning of a line shorter than three letters.
- Check "Break Capitalized Words." Traditionalists might say breaking capitalized words is poor practice, and they'd be at least partly right. It would be nice not to have to do this, but most text will end up with gaping spaces if you don't break capitalized words.

> **Tip**
>
> To keep a word from hyphenating even when automatic hyphenation is turned on, place your cursor at the beginning of the word and press (Command-hyphen)[Control-hyphen]. This inserts an invisible character that suppresses hyphenation for that word alone. To remove the character, place your cursor to the right of it (but before the word itself) and press (Delete)[Backspace]. Use this technique to avoid breaking people's names.

- Set Hyphens in a Row to two to ensure that QuarkXPress won't end more than two consecutive lines with an automatically hyphenated word. Unfortunately, the program doesn't pay attention to hyphens you insert yourself, so you'll still have to check for these manually.
- Set the Hyphenation Zone to 0; this setting won't affect the text in this document, since it's mostly full-justified. In ragged-right (left-justified) or ragged-left (right-justified) text, the Hyphenation Zone value determines where QuarkXPress can hyphenate words at the ends of lines—all hyphens must be placed within that distance from the paragraph's right indent, and the word before the hyphenated word must end before the zone begins. A setting of 0 lets QuarkXPress place hyphens anywhere on an unjustified line, while higher settings shift the balance toward using spacing to justify a line rather than hyphenation.

6. On the right-hand side of the dialog box, make the following changes to the Justification Method settings:
   - Under Space, change the Minimum value to 85 percent, the Optimal value to 95 percent, and the Maximum value to 105 percent. This affects

how much QuarkXPress "squeezes" and "stretches" spaces between words as it justifies the text. 100 percent is a standard word space, which is usually a bit large, so with these settings the smallest space between words will be 85 percent of the standard space and the largest will be 105 percent. The Optimal value for a space, the value QuarkXPress strives to maintain in as many cases as possible, will be 95 percent, slightly narrower than the standard space for this font. In centered, left-justified, or right-justified text, the Optimal value is used for all spaces.

Note

QuarkXPress's default word space settings are pretty outrageous. In Figure 6.4, you can see that the Optimal value is 110 percent—wider than the standard space—and the Maximum value is 250 percent. That's right, two and a half times as wide as the standard space. Leaving these values as is will result in spacy, unattractive, and amateurish type.

- Under Char (or Character), change the Minimum value to -1 percent, the Optimal value to 0 percent, and the Maximum value to 1 percent. This tightens up the spacing between characters within words; ideally, QuarkXPress will use the built-in spacing values for the font, and you're allowing the program to squeeze or expand intercharacter spacing by just a tiny amount—1 percent of an en space in either direction. These settings ensure that individual words won't be too spaced out. In centered, left-justified, or right-justified text, the Optimal value is always used.

Note

The Maximum values in the character and word spacing fields are, in a way, meaningless. If it runs out of other options when justifying a line, QuarkXPress uses a higher value than the Maximum to space out the line.

- Set the Flush Zone value to 0 to prevent the last lines of paragraphs from being justified. Larger values would allow XPress to justify the last line of a paragraph if it ended within that distance of the right indent. Like the Hyphenation Zone value, this number is expressed in whatever units are specified in your Application Preferences (inches, picas, millimeters, and so on).

- Click Single Word Justify off. If left on, this setting enables QuarkXPress to justify a line that contains a single long word by adding space between the word's letters to stretch it to the full column width. While newspapers are sometimes forced to justify lines this way, because of their narrow column width, it certainly won't be necessary for this book chapter.

7. The Standard H&J settings should now look like those in Figure 6.5. Click OK to save your changes.

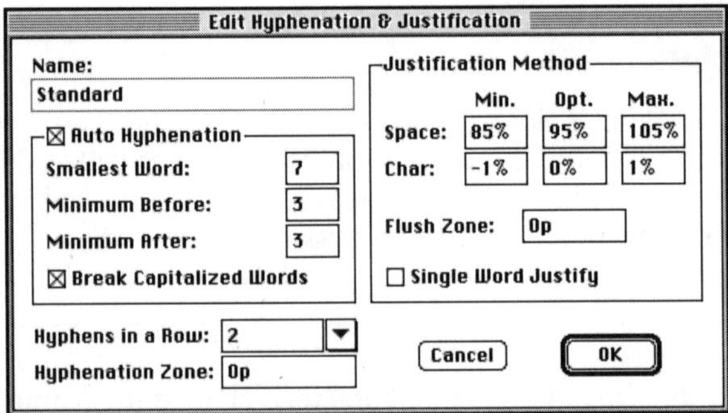

Figure 6.5

The revised H&J settings.

Now that you've adjusted the H&J settings for script.qxd, take a look at where the text ends—the revised spacing should change the number of lines in the document. Figure 6.6 shows how one paragraph in the text changed when the settings were changed—it tightened up enough to lose a line.

The spacing settings used for this document are appropriate for the situation, but remember that the settings you need to use will vary depending on two things: the fonts that are used and the designer's preference (your own, if you're the designer). Most designers prefer tighter spacing over looser spacing, in general, and XPress's default settings for spacing are too loose for most applications.

Hyphenation settings are also subject to your preference—if you don't have a problem with two-letter hyphenation, then go for it (I'll try not to cringe). To see the effects of different settings, create a document containing several copies of the same paragraph, each with a different H&J setting, and print it out to compare the "color" of the text—the effective darkness or lightness produced by looser or tighter spacing.

Obviously, newspapers and glossy, expensive coffee-table books will have different requirements for H&Js. Newspaper production people can't afford to spend all day inserting discretionary hyphens and fiddling with letterspacing in individual paragraphs, while publishers of high-end books do have the time to do this—and owe it to their readers, who are paying for the beauty of the books as well as their textual content.

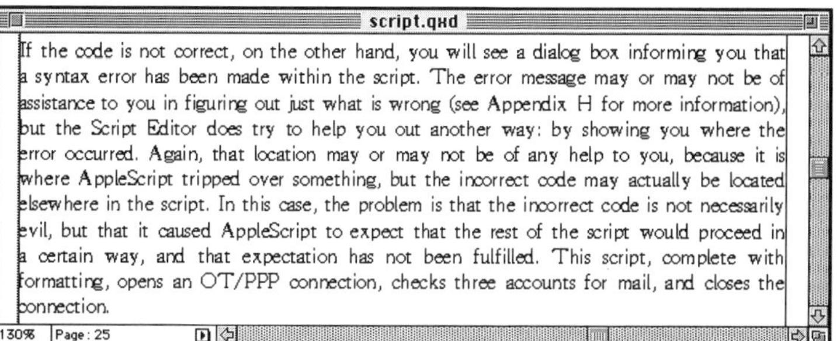
script.qxd

If the code is not correct, on the other hand, you will see a dialog box informing you that a syntax error has been made within the script. The error message may or may not be of assistance to you in figuring out just what is wrong (see Appendix H for more information), but the Script Editor does try to help you out another way: by showing you where the error occurred. Again, that location may or may not be of any help to you, because it is where AppleScript tripped over something, but the incorrect code may actually be located elsewhere in the script. In this case, the problem is that the incorrect code is not necessarily evil, but that it caused AppleScript to expect that the rest of the script would proceed in a certain way, and that expectation has not been fulfilled. This script, complete with formatting, opens an OT/PPP connection, checks three accounts for mail, and closes the connection.

130% Page: 25

a

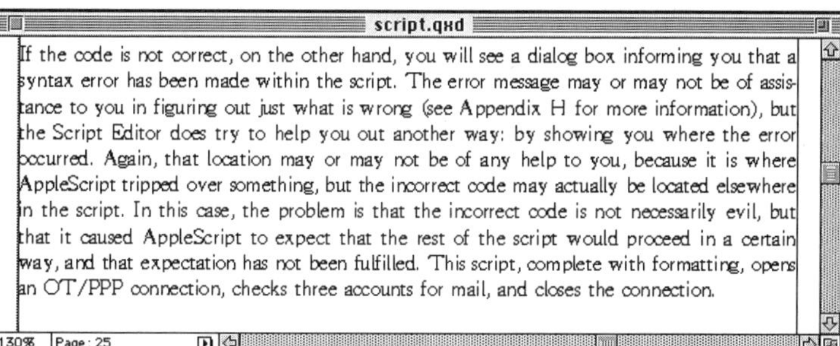
script.qxd

If the code is not correct, on the other hand, you will see a dialog box informing you that a syntax error has been made within the script. The error message may or may not be of assistance to you in figuring out just what is wrong (see Appendix H for more information), but the Script Editor does try to help you out another way: by showing you where the error occurred. Again, that location may or may not be of any help to you, because it is where AppleScript tripped over something, but the incorrect code may actually be located elsewhere in the script. In this case, the problem is that the incorrect code is not necessarily evil, but that it caused AppleScript to expect that the rest of the script would proceed in a certain way, and that expectation has not been fulfilled. This script, complete with formatting, opens an OT/PPP connection, checks three accounts for mail, and closes the connection.

130% Page: 25

b

Figure 6.6

A single paragraph from "AppleScript Structure" (a) before and (b) after the H&J settings were revised.

Tip

It can be a pain making changes to H&J settings for every document you work with. To create default H&J settings that will be applied to any new document you create, start QuarkXPress and choose Edit➡H&Js while no documents are open.

Creating Custom H&J Settings

Different kinds of text in a document call for different H&J settings; to do justice to an entire design, you may need several different settings in one file. For example, it's a good idea to have a setting called something like "No hyphenation" that prevents text from being hyphenated at all—you would use this setting for headlines, bylines, and other text that you don't want to hyphenate, such as, perhaps, captions or lists.

Using the script.qxd file again, we'll make several custom H&J settings for different purposes.

1. If lessons/chap6/script.qxd isn't still open, open it again.

2. Choose Edit➡H&Js or press (Command-Option-H)[Control-Shift-F11] to open the H&Js dialog box.
3. Click the New button.
4. In the Edit Hyphenation and Justification dialog box, first type a name for the new H&J setting: "Mono." This setting will be used for computer code that's set in a **monospaced** font. The idea is that the letters in each line of code line up under the letters above as they would on a computer programmer's screen, so all the spaces must be exactly the same width.
5. In the hyphenation section of the dialog box, check the Auto Hyphenation box to turn off hyphenation completely. You can ignore the rest of the settings in the hyphenation section.
6. On the right-hand side of the dialog box, make the following changes to the Justification Method settings:
   - Under Space, change the Optimal value to 100 percent. This ensures that spaces will be the same width as letters, which is essential for a monospaced font. You can ignore the Minimum and Maximum values since all the text that will use this setting will be left-justified.
   - Under Char (or Character), change the Optimal value to 0 percent. This prevents XPress from adding or subtracting any space between letters within words. You can ignore the Minimum and Maximum values since all the text that will use this setting will be left-justified.
   - You can also ignore the Flush Zone value and Single Word Justify, since this text will be left-justified.
7. Click OK to save your changes and return to the H&Js dialog box.
8. Click Standard and then on the Duplicate button to create a copy of the Standard settings and open the Edit Hyphenation and Justification dialog box.
9. Name this setting "No hyphenation"; we'll use it to keep headings and bylines from hyphenating.
10. The only change that needs to be made to the "No hyphenation" setting is to uncheck the Auto Hyphenation box so that hyphenation won't be used. The spacing settings are just fine—they're copied from the Standard setting you modified earlier in the chapter. Again, click OK to save your changes and return to the H&Js dialog box.
11. Click on Standard and then the Duplicate button again. This time, in the Edit Hyphenation dialog box, name the new setting Tight.
12. The only settings you'll change here are the spacing values. For Space, change the values to Minimum: 70 percent, Optimal: 85 percent, Maximum: 95

percent; for Char change the values to Minimum: -3 percent, Optimal: -1 percent, Maximum: -1 percent. These values, particularly the Minimum and Optimal values, will force any paragraph using this H&J setting to be more tightly spaced. Click OK to save your changes and return to the H&Js dialog.

13. Duplicate Standard one more time and name the new setting Loose in the Edit Hyphenation dialog box.
14. Here, change the spacing values as follows: for Space, use Minimum: 100 percent, Optimal: 110 percent, Maximum: 150 percent; for Char change the values to Minimum: 0 percent, Optimal: 1 percent, Maximum: 1 percent. These values will loosen the spacing of any paragraph to which the Loose H&J setting is applied, stretching it to fill more lines. Click OK to save your changes and return to the H&Js dialog box.
15. Click Save to save your changes.
16. Now you'll use these new settings in the document's text. First, choose Edit➥Style Sheets and double-click on the Head1 style sheet to open the Edit Style Sheet dialog box.
17. Click the Formats button to bring up the Paragraph Formats dialog box and choose No hyphenation from the H&J pop-up menu. This will prevent paragraphs using the Head-1 style from being hyphenated, and it will also affect all the other heading style sheets, since they're all based on Head1. Click OK in this dialog box to return to the Edit Style Sheet dialog box; then make the same change to the Chapter Title and Chapter Objectives styles.
18. Back in the Edit Style Sheet dialog box, double-click the Code style to edit it and click the Formats button. In the Paragraph Formats dialog box, choose Mono from the H&J pop-up menu. Click OK and then click OK again in the Edit Style Sheet dialog box. This change will affect Code first as well as Code itself, since the other style was based on Code when it was created.
19. Click Save to save your changes and return to the document window. Any headings that were hyphenated suddenly aren't any more and the monospaced code sections tighten up.
20. The Tight and Loose H&J settings can be used on individual paragraphs for **copyfitting.** To apply one of these settings to a paragraph, click in the paragraph and choose Style➥Formats to bring up the Paragraph Formats dialog box. Choose the H&J setting you want to apply from the pop-up menu and click OK. Try applying these H&J settings to various paragraphs to improve the look of the document's text by bringing up short lines at the ends of paragraphs and evening out the page lengths.

Figure 6.7 shows a page in script.qxd before and after applying these new H&J settings both globally and locally. The Tight setting was applied to two body paragraphs to bring the end of the second paragraph onto this page.

Figure 6.7

Before (a) and after (b) creating and applying new H&J settings.

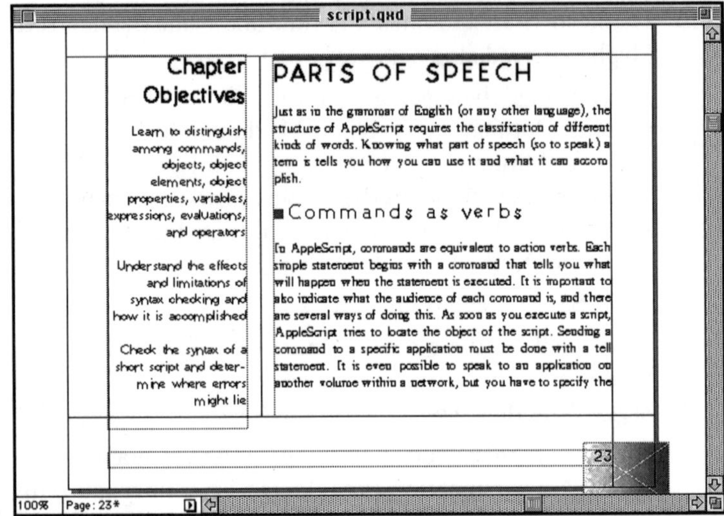

a

b

Appending H&J Settings from Other Documents

If you've already created H&J settings in another document that you want to add to the current document, you can do so by appending them.

1. Choose Edit➡H&Js or press (Command-Option-H)[Control-Shift-F11] to open the H&Js dialog box.
2. Click the Append button and navigate to the document whose H&J settings you want to add. Click Open to view its H&J settings.
3. In the Append H&Js dialog (see Figure 6.8), double-click each setting in the left window that you want to add to the current document, or click each setting and then click the right arrow in the middle of the dialog box. The ones you choose move to the right window. To change your mind, double-click a setting in the right window to move it back, or click it and then click the left arrow.

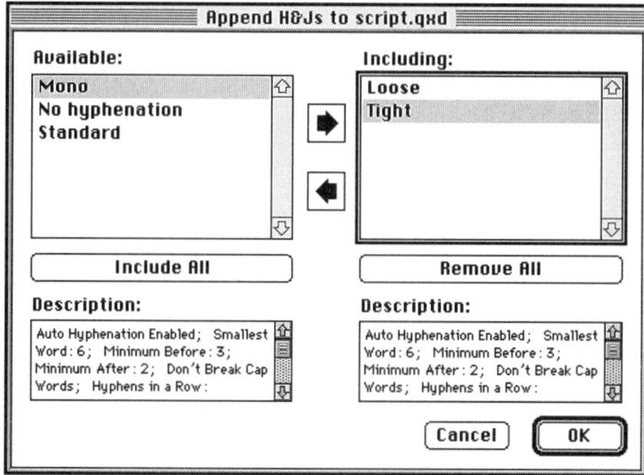

Figure 6.8

You can append any or all of the H&J settings from another document.

4. Click OK to append the H&J settings.

That's all there is to it. If you try to append a H&J setting with the same name as one that already exists in your document, you'll see a dialog box asking what you want to do about it (see Figure 6.9). Your choices are as follows: Forget about the new H&J and continue to use the old one, or go ahead and append the new one, but change its name. If you elect to change the new H&J setting's name, QuarkXPress adds an asterisk to it; by clicking the Edit button, you can then change the name to anything you want.

If you want to substitute one of the new settings for one that's used in your document, you can delete the old setting as described in the next section. When you do that, you'll be asked what setting you want to substitute for it, and you choose the new setting. The time you're likely to run into problems with this procedure is if you want to substitute a new Standard setting for the old one, because you can't delete the Standard setting. In this case, you'll just have to manually change the setting in the Paragraph Format dialog box for affected paragraphs.

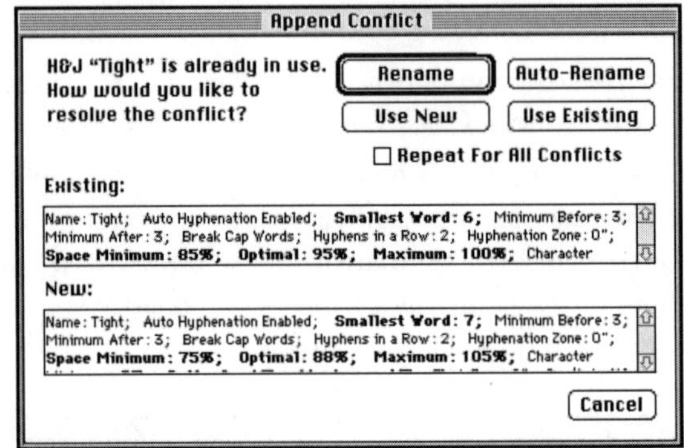

Figure 6.9

XPress warns you if you try to append an H&J setting to a document that already has a setting with the same name.

Deleting H&J Settings

There are two reasons you might want to delete H&J settings; the first is if your H&Js dialog is so full of old settings you're not using any more that it's getting confusing, and the second is if you want to substitute another setting for one that's used in the document.

1. Choose Edit➡H&Js or press (Command-Option-H)[Control-Shift-F11] to bring up the H&Js dialog.
2. Click on the setting you want to delete, then click the Delete button.
3. If the setting is used in your document, then you'll see the dialog box in Figure 6.10. Either cancel the deletion, or choose another setting to be used in the deleted one's place, and click OK.

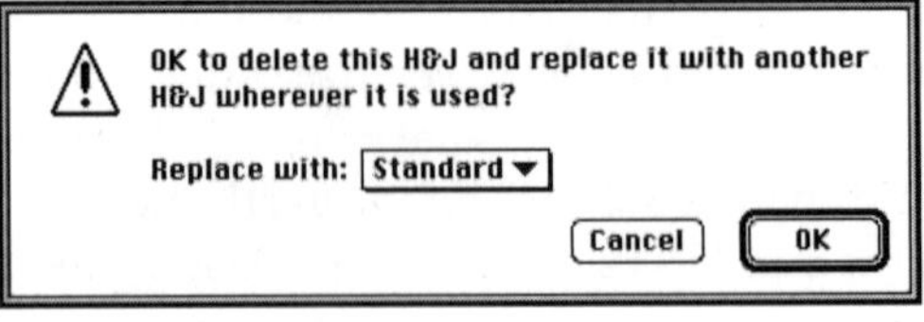

Figure 6.10

When you delete an H&J setting, you may need to specify a new setting to be used wherever the deleted setting was used.

4. Click Save to exit the dialog box and save your changes.

Do-it-yourself Hyphenation

You can force QuarkXPress to hyphenate a word at a specific point (rather than the point the software has chosen) by inserting a discretionary hyphen (press (Command-hyphen)[Control-hyphen]). This is the same character that suppresses hyphenation if it's used at the beginning of a word; if inserted in the middle of the word, it forces QuarkXPress to hyphenate the word only at that point. If the first part of the word won't fit at the end of the line, the whole word will be bumped to the next line.

While they're very useful, discretionary hyphens should only be used when you don't expect to encounter that word again—or if there's nothing wrong with the way XPress hyphenated the word, and you're making the change for copyfitting purposes. Otherwise, it's better to add the word to your Hyphenation Exceptions.

None of this H&J discussion has mentioned another kind of hyphen, the kind you insert yourself, such as in phone numbers or compound terms like "pre-existing condition." That's because you already know how to use those hyphens. However, QuarkXPress does have one variation on regular hyphens that comes in handy when you don't want lines to break after them: the non-breaking hyphen (press (Command-=)[Control-Shift-hyphen]), which looks just like a regular hyphen. See Figure 6.11 for one use of this character.

non-breaking hypen
Quality Dry Cleaning, 948-3678
Springfield Foreign Auto, 948-
8211
Top-of-the-Town, Inc., 948-7729
Zyla's Auction House, 948-7765
Quality Dry Cleaning, 948-3678
Springfield Foreign Auto,
948-8211
Top-of-the-Town, Inc., 948-7729
Zyla's Auction House, 948-7765
222.7%
Page: 1

Figure 6.11

Using a non-breaking hyphen in the lower version of this paragraph prevents the phone number from being broken over two lines.

Tracking and Kerning

While the spacing values in the H&Js dialog determine how space is added and subtracted when text is justified, QuarkXPress's kerning and tracking values control how text is spaced even when it's not justified. Tracking governs how text at different sizes is spaced, while kerning refers to how pairs of letters can be adjusted to fit together neatly. XPress offers two ways to control each of these, either locally or throughout entire documents.

Tracking and Kerning On-the-Fly

Tracking is also often called **letterspacing** (actually, tracking is the software engineer's term, while letterspacing is the typesetter's term). Large amounts of tracking are used for special effects, such as in the logo shown in Figure 6.12, while smaller amounts are usually used for copyfitting—squeezing a range of text a bit to make it fit in fewer lines. The unit used in QuarkXPress for both tracking and kerning is 1/200th of an em space, which means that applying a tracking value of 200 to a range of text or applying a kerning value of 200 between two letters has the same effect as inserting an em space after each letter.

Figure 6.12

This logo uses tracking to space out the letters in the company's name.

The main difference between tracking and kerning in QuarkXPress is how they're applied. Tracking is applied when you have a range of text selected and it affects every letter in the selection, while kerning is applied when your cursor is between two letters and only affects the relationship between those two letters. In the following example, you'll use both tracking and kerning to create the type for a logo that's intended to be used on a sticker advertising a brand of make-up.

1. Open lessons/chap6/io.qxd on the CD that accompanied this book. This file contains only a kite-shaped graphic created by placing two triangles next to each other (see Figure 6.13).

Note

This file uses Patrician (in the Scriptorium folder on the CD) and Mona Lisa (in the SoftMaker folder on the CD), so make sure that font family is installed in your system.

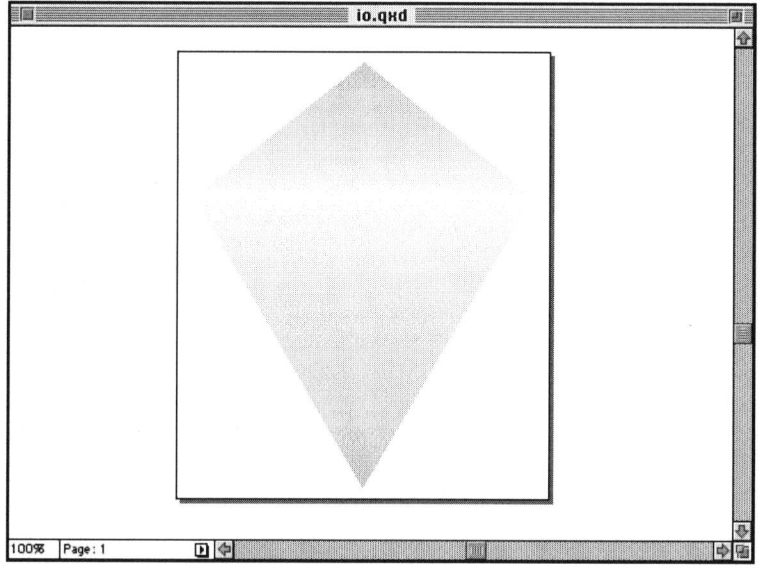

Figure 6.13

Two triangles containing linear blends from pink to white form a kite shape for this logo.

2. Press (Command-Y)[Control-Y] to bring up the General Preferences dialog box and make sure that both Horizontal Measures and Vertical Measures are set to picas.
3. Choose the Text Box tool from the Tool palette and draw a text box 18 picas wide and 16 picas deep.
4. Switch to the Content tool and type the following text in the box, just as it's printed here:

   IO

   all-natural make-up

   for the natural you
5. Select the first line and make it Patrician, either by choosing Style➡Font and picking the font from the submenu, or by entering the new font name in the Measurements palette. Select the second and third lines and make them Mona Lisa. Finally, select all (press (Command-A)[Control-A]) and center the text by pressing (Shift-Command-C)[Shift-Control-C] (see Figure 6.14).
6. Select the "I" and make it 144 points, either by pressing (Command-Shift-\)[Control-Shift-\] and entering the new size in the Paragraph Format dialog box or by entering the new value in the size field of the Measurements palette. Leave the letter selected and make its color Pantone 675 CV by clicking the content icon in the Colors palette and then clicking on the name of the color. If the Colors palette isn't visible, press F12 to bring it up.

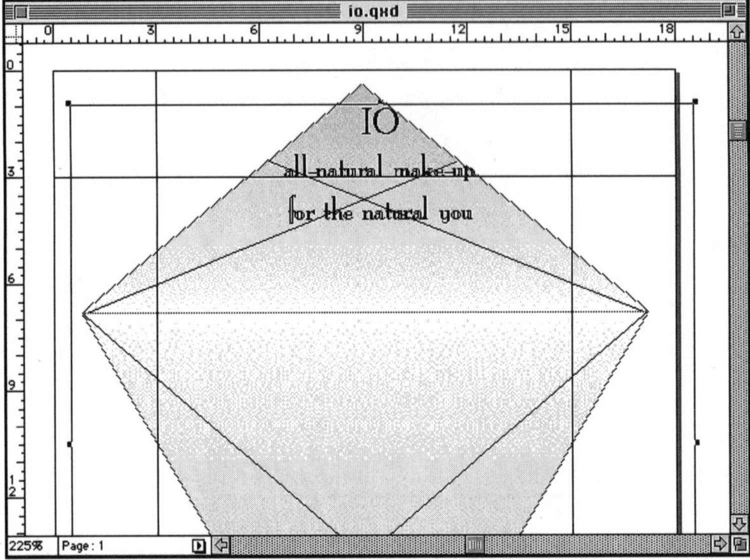

Figure 6.14

The logo text has been centered and changed to Patrician and Mona Lisa.

7. Now select the "O" and make it 110 points; then make its color Pantone 293 CV (see Figure 6.15). Set the leading for this line to 12.5 by entering the new value in the Measurements palette or by pressing (Command-Shift-E)[Control-Shift-E] and entering the new value in the Leading field of the Paragraph Format dialog box.
8. Place the cursor between the "I" and the "O" and make the kerning -94, either by entering the new value in the tracking field of the Measurements palette or by choosing Style➡Kern and entering the new value in the Kern Amount dialog box. This kerns the "O" to the left so that it's positioned over the "I" (if it's not centered over the "I," adjust the kerning value until it is). The "IO" line should now look like Figure 6.16.
9. Select the second and third lines of text and make them 20 points. Place the cursor in the second line and make the leading 24 points, then move to the third line and make its leading 20 points.
10. Select both the second and third lines and change their text color to Pantone 293 CV. Then apply tracking of +10 to give these lines an airier look, either by entering the new value in the tracking field of the Measurements palette or by choosing Style➡Tracking. Make sure you have both lines of text completely selected, or the tracking will be applied only to those letters that are selected.

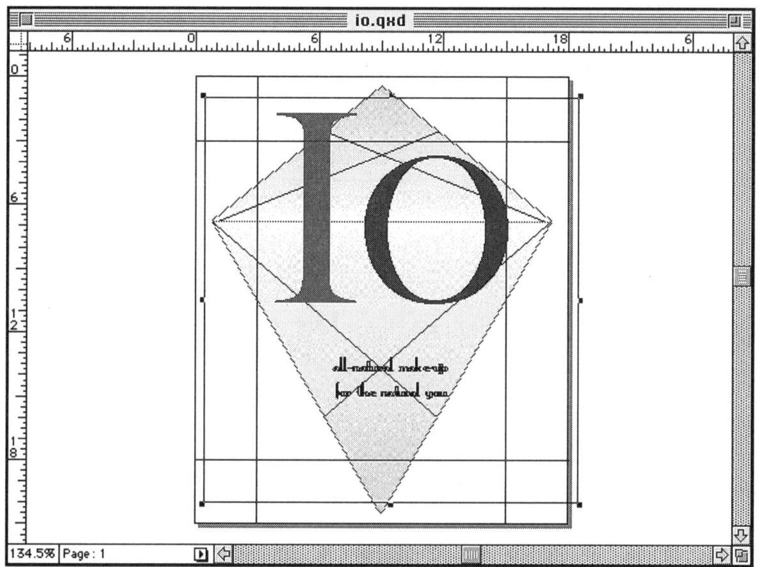

Figure 6.15

The two letters in the word "IO" are different point sizes.

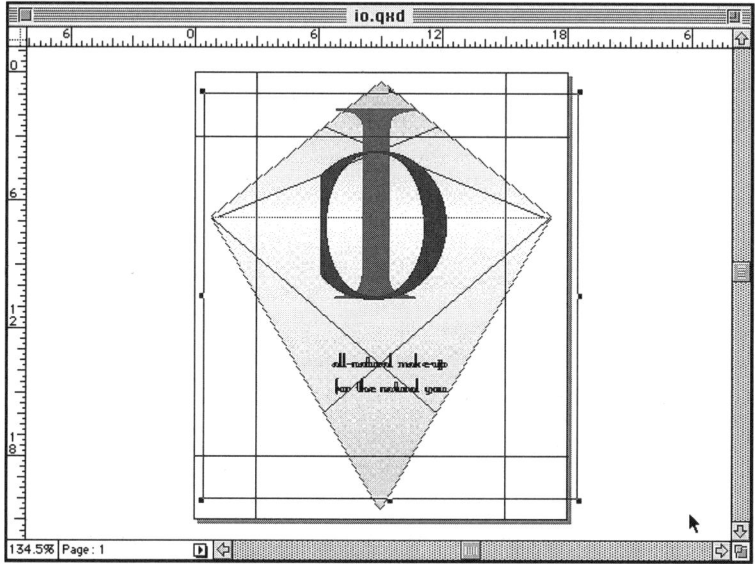

Figure 6.16

Locally applied kerning moves the "O" into place directly over the "I."

11. The kerning applied to the word "IO" has made it off-center. To fix this, type a space and—without moving the cursor—set the kerning to -59 to move the word back into the center of the box.

12. Now that the text part of the logo is complete, switch to the Item tool and select both the kite-shaped graphic (which is composed of two grouped picture boxes) and the text box. Choose Item➡Space/Align (or press Command-,) and click the Horizontal checkbox on (make sure the Vertical check box is off); set Space to 0 and choose Centers from the Between pop-up menu, then click OK to center the text box and the triangles.
13. While both the text box and the triangles are still selected, press (Command-G)[Control-G] to group them, and then type the following position values into the Measurements palette: X 0, Y 6. If the Units in your General Preferences are set to picas, then this will center the items both horizontally and vertically within the document (see Figure 6.17 for the final results).

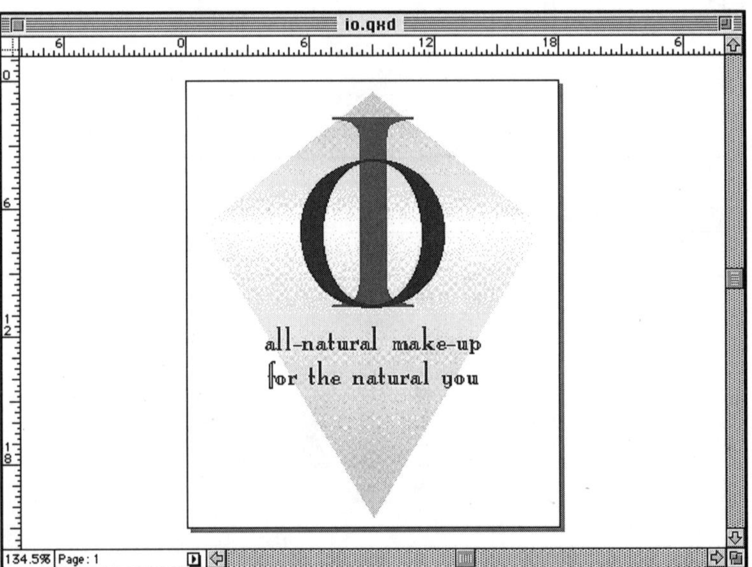

Figure 6.17

The final design.

The IO logo sticker uses local tracking and kerning to achieve what could be called special effects. Tracking (but not kerning) can also be via character attributes within style sheets, either for effect or to compensate for overly spacy or tight text throughout a design. A third way to apply tracking, in this case on a document-wide basis, is through the use of tracking tables (see the next section, "Using Tracking Tables").

Traditionally, kerning is used to adjust specific letter pairs so that they *appear* evenly spaced, although they may actually be irregularly spaced (see Figure 6.18). While kerning can be done locally (as in the IO example) for small amounts of text, such as headings and logos, kerning tables let you apply changes to kerning pairs in a particular typeface throughout a document's text (see "Using Kerning Tables" later in this chapter).

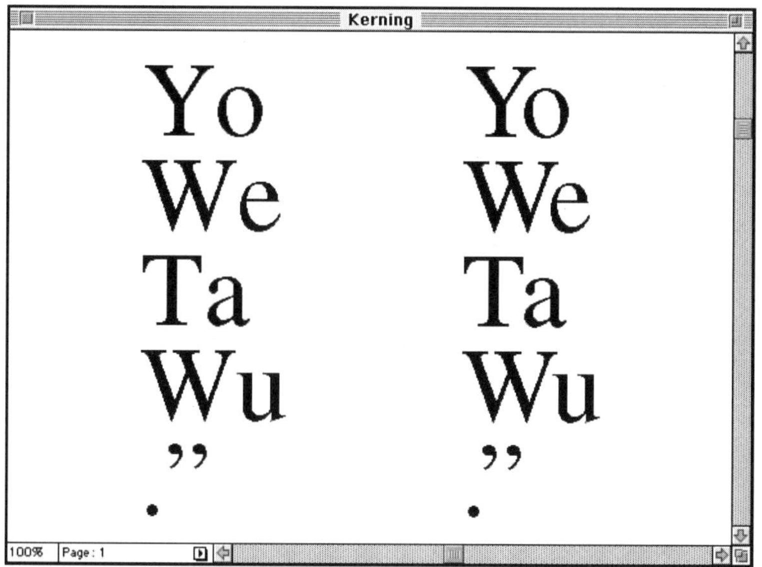

Figure 6.18

These are five two-character combinations that are commonly kerned to improve their appearance; the left-hand column shows the letters before manual kerning, and the right-hand column shows them after.

Using Tracking Tables

To keep letters from touching, fonts include extra white space on either side of each letter. At text sizes, the amount of white space is usually just right, but at smaller sizes it can be too little and at larger sizes it can be too much (see Figure 6.19). Tracking tables let you compensate for this typographical phenomenon by specifying amounts of tracking to be applied throughout all your documents wherever a font is used at a particular size.

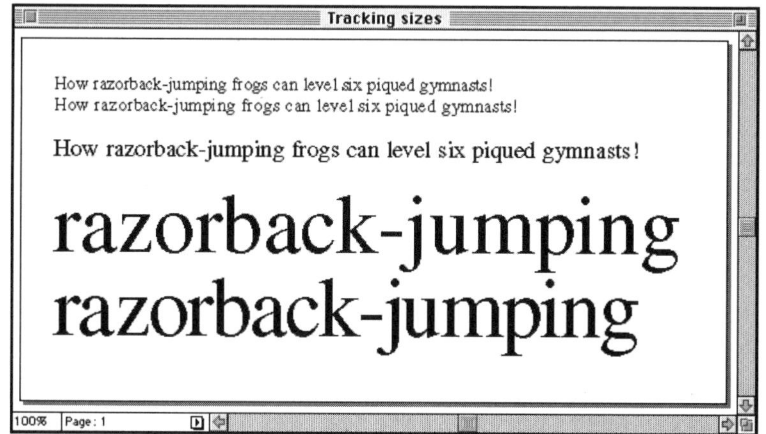

Figure 6.19

Positive tracking (second line) makes the smallest text more readable, while the medium-sized text doesn't have any tracking; the largest line of text has negative tracking (last line) to keep it from appearing too open.

The changes you make to tracking values are stored both in the current document (if you have one open) and in your XPress preferences file, so they'll apply to the current document and to all documents you create after making the changes. If you open a document created by someone else or one you created before editing the tracking values, you'll see a dialog telling you that the preferences for this document are different from your QuarkXPress preferences and asking you which set to use (see Figure 6.20).

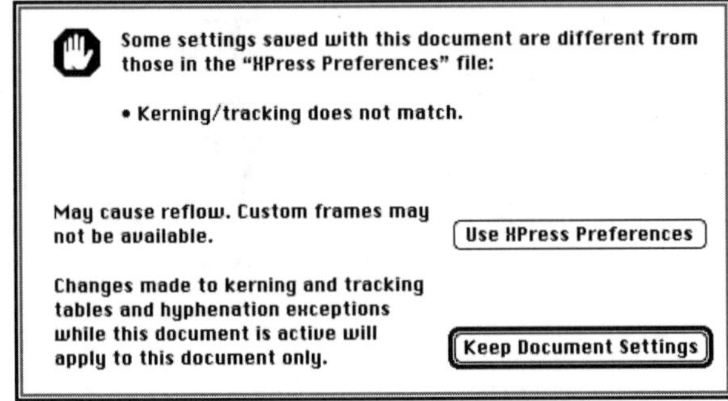
Some settings saved with this document are different from those in the "XPress Preferences" file:
• Kerning/tracking does not match.
May cause reflow. Custom frames may not be available.
Use XPress Preferences
Changes made to kerning and tracking tables and hyphenation exceptions while this document is active will apply to this document only.
Keep Document Settings

Figure 6.20

If a document's preferences don't match the settings for your copy of QuarkXPress, these are your choices.

Tip

Unless you're very sure that you know what the different preferences are and that you want to override them, always choose Keep Document Settings in this situation. It's especially important to keep the document's preferences if you're outputting a file created by someone else, since using your own preferences to override the document's kerning and tracking tables can reflow the text.

In this example, we'll edit the tracking values for Times (or any font you prefer). If you don't want these changes to be permanent, find your XPress preferences file and make a copy of it so you can restore it later. For Windows users, the file is called XPRESS.PRF, and for Mac users it's called XPress Preferences. In both cases, it's located in the same directory or folder as the QuarkXPress application.

1. Create a new file, draw a text box, and use the Content tool to enter a line of text in it—any text at all. Copy and paste the text a few times on separate lines, and make each line a different size by selecting it and either entering a new size value in the Measurements palette or pressing (Command-Shift-\)[Control-Shift-\] and entering the new size in the Font Size dialog. Good sizes to use might be 5 points, 10 points, 30 points, and 42 points.
2. Select all the text with the Content tool and make it Times (or another font of your choice) by entering the font in the Measurements palette or by choosing Style➥Font and scrolling to the correct font in the submenu.

3. Print your document so you'll have a "before" version to compare your final version with (choose File➡Print or press (Command-P)[Control-P]).
4. Choose Utilities➡Tracking Edit to bring up the Tracking Edit dialog box (see Figure 6.21).

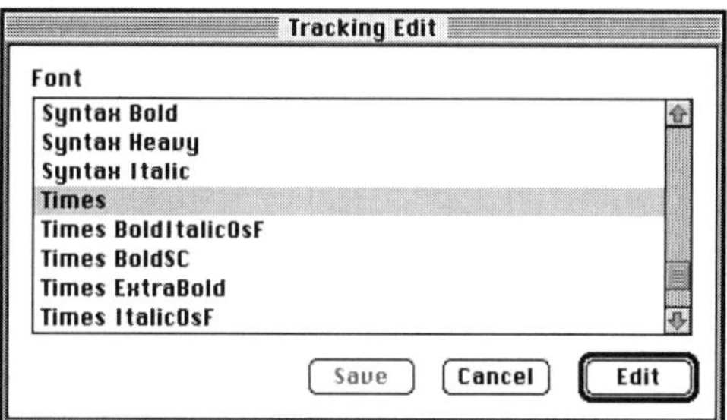

Figure 6.21

Choose a font to edit in the Tracking Edit dialog box.

5. Scroll through the list and double-click the name of a font to edit, or click its name and then click the Edit button. Use Times, or whatever font you used for the text in Step 2. Each screen font has a separate listing, so you'll need to edit each variation of a typeface separately (roman, bold, italic, bold italic, and so on).

Tip

To find the font you want quickly, type the first letter or two of its name. Mac users: Remember to type "I" first if you're looking for, say, I Times Italic.

6. The Tracking Values dialog box shows a line graph with tracking values on the left and font sizes across the bottom (see Figure 6.22). You can create a curve (well, a kind of angular curve) by clicking the line at up to four different points and dragging the each point to position it at the intersection of a font size and a tracking value.

   Start by clicking the line at about five points and dragging that point up to a tracking value of about +4. By doing this, you'll apply a tracking value of +4 to any type in this font set at seven points or smaller.

   As you move the point around, the point size and tracking value represented by your current location on the grid are displayed in the upper-right corner of the dialog box.
7. Now click the line at about 10 points and move the mouse down to the 0 level, so that no tracking will be applied to 10-point type.

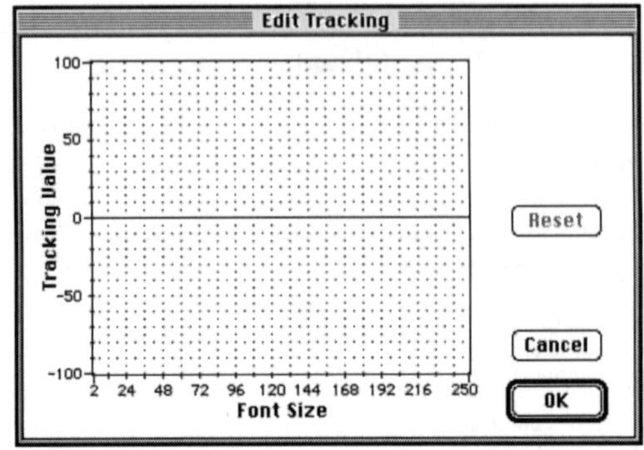

Figure 6.22

The tracking values for each font start out as a flat line at 0, meaning that tracking is set to 0 for all sizes of that font.

8. Click to make another point on the line for 30-point type, positioning it at a tracking value of -4, and finish the "curve" by adding a final point for 42-point type at -6 tracking. That's the amount of manual tracking I applied to the 42-point type in Step 1.
9. Click OK to save your changes, and then click Save in the Tracking Edit dialog box to return to the document window. See Figure 6.23 for the final settings.

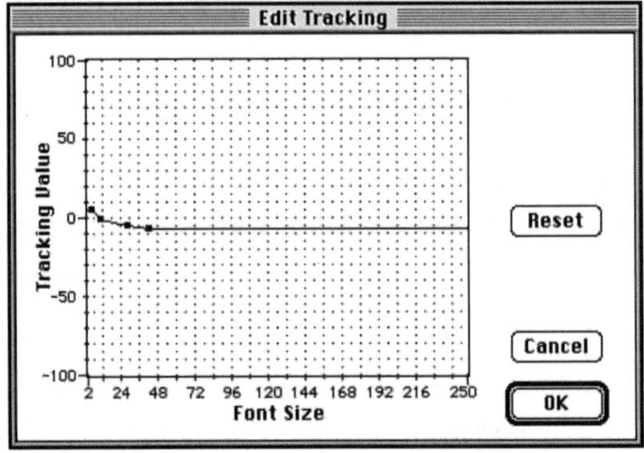

Figure 6.23

The new tracking values for Times.

10. Make another printout of the document with your changes and compare the two. The smallest type should be spaced a bit more widely than it was and the largest type should be tighter than it was. The line of 10-point should not have changed at all. Figure 6.24 shows before and after versions.

How razorback-jumping frogs can level six piqued gymnasts!

How razorback-jumping frogs can level six piqued gymnasts!

razorback-jumping *a*

How razorback-jumping frogs can level six piqued gymnasts!

How razorback-jumping frogs can level six piqued gymnasts!

razorback-jumping *b*

Figure 6.24

The various sizes of Times show the difference that editing tracking tables makes: (a) before and (b) after.

Note

If you don't see the Tracking Edit or Kerning Table Edit commands in your Utilities menu, it's because you don't have the Kern/Track Editor XTension installed. Make sure this XTension (called KTEDIT.XXT in the Windows version) is in the same directory or folder as your other XTensions. If you can't find it on your QuarkXPress disks, then you can download it from the QuarkXPress Web site at `http://www.quark.com`.

You can get rid of these changes to your tracking tables in two ways. First, if you want to remove all alterations and start fresh, replace your QuarkXPress preferences file with the copy you made earlier. Or, if you just want to return one font to its previous, pristine state, choose Utilities➡Tracking Edit, double-click the name of the font you want to change, and click on the Reset button in the Tracking Values dialog box. This returns the tracking values to a flat line at the 0 mark.

Tracking applied through tracking tables is "invisible" in the sense that it won't show up in the Measurements palette or the Tracking dialog box (Style➡Track). If you manually track text that's already tracked via a tracking table, the manual tracking is added to the tracking that's already there.

For example, if you applied manual tracking of -10 to 42-point Times after making the changes outlined above to the tracking table for that font, the total tracking would be -16, but the tracking value displayed in the Measurements palette and the Tracking dialog would be only -10.

Note

The tracking values in tracking tables will only be applied if automatic kerning is turned on in your preferences. See "Customizing QuarkXPress with Preferences" in Chapter 1 for more information on setting this preference.

Using Kerning Tables

Quark's automatic kerning, which you can activate in the Typographic Preferences (see "Customizing QuarkXPress with Preferences" in Chapter 1), will go a long way toward making sure that each individual letter combination has the best-looking spacing. But sometimes Quark's ideas of proper kerning and yours won't coincide. That's where kerning tables come in.

Using kerning tables, you can enforce your own vision of how specific letter pairs should be kerned throughout a document. Like tracking tables, kerning tables are stored both in the document that's open when you make the changes and in your preferences file. So if you're sending a file with kerning table changes to someone else, you'll need to make sure that the other XPress user chooses to keep document preferences when opening the file (see Figure 6.18).

Creating and editing kerning pairs is a time-consuming procedure, so you'll probably want to concentrate on, first, display fonts that will be used in larger sizes where kerning problems will be more noticeable, and, second, kerning pairs that you notice a lot. In other words, if you don't have a problem with a kerning pair, don't mess with it.

Once you've decided that you do want to edit some kerning pairs, here's how to go about it. Just as with the tracking table editing, if you're not sure that the changes you're about to make will be ones you want to keep, make a backup copy of your preferences file first and replace it once you're done experimenting.

1. Choose Utilities➡Kerning Table Edit to bring up the Kerning Table Edit dialog (see Figure 6.25).
2. Double-click the name of a font to edit (or click a name and then click the Edit button). This brings up the Edit Kerning Table dialog box (see Figure 6.26), where you can do one of four things:

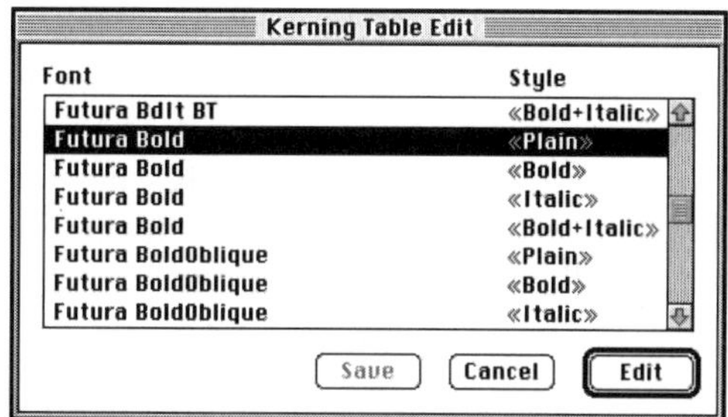

Figure 6.25

The Kerning Table Edit dialog box.

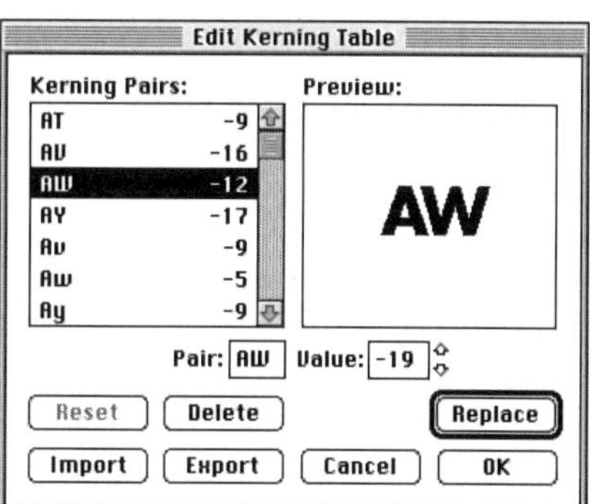

Figure 6.26

In the Kerning Values box, you can see and change the kerning values that will be applied to automatically kerned text.

- Edit an existing kerning pair. These pairs reflect the values that XPress uses when automatic kerning is turned on and they're built into the font itself by the type designer. Your changes won't affect the font file itself, just how QuarkXPress uses it.
- Create a new kerning pair.
- Export the kerning values shown here into a file that can be imported for use with this font or any other font.
- Import kerning values from a previously created export file.

The list of fonts contains all the screen fonts currently installed on your system, as well as added bold, italic, and bold italic versions of each of them. So for Times you might see Times, Times Italic, Times Bold, Times Italic Bold—the real Times fonts—as well as versions of each of those with XPress's built-in styles applied, such as Times Bold <Bold> and Times Italic <BoldItalic>. Don't bother editing anything but the real versions of the fonts, since it's bad practice to use XPress's built-in font styles anyway.

3. To edit an existing kerning pair, click it in the list at the left of the dialog. The value of the kerning that's applied to that pair shows up in the Value field, while the pair itself shows up in two places: a Pair field and a preview box below the Value and Pair fields. To change the kerning value, enter a different number in the Value field and watch the preview box change. Once you've got the value where you want it, click the Replace button to change the value in the list.

Note

For the most accurate view of the effects of a kerning value, you'll have to rely on hard copy rather than an onscreen preview—at least, until computer monitor resolutions (usually 72 dpi to 96 dpi) equal those of the output devices we use (generally at least 300 dpi).

4. To add a new kerning pair, type it in the Pair field and then type a number in the Value field. Just as when you're editing an existing pair, the preview box shows the effects of your changes to the kerning value. When you're done, click the Add button (this is what the Replace button turns into when you enter your own letters in the pair field).
5. To export the kerning values for a font, just click the Export button and assign the new file a name and a location in the resulting dialog box.
6. To import kerning values, click the Import button and find the file you want to import. The imported values can come from any font; you can export values from one font and import them into another font entirely. If you do that, though, you will definitely need to look at each pair and adjust it to correct value for the font you've imported the values into.
7. If you decide you don't like your changes to an existing kerning pair and you want to revert to the type designer's defaults, click the Reset button (it's only available after you've clicked the Replace button to make your kerning change in the list).
8. After you're done editing kerning pairs (beware—it can get addictive), click either the Cancel button (to abandon your changes) or the OK button to return to the Kerning Table Edit dialog box.
9. Choose another font to work on, or click Save (to save your changes) or Cancel (to abandon them).

"Watch the preview box" may seem like pretty bare-bones instructions for creating and editing kerning pairs, but the key is that it's all done by eye—you just work with the value until the pair looks right. That's the only way anyone knows how to do it; there's no scientific formula for kerning pairs.

Using Special Characters

Using the right character in the right place is one of the most important keys to producing professional-looking typeset copy, whether you're working with ads that contain only a few words or books that run thousands of pages. Here's a rundown of characters to watch out for:

- *Spaces*

  En spaces (press (Option-space)[Control-Alt-6]) are the width of a zero in the font they're used in (the name comes from the fact that they're usually about the same width as a capital "N" in that font as well). Although this is a break from typographical tradition (in which an en space is half as wide as the point size it's set in), it does mean that you can use en spaces as an alternative to decimal tabs to line up numbers in a numbered list. Press (Command-Option-space)[Control-Alt-Shift-6] to type a non-breaking en space.

  Em spaces are twice as wide as en spaces, about the width of a capital "M." A common use for em spaces is to separate a run-in heading from the beginning of the body type in the paragraph. QuarkXPress doesn't have a keyboard combination for typing an em space, so you have to make one by typing two en spaces.

Note

In noisy print shops, where it's hard to tell if someone's saying "em" or "en," people sometimes say "nut space" (en space) and "molly" (em space) instead.

Flex spaces (press (Option-Shift-space)[Control-Shift-5]) can be any width you want them to be. You determine the width for all flex spaces in a document by setting the value in the Character tab of the Document Preferences (press (Command-Y)[Control-Y] and click the Character tab). Professional typesetters often use this feature of QuarkXPress to give themselves access to a "thin space," traditionally defined as 1/4 or 1/5 of an em space. The default value for flex spaces is 50 percent of an en space (watch those ems and ens), which makes it 1/4 of an em. You could also use the flex space as a "hair space," which is anything smaller than 1/5 of an em, or as a humongous space (as big as you want it to be!).

Non-breaking spaces (press (Command-space)[Control-space]) are the same size as normal spaces, but they keep QuarkXPress from separating two words with a line break. They're sometimes used to keep people's first names on the same line with their last names; they're also useful with phone numbers, if you use the format "(508) 555-1212," to keep the area code on the same line with the rest of the number.

- *Dashes*

  En dashes (press (Option-hyphen)[Control-Alt-Shift-hyphen]) are wider than a hyphen, and they're used for ranges of numbers. For example, you'd use an en dash in "January 12–18" to indicate that you're talking about January 12, January 18, and all the days in between. Or, in a recipe, you might write "1–2 liters of milk" to indicate that the cook can use one liter of milk, two liters, or any amount in between, as she deems fit.

  Em dashes (press (Option-Shift-hyphen)[Control-Shift-=]) are wider yet, and they're used more like colons and parentheses, depending on the writer's whim.

- Quotation marks must be "curly" or "typographer's" quotes, rather than straight quotes (see Figure 6.27). Make sure that Smart Quotes is checked on in the Application Preferences (press (Command-Option-Shift-Y)[Control-Alt-Shift-Y], and when you need inch and foot marks (straight quotes), press (Control-')[Control-'] to get foot marks (single straight quotes) and (Control-Shift-')[Control-Alt-'] to get inch marks (double straight quotes).

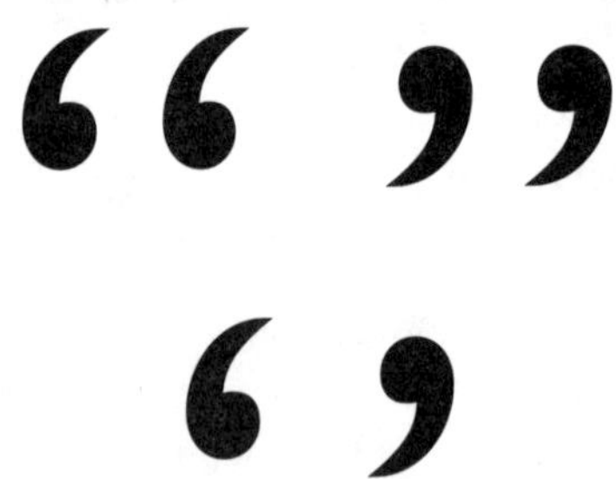

Figure 6.27

Typographer's quotes and apostrophes have a distinct orientation—you can tell an open quote mark from a close quote mark.

- Ligatures are letter combinations built into fonts for letters that tend to bump into each other in their ordinary forms, such as "fi," "ff," and "fl." Ligatures are extremely classy, and fortunately they're easy to use—just turn them on in the Character tab of the Document Preferences (press (Command-Y)[Control-Y] and click the Character tab). Ligatures will be automatically inserted wherever those letter combinations occur.

This is usually great, but it can cause a problem if you're typesetting a computer book with code sections in a monospaced font (which is supposed to line up vertically). There are two ways of getting around this: Either don't use ligatures (boo, hiss), or type a space in the middle of each occurrence of these letter combinations within code, then use negative kerning to push the two letters back together (not much fun).

- **Diacritical marks** and special foreign letters (such as "é" and "ß") should be used throughout an entire job or not at all. Check the Windows Character Map or the Mac Key Caps DA to find out how to enter a specific character. The same goes for currency symbols—if you use "¥" for yen, be consistent by using £ for English pounds—or avoid the issue altogether by using words, rather than symbols, for all references to money.
- Copyright, trademark, and registered trademark symbols are included in most fonts; press, respectively, (Option-G)[Alt-Shift-C], (Option-2)[Alt-Shift-2], and (Option-R)[Alt-Shift-R].
- Mathematical and scientific symbols aren't a big deal for most designers, who never have to go beyond "+" and "–" most of the time. There are a couple of things everyone should know, though. Use Symbol, the one math font almost everyone has, for plus and minus signs; Symbol's plus and minus signs are the same width, so columns of numbers will line up correctly. And use Symbol's multiplication sign ("×", rather than a lowercase "x,") for multiplication.
- Fractions can be set in several ways (see Figure 6.28). "Built-up" fractions use a horizontal fraction bar, with numerator above and denominator below. "Shilling" fractions use a slash, or "solidus," again with numerator above and denominator below. In running text, it makes life much easier if you set fractions smaller than the surrounding text so that they don't interfere with the lines above and below; you can accomplish this by using the superscript and subscript characters, together with a little judicious kerning.

¾ $\frac{3}{4}$ 3/4 $\frac{3}{4}$ Text

Figure 6.28

Fractions can be set as shilling or built-up fractions, with the numbers set at the size of the text or reduced to fit better within running text.

Fortunately, Quark makes a free XTension called Thing-a-ma-bob that automates the creation of shilling fractions. If Thing-a-ma-bob is installed, all you do is type the numerator, a slash, and the denominator, select them, and choose Style➡Type Style➡Make Fraction. The first fraction in Figure 6.28 was created using the Make Fraction command.

Summary

Setting type correctly is what distinguishes the professional designer or typesetter from everyone else who has access to desktop publishing software. It's not hard to do, but it takes attention to detail. While spacing and hyphenation are the most complex issues to deal with, creating H&J settings for a design only has to be done once per job—and then you can forget about it. Likewise, editing tracking and kerning tables only needs to be done once per font, but it provides a big pay-off in terms of improved typography. Finally, using the right special characters means memorizing their keystrokes and knowing what character to use when.

Importing and Editing Graphics

- Importing images
- Scanning from within QuarkXPress
- Using different file formats
- Changing images' brightness, contrast, and color

Along with creating graphic elements using the various box and line tools, QuarkXPress lets you import scanned images and images created in other applications, like Photoshop and Illustrator. Imported images can be manipulated to some degree, and you can integrate images into your designs by resizing them and running text around them (see "Running Text Around Objects" in Day 3, "Creating Text and Graphic Elements"). In this chapter you'll create a catalog cover design that uses several versions of one imported image to convey a feeling of the variety of products the catalog offers. Keep in mind, though, that QuarkXPress can't replace a dedicated image editor or illustration program; its tools aren't powerful enough and it doesn't offer the fine control that these other kinds of programs do.

Importing Images

Importing pictures into a QuarkXPress document is about as simple as it gets—the only thing you have to remember is that each picture needs a box to live in, and a box can hold only one picture. If you import a picture into a box that already holds an imported image, the second picture will replace the first one.

1. Create a picture box of any type.
2. Choose either the Item tool or the Content tool; previous versions of QuarkXPress required you to use the Content tool to import pictures, but version 4.0 lets you use either.
3. Choose File➡Get Picture or press (Command-E)[Control-E] to bring up the Get Picture dialog box (see Figure 7.1).

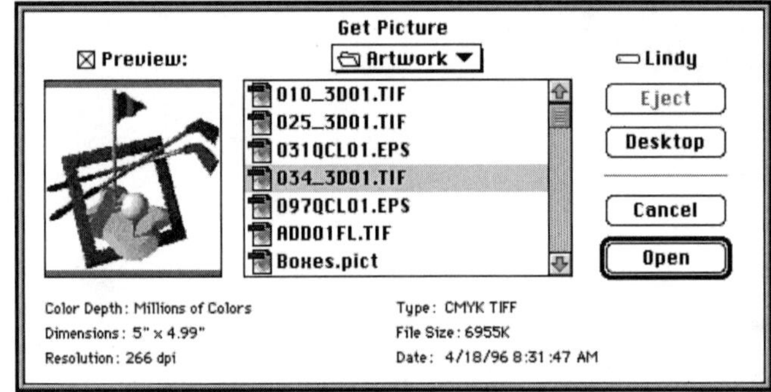

Figure 7.1

At the bottom of the Get Picture dialog box, XPress displays the color depth, size, resolution, format, file size, and modification date of each picture you click.

4. View a **preview** of an image by clicking Preview. The larger the image file, the longer the preview will take to display, so if you're using large files and are in a hurry, make sure to disable Preview before navigating to the folder or directory containing the image files.
5. Click the name of the picture you want to import and click Open to bring it into the picture box. As it's imported, the page number in the corner of the document window changes to a percentage that indicates the amount of the file that's been imported so far. When the picture is completely imported, it's placed in the upper left corner of the box at 100 percent (see Figure 7.2). Resize the box to show all of the picture, if you need to.
6. To move a picture, choose the Item tool, click the picture and hold down the mouse button. Once the cursor changes to a hand, keep holding the mouse button as you move the picture to change its position within the box. The image's coordinates on the right side of the Measurements palette change to reflect your movements (see Figure 7.3). You can also move pictures numerically by double-clicking the X or Y coordinate and entering a new value, by clicking the arrows next to the X and Y coordinates, or by pressing the arrow keys on your keyboard.

X:-24p1.759	W:17p3.236	0°	X%:100%	X+:0p	0°
Y:-47p6.949	H:15p9.778	0p	Y%:100%	Y+:0p	0°

Figure 7.2

The picture starts out at 100 percent, in the upper-left corner of the picture box.

X:0.5"	W:4.783"	0°	X%:100%	X+:-0.014"	0°
Y:0.5"	H:4.549"	0"	Y%:100%	Y+:-0.014"	0°

Figure 7.3

The controls on the right side of the Measurement dialog for picture boxes enable you to adjust the box's contents rather than the box itself.

Tip

Place a picture in the exact vertical and horizontal center of a picture box by pressing (Command-Shift- M)[Control-Shift-M].

7. To resize a picture, double-click the percentage fields in the Measurements palette and enter new percentages. QuarkXPress will not automatically change one dimension if you change the other, so remember to change both the X and Y percentages if you want to maintain the image's original proportions. To increase both percentages simultaneously, five percentage points at a time, press (Command-Option-Shift->)[Control-Alt-Shift->]; use (Command-Option-Shift-<)[Control-Alt-Shift-<] to decrease both percentages.

Tip

Resize an image to fit perfectly in its box by pressing (Command-Shift-F) [Control-Shift-F]. Add (Option)[Alt] to maintain the image's proportions—this will make the image as big as it can be in the box without having different X and Y percentages.

8. To delete a picture from a box, click the box with the Content tool and press (Delete)[Backspace]; to delete or move the box, use the Item tool. Use either tool to resize the box.

Although you can scale imported images from 10 percent to 1000 percent, doing so isn't always a good idea. While **vector** images (see "File Formats," below) can be resized to any percentage without harm, enlarging **raster** images more than a few percentage points over 100 percent can reduce image quality (see Figure 7.4).

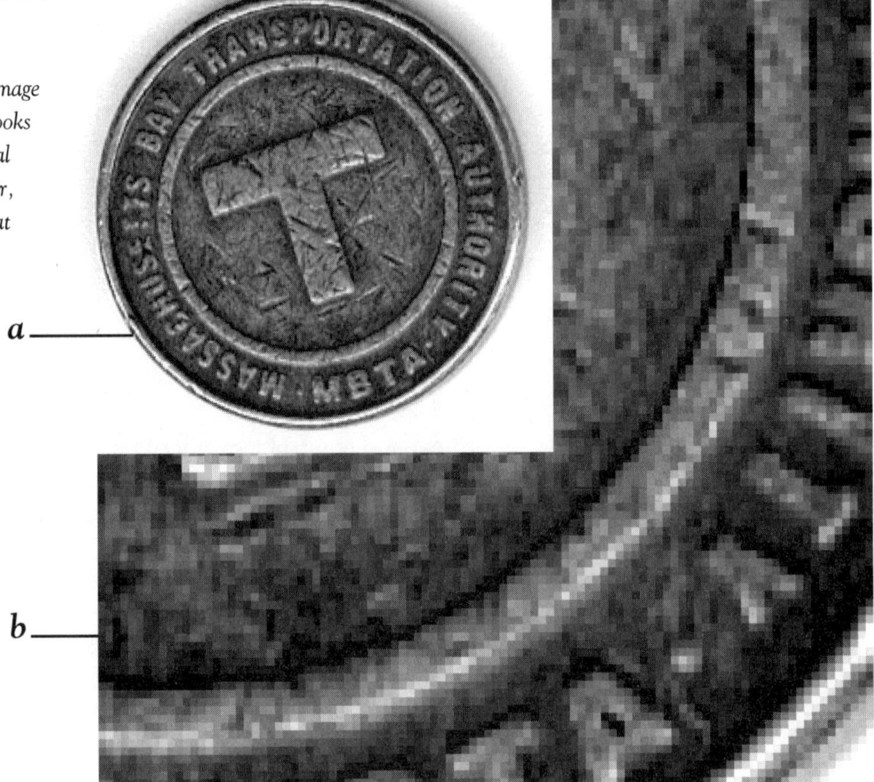

Figure 7.4

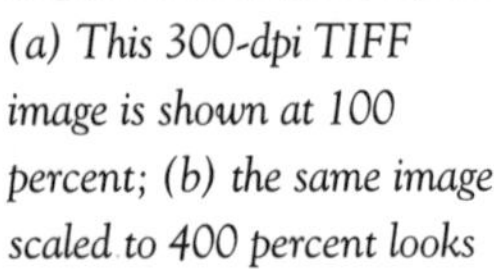
(a) This 300-dpi TIFF image is shown at 100 percent; (b) the same image scaled to 400 percent looks pixilated—the individual pixels, or blocks of color, are enlarged enough that they start to show.

If a larger image is needed, it's best to rescan the original photo at a larger size. One technique that a lot of designers use is to scan all photos at a low resolution (like 100 dpi) and resize the images at will within QuarkXPress. Once the design has been finalized, all the scans are redone at the proper size and a higher resolution.

Tip

Normally, resizing a box doesn't affect an imported picture; resize both a box and its picture by pressing (Command)[Control] as you resize the box. That doesn't maintain the box's or the image's original proportions; to do that, press (Command-Option-Shift)[Control-Alt-Shift] as you drag. To make the box and image square, press (Command-Shift)[Control-Shift] as you drag.

Scanning in QuarkXPress

The free Photoshop Plug-In XTension enables you to use some Photoshop-compatible plug-ins from QuarkXPress, primarily those used for scanning images. If this XTension is installed, an Acquire submenu in the File menu provides access to any acquire modules in your Photoshop plug-ins folder (see Figure 7.5); choose a module from the submenu to open the scanning software and scan as you ordinarily would. You can download the XTension from Quark's web site at `www.quark.com`.

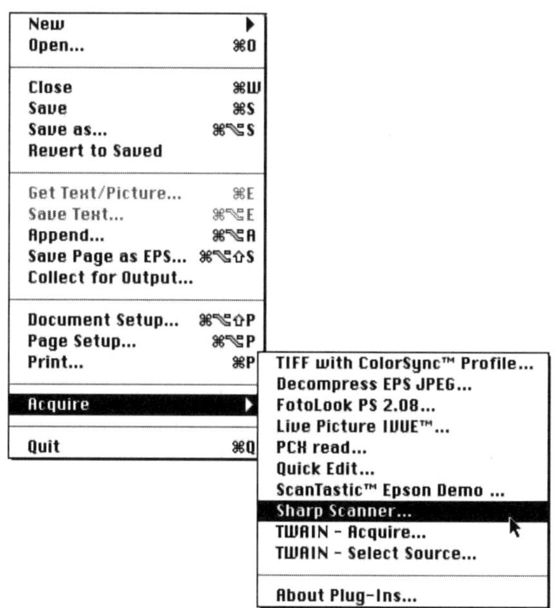

Figure 7.5

All of these Photoshop acquire plug-ins are accessible from QuarkXPress using the Photoshop Plug-In XTension.

File Formats

QuarkXPress recognizes various graphics file formats, in two basic categories:

- Raster formats: BMP, EPS, EPS DCS, JPEG, Paint, PCX, Photo CD, PICT, Scitex CT, TIFF
- Vector formats: EPS, PICT, WMF

For professional design and prepress, the most common—and trouble-free—formats are TIFF or EPS for raster images (such as photographs and other scans) and EPS for vector images. If you're not using a PostScript printer, PICT (for Mac OS) or WMF (for Windows) are alternative vector formats.

Images in formats that XPress can't import either won't be visible in the Get Picture dialog or will result in a "Bad file format" dialog when you try to import them. Convert these images to another format by resaving them in the original application or using a graphics conversion program.

Tip

Support for JPEG, PCX, and Photo CD images isn't built into the QuarkXPress application; it's supplied by XTensions. If you have trouble importing these images, check to make sure the PCX Import, PhotoCD, and JPEG Import XTensions are installed in your XTensions folder.

Managing Imported Graphics

Some page layout programs enable you to either link to an imported graphic, without copying it into the page layout document, or embed the image in the page layout document, so that there's no link to the original graphic file. XPress, on the other hand, doesn't allow you to **embed** graphics; all imported images are **referenced**, meaning that the only information about them that's stored in an XPress document is the image preview and the graphic file's pathname.

While it's convenient to embed graphics in page layout documents, because then you don't have to keep track of any files but the page layout file, there are advantages to referencing as well. First, XPress document sizes are smaller, because page layout documents don't have to contain entire images. Second, you can make changes to the original image at any time and see those changes reflected in the XPress file, whereas embedded images often aren't editable. And third, the graphics files remain separate from the page layout file and can be used more easily in other projects and distributed to other people.

Maintaining links between XPress documents and imported graphics is a simple, but necessary task. If XPress loses track of the original file for an imported graphic, the program can only print the image's preview, which is generally not of reproduction quality. The Usage dialog box enables you to track the status of imported images, as well as the fonts used in a document, so that you can be sure that these images always accompany the document file.

1. To check on the status of imported pictures, choose Utilities➥Usage and click the Pictures tab (see Figure 7.6).

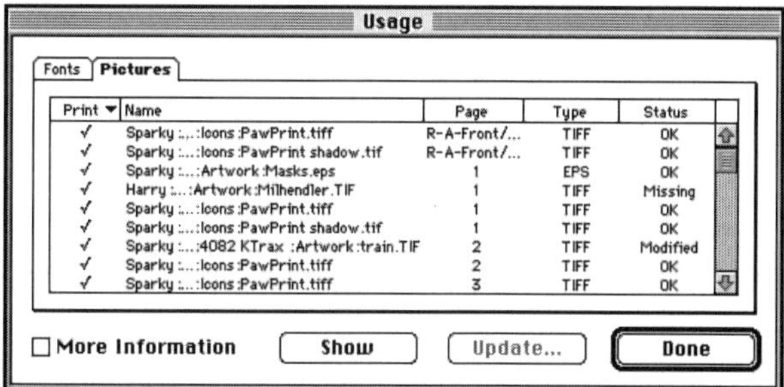

Figure 7.6

The Pictures tab of the Usage dialog shows where pictures are located in the document and whether XPress can find the original files on your drive.

2. The Pictures tab shows a list of all the imported graphics in the document. Five columns contain different information about each graphic.
   - The Print column indicates whether the graphic is set to print.
   - The Name column shows the file's name and path on the disk where it's stored; if the image was pasted in, "No Disk File" appears in the Name column.
   - The Page column indicates which document page the graphic appears on; a dagger next to the page number means that the graphic is on the pasteboard and doesn't touch the page itself.
   - The Type column shows what file format the graphic is saved in (TIFF, EPS, and so on).
   - The Status column contains one of the following comments: OK, Modified, Missing, Wrong Type (the graphic's file format has changed or the proper import filter is not installed), In Use (the file is open in another application), No Access (you don't have access privileges for the file), or Can't Open (XPress doesn't have enough memory left to open the file).

Click a graphic's name and then the Show button to view that image; click More Information to display the image's full pathname, file size, modification date, dimensions, resolution, and colors (the same information displayed in the Get Picture dialog box).

3. You can update and change the print status of more than one picture at a time; click the first picture, then Shift-click the last one to select a group of pictures, or (Command-click)[Control-click] individual pictures to select multiple pictures that aren't next to each other in the list (see Figure 7.7).

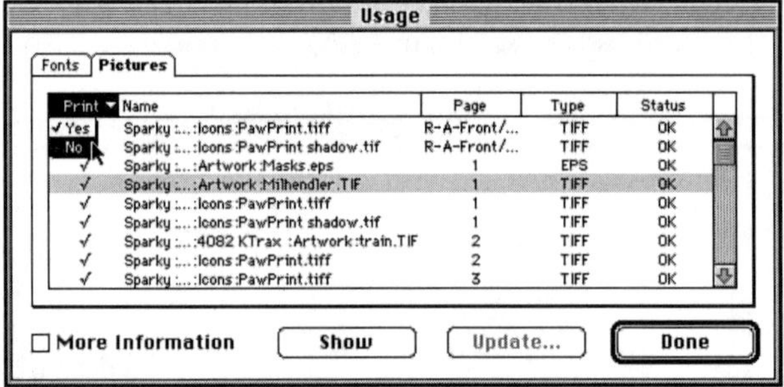

Figure 7.7

The print status of the selected pictures can be changed by choosing an option from the Print menu at the top of the column.

4. To suppress the printout of a graphic, click its name and choose Yes or No from the Print menu at the top of the list. Pictures with a checkmark will print; those with no checkmark won't print.

Tip

A quicker method of toggling the print status of a picture is just to click its checkmark to remove the checkmark (suppress printing) or click where the checkmark should be to add a checkmark (enable printing).

5. To locate a picture showing as missing, click its name in the list and click the Update button. In the Find dialog box (see Figure 7.8), locate the graphic file and click Open to return to the Picture Usage tab. If there are any other missing files in the same directory or folder, XPress will ask if you want to update those files as well (see Figure 7.9).

6. To update a picture showing as modified, click its name in the list and click the Update button. A dialog box confirms that you want to update the graphic; click OK to update the picture or Cancel to skip the update (see Figure 7.10).

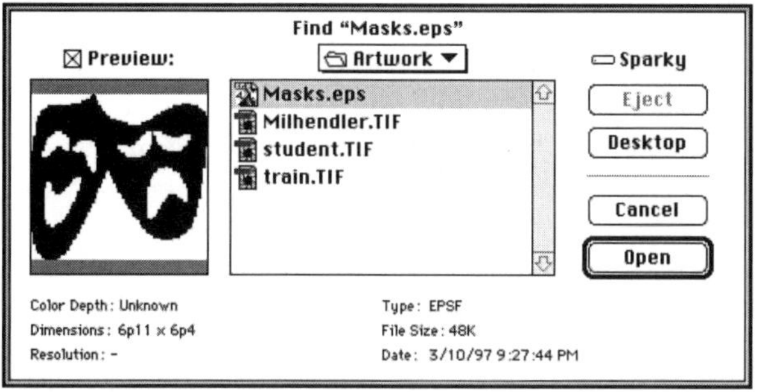

Figure 7.8

The Find dialog box looks and works just like the Open and Get Picture dialog boxes, except that it shows the name of the missing file at the top.

Figure 7.9

XPress notices when more than one missing picture is located in a folder or directory and asks you to let it update all the images at once.

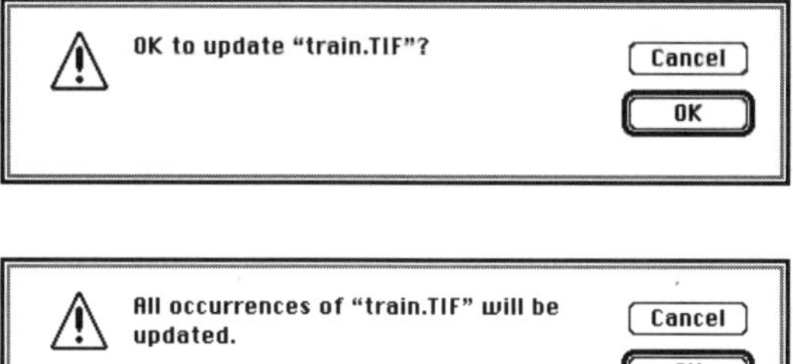

Figure 7.10

(a) If the picture is only used once in the document, XPress just asks if it's OK to update it; (b) if it appears more than once, XPress lets you know it'll be updated throughout the document.

Note

If a picture's boundaries have changed in its original file—if it's larger or smaller or shaped differently than it was when it was imported into QuarkXPress, updating the picture may cause it to move within its box—use the Show Me button to watch as the picture is updated so you'll know if its position changes.

QuarkXPress generally won't bother you about moved or modified pictures until you try to print. If there are moved or modified pictures in a document, after you click the Print button in the Print dialog another dialog box comes up warning you about the altered or missing images (see Figure 7.11). At that point, you can cancel the printing, or you can choose to print anyway, in which case the screen preview will be substituted for missing images and the modified images will be printed. The alternative is to go directly to Picture Usage by clicking the List Pictures button. Once you've updated the pictures, click OK in Picture Usage to resume printing.

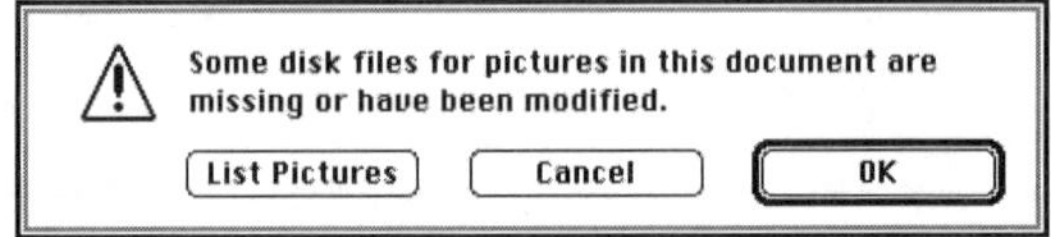

Figure 7.11

Before it prints, XPress warns of any missing or modified images.

XPress does offer the option of updating modified pictures every time you open a document, either with or without a warning dialog. See "Document Preferences" in Day 1, "XPress Basics," for how to set this preference.

On Mac OS systems, the **Publish and Subscribe** feature duplicates XPress's picture importing and updating features, so there's generally no reason to use them. If you need to import an image from an application that can't save an image file, however (such as a spreadsheet), try publishing the image and then subscribing to it in XPress. When publishing, choose EPS rather than PICT or TIFF if you're using a PostScript output device; otherwise, choose PICT. Check the other application's documentation, or the manuals that came with your system software, for information on using the Publish feature.

The same goes for **OLE**, Object Linking and Embedding, on the Windows side of the aisle. Instead of Publish and Subscribe, Windows users have Paste Special, Paste Link, and Links commands in the Edit menu. These commands allow you to link graphics to their originating applications so that double-clicking on a graphic opens the program in which it was created. You can then edit the graphics and return to QuarkXPress, where your changes are reflected in the XPress document. The other feature of OLE is that it enables you to embed a graphic in an XPress document so that you don't need to keep the original file around. Check your Windows documentation for more information on using OLE.

One more way of getting an image into QuarkXPress is to simply copy it in its original application and paste it into a picture box in XPress. The image will appear in the Picture Usage dialog box, but it won't be linked to a file. Images placed in XPress this way don't always print as you'd expect, so only use this feature if you can't get an image into the file any other way.

Editing Images

Although XPress doesn't offer the power of a dedicated image editor like Photoshop, it does allow you to modify imported images to some extent, in addition to scaling them and moving them around in their boxes. This example uses one photograph six times, with different effects applied, to create a design.

1. Open lessons/chap07/homelife.qxd on the CD-ROM that accompanies this book (see Figure 7.12). This is the cover of a catalog selling home furnishings; the file is a blank page, but it contains the colors and paragraph styles that will be needed for the design.

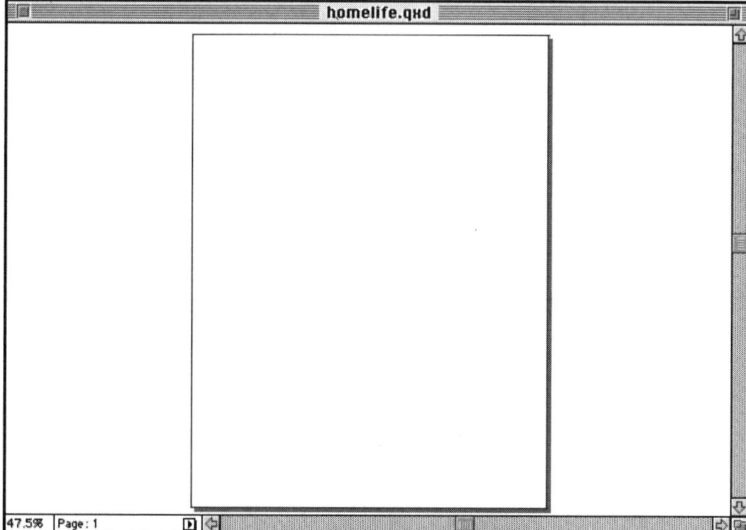

Figure 7.12

The empty catalog cover document.

2. Press F7 to show guides. The margin guides for this document are on the edge of the page.
3. Press (Command-Option-Shift-Y)[Control-Alt-Shift-Y] to bring up the Document Preferences. Click the Display tab and choose 32-bit from the Color TIFFs pop-up menu (see Figure 7.13). This ensures that screen preview of the picture you're about to import will be the highest possible quality. While this setting doesn't affect the way the image will output, it's a nicety that gives you an accurate idea of what the picture looks like. Click OK to return to the document.

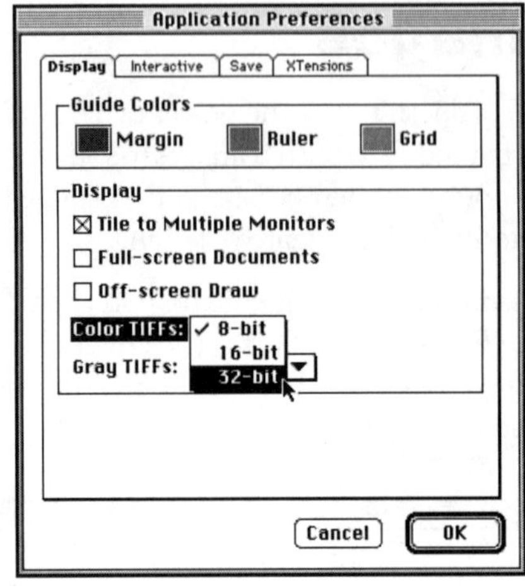

Figure 7.13

Setting the Color TIFFs menu to 32-bit allows for the best-quality screen previews of imported images.

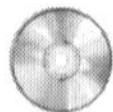

4. Draw a rectangular picture box covering the entire page. Choose Edit➡Get Picture or press (Command-E)[Control-E] to bring up the Get Picture dialog box. Choose lessons/chap07/house.tif and click Open to import the picture.
5. Double-click in the X percentage field of the Measurements palette, type 200, and press Tab to move to the Y percentage field. Enter 200 there as well, and press (Return)[Enter] to apply the change. The picture is scaled to 200 percent, twice its original size (see Figure 7.14).

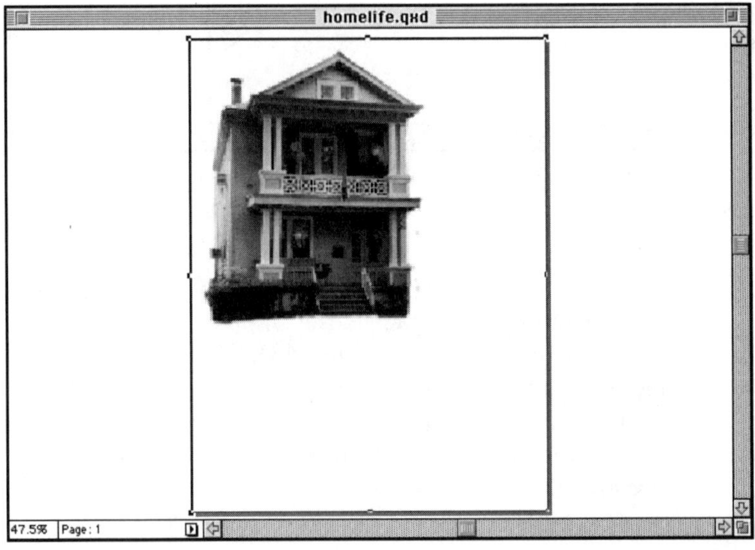

Figure 7.14

Scaling the picture to 200 percent will reduce its output quality—but that doesn't matter here since this is just a design layout, not the final document.

6. Press (Command-Shift-M)[Control-Shift-M] to center the picture in the box, then double-click in the Y coordinate field on the right side of the Measurements palette, type 0 (zero), and press (Return)[Enter] to apply the change, moving the picture to the top of the picture box. This value controls the vertical position of the picture within the box; the Y coordinate on the left side of the palette controls the position of the box itself.

Tip

You can remember this shortcut by thinking "M" for "middle."

7. Press F12 to view the Colors palette if it's not visible. Click the third icon at the top of the palette, which controls the background color of the box, and then click Cream process in the list of colors. This makes the box cream, but the area around the house is still white, as it is in the original TIFF file (see Figure 7.15).

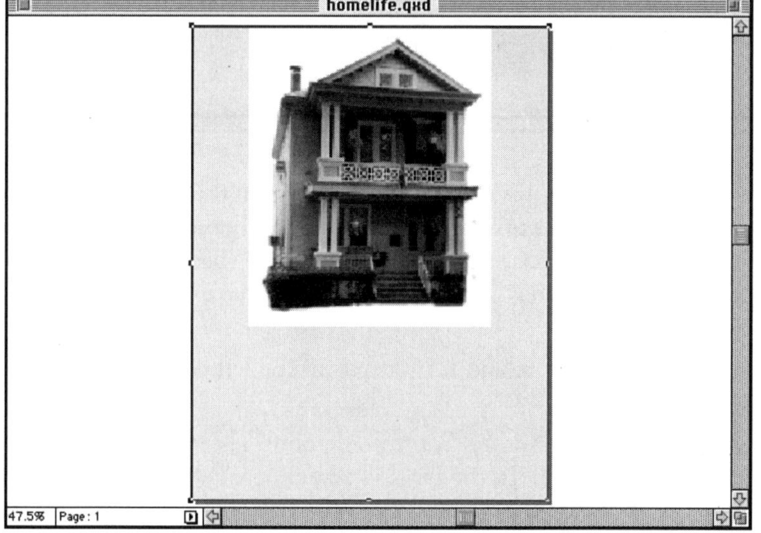

Figure 7.15

The box's background is cream-colored, but the white background of the image itself still shows.

8. To "clip" the white area around the house, press (Command-Option-T) [Control-Alt-T] to bring up the Clipping tab of the Modify dialog box. Choose Non-White Areas from the Type pop-up menu; this option creates a path around the edges of the house that will hide any white areas outside the house. Click OK to create the clipping path.

9. Edit the clipping path to bring it as close as possible to the edges of the house. Choose Item➥Edit➥Clipping Path to show the clipping path in the picture box, and adjust the points and curves so that the clipping path follows the edge of the house without allowing the white to show through (see Figure 7.16).

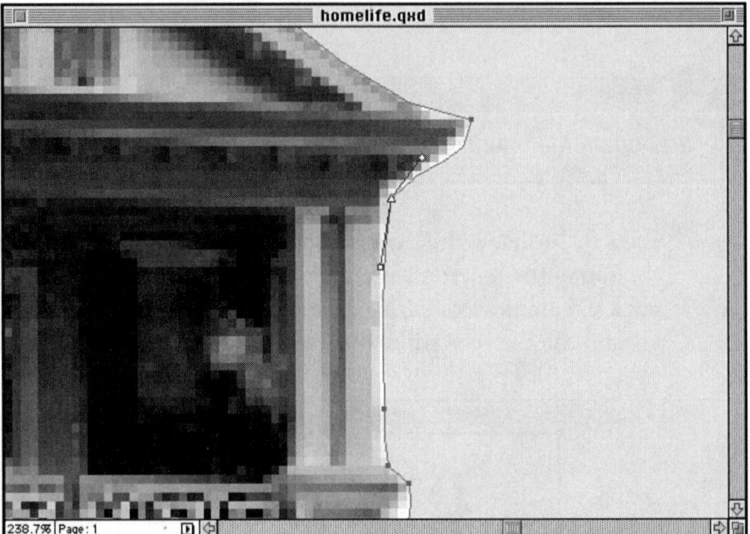

Figure 7.16

You can edit the image's clipping path just as you would edit a Bézier object.

10. Draw a rectangular box 8.5" wide and 2" deep 8.5" from the top of the page. It doesn't matter whether it's a text box or picture box; choose Item➥Content➥None to make it an empty box, then click on the third (background color) icon in the Colors palette and click Dark green process to make the box green (see Figure 7.17).
11. Draw a picture box 1.25" wide and 1.5" deep near the left edge of the green box.
12. Press (Command-Option-Shift-Y)[Control-Alt-Shift-Y] to bring up the Document Preferences again. In the Display tab, choose 8-bit from the Color TIFFs pop-up menu. While the 32-bit preview used for the first house picture looks better, it doesn't allow you to adjust the image's brightness and color. Click OK to return to the document.

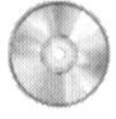

13. Click the small box and press (Command-E)[Control-E] to bring up the Get Picture dialog box. Choose the house picture again and click Open to bring it into the box.

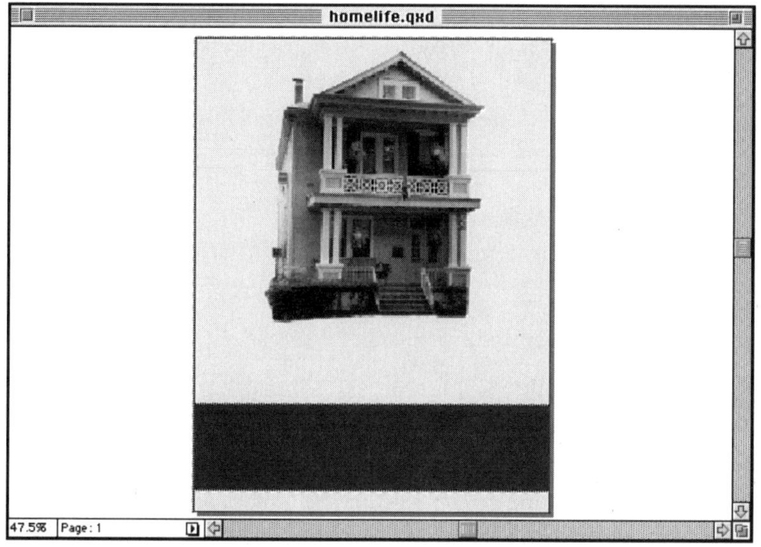

Figure 7.17

The green box can be an empty box to keep the document's file size down.

14. Enter 40 in the X and Y percentage fields of the Measurements palette, and press (Return)[Enter] to scale the picture to 40 percent. Press (Command-Shift-M)[Control-Shift-M] to center the picture in the box (see Figure 7.18).

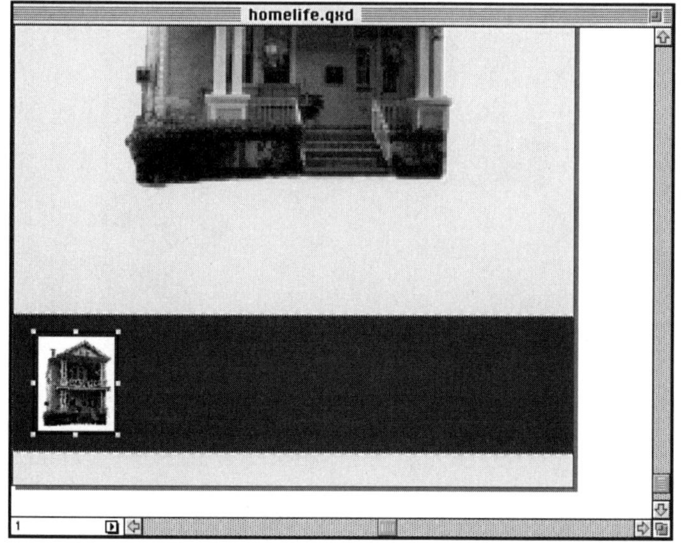

Figure 7.18

Another copy of the house picture is imported and scaled to 40 percent.

15. Choose Style➡Flip Horizontal or click the Flip Horizontal arrow in the Measurements palette (see Figure 7.19).

X: 0.328"	W: 1.258"	∠ 0°	X%: 40%	X+: 1.209"	∠ 0°
Y: 8.754"	H: 1.492"	0"	Y%: 40%	Y+: 0.05"	0°

Figure 7.19

These two arrows in the middle of the Measurements palette let you flip images horizontally or vertically; they turn black if an image has been flipped.

16. Press (Command-Option-T)[Control-Alt-T] to bring up the Clipping tab of the Modify dialog box and choose Non-White Areas from the Type pop-up menu. Then edit the clipping path as you did in Step 9.
17. Click on the third (background color) icon in the Colors palette and click Dark green process to make the box's background green.
18. Press (Command-D)[Control-D] twice to create two copies of the box. Move the third box close to the right edge of the green box and the second one to the center of the row (see Figure 7.20). Don't worry about positioning the boxes precisely yet; that will be taken care of later.

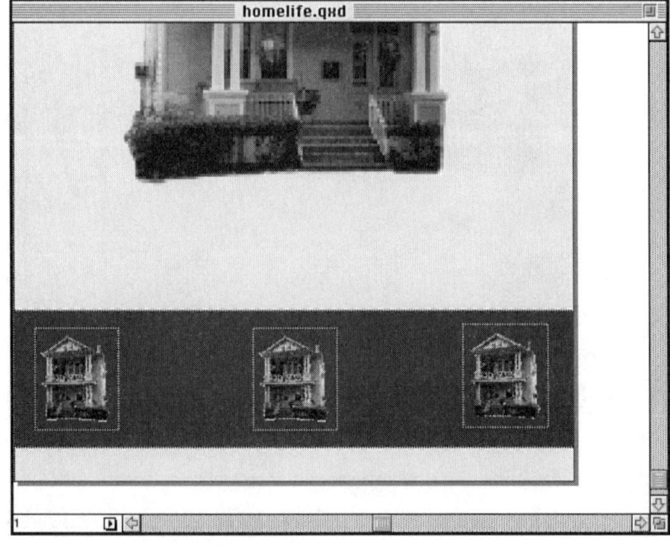

Figure 7.20

The three copies of the small house image are placed across the green bar.

19. Click on the first small house picture and press (Command-Shift-C)[Control-Shift-C] to bring up the Picture Contrast Specifications dialog box.
20. Edit the contrast curve as shown to turn the house a mossy, greenish black color (see Figure 7.21). If you're familiar with Photoshop's curves feature, or that of another image editor, this will all be familiar to you; if not, see the sidebar, "Adjusting the Color Curve," for more information. When you're done adjusting the curve, click OK to apply the changes and return to the document.

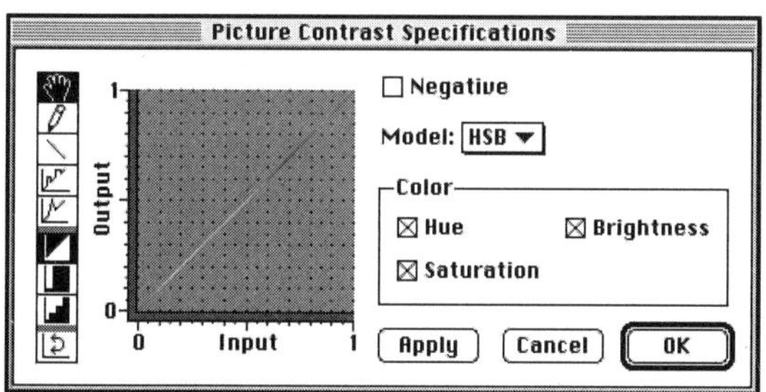

Figure 7.21

These settings turn the house dark green and black.

Adjusting the Color Curve

The contrast curve is a graph of the relationship between the picture's original color values and the values you want it to have when you print it. The original values are shown on the curve's horizontal axis (left = white, right = black), and the new values are shown on the vertical axis (bottom = white, top = black).

The tools on the left of the dialog box let you adjust the curve in several different ways (see Figure 7.22).

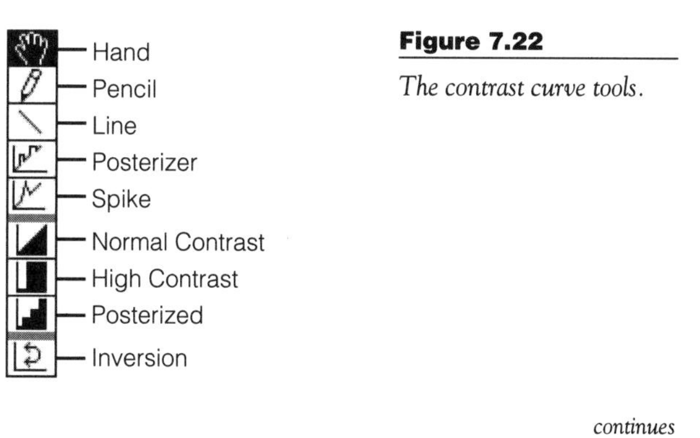

Figure 7.22

The contrast curve tools.

continues

- Choose the Hand tool to drag the entire curve without altering its shape; hold down the Shift key as you drag to keep the movement exactly horizontal or vertical.
- Choose the Pencil tool to draw a new curve or modify portions of an existing curve freehand.
- Choose the Line tool to add straight line segments to the curve; hold down the Shift key as you drag to make the line segments horizontal or vertical.
- Choose the Posterizer tool to place handles between the 10 percent increments along the curve, then drag the handles.
- Choose the Spike tool to place handles between the 10 percent increments along the curve, then drag the handles.
- Choose the Normal Contrast tool to reset the curve to its normal setting.
- Choose the High Contrast tool to create a curve that increases the contrast in the image.
- Choose the Posterized tool to create a posterized curve, one that reduces the number of colors in the image.
- Choose the Inversion tool to invert the curve; because it flips the modified curve, this command doesn't necessarily create a true negative of the original image. If you want to create a negative image, check on the Negative box; this command takes into account the changes in the curve to create the negative but doesn't modify the curve visibly.

The Model area lets you choose a color model to use when changing contrast: HSB, RGB, CMY, or CMYK. The color model determines what aspects of the image you can adjust with the curve. For example, if you choose HSB, the Color checkboxes will be labeled Hue, Saturation, and Brightness. If all three boxes are checked, all three aspects of the image will be changed when you alter the curve. If only Brightness, say, is checked, only the image's brightness will be altered when you adjust the curve.

Because these changes are made while you're looking at a low-resolution preview image that doesn't necessarily exactly match the actual image, it's best to make picky image adjustments in Photoshop or a similar program. Use XPress's contrast curve for special effects or for last-minute, quick-and-dirty adjustments when a true image editor isn't available.

21. Click on the second small house picture and press (Command-Shift-C) [Control-Shift-C] to bring up the Picture Contrast Specifications dialog box. Adjust this contrast curve as shown to turn the house red and yellow (see Figure 7.23). Click OK when you're done.

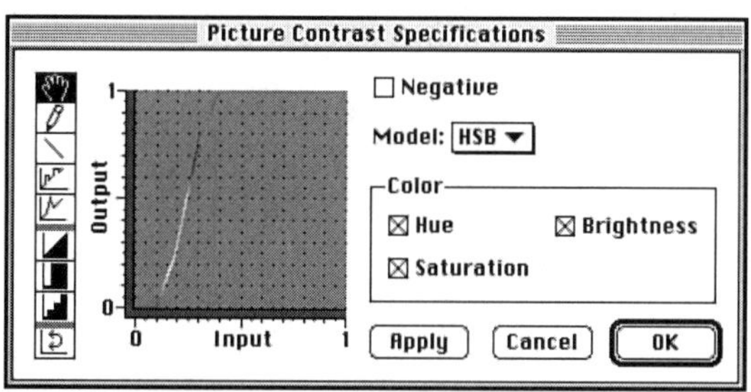

Figure 7.23

These settings turn the house red and yellow.

22. Click the third small house picture and press (Command-Shift-C)[Control-Shift-C] to bring up the Picture Contrast Specifications dialog box. Adjust this contrast curve as shown to turn the house purple and blue (see Figure 7.24). Click OK when you're done.

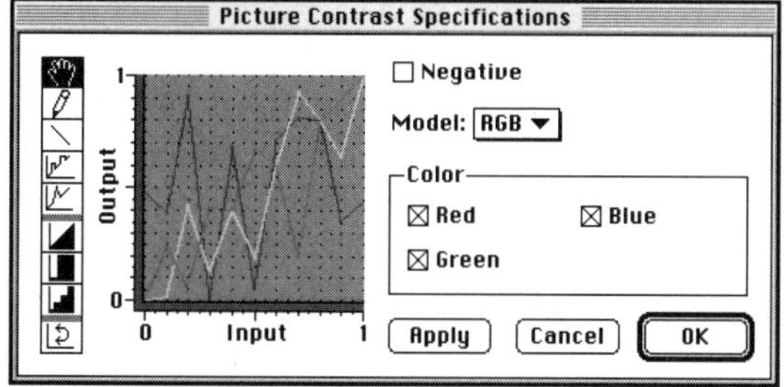

Figure 7.24

These settings turn the house purple and blue.

23. Now add another house; click the first small house and press (Command-D)[Control-D] to duplicate the picture. Move the new box to a position between the first and middle boxes; choose the Content tool and press (Delete)[Backspace] to delete the picture from the box.
24. Choose Edit➡Get Picture or press (Command-E)[Control-E] to bring up the Get Picture dialog. Choose lessons/chap07/house.tif again and hold down the (Command)[Control] key as you click Open to import the picture. This imports the picture as a grayscale image instead of as a color image.
25. Enter 40 in the X and Y percentage fields of the Measurements palette and press (Return)[Enter] to scale the picture to 40 percent. Press (Command-Shift-M)[Control-Shift-M] to center the picture in the box.

26. Now you can apply color to the image. Click the middle (image) icon on the Colors palette and click Dark purple process in the color list to turn the black areas of the image purple (see Figure 7.25).

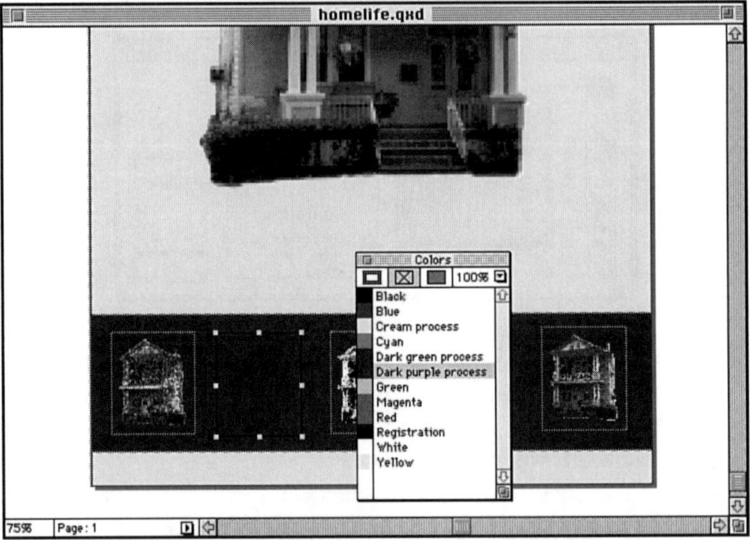

Figure 7.25

Because this version of the house picture is a grayscale image, you can change the black and gray areas of the image to another color.

Note

You can adjust the background color of a color TIFF but not the image color. To be able to adjust the image color, import it as grayscale.

27. Press (Command-D)[Control-D] to duplicate the picture and move the new box to a position between the middle and last boxes.
28. Shift-click to select all five small house picture boxes. Choose Item➥Space/Align or press (Command-,)[Control-,] to bring up the Space/Align dialog box (see Figure 7.26). Click both Horizontal and Vertical. On the Horizontal side, click Distribute Evenly and choose Items from the Between pop-up menu. On the Vertical side, click Space (0") and choose Top Edges from the Between pop-up menu. Click OK or press (Return)[Enter] to apply the changes.
29. Now that the boxes are spaced and aligned evenly with respect to each other, press (Command-G)[Control-G] to group them, then Shift-click the green box so that both it and the group are selected. Press (Command-,)[Control-,] to bring up the Space/Align dialog box again. This time, click both Horizontal

and Vertical, click Space (0"), and choose Centers from the pop-up menu. Click OK or press (Return)[Enter] to center the group and the green box vertically and horizontally with respect to each other (see Figure 7.27).

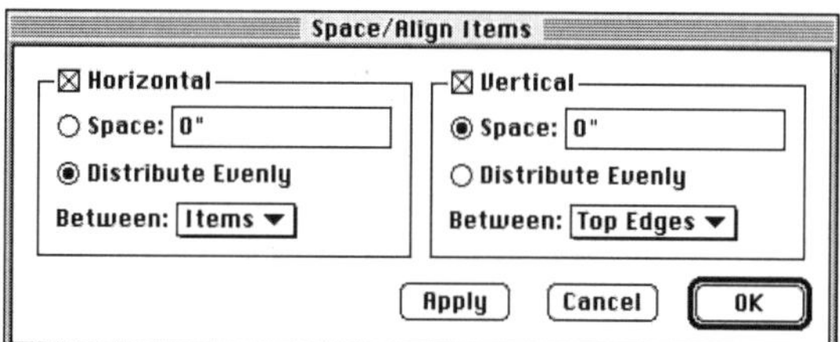

Figure 7.26

The Space/Align dialog box lets you adjust the position of elements with respect to each other.

Figure 7.27

The grouped picture boxes are centered on the green box.

30. To finish off the catalog cover, add the title. Draw a rectangular text box the width of the page and 1" deep, flush with the left and right edges of the page and 7" from the top of the page. Type **HomeLife** in the box.
31. Double-click to select the title and click the middle (text) icon in the Colors palette; click Dark purple process in the list to turn the type purple. Then choose a font you like (I used Goudy Handtooled) from the font menu and choose a size (mine is 72 points) from the point size menu in the Measurements palette (see Figure 7.28).

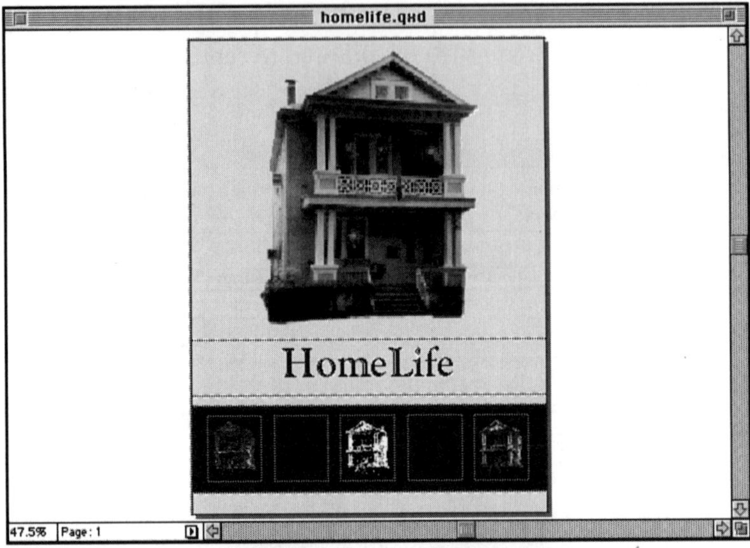

Figure 7.28

The final layout.

Tip

To speed up screen redraw as you move around a document, greek the images by clicking Greek Pictures in the Document Preferences (Command-Y)[Control- Y]. Imported pictures will be replaced with gray boxes onscreen, but they'll print correctly.

Summary

Some of the best designs depend on the power of a single image created in another program, and almost every design has imported images of some kind—logos, special type treatments that you can't achieve in QuarkXPress, photographs, clip art. Although there are several ways to bring images into an XPress document, the best way is the old-fashioned way: the Get Picture command. You can keep track of what images are where and their status with the Pictures tab of the Usage dialog box, so you'll always know what images you've used, where they are in the document and on your hard drive, and what format they are. Finally, sticking to a few major file formats—preferably those recommended by your prepress house or printer—enables you to get consistent results and stop worrying (for the most part) about output problems related to imported images.

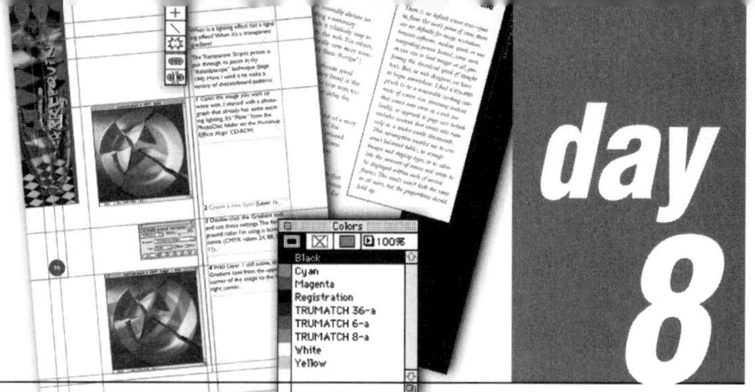

Creating and Using Master Pages

- Creating master pages
- Adding elements to master pages
- Applying master pages
- Using automatic page numbering
- Using automatic text boxes
- Moving and deleting master pages

Unless every document you create is unique, with each page unlike any other, you should be using master pages. They're particularly helpful in producing longer documents, such as books, magazines, and catalogs. In fact, you can combine master pages, style sheets, database information storage, scripting, and precoding to almost completely automate production of any long document. There's a lot of work to be done up front, setting up the system, but it can save time in the long run. In this chapter, you'll create and use several different master pages; for information on style sheets, see Day 5, "Formatting Text and Using Style Sheets."

Building Master Pages

A master page contains a master layout that can be applied to any document page and then used as the basis for a final layout. In QuarkXPress, master page items on document pages can be selected, modified, and deleted, and a new master page can be applied to document pages without deleting the main text flow on those pages.

There are two kinds of master page elements: automatic text boxes, which enable you to position the main text flow on each page, and everything else. That "everything else" is a pretty big category because you can place anything on a master page that you can place on a document page. That includes:

- Text
- Imported graphics
- Automatic page numbers (special characters that insert a page number in the text)
- XPress graphic elements such as boxes, Bézier shapes, and rules

After you've created a master page, you apply it to document pages so that the document pages will conform to the layout of the master page. This project is a marketing brochure for a cookbook that uses essentially the same layout as the cookbook.

1. Open lessons/chap10/cookbook.qxd on the CD that accompanies this book (see Figure 8.1). This file contains all the style sheets needed to format the cookbook, but not the master pages. As with all documents, though, it starts out with a blank master page A, which contains a two-page spread because this document has facing pages.

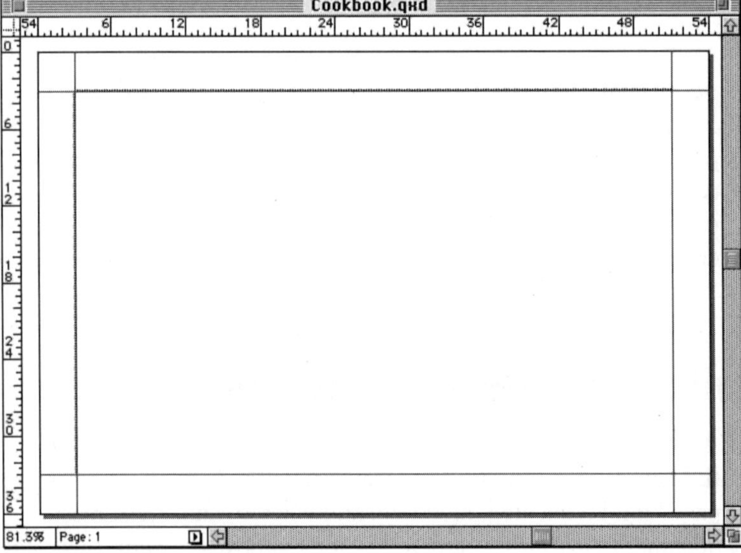

Figure 8.1

The cookbook file starts out with only one blank page.

Note

This file uses Salut and Vendome (both in the Title Wave folder on the CD), so make sure those font families are installed in your system.

2. Press (F10)[F4] to show the Document Layout palette if it's not visible, then double-click the A-Master A icon to view the default master page spread.
3. This spread will become the master page for the covers. The default automatic text box is fine as is, but a colored background is needed. Create a picture box 6p by 36p and position it at the zero coordinates of the spread—at the left edge of the left-hand page (see Figure 8.2).

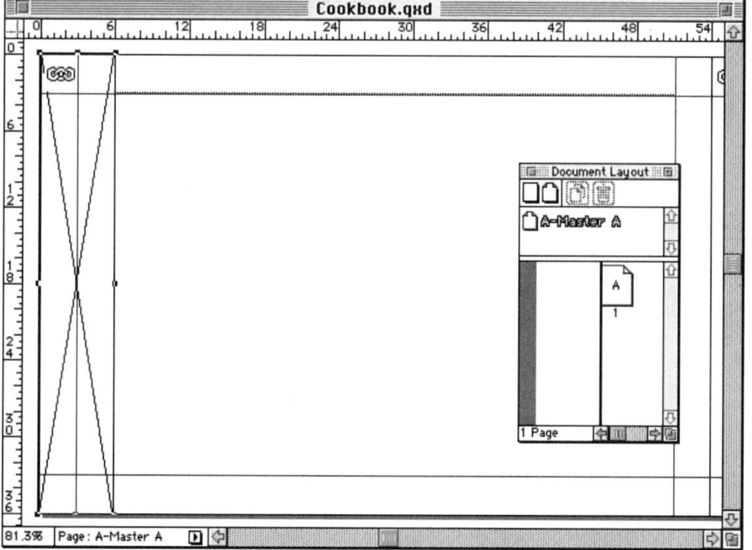

Figure 8.2

The first picture box will form the basis for a striped design on the book's cover.

4. Choose Item➡Step and Repeat to create several copies of the box. Enter 17 for Repeat Count, 6p for Horizontal Offset, and 0p for Vertical Offset, then click OK or press (Return)[Enter]. This creates 17 more boxes, positioned edge to edge and aligned vertically (see Figure 8.3).
5. Switch to the Item tool and drag to select all the boxes except the main text box, then press F12 to view the Colors palette if it's not visible. Click the third (background color) icon in the Colors palette and choose PANTONE 1785 CV from the list of colors, then enter 20% in the screen field. All the boxes are now a light melon color.

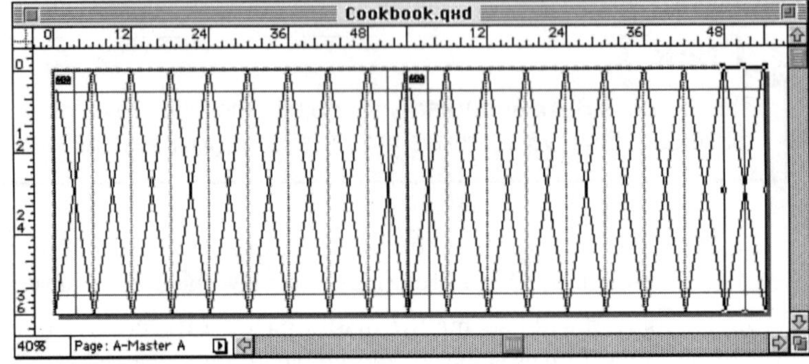

Figure 8.3

The Step and Repeat command creates 17 copies of the box.

6. Select the second box from the left, then Shift-click to select every other box on that page, along with the second box on the right-hand page and every other box on that page. Because there are nine boxes on each page, the second, fourth, sixth, and eighth boxes on each page should be selected. Choose PANTONE 326 CV in the Colors palette to make these boxes light green (see Figure 8.4).

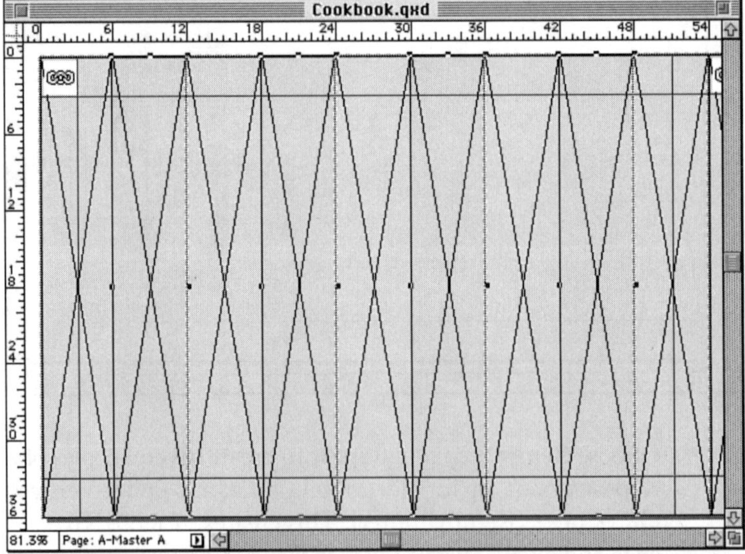

Figure 8.4

The alternating colors used for the boxes make a stripe pattern.

7. Select all the boxes on the left-hand page except the main text box and group them ((Command-G)[Control-G]), then choose Item➡Send to Back to make sure the text box is in front of the stripe boxes. Lock the group ((Command-L)[Control-L]). Do the same with the boxes on the right-hand page. This will

keep them from moving around when you edit the document pages that use this master page.

8. In the Document Layout palette, double-click the icon for the first (and only, so far) document page to return to the main document. Because its master page was edited, this page shows all the changes just made to the right-hand page in the A master spread (see Figure 8.5).

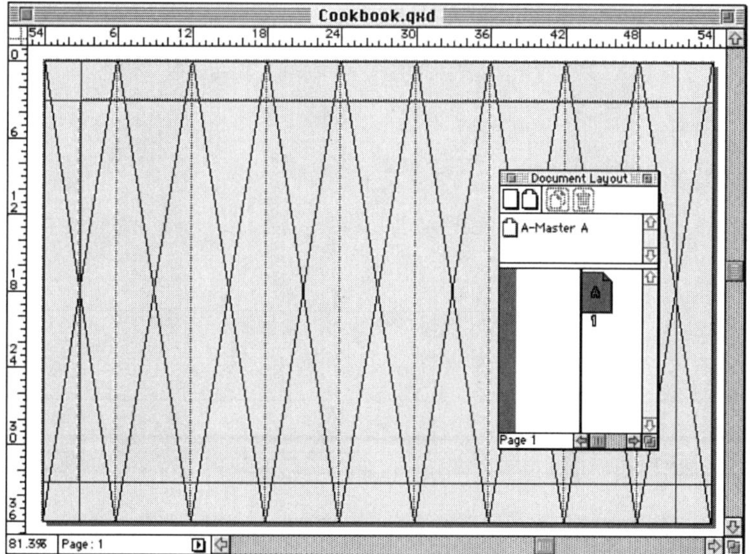

Figure 8.5

The single document page looks just like the corresponding page on the master page spread.

9. Drag a generic facing pages master page icon from the top of the palette into the master page area of the Document Layout palette to create a new master page spread. It's automatically named B-Master B. Double-click the B master page icon to view the master page spread—it looks just like the A master page spread before you started working on it, only without the text box.

   Annoyingly, XPress only places automatic text boxes on the default A master page or spread. When you create new master pages from scratch, you have to add your own automatic text boxes.

Note

Before you start creating text boxes, you may need to change your tool preferences. Double-click the Text Box tool in the Toolbox to bring up the Text Box tool Preferences dialog. Click the Modify button, then click the Text tab and make sure the Text Inset value is 0 (Quark's default is 1 point).

10. Make a 32p by 11p text box on the left-hand page, and position it flush with the top and right margin guides. Choose the Linking tool and click the Link icon in the upper left corner of the left-hand page, then click the new text box. That makes it an automatic text box (see Figure 8.6).

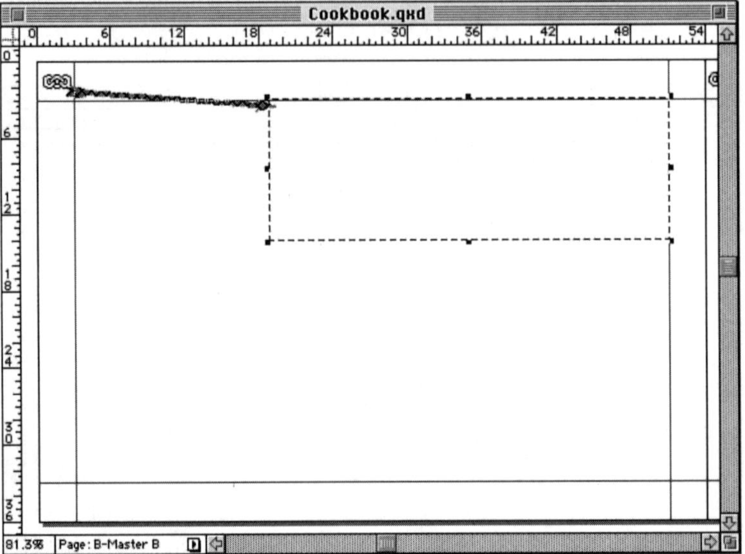

Figure 8.6

The gray arrow from the Link icon to the text box indicates that this is an automatic text box.

11. The right-hand page will have several linked boxes. Ordinarily, after you draw a text box QuarkXPress reverts to the Item or Content tool, whichever was active before you chose the Text Box tool. To keep that from happening so that you can draw several text boxes in quick succession, (Option-click)[Alt-click] the Text Box tool in the Toolbox.
12. Draw four text boxes on the page (see Figure 8.7):
    - Start at the top of the right-hand page and draw a text box about 3p6 deep, flush with the top margin guide and running from the left margin guide to the right one (48p wide). Hold down the (Command)[Control] key to position the box before drawing the next one.
    - Then draw another box 12p wide by 25p6 deep, flush with the left and bottom margin guides.
    - Make a third box 30p wide by 19p6 deep and position it about halfway between the edge of the previous box and the right margin guide (X coordinate about 17p6).

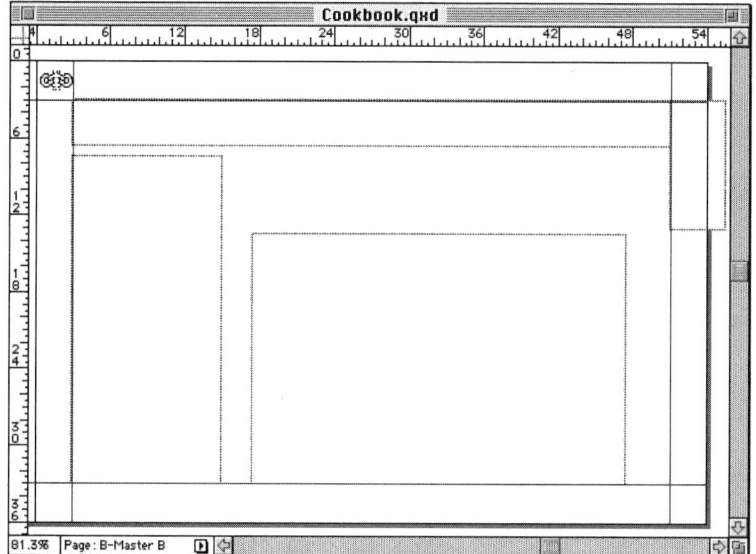

Figure 8.7

Master pages can contain several linked text boxes.

- Finally, draw a box 10p wide by 4p6 deep, switch to the Item tool, and turn the box on its side by entering -90° in the angle field of the Measurements palette (press F9 to bring up the palette). Then position the box bleeding off the right edge of the page by first moving it completely off the right edge of the page then entering 1p6 in the X coordinate field of the Measurements palette and 3p in the Y coordinate field.

Note

If you don't move the box off to the right before positioning it, entering 1p6 for the X coordinate places it on the left side of the page, not the right.

13. (Option-click)[Alt-click] the Linking tool to prevent XPress from giving you back the Item tool after each link, and link the four boxes as automatic text boxes by clicking in turn on the Link icon, the top box, the left-hand box, the middle box, and the box on the edge of the page. Arrows connect the end of each box to the beginning of the next box in the flow (see Figure 8.8).
14. Click the left-hand box and give it a plain border by pressing (Command-B) [Control-B] to open the Frame panel of the Modify dialog box. Enter 2 points for the width of the border, choose Solid from the Style pop-up menu, and choose PANTONE 1785 CV for the border's color.

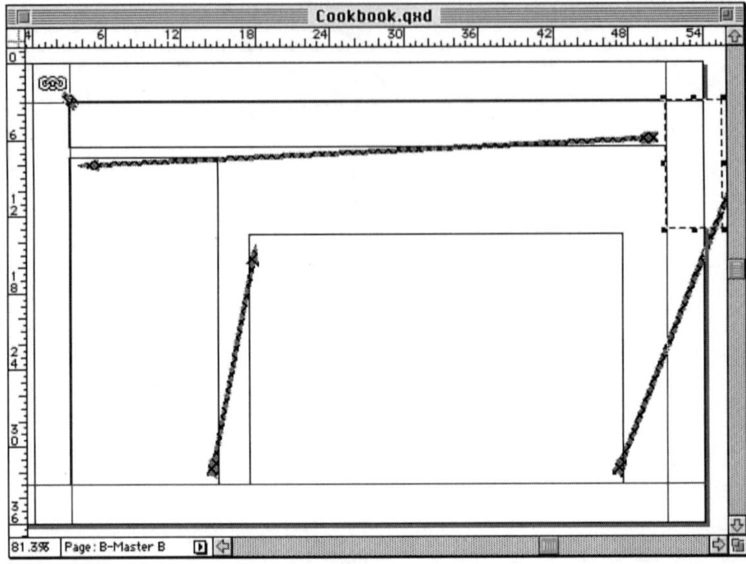

Figure 8.8

The four boxes are linked to each other and to the Link icon, so the text will flow into each box in turn.

15. Click the box at the edge of the page (this box is called a side tab) and make the box's background color PANTONE 1785 CV (see Figure 8.9).

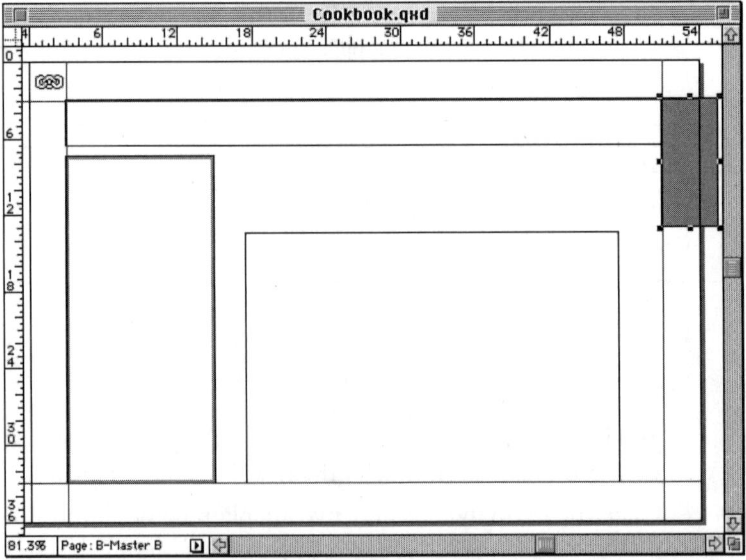

Figure 8.9

Automatic text boxes on master pages have all the same attributes as text boxes on document pages, including color.

16. With the side tab still selected, press (Command-M)[Control-M] to bring up the Modify dialog box and click the Text tab. In the Vertical Alignment section, choose Bottom from the Type pop-up menu. This will force the text in the box to the bottom, rather than keeping it at the top (which would be off the edge of the page).
17. Now add an element that won't be an automatic text box: a running footer. Although running headers and footers can contain text such as the book title, chapter title, or the text of the last first-level heading, this one will have only a page number, or folio. Create a text box 2p wide by 1p deep and position it 1p inside the left margin guide on the left-hand page and at a Y coordinate of 34p. Click in the box with the Content tool and type (Command-3)[Control-3] to insert an automatic page number character. Select the page number character and format it as 9-point Salut (see Figure 8.10).

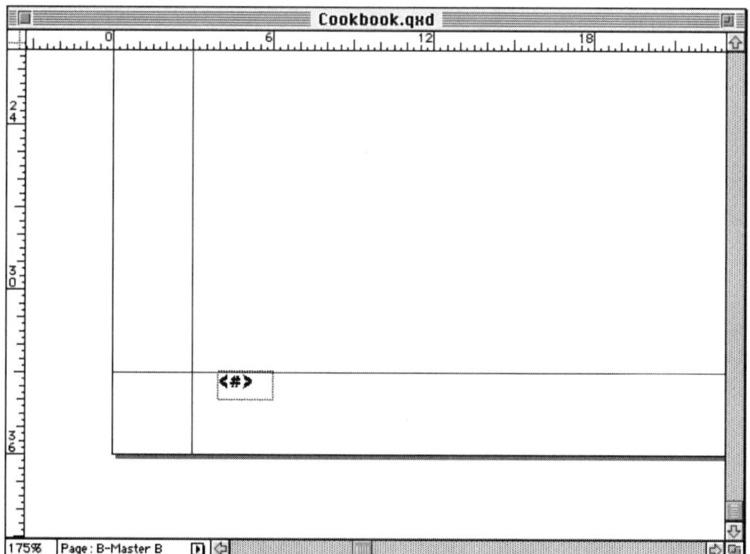

Figure 8.10

This special character will appear as the page number on document pages.

Tip

In addition to (Command-3)[Control-3] to insert the current page number, you can use (Command-2)[Control-2] to insert the page number of the previous text box and (Command-4)[Control-4] to insert the page number of the next text box in the flow. Use these characters on document pages for continuation lines ("Continued on page 37" and "Continued from page 23"). They'll automatically update if page numbers change.

18. Press (Command-D)[Control-D] to duplicate the folio box and drag the copy over to the corresponding position at the right side of the right-hand page. Click in the box with the Content tool and press (Command-Shift-R)[Control-Shift-R] to right-justify the text.
19. Now that the document's main master page is done, return to the first page of the document by double-clicking its icon in the Document Layout palette. Add another page to the document using the B master page spread you just created by dragging the B-Master B icon into the left side of the Document Layout palette below the icon for page 1 (see Figure 8.11).

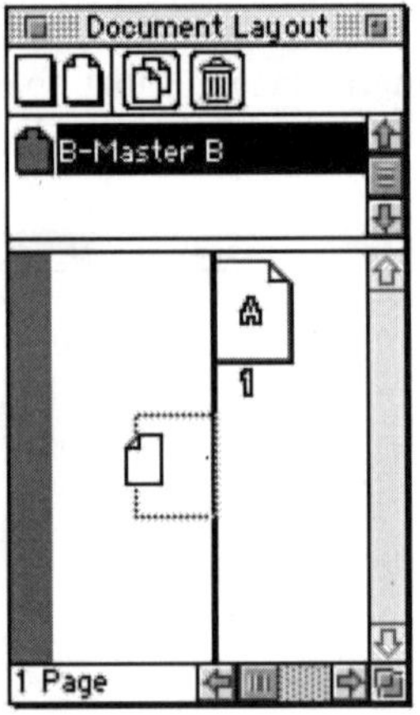

Figure 8.11

Document pages are added by dragging the appropriate master page icons into the document page area of the Document Layout palette.

20. Because you added this second page manually, you need to link it with the first page. Choose the Linking tool and click in the text box on the first page, then in the main text box (not the folio box) on the second page. An arrow connects the two boxes to indicate that they're linked (see Figure 8.12).

21. Click in any text box on either page of the document; because they're linked, clicking in any of them selects the text flow. Choose File➡Get Text (or press (Command-E)[Control-E]) and navigate to lessons/chap10/cookbook.xtg on the CD that came with this book. Make sure Include Styles is checked on and click Open to import the text. It comes in completely formatted because the text file is an XPress Tags file that contains all the character and paragraph formatting codes (see Figure 8.13).

    When the text is imported, XPress adds several pages to hold it. The document now has eight pages, with the first one using the A master and all the rest using the B master (because that's the master of the last page in the text flow before you imported the text).

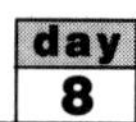

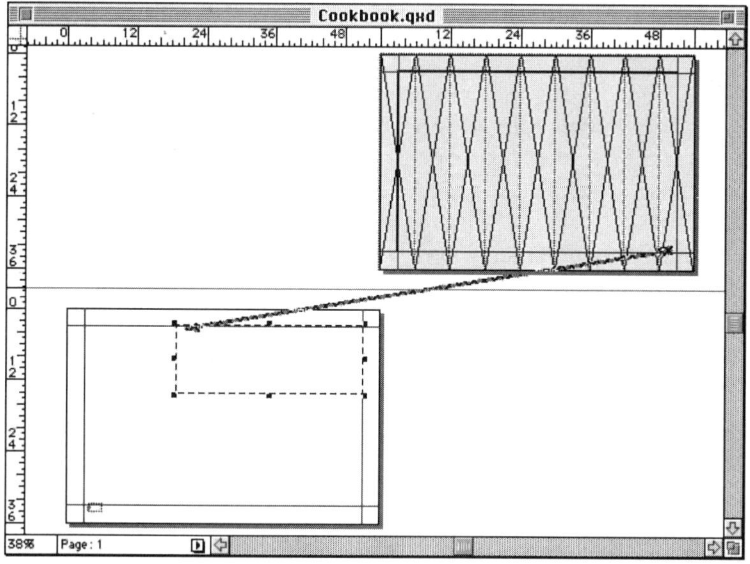

Figure 8.12

The gray arrow shows that the text boxes on the two pages are linked.

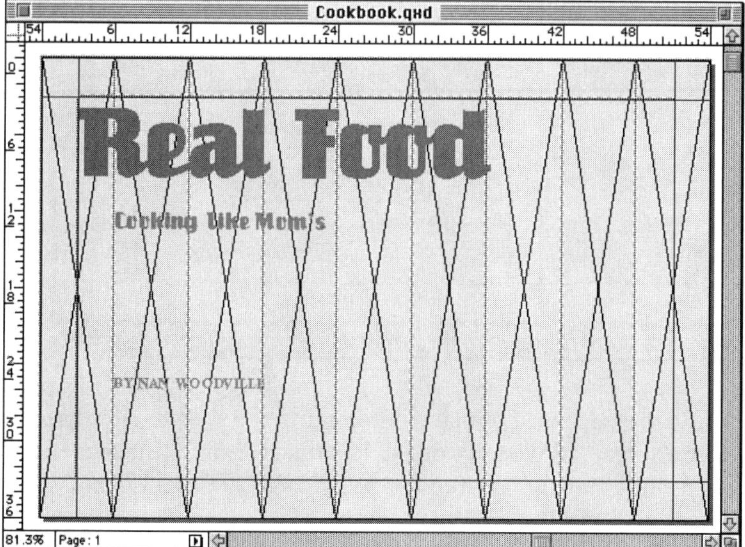

Figure 8.13

The text was styled in XPress, then exported in XPress Tags format, so it comes in completely formatted.

22. Now create master pages for the different sections of the cookbook. Each section will have a different kind of dish (such as desserts or side dishes) and use a similar layout. Click the B master page icon in the Document Layout palette, then on the Duplicate icon at the top of the palette to make a copy called C-Master C.

Tip

Drag down the boundary between the master page area and the document page area to see more master pages. The bigger the Document Layout palette is, the bigger you can make the master page area.

23. Double-click the C-Master C icon to view the new master spread. There's only one change to make for this spread; move the side tab box down 10p so its Y coordinate is 13p, then change its color to PANTONE 326 CV, the green (see Figure 8.14).

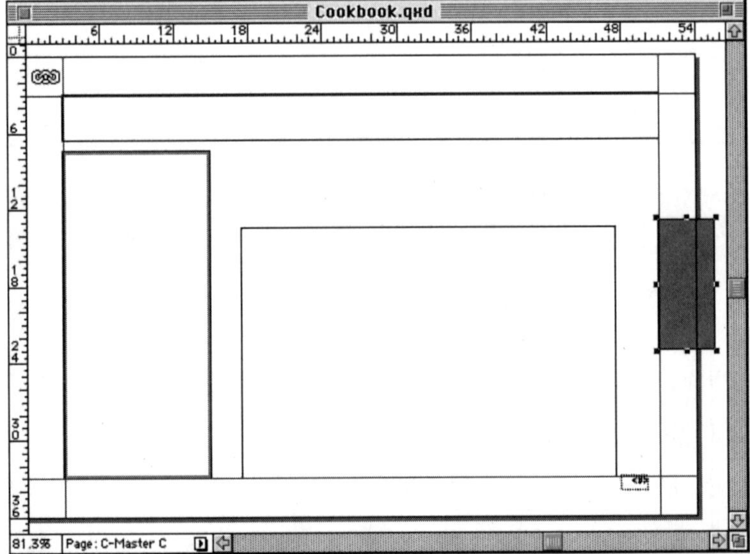

Figure 8.14

The side tab for the C master page is at a second side tab position.

24. Duplicate the C master spread to make D-Master D and double-click the new D icon to view the spread. Move the side tab box down again, flush with the bottom margin guide and change its color back to PANTONE 1785 CV (see Figure 8.15).
25. Apply the new master pages to the second and third complete spreads in the document. Apply C-Master C to pages 4 and 5 and D-Master D to pages 6 and 7 by dragging the appropriate master page icon onto the document page icons (see Figure 8.16).

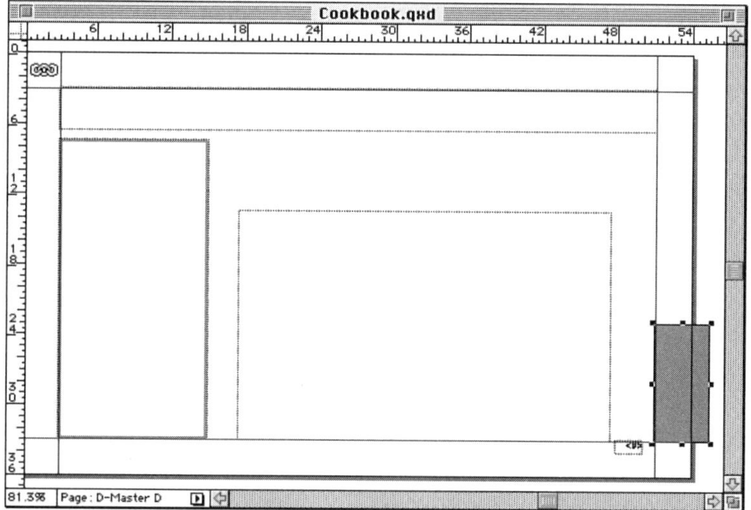

Figure 8.15

The side tab for the D master page is at a third side tab position.

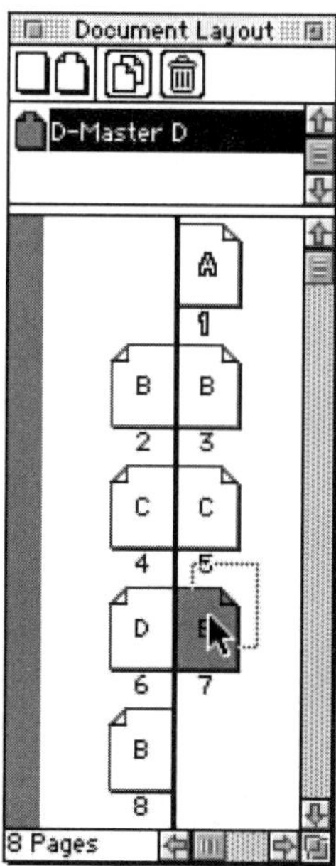

Figure 8.16

Dragging a master page icon onto an existing page changes that page to match its new master.

Because the left-hand pages of the C and D master spreads are just like the left-hand page on the B spread, no change occurs when you apply the C and D master pages to pages 4 and 6. If you decide later that you want the left-hand pages in each section to have a distinctive color or element, you can just change the master pages to have that change made automatically in the document pages.

26. Apply the A master page to the last page in the document, the back cover, then return to the front cover by double-clicking the page's icon in the Document Layout palette.

27. The artwork for the cookbook has been stored in a library. Choose File➡Open and navigate to the library file lessons/chap10/cookbook.qxl, then click Open (see Figure 8.17).

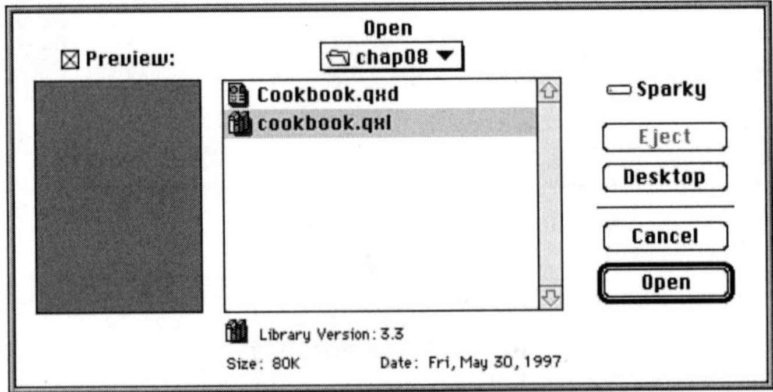

Figure 8.17

Opening the library file.

28. Click the first element in the library, the ripple graphic, and drag it into the document. Position it flush with all four margin guides on the first page.

29. Drag the second library element onto the page and position it flush with the right and bottom margin guides. The cook figure should fit in the gap in the ripple (see Figure 8.18).

30. Move to the second page of the document; this is the left-hand page of the spread for the macaroni and cheese recipe. Using the Item tool, not the Content tool, drag the macaroni graphic out of the library and position it flush with the right and bottom margin guides on the page (see Figure 8.19).

31. The fourth page of the document faces the potato salad recipe. Using the Item tool, position the potatoes and chives graphic from the library flush with the right and bottom margin guides on the page (see Figure 8.20).

32. The sixth page of the document faces the cake recipe. With the Item tool, position the cake graphic from the library flush with the right and bottom margin guides on the page (see Figure 8.21).

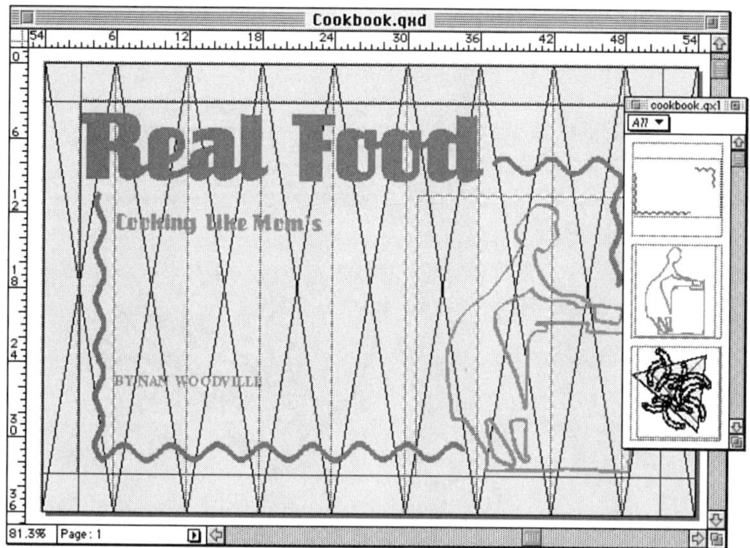

Figure 8.18

Place the artwork by dragging it from the library onto the page.

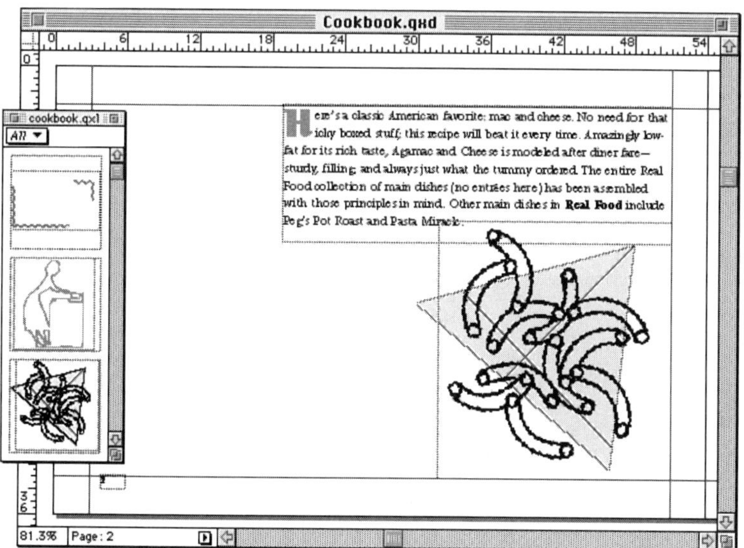

Figure 8.19

Add different artwork for each recipe.

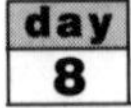

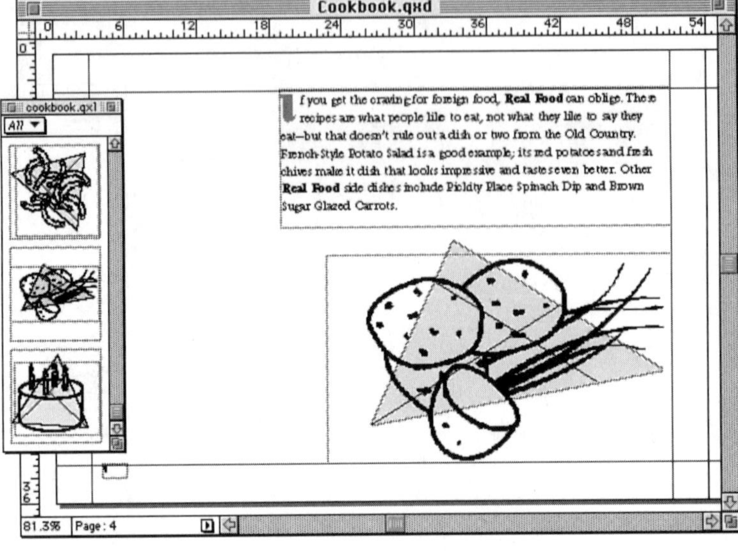

Figure 8.20

The potatoes and chives artwork is placed facing the potato salad recipe.

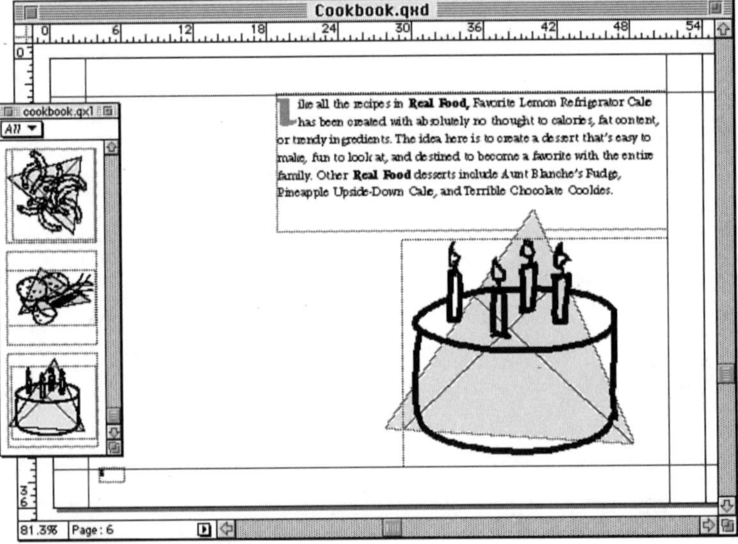

Figure 8.21

The final artwork is the cake image, facing the cake recipe.

After the master pages are created, they can be applied to as many pages as necessary. If this were a real-life project, the cookbook itself would have far more pages than the brochure and the efficiency inherent in using master pages would really show up.

Managing Master Pages

Master pages aren't set in stone after they're created. Of course, you can edit them as needed—that's the whole point, but you can also give them your own names, reorder them, delete them, and even add master pages from other documents.

- To delete a master page, click its icon then on the (trash can)[**X**] icon at the top of the Document Layout palette.
- To rename a master page, click its name and type a new name. If the new name doesn't contain a hyphen, QuarkXPress will retain the letter and hyphen that originally started the master page's name. You can substitute numbers or words before the hyphen, or you can type a different letter, by typing the number, word, or letter and a hyphen, then the rest of the name. In a book, for example, you might use the names "Text-page" and "Chapter-opener."
- To reorder master pages, drag their icons in the Document Layout palette to a new position above or below another master page icon.

When both documents are in Thumbnail view, you can drag pages from one document to another. When you do this, any associated style sheets and master pages come along for the ride. So if you want to copy a master page to another document, drag a page that uses that master page to the second document, then delete the document page; the master page stays there.

Troubleshooting

Master pages are useful, but their behavior in XPress is sometimes unpredictable. Here are two common questions brought up by those working with master pages for the first time.

Why Did My Text Go Away When I Applied a Master Page?

Either the new master page or the document page doesn't have an automatic text box and the Delete Changes option is chosen in the Master Page Items pop-up menu of the Document Preferences dialog box. The only way to maintain the text flow on a document page when applying a different master page (or reapplying the current master page) is to make sure that the master page and document page both have automatic text boxes. You can't undo a master page application, so it's important to be sure of this before you start.

If the text box on the document page was linked to another page, then the text that disappeared has moved to the next page in the flow. You can put it back where it belongs by selecting all, cutting the text, linking its original page to the next page, and pasting the text into the flow again.

Why Didn't the Extra Elements Go Away When I Applied a Master Page?

You can change the layout of a page by applying a different master page, but XPress plays it safe by only changing master page items. If you add extra elements—such as artwork in the example above—to a page, these items stay on the page until you delete them.

In addition to placing extra elements on a page, you can modify the master page items that are there. How master page items are dealt with when you change master pages depends on your preferences. Press (Command-Y)[Control-Y] to bring up the Document Preferences dialog.

- To leave master page items in their altered state, choose Keep Changes. With this setting, if you've changed the size of the automatic text box on the document page, the master page's own automatic text box is added to the page instead of replacing the previous one, so you end up with two text boxes on the page.
- To restore them to their original state when you apply a master page, choose Delete Changes from the Master Page Items pop-up menu. With this setting, the new master page's automatic text box replaces the old automatic text box, whether it's modified or not.

Summary

Although they don't seem very glamorous, master pages are one of the most powerful functions in QuarkXPress. They help you speed up your work, ensure consistency throughout a publication or multiple publications, and make changes to multiple pages quickly and easily. When you're planning a project, decide if master pages are appropriate for that job—if more than one or two pages in the publication will have the same basic design, then take a minute to create a master page for that layout. Don't forget to use automatic text boxes and page numbering where appropriate. Renaming master pages with descriptive titles can help you remember how you planned to use them, and it can be even more useful for other designers who may work on the same files later on.

Using Color

- Defining process colors
- Defining spot colors
- Applying colors to objects
- Using color management
- Making sure colors print correctly

A little bit of color can make a document a lot more expressive. Color can add prestige, warmth, and excitement to a design, but you have to know how to use it. This chapter doesn't cover the design theory of color, but rather the mechanics of using color in QuarkXPress. Used correctly, color can fool readers into thinking a document cost more to produce than it did; used incorrectly, color can cost *you* more to produce a document than you expect. In this chapter, you'll create and edit different kinds of colors, apply them to elements in a design, and learn how XPress's color management features can help ensure that the color you see in the final printed piece matches what you saw on your screen as you created the design.

Color Basics

If you're familiar with color publishing, then you can skip this section and move directly to the sections dealing with using color in QuarkXPress. On the other hand, a refresher course never hurt anyone.

For the most part, colors in QuarkXPress represent colored inks that will be applied to paper. That may seem like stating the obvious, but it's easy to lose sight of that concept when we spend so much time looking at colors onscreen. Colors on a computer monitor are made up of colored light, rather than colored inks, and the gamuts, or ranges of available colors, of these two ways of representing colors aren't completely equivalent. That means that you can't reproduce all onscreen colors correctly when you print a document, and you can't show all ink colors accurately onscreen.

Process and Spot Colors

Printing inks come in two basic varieties—process colors and spot colors. If a document contains a dark blue box, for example, that box can be printed with a dark blue ink, or with a combination of cyan, magenta, yellow, and black inks that will fool the eye into thinking it sees dark blue. The latter method is four-color process printing, and it's what we most often see in magazines, newspapers, and other printed pieces with color photos.

Spot colors are produced by using single inks rather than combinations of the four process inks. Generally, spot colors are used for two reasons. First, they're the only way to be sure a color is reproduced exactly as it should be, so they're often used for corporate logos and other identity designs. Second, if a printed piece contains fewer than four colors (counting black as a color), then it's often cheaper to print it with spot colors, because fewer printing plates and less press set-up are required.

Because computer monitors can't accurately reproduce printed colors, designers use color **swatchbooks** to choose colors for their designs. These swatchbooks show how colors will reproduce on press, whether they're spot colors or process colors. Spot color matching systems include **Pantone**, Toyo, and DIC. These systems identify colors by numbers that correspond to ink colors, so designers using these systems specify colors by their numbers, such as Pantone 549, a light blue. Process color matching systems include Pantone Process, **TruMatch**, and Focoltone. Colors in these systems are made up of varying percentages of process ink colors, so these colors can be identified by either their system numbers (such as TruMatch 26-a7) or their CMYK percentage breakdowns (such as C90, M6, Y30, K42—which is the same color).

Hexachrome Color

If you look at a Pantone process color swatchbook, which shows Pantone ink colors and their CMYK equivalents, you'll notice that the CMYK versions of a lot of the colors aren't really all that equivalent. If you've got a Pantone process swatchbook handy, take a look at Pantone 527 for a good example. It's a lovely bright purple, but the CMYK version is muddy and brownish. That's because the four process colors can't really make all colors of the rainbow, no matter how you combine them.

In an effort to come up with a better system, Pantone has created **Hexachrome**, a process color system that uses six colors instead of four. Hexachrome uses the four traditional process colors and adds orange and green. Printing in Hexachrome costs more, because there are more plates and more inks, and most printers don't offer it yet. Another concern is the increased possibility of **moiré** patterns, because more colors have to share the same possible number of screen angles. But the results of printing with Hexachrome are amazing—bright, vivid colors that could never be achieved using traditional four-color process printing. Hexachrome can simulate more than 90 percent of the Pantone spot colors, more than twice as many as CMYK printing.

Note

Alternative printing processes like Hexachrome are part of achieving **hi-fi (high fidelity) color**. Another technology that's part of the mix is **stochastic**, or frequency modulation, screening, which uses randomly placed **halftone** dots instead of rows. Using stochastic screening virtually eliminates moiré patterns, and images screened this way often look more like continuous-tone photographs than printed halftones.

QuarkXPress 4.0 includes the Hexachrome color system, along with Pantone, TruMatch, and other systems. You can turn color Photoshop images into Hexachrome images with the HexWrench Photoshop plug-in (Mac OS, Pantone), which lets you save images in six-color EPS DCS format.

Using Color Management

How a color appears when you're looking at depends on so many factors that it's nearly impossible to ever predict the exact results. Just a few of those factors:

- The ambient light
- The type of color—subtractive or additive (video or printed)
- The type of colorant (ink, wax, or something else)
- The medium or **substrate** (paper)
- Your own color vision
- The surrounding colors

Given all that, there are a few ways of trying to keep color predictable, so that what you see in an image is what you get onscreen after you've scanned that image, and what you see onscreen is what you get when you print the image. Swatchbook systems work reasonably well for spot color; although they're not perfect, they can bypass the difference between monitor colors and printed colors.

Color management software attempts to go a huge step further by actually adjusting what you see and what you print to make up for the differences between how your monitor, printer, and scanner recognize and reproduce color. QuarkXPress's built-in color management feature uses the Kodak Digital Science Color Management System (**CMS**) to accomplish this. The software uses device profiles that contain information about the color characteristics of each piece of hardware in a system, including a monitor, a composite color printer, a scanner, and an imagesetter.

Note

The Kodak CMS used by QuarkXPress uses industry-standard **ICC** (International Color Consortium) profiles; it's compatible with any ICC profiles, whether or not they were designed to be used with Kodak's CMS.

To use XPress's color management features:

1. First make sure that the Quark CMS XTension is in the XTension folder. Windows users also need to look for several DLL files:
   - Cms303.dll
   - Kcm2sp.dll
   - Kpcp32.dll
   - Kpsys32.dll
   - Sprof32.dll

   Mac OS users need to make sure that ColorSync and the Kodak Color Matching Module (CMM) are installed in the System Folder, which includes the following:
   - KODAK PRECISION Startup in the Startup Items folder
   - KODAK CMM, KODAK PRECISION CP1, KODAK PRECISION ProfileAPI, ColorSync™, and the CMSCP folder in the Extensions folder
   - ColorSync™ System Profile in the Control Panels folder
   - ColorSync Profiles folder in the Preferences folder

   If the Mac OS software isn't installed, you'll need to restart your system after installing it. Then start up QuarkXPress (or quit and restart it).
2. If this is the first time you're starting XPress with the color management software installed, you'll see the Auxiliary Profiles Folder dialog (see Figure 9.1). Navigate to the folder that contains ICC profiles on your computer and click the Select [Folder Name] button when you can see the profiles in the file list. If you later move the profiles folder or the XPress folder, you'll see this dialog again and will need to let XPress know once more where to find the profiles.

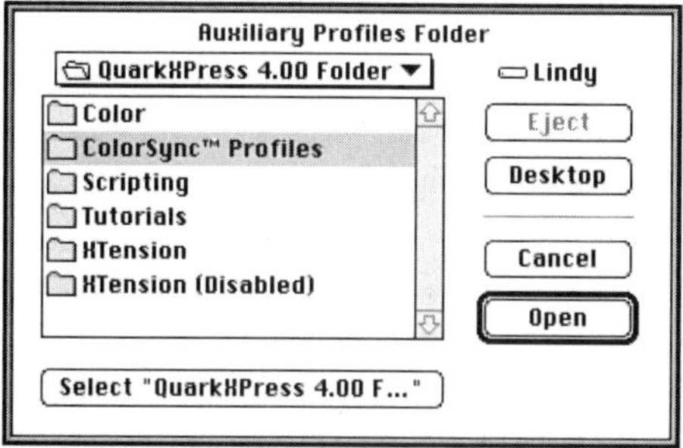

Figure 9.1

The Auxiliary Profiles dialog box.

3. Choose Edit➥Preferences➥Color Management to bring up the Color Management Preferences (see Figure 9.2).

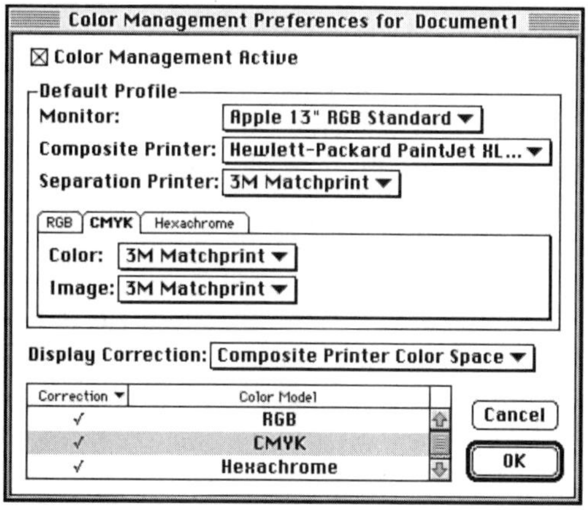

Figure 9.2

The Color Management Preferences dialog box.

4. Click Color Management Active to turn on the color management features.
5. In the Default Profile area, first choose profiles for the devices in your system—the ones you normally use. If the profile you need isn't in the list, contact the device's manufacturer to see where you can find the profile (the company's web site is usually a good place to start). In the top three pop-up menus, choose the "destination" profiles—the ones for the devices that output or display color. Choose a Monitor profile for the monitor on which you will display files. Then choose profiles for Composite Printer (the color printer you plan to use for proofing) and Separation Printer (the imagesetter that will produce film separations of the piece).
6. The RGB, CYMK, and Hexachrome tabs let you specify profiles for the source devices—the ones that created the color in your files. Each tab indicates a different **color space**, so you can specify profiles separately for RGB colors and

images, CMYK colors and images, and Hexachrome colors and images. Each tab has two pop-up menus containing profiles; choose the profiles that should be used for colors created in QuarkXPress from the Color menus, and choose the profiles that should be used for imported images from the Image menus.

In general, you'll choose the appropriate monitor profile from the Color menus, because theoretically you choose XPress colors based on how they look onscreen. And you'd choose the appropriate scanner profiles from the Image menus. For RGB Image, you would probably choose your desktop scanner profile, while for CMYK Image you would choose the profile for your separator's drum scanner.

If you color-correct scanned images based on how images look on your monitor, then you would choose your monitor profile from the Image menu for the appropriate color space. If you convert RGB scans to CMYK in Photoshop using a specific output profile for the device you'll print to, then you would use that profile for CMYK Image.

7. In the Display Correction, choose Off, Monitor Color Space, Composite Printer Color Space, or Separation Printer Color Space. If you choose Off, XPress won't alter the colors displayed on your monitor to reflect the profile information. If you choose one of the other three options, XPress will change its display of color to match as closely as possible the device profile specified in that pop-up menu. For example, if you want to see how the colors in a design will look when it's printed on your color inkjet, you would choose the profile for that printer in the Composite Printer menu and then choose Composite Printer Color Space in the Display Correction menu.
8. Finally, choose which color models XPress should correct. Click a checkmark to turn it off and on, or click the name of a color and choose Yes or No from the Correction pop-up menu.

As with XTensions and PPDs, you can control which device profiles appear in these menus with the Profile Manager. To add or remove profiles from the lists:

1. Choose Utilities➥Profile Manager to bring up the Profile Manager (see Figure 9.3).
2. To determine whether a profile will be included in profile menus, click its name and either click the checkmark off or on or choose Yes or No from the Include pop-up menu.

   Information about each profile is displayed below the list: the profile's location on your system, its filename, and its color space (such as RGB or CMYK). Most monitors and scanners use the RGB color space, while most color printers use CMYK. Kodak's Photo CD images use a special color space called YCC; it has one brightness channel (Y) and two color channels (C and C).

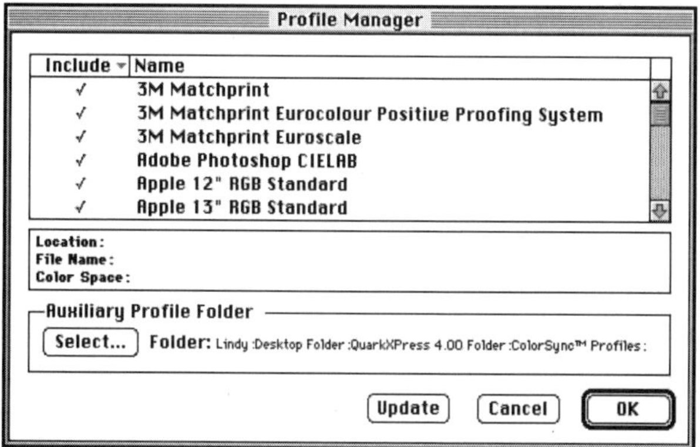

Figure 9.3

The Profile Manager.

3. To change the location of your Auxiliary Profile Folder, click Select and navigate to the correct folder.
4. If you've added profiles to the profile folder since you started QuarkXPress, click Update to add those profiles to the list in the Profile Manager.

Regardless of your preferences, you can specify the profile to be used for any given imported image in the Get Picture dialog box, which adds a section when the color management software is installed (see Figure 9.4). Click Color Correction on and choose the profile you want to use from the Profile pop-up menu.

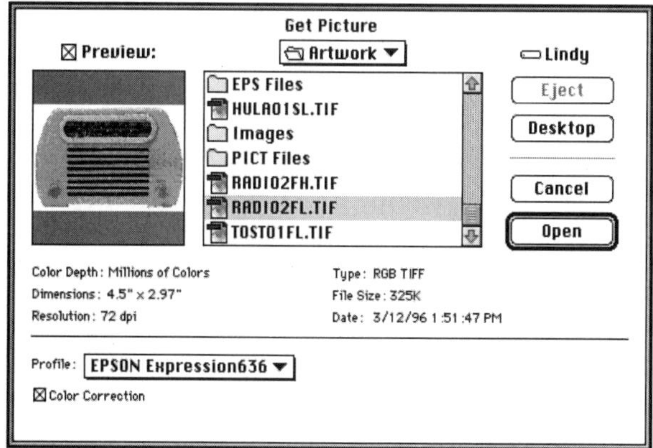

Figure 9.4

The Get Picture dialog box has an extra section when Quark CMS is installed.

Then, once images are imported, you can change their profiles again in the Usage dialog box, which adds a Profiles tab (see Figure 9.5). You can choose a profile from the Profile pop-up menu to see what imported images use that profile. To change the profile used for an image or in the preferences, click it and then click the Replace button. In the

Replace dialog box, choose a new profile and click OK (see Figure 9.6). The area at the bottom of the Profiles Usage tab shows information about the profile, if the profile's manufacturer has embedded any information.

Another way to monitor the profile used for each image is to click on an image and then take a look at the Profile Information palette (choose View➡Show Profile Information). Choose a different profile from the Profile pop-up menu if you want to change the profile. To turn off color correction for that image, click off Color Correction.

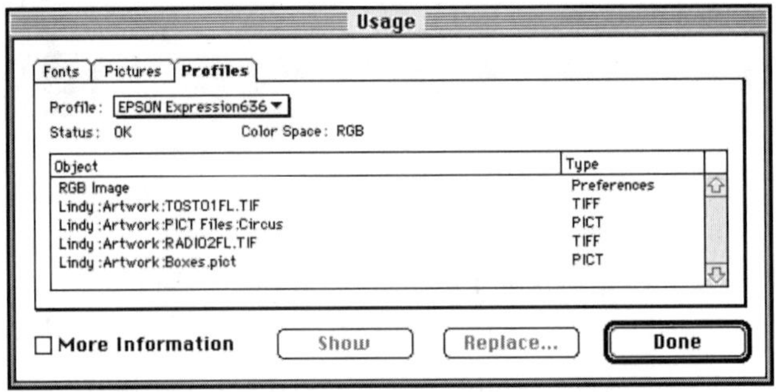

Figure 9.5

The Profiles tab of the Usage dialog box.

Replace Profile

Current Profile: 3M Matchprint

Replace with: Canon CLC500/EFI

Cancel OK

Figure 9.6

The Replace Profile dialog box.

Finally, there's a new Color Management tab in the Print dialog box (see Figure 9.7). These settings give you another chance to change your mind about the profiles specified in the preferences. To change the Separation or Composite Profile, choose another profile from the list. A note at the bottom of the tab tells you that the choices you make here will be used in the preferences. If you want to simulate the results of printing to your chosen separation printer when you're printing to a composite printer, click Composite Simulates Separation.

Although all this is quite impressive, and it gives us much more control over color reproduction than we had just a couple of years ago, it's not yet perfect. For one thing, most people use device profiles supplied by equipment manufacturers, which can characterize the color fidelity of a class of devices but can't take into account quirks that one particular device may have. You can create your own device profiles using extra software, like ColorSynergy (Mac OS, Candela) or ColorBlind ICC Print (Mac OS/Windows, Color Solutions), and equipment, like the Colortron II (Mac OS/Windows, Light Source).

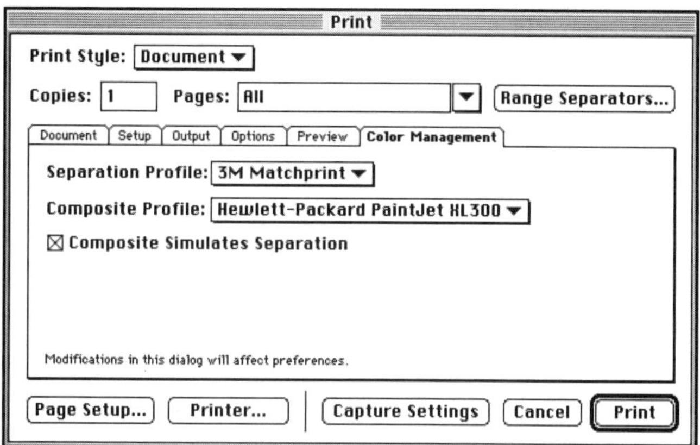

Figure 9.7

The Color Management tab of the Print dialog box.

This system also doesn't take into account ambient lighting or many other factors that can influence color. Bottom line: Don't rely on color management software until testing under your typical working conditions has proved it accurate.

Defining and Using Colors

Every QuarkXPress document starts out with a set of default colors, including the four process colors (cyan, magenta, yellow, and black), the three video colors (red, green, and blue), and white. Before you can use other colors, such as spot colors from systems like Pantone's or process mix colors, you have to define them. You can also combine colors you've defined to create multi-ink colors. Once you've defined a color, you can apply it to text, boxes, box borders, lines, and even imported pictures. When you're defining colors, it's best to have the appropriate printed swatchbook next to your computer so you can see what each color will look like when it's printed. Judging colors by their appearance on a computer monitor—even if it's very expensive and perfectly calibrated—can lead to expensive mistakes.

This project is a book cover that uses both process colors and a Pantone spot color.

1. Open lessons/chap09/voodoo.qxd on the CD that came with this book (see Figure 9.8). This is the front cover of an imaginary novel by a Louisiana writer; if it were a real book cover this file would also include the book's back cover, spine, and flaps.

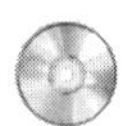

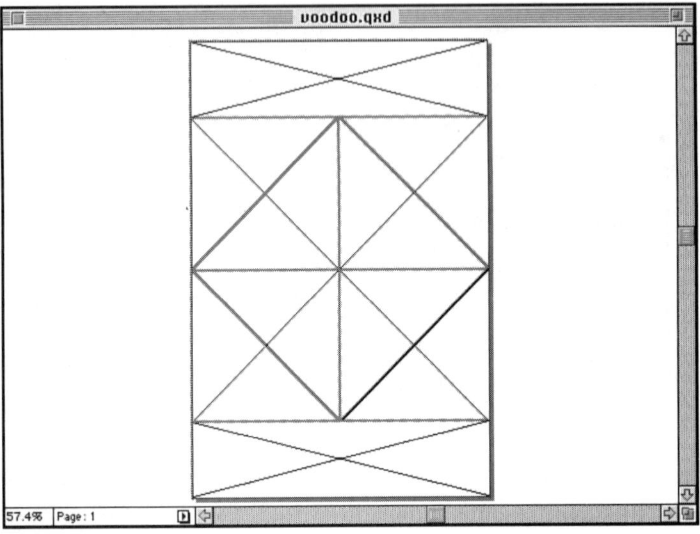

Figure 9.8

The boxes that become a book cover.

Note

This project uses the Mondõ Kaizen (in the Synstelien folder on the CD) and VT Nervous Reich (in the Vintage folder on the CD) fonts included on the CD that accompanies this book, so you'll need to make sure those fonts are installed before starting.

2. Make sure guides are on (choose View➡Show Guides or press F7) so that you can see the edges of the boxes on this page. Choose View➡Show Colors or press F12 to show the Colors palette if it's not visible. The default colors in the Colors palette list are Black, Blue, Cyan, Green, Magenta, Red, White, and Yellow (see Figure 9.9). None appears at the top of the list when it's an option—for example, a box's background can have a color of None, but type can't.

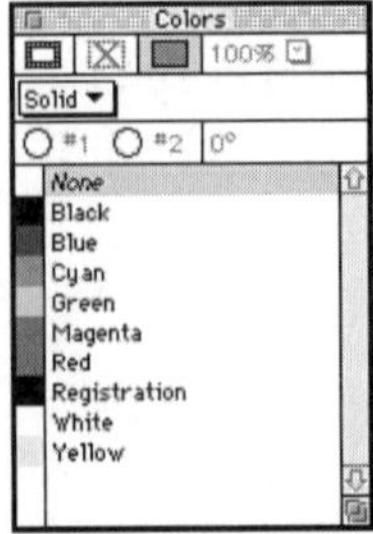

Figure 9.9

The Colors palette.

3. With either the Item tool or the Content tool, click the rectangular box at the top of the page and Shift-click the matching box at the bottom of the page. Click the third (background color) icon at the top of the Colors palette, and click Black in the color list to turn both boxes black (see Figure 9.10).

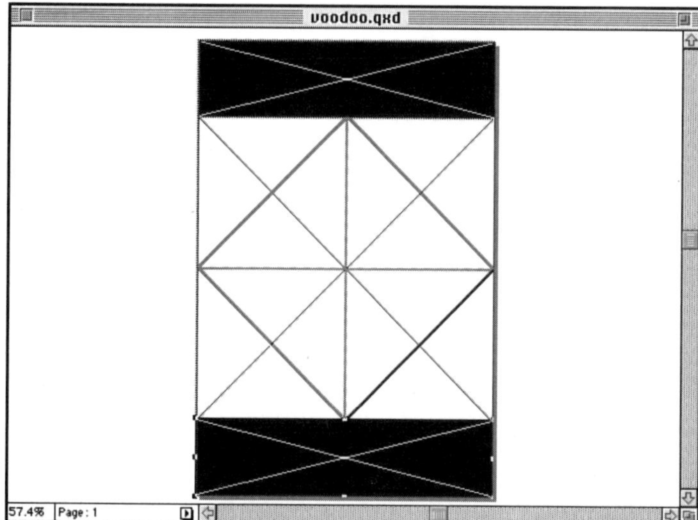

Figure 9.10

The top and bottom boxes are black.

4. Choose Edit➡Colors or press Shift-F12 to bring up the Colors dialog box (see Figure 9.11, which works like the Styles dialog (see Day 5, "Formatting Text and Using Style Sheets"). A window shows all the colors defined in the documents, and buttons let you create new colors, duplicate or edit existing ones, delete them, append colors from other documents, and, of course, cancel or save your changes. A second window shows the description of the color you've clicked, and a Show menu lets you choose to view All Colors, Spot Colors, Process Colors, Multi-Ink Colors, Colors In Use, or Colors Not Used in the document.

Tip

A quick way to open the Colors dialog box is to (Command-click)[Control-click] one of the colors in the Colors palette. The dialog box will open with that color selected, so you can just press (Return)[Enter] to edit it. This trick works with the Style Sheets and Lists palettes, too.

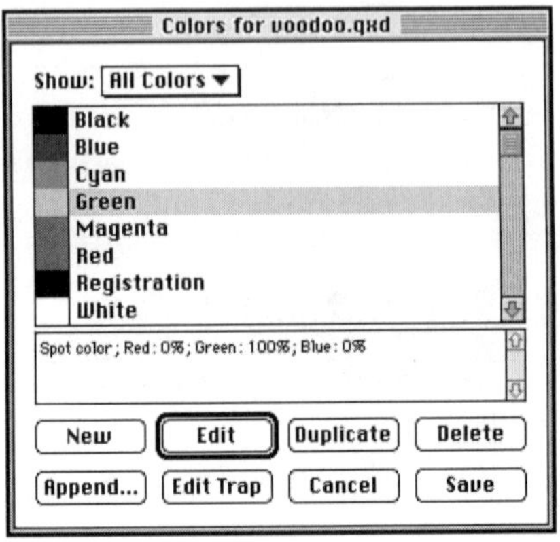

Figure 9.11

The Colors dialog box.

5. Click New to bring up the Edit Color dialog box (see Figure 9.12). The first four colors to be defined are process colors, made up of the CMYK inks. Choose TRUMATCH from the Model pop-up menu and click Spot Color off; this lets you use the TruMatch system to choose process colors. Click in the TRUMATCH field and type "20-b7" to skip quickly to the first TruMatch color we need in the color swatch area. XPress automatically fills in the Name field with "TRUMATCH" and the color's number. Click OK to return to the Color dialog, where TRUMATCH 20-b7 (a dark green) has been added to the list of defined colors.

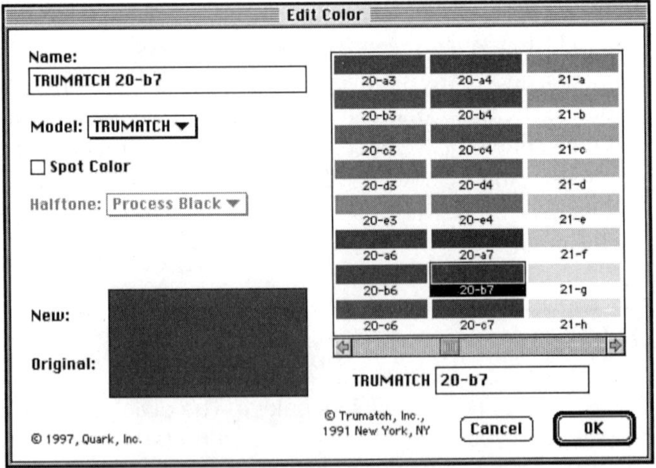

Figure 9.12

The Edit Color dialog box.

6. Define three more colors the same way: TRUMATCH 35-b1 (dark blue), TRUMATCH 39-b (dark purple), and TRUMATCH 48-a6 (dark red). Be sure

to click Spot Color off for each color, and don't skip the hyphen in each color number. When you're done, click Save to save the new colors and return to the document.

Note

You can also choose colors by just clicking in the color swatch area, which is fine when you're just working out design ideas. Be sure to consult a swatch-book before finalizing colors, though, to be sure of what each color will look like when it's printed.

7. The central portion of the book cover consists of four colored squares with a diffused black diamond shape drawn over them. To achieve this effect, the design actually uses eight triangles with blended fills. To create the first square, click in the upper-left triangle and choose Linear Blend from the blend pop-up menu on the Colors palette.
8. Objects with blended fills use two colors, the background color (#1) and the blend color (#2). To specify the background color for the first triangle, click the #1 radio button and choose TRUMATCH 48-a6 in the Colors palette. Then click the #2 radio button and choose Black. In the Colors palette's angle field, enter 225° so that the black runs along the triangle's diagonal edge (see Figure 9.13).

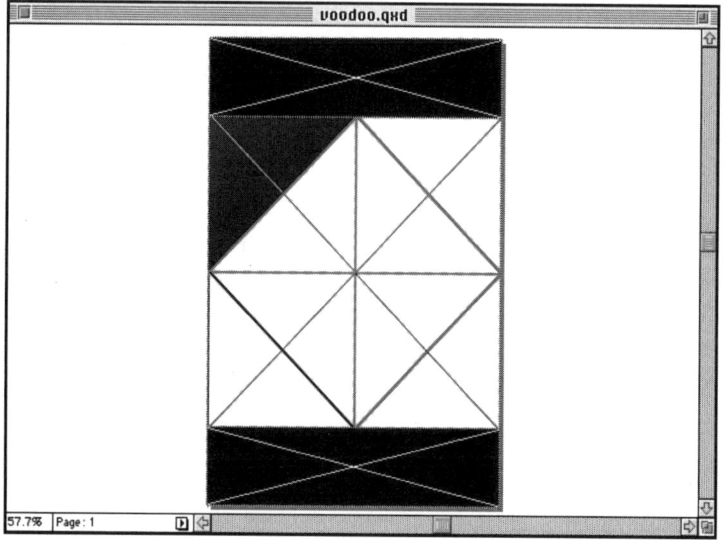

Figure 9.13

The blend can run in any direction.

9. Click in the triangle whose diagonal edge abuts the black edge of the first triangle and choose Linear Blend. Enter 45° in the angle field, and choose the same colors as in Step 8 (#1: TRUMATCH 48-a6, #2: Black). The black edge of this triangle should be adjacent to the black edge of the first triangle so that the two triangles look like a square with a soft black line running diagonally across it (see Figure 9.14).

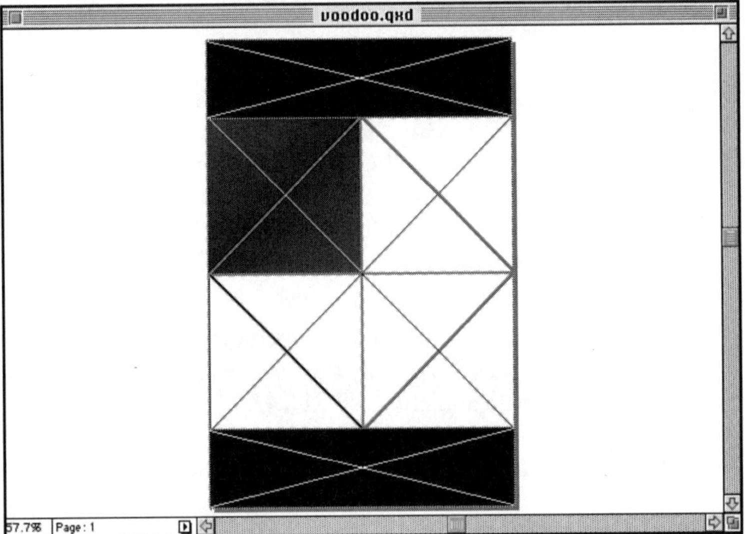

Figure 9.14

The two triangles form a square.

10. Click in the upper right triangle and give it a linear blend with an angle of 135°, then choose TRUMATCH 35-b1 for color #1 and black for color #2. Click in the adjacent triangle and give it a linear blend with an angle of 315°, then choose the same colors. This results in a blue square similar to the red one except that the black line runs from the top left to the bottom right (see Figure 9.15).
11. Click in the lower left triangle and give it a linear blend with an angle of 315°, then choose TRUMATCH 39-b for color #1 and black for color #2. Click in the adjacent triangle and give it a linear blend with an angle of 135°, then choose the same colors. This results in a purple square with a black line running from the top left to the bottom right (see Figure 9.16).

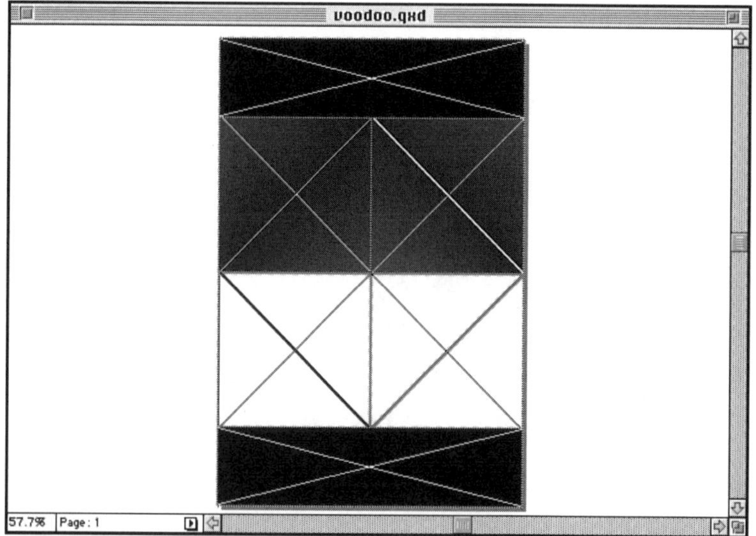

Figure 9.15

The black line in this square runs down instead of up.

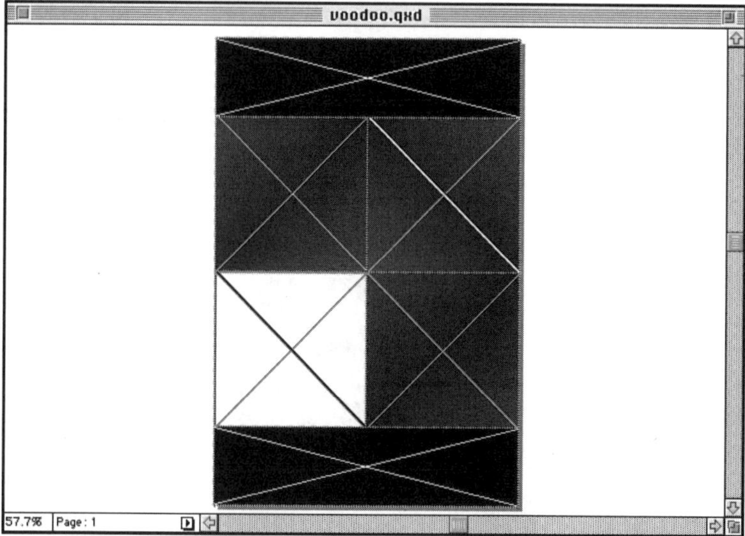

Figure 9.16

The black line in this square is at the same angle as in the first square.

12. Click in the lower right triangle and give it a linear blend with an angle of 45°, then choose TRUMATCH 35-b1 for color #1 and black for color #2. Click in the adjacent triangle and give it a linear blend with an angle of 225°, then choose the same colors. This results in a green square with a black line running from the top right to the bottom left (see Figure 9.17).

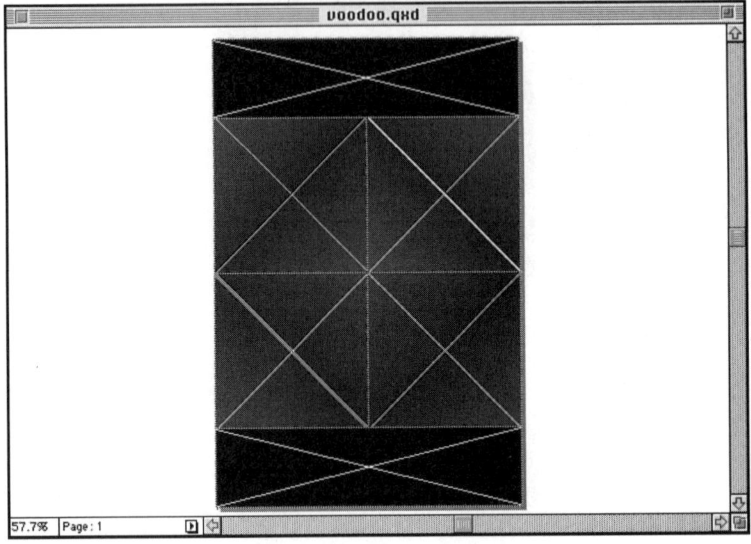

Figure 9.17

The black line in this square is at the same angle as in the second square.

13. Draw a text box over the top black box, slightly smaller than the black box. Shift-click to select both the text box and the black box and press (Command-,)[Control-,] or choose Item➡Space/Align. In the Space/Align dialog box, click Horizontal; leave the Space value at 0 and choose Centers from the Between pop-up menu. Click OK to center the text box on the black box (see Figure 9.18).

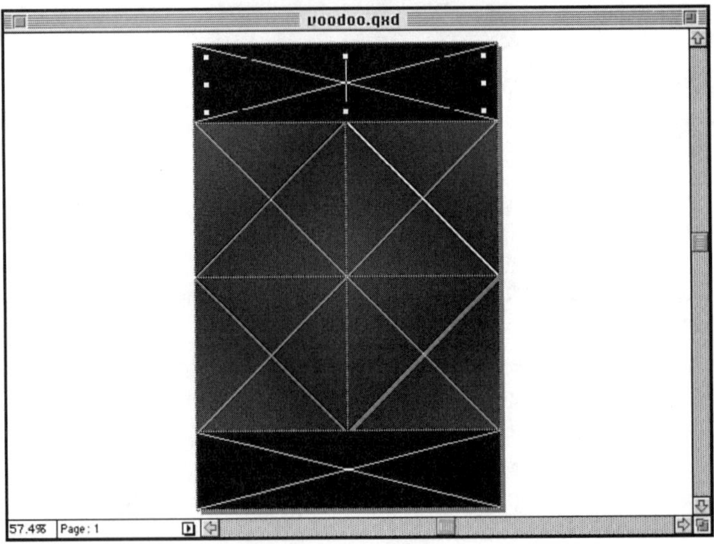

Figure 9.18

This text box will hold the book's title.

14. Press Shift-F12 to bring up the Colors dialog box and click New to define the color for the book's title. Choose Pantone from the Model pop-up menu and scroll through the swatch area until you see the swatch for Purple (or type "purple" in the PANTONE field). Make sure that Spot Color is clicked on, and click OK to add the color to the color list, then Save to save changes.

Note

Here's a good example of a color that just can't be produced using traditional process color—Pantone Purple. It's brighter and more intense than any process purple.

15. Type "Voodoo Loco" in the text box. Select the text and make it 48-point VTNervouzReich-Boots. With the text still selected, click the middle (type) icon at the top of the Colors palette and choose PANTONE Purple CV from the color list, then press (Command-Shift-C)[Control-Shift-C] to center the text (see Figure 9.19).

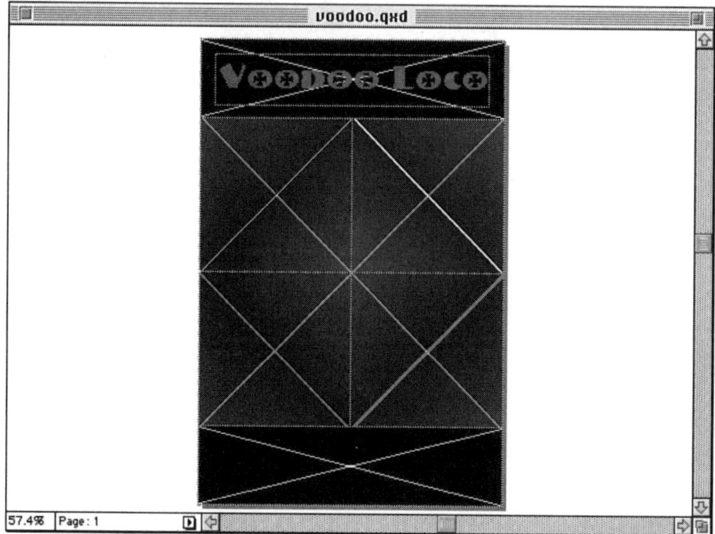

Figure 9.19

The book's title is a Pantone color, not a process mix.

16. With the Item tool, click and drag to select all eight triangles, then press (Command-G)[Control-G] to group them.

17. Draw a text box about one inch square in the center of the grouped triangles. Type "r" in the box, then select it and change the font to Mondõ Kaizen and the size to 48 points. With the type still selected, choose Yellow from the Colors palette to change its color to yellow.
18. With the Item tool, Shift-click the new text box and the triangle group to select both. Press (Command-,)[Control-,] to bring up the Space/Align dialog. Click both Horizontal and Vertical; leave the Space value on both sides at 0 and choose Centers from both Between pop-up menus. Click OK to center the text box on the triangle group (see Figure 9.20).

Figure 9.20

The heart icon is 100 percent process yellow.

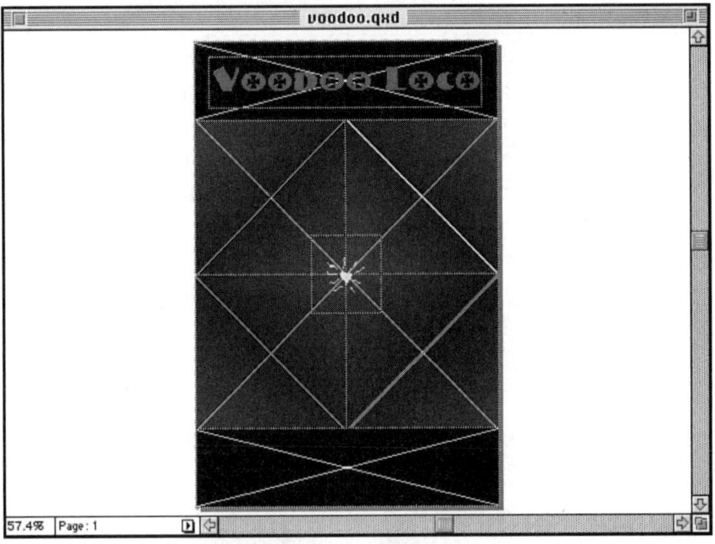

19. Draw another text box over the bottom black box and center it horizontally on the black box, as in Step 13, then position it slightly closer to the top of the black box than to the bottom. In the box, type "a novel by" then press (Return)[Enter] and type "Jefferson Parrish" on the next line.
20. Press (Command-A)[Control-A] to select all, then change the font to VTNervouzReich-Boots, the size to 18 points, and the color to Pantone Purple. Triple-click in the second line to select it and change the size to 24 points (see Figure 9.21).

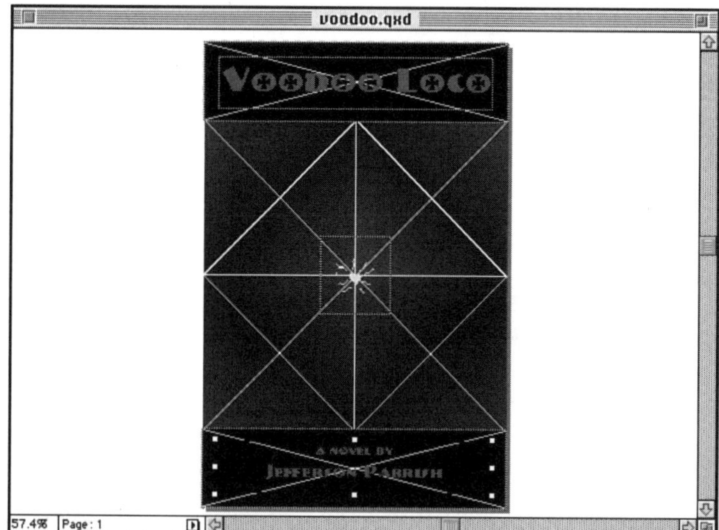

Figure 9.21

The name of the book's author is the same purple as the title.

21. Make a darker color for the line "a novel by" by pressing Shift-F12 to bring up the Colors dialog box, then clicking New. In the Edit Colors dialog box, choose Multi-Ink from the Model pop-up men and make sure Spot Color is clicked off (see Figure 9.22).

    All the ink colors defined in the document so far appear in a color list at the right of the dialog box; choose CMYK or Hexachrome from the pop-up menu above the list to view either the traditional process colors or the Hexachrome ones. The TruMatch colors don't show in this list because they're mixtures of process inks.

    The new color will be composed of part Pantone Purple and part black, so enter "Dark purple" in the Name dialog box. Click PANTONE Purple CV in the color list and choose 100 percent from the Shade pop-up menu, then click on Process Black and choose 40 percent from the Shade pop-up menu. Click OK to create the color, then click Save to return to the document.

22. Triple-click in the "a novel by" line to select the text, then click Dark purple in the Colors palette to apply the color to the text. That finishes the design (see Figure 9.23).

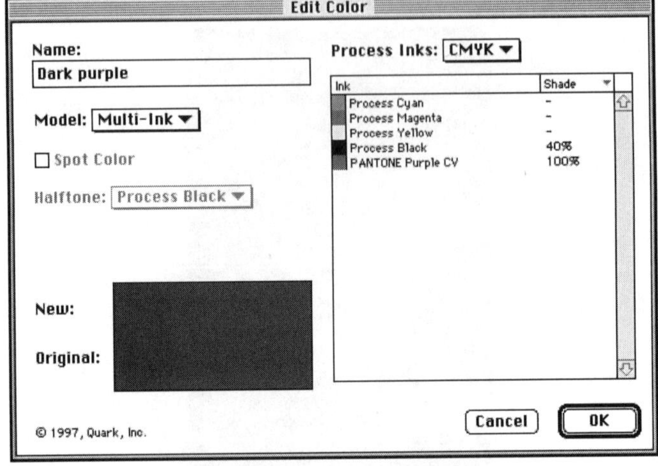

Figure 9.22

Rather than showing color swatches or a color wheel, the Multi-Ink model lets you combine inks already defined in the document.

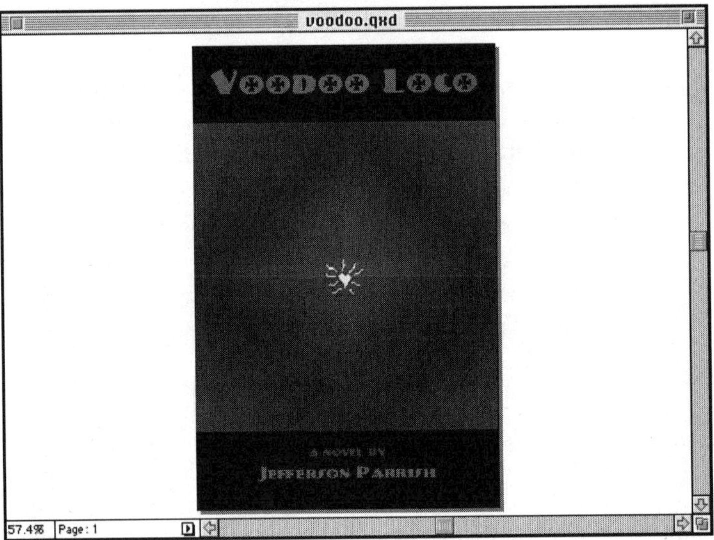

Figure 9.23

The design is complete.

23. To change any of the colors used, (Command-click)[Control-click] the color in the Colors palette, then press (Return)[Enter] to bring up the Edit Color dialog box. Choose another model if you prefer, and then choose a color from the color swatch area. You can also change a process color by moving the sliders to change the percentages of cyan, magenta, yellow, and black that make up the color. Color swatches at the left of the dialog box show the difference between the original color and your changed version. Click OK to change the

color and, in the Edit Colors dialog box, click Save to save your changes. Every instance of the original color, whether it's used in the document or in a style sheet, is changed to the new color.

Note

The only colors you can't edit are the four process colors and white.

If you used the colors listed here, everything on the cover except for the purple type is a process color. When this piece is printed, there will be five color plates—one for each of the four process colors, and one for the purple type (see Figure 9.24). You could save money by changing the purple type to a process color, or you could spend more money by using spot colors for the yellow heart and the eight colored triangles. Spot colors might be more vivid, depending on the colors used, and they would be easier to match when printing other pieces.

As with style sheets, you can append colors from other documents. In the Colors dialog box, click Append, then choose the document from which you want to add colors. In the Append Colors dialog box, choose the colors you want to add, then click Append to bring them into the current document. If identical color names are already used in the document, you can choose to cancel the operation, use the new colors, use the old colors, or rename the new colors.

a

b

Figure 9.24

The negatives that would be used to make printing plates for the book cover: (a) cyan, (b) magenta...

Figure 9.24

...(c) yellow, (d) black, and (e) Pantone Purple.

c

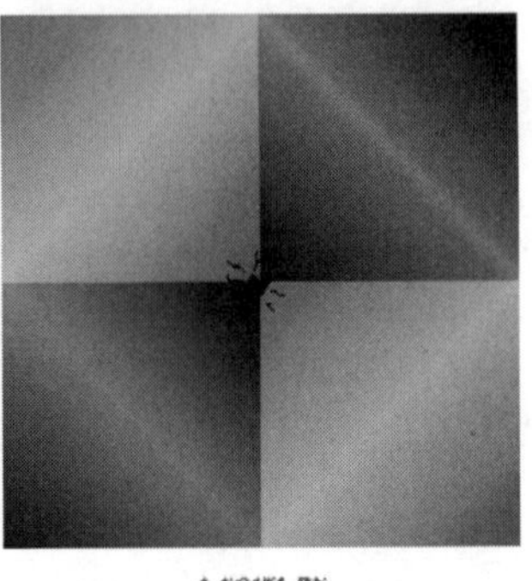

d

e

You may notice colors that you didn't define appearing mysteriously in the Colors palette. This is due to a truly handy feature of QuarkXPress—adding custom colors used in imported graphics. Any time you import a graphic that uses a spot color not defined in the XPress document, that color is automatically added to the document's color list. (See "Why Do I Have Two Spot Plates for the Same Color?" later in this chapter, for a common problem this feature creates.)

Troubleshooting

Using color in your documents costs money, whether you're printing them on a color printer or having film separations or printing plates output from your files. If you're printing separations, it's wise to check that colors are separating the way you want them to by printing separations on a laser printer first. Then there's the perennial problem of getting what you see to match what you get in terms of color. Here are a few of the most common questions that using color in QuarkXPress can prompt.

Why Aren't the Spot Colors Printing on Separate Plates?

The spot colors are separating into their CMYK equivalents. There are three reasons this might be happening.

- The spot colors are used in an imported graphic and they're not properly specced as spot colors in the image file. You'll need to open each graphic in its original application and make sure that the colors are specified as spot colors rather than process colors.
- The spot colors are specced as process equivalents within QuarkXPress. To change them back to spot colors, choose Edit➡Colors, click a spot color to change, and click Edit. In the Edit Color dialog box, click Spot Color to make sure that this color is treated as a spot color—in other words, that it will print on its own plate.
- In the Output tab of the Print dialog box, Convert to Process is chosen from the Plates pop-up menu, rather than Process & Spot. This option converts all spot colors to their process equivalents on-the-fly, while printing, without changing the colors' definitions.

Why Do I Have All Spot Color Plates Instead of Process Color Plates?

This is the opposite of the previous problem and the answer is that the colors used are specced as spot colors rather than process equivalents in either the graphics used, the XPress colors, or both. You'll need to uncheck Spot Color in the XPress Edit Color dialog box to fix XPress colors, and you'll need to open each image file in its original application to change its color definitions.

Why Do I Have Two Spot Plates for the Same Color?

This one gets everyone sooner or later. The answer is that the two plates aren't really for the same color. Look closely at the color names printed next to the filename by the upper left cropmarks—chances are, they're not *exactly* the same. One common difference is with Pantone colors; some applications add a "C" after the number, while others add "CV." So if you're using Pantone 273 CV in an XPress document, and you import a graphic from an application that calls that same color Pantone 273 C, you're in trouble. The answer is simply to edit the name of the color in either the graphics application or XPress so that it matches the other version.

If you change the color name in the graphics application, you can make sure the problem is solved by deleting the non-Quark version of the color in the Colors dialog box, then reimport the graphic. If the color is still different, you'll have two versions of the color name in the Colors palette again. If it's the same as the color used in the XPress document, the Colors list will stay the same.

Why Don't the Printed Colors Look the Same as When I Specced Them Onscreen?

Computer monitors use light to represent colors, while printers and printing presses use liquid or solid coloring agents like ink and colored wax. Because of this inescapable fact, it's impossible to have a perfect match between the colors you see onscreen and the ones you get from your printer. With expensive high-end monitors (like the Radius PressView), precise calibration, and color management software, you can come pretty close, but most people's systems don't have these advantages.

Color management software attempts to "translate" colors from RGB to CMYK and back again as closely as possible. QuarkXPress's built-in color management features can help you achieve better results, but it's still best to rely on swatchbooks and contract proofs rather than your monitor. Contract proofs are color proofs supplied by a printer that are so accurate that the printer will promise to match those colors on-press. For four-color printing work, consult with your printer to see how you can improve color fidelity throughout the design and production process.

Summary

Color is one of the reasons QuarkXPress has reigned supreme in the world of page layout software. XPress uses the color models to which professionals expect to have access, and its built-in trapping has simplified production, since little additional work is required on film output directly from XPress. With version 4.0, color management will make the results of the color production process more predictable. As always, though, it's important to understand the differences between spot and process color and make sure that you communicate with your service bureau or printer about what your color expectations are.

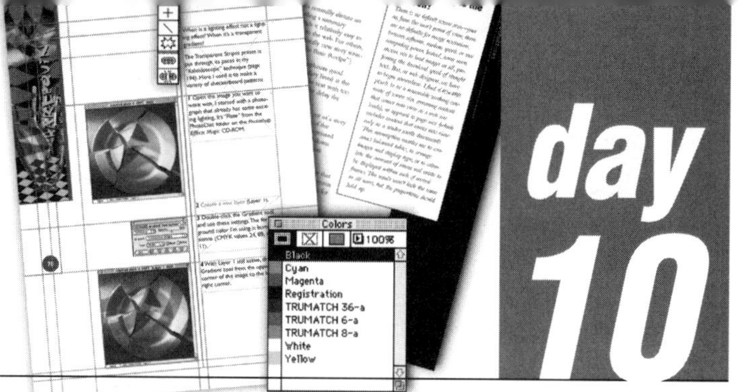

Managing Long Documents

- Organizing chapter files with books
- Creating indexes
- Creating tables of contents

During the last few years, as software publishers have run out of layout features to add to page layout programs, they've turned to other features, like HTML export and better integration with their other products. Another set of features that's gotten more popular is long-document management features, which let you keep track of and organize files that make up long documents like books and journals. QuarkXPress 4.0 includes three features in this category: multi-file books, indexing, and list generation.

These features work together to assist in the creation of long documents. First, book files let you keep the separate chapter files that make up a book stylistically consistent and numbered correctly. Then the indexing and list generation features let you create indexes, tables of contents, lists of figures and tables, and the other peripheral files that books require. In this chapter you'll create a book file containing several chapters, synchronize the chapters' styles and page numbering, then generate a table of contents and an index for the book.

Coordinating Multi-File Books

A book file doesn't contain any document pages; instead, it holds information about a collection of XPress files that together make up one long document. These can be chapters in a book, articles in a journal, or any other components of a larger whole. Grouping files together in a book lets you control their formatting and numbering, two functions that are vital in creating books and other long documents.

Here you'll create a book file composed of five sample files.

1. Choose File➡New➡Book (see Figure 10.1).

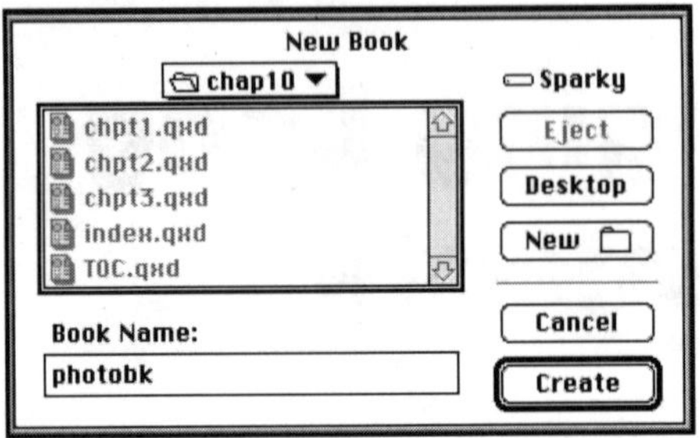

Figure 10.1

The New Book dialog box.

2. Enter a name for the new book (this example uses "photobk") and click Create to save the book file and display the Book palette (see Figure 10.2). Several buttons across the top of the palette control the book's functions, and each file in the book is listed. The M column indicates which chapter is the master chapter. The Document column shows the name and path of the chapter files. The Pages column lists the chapters' page numbers, and the Status column indicates whether the chapter files are open or available to be opened.

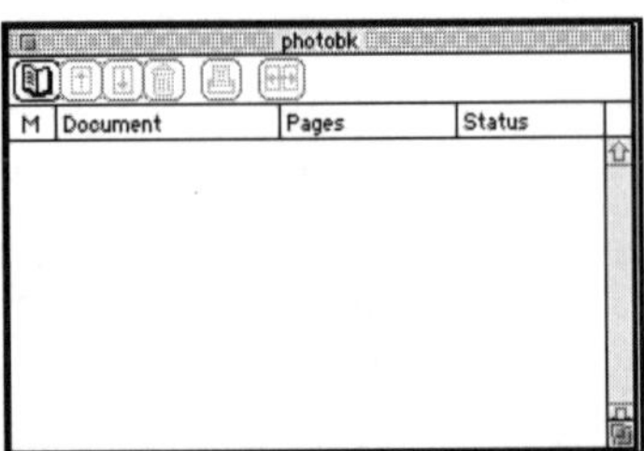

Figure 10.2

The Book palette.

3. Click the open book button at the top left of the palette to add chapters to the book (see Figure 10.3). Navigate to lessons/chap10/chpt1.qxd and click Add to make this file part of the book.

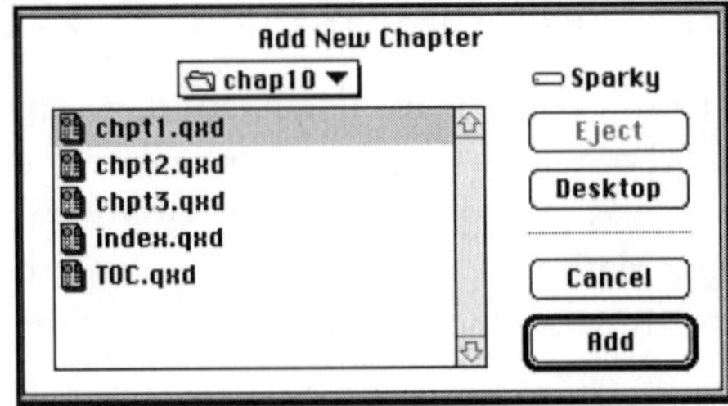

Figure 10.3

Adding a new chapter.

The first chapter you add is the master chapter, and this status can't be changed except by deleting that chapter from the book. When you synchronize the book to make its styles consistent, this is the chapter that XPress will base its changes on, so any formatting changes that you want applied to the whole book will need to be made in this chapter.

Warning

Always be sure that the master chapter is correctly formatted before you update the book, and don't use a chapter for the master that has different formats from the rest of the book, such as the front matter.

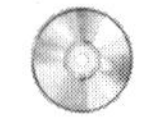

4. Add chpt2.qxd, chpt3.qxd, and frntmat.qxd to the book. Place the chapters in the desired order by clicking a chapter name and then clicking the up or down arrow button to move the chapter in the list. When you're done, the Book palette should look like Figure 10.4.

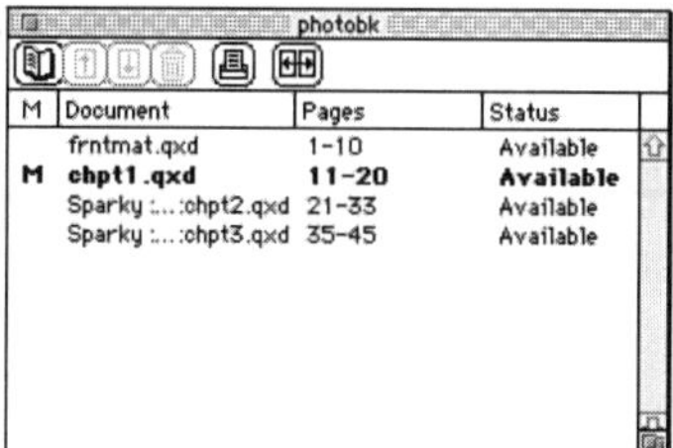

Figure 10.4

The Book palette, complete with chapters of the book.

As you add chapter files to the book, their pages are automatically renumbered in consecutive order. XPress takes into account whether a chapter begins with a left- or right-hand page, assigning numbering accordingly. So if Chapter 1 ends on page 7, a right page, and Chapter 2 starts with a right page, the first page in Chapter 2 will be page 9.

Note

If a chapter contains page numbers that have been specified in the Section dialog, those pages won't be renumbered.

You can delete a chapter from the book by clicking its name and then clicking the (trash can)[**X**] button.

5. Double-click chpt1.qxd in the Book palette to open it, then press (F10)[F4]to show the Document Layout palette if it's not visible.
6. Click the icon for the first page of the file, then click the page number field in the lower left-hand corner of the Document Layout palette to bring up the Section dialog (see Figure 10.5). Click the Section Start box and enter 1 in the Number field, then click OK to apply the change. Before, this file started on page 3, because the frntmat.qxd file was two pages long; now it starts on page 1. It's customary to start numbering book pages at the beginning of the first chapter rather than on the first page of the book.

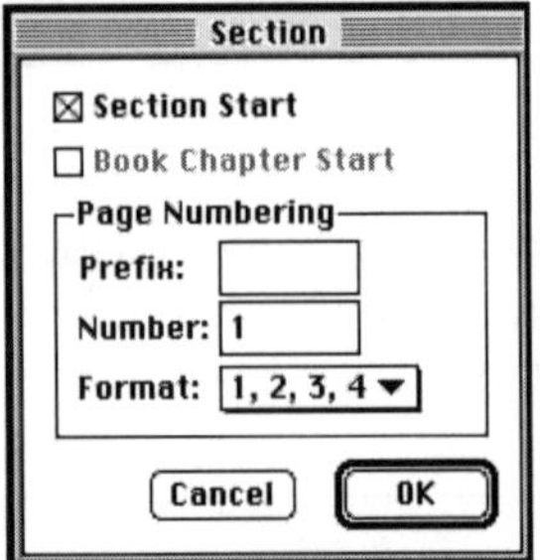

Figure 10.5

Change the page numbering of Chapter 1 in the Section dialog.

7. Double-click frntmat.qxd in the Book palette to open it.
8. Click the icon for the first page of the file, then click the page number field in the lower left-hand corner of the Document Layout palette to bring up the Section dialog. Click the Section Start box and enter 1 in the Number field, then choose lower-case Roman numerals from the Format pop-up menu and click OK to apply the change. Now this file starts with page i and ends with page ii, which is the customary way to number front matter pages in books.

Note

"Front matter" consists of the pages that come before the first chapter in a book. Elements of a front matter section might include a half-title page (with just the book's title), a title page (with the title, author, publisher, and other information), a copyright page, a table of contents, a dedication, and an introduction. Conversely, "back matter" includes pages that come after the last chapter in a book, such as an index.

9. Double-click chpt2.qxd in the Book palette to open it. The formatting in this chapter is slightly different from the formatting in chpt1.qxd—different fonts have been used for the text and headings (see Figure 10.6).

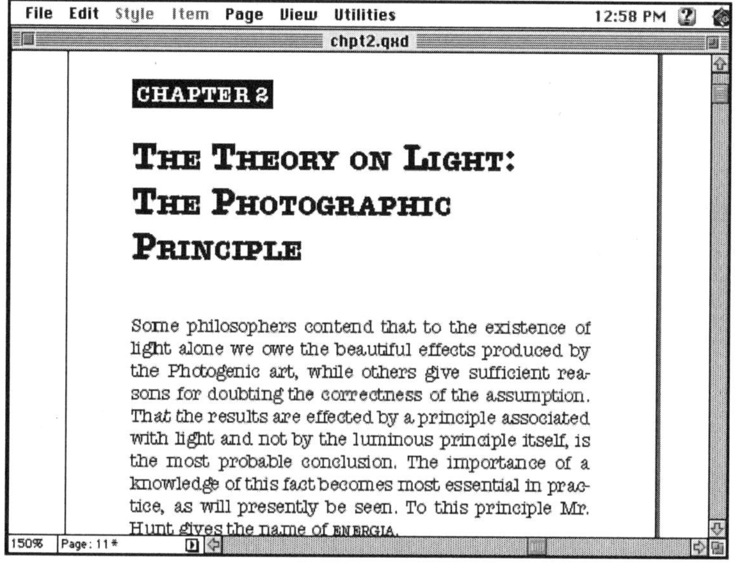

Figure 10.6

Chapter 2 has been incorrectly formatted with Typewriter instead of Vendome.

10. Synchronize the chapters by clicking the double-arrow button in the upper right-hand corner of the Book palette. The style sheet, color, H&J, lists, and dashes and stripes settings of chpt2.qxd and the other chapters in the book will be changed to match those in the master chapter, chpt1.qxd (see Figure 10.7). If the other chapters include styles that aren't in the master chapter, those styles won't be changed or deleted.

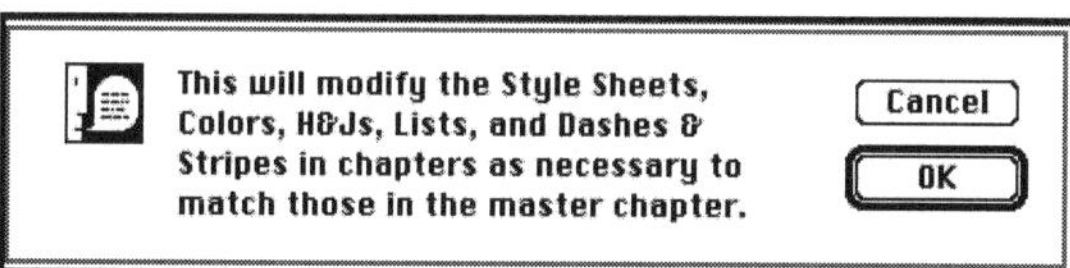

Figure 10.7

XPress lets you know exactly what it's about to do when you synchronize a book.

11. To print the book, click the printer button at the top of the palette to bring up the Print dialog. Change the settings, if needed, and click Print to print all the chapter files in the order in which they appear in the Book palette.

Once a book has been created, you can open it by choosing File➡Open and navigating to the book file. While chapters can belong to more than one book, changes made by one book file will override previous changes made by another book file. If you add a chapter that already belongs to another book, you'll see a warning dialog to remind you of this (see Figure 10.8).

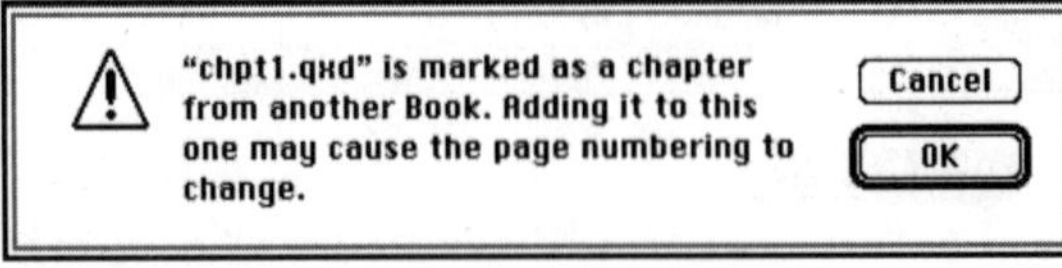

Figure 10.8

It's generally not a good idea to add chapters to two different books.

Creating an Index

There are three basic steps to creating an index for a book. First, you insert index markers in the chapter files, indicating what terms should be included in the index. Then, you create an index file, with the appropriate master pages and style sheets. Finally, you use the Build Index command to actually generate and format the index text. This example uses the same chapters and book file from the previous example.

1. If the photobk Book palette isn't visible, choose File➡Open and navigate to the book file on your hard drive. Click Open to open the book.
2. Double-click its name in the Book palette to open chpt1.qxd.
3. Choose View➡Show Index if the Index palette isn't visible (see Figure 10.9). On the first page of the file, double-click to select the words "Photogenic drawing" and click Add on the Index palette to insert an index marker for this text.

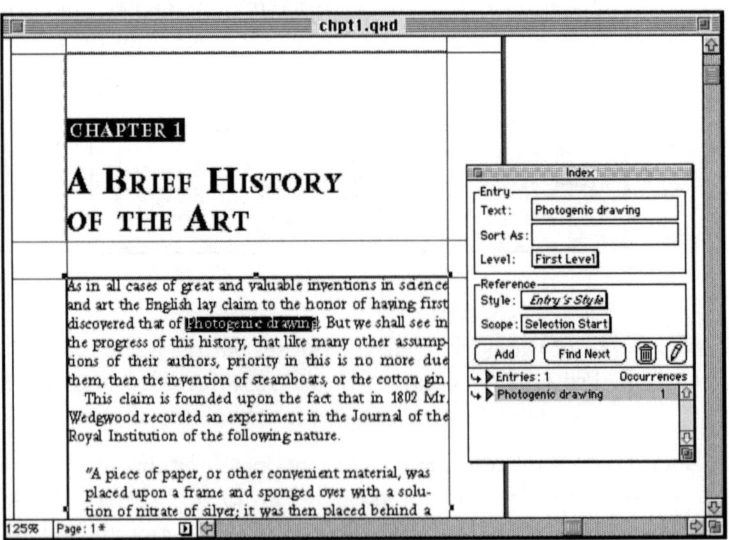

Figure 10.9

Add an index marker at the term "Photogenic drawing."

4. Use the Find command ((Command-F)[Control-F]) to find all the other occurrences of "Photogenic drawing" in the document and insert index markers at those points. Click Whole Word on in the Find/Change dialog box to make sure you'll find those exact words each time. You don't need to click in the document to add the words—just click Find Next in the Find dialog and then click Add. Repeat until all occurrences of "Photogenic drawing" have been added to the Index palette. The number next to that entry in the palette increases as you mark additional occurrences.
5. Return to the first page of the chapter and select the name "Sir Humphry Davey." In the Text field of the Index palette, retype the name as "Davey, Sir Humphry," then click Add on the Index palette to insert an index marker for this name (see Figure 10.10). When you generate the index for the book, this name will appear as "Davey, Sir Humphry" rather than "Sir Humphry Davey."

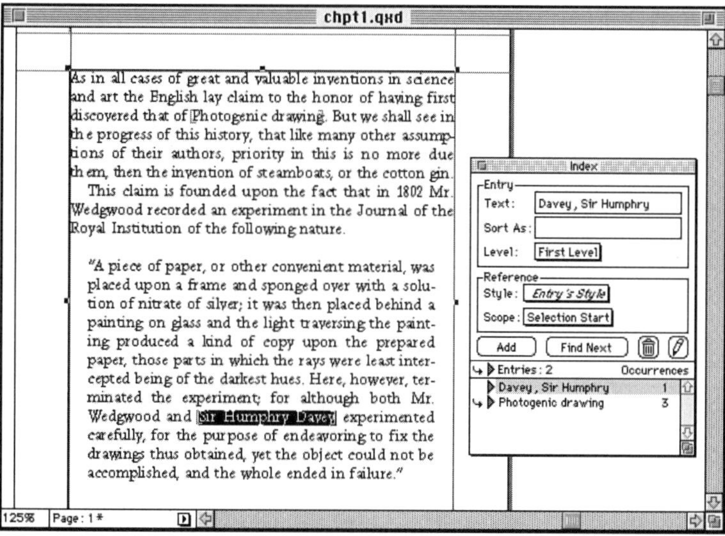

Figure 10.10

Index text doesn't have to match the text where the marker is inserted.

6. "Photogenic art" appears on the third page of the chapter, but if you just select it and click Add, it will appear in the index just that way, rather than as an additional reference to "Photogenic drawing." To sort this text properly, first select it, then click the correct entry in the Index palette—"Photogenic drawing"—before clicking Add.

7. On pages 5 and 6 of the chapter, there's a discussion of early experiments in portrait photography. While these words don't actually appear as such in the text, you can use "portrait photography" as the index entry. Select the range of text that starts with "The process was a secret" and ends with "this splendid discovery" and type "Portrait photography" in the Text field of the Index palette. Then choose Selection text from the Scope pop-up menu to make sure that the index entry references both pages containing this text. Click Add to add the entry.

Tip

You can choose the character style that will be used in the index for each entry. Choose Entry's Style from the Style pop-up menu to leave the entry as it is in the document, or choose from the list of character styles available in the document.

8. All the entries added to the index so far have been first-level entries, rather than subentries. Select "Daguerreotype portrait" on page 6 and choose Second Level from the Level pop-up menu. Type "Daguerreotype" in the Text field, then click in the left column of the palette list next to "Portrait photography" and click Add. A curved arrow appears next to "Portrait photography," indicating that it has a subentry, and "Daguerreotype" appears in the entry list indented slightly under "Portrait photography" (see Figure 10.11). When you generate the index, this entry will appear as a subentry under the first-level entry "Portrait photography."

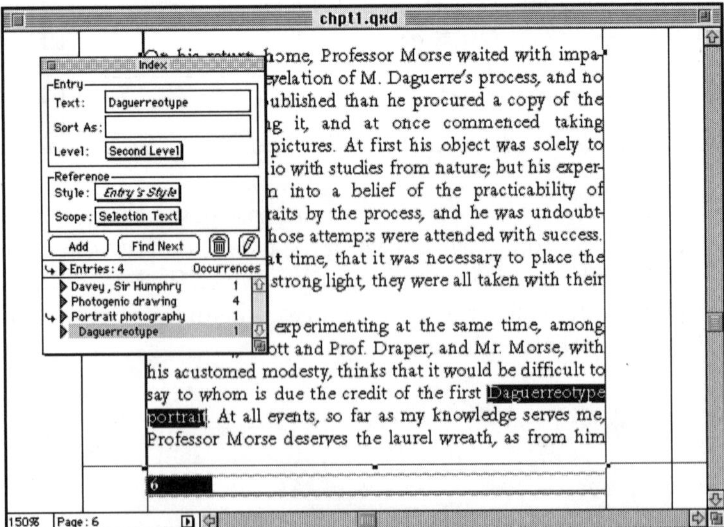

Figure 10.11

XPress allows for four levels of entries in an index.

9. Continue adding as many index entries as you like in all three chapters of the book. To specify that an entry should appear out of alphabetical order in the index, type the text that you want used to alphabetize the entry in the Sort field. For example, entries starting with numbers will be placed before the entries starting with "A," but you can place them in alphabetical order by spelling them out in the Sort field. That won't affect the way they appear in the index, only where they're placed.

Tip

To see where index markers are on the pages, click the (triangle)[plus sign] next to their names in the Index palette to view a list of the individual markers (see Figure 10.12). Click a marker in this list to view the entry in the text. To move to the next index marker, click the Find Next button on the Index palette.

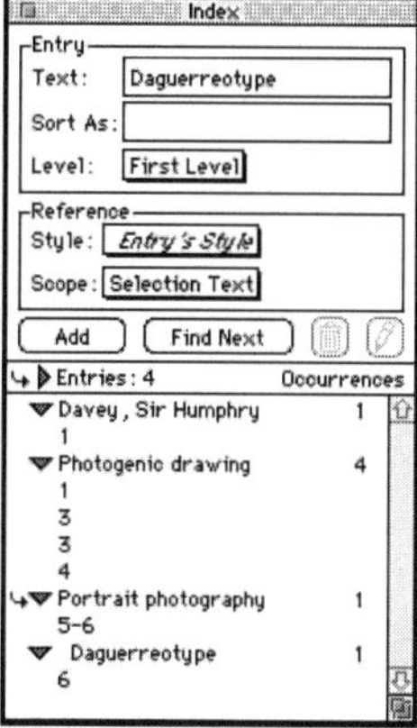

Figure 10.12

The individual marks can be displayed or hidden in the Index palette.

10. To edit index entries after you've added them, click the name of the entry you want to change and click the pencil button. Make your changes and click the pencil button again to apply them.
11. To delete an entry or one marker for an entry, click that item in the Index palette list and click the (trash can)[**X**].
12. When all your index markers are placed, you're ready to generate the index. Click the book button at the top of the Book palette, navigate to /lessons/chap10/index.qxd, and click Add to add the index file to the book. Double-click on index.qxd in the Book palette to open the file (see Figure 10.13).

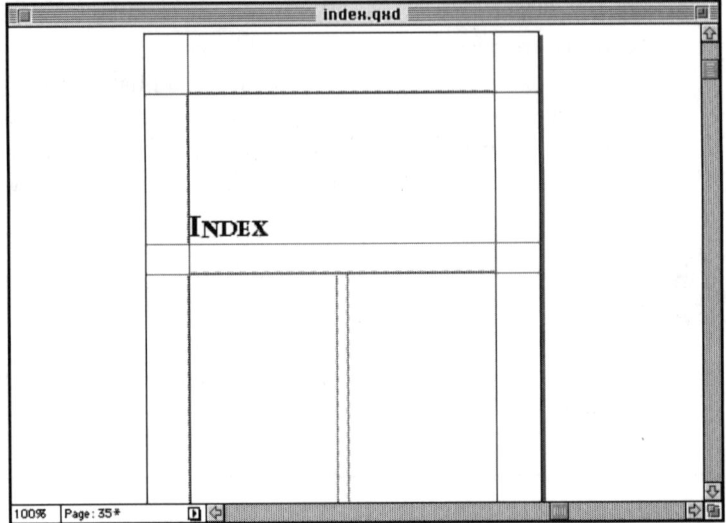

Figure 10.13

The index file contains the master pages and styles necessary to format the index, but no text.

This file contains the style sheets and master pages that will be used to format the index. The extra style sheets are as follows:

- Index 1, for first-level entries
- Index 2, for second-level entries
- Index 3, for third-level entries
- Index letter, for the letters that will introduce each section of the index

The master pages for the index are just like the ones used in the chapter files, except that the main text box on each page has two columns instead of one.

13. Choose Edit➡Preferences➡Index to bring up the Index Preferences dialog box (see Figure 10.14). Next to Between Page Range, enter an en dash ((Option-hyphen)[Control-Shift-Alt-hyphen]) instead of the hyphen that's there by default.

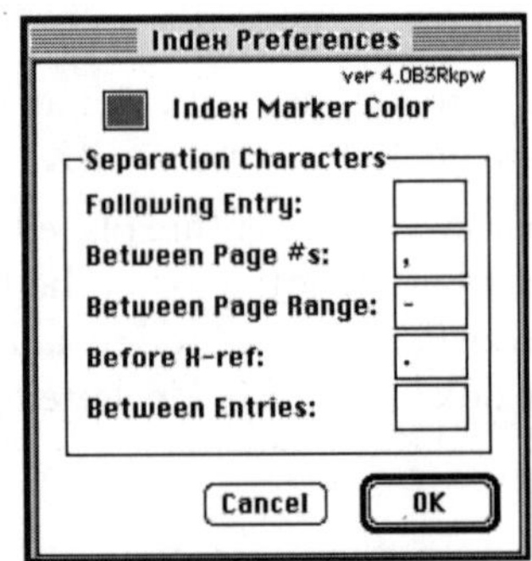

Figure 10.14

Change the Index preferences to use an en dash instead of a hyphen in a range of pages.

14. Make sure the Index palette is still visible, and choose Utilities➥Build Index to bring up the Build Index dialog box (see Figure 10.15).

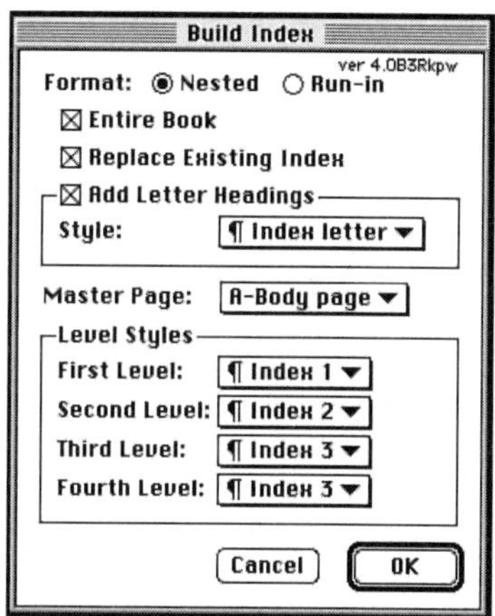

Figure 10.15

The Build Index dialog box.

15. Choose a format: Nested or Run-in. Most indexes use a nested format; the run-in format places all subentries at the end of the main entry rather than on the next line. If you choose Run-in, the style menus for Second, Third, and Fourth Level are not available, since the levels will all appear as part of the same paragraph.
16. Click Entire Book so that XPress will use index markers in all the current book's chapter files to create the index.

Note

Since this is the first index you've generated for this book, it doesn't matter if Replace Existing Index is checked.

17. Click Add Letter Headings and choose Index letter from the Style menu. XPress will add a letter heading before each section of the index and apply the Index letter style to those headings.
18. Choose A-Index body from the Master Page menu. This is the master page that will be applied to the document pages added to hold the index.
19. Choose the appropriate paragraph styles in the Level Styles section. Choose Index 1 from the First Level menu and Index 2 from the Second Level menu. It doesn't matter which styles are chosen in the Third and Fourth Level menus, since there are no third- or fourth-level entries marked.

20. Click OK to generate the index. XPress places the index on new pages at the end of the file, with the first new page being a right-hand page. Although this would be appropriate if you were indexing a single document, in this case, the index text needs to start at the beginning of the file.
21. Press F10 to view the Document Layout palette. Click the master page icon B-Index chapter opener and drag it over the first new page in the document, page 3 (see Figure 10.16).

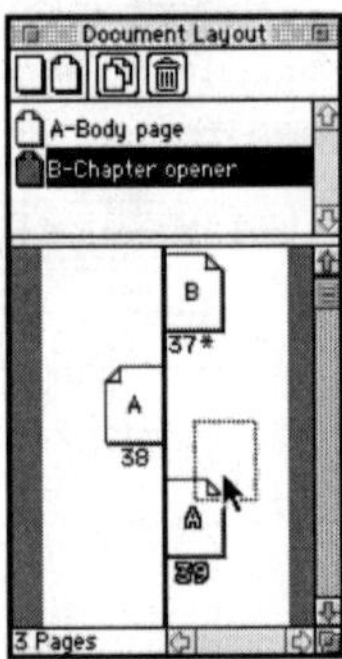

Figure 10.16

Change the first page of index entries to use the Index chapter opener master page.

22. Click page 1 in the Document Layout palette, then Shift-click page 2 and click the (trash can)[**X**] button to delete the pages that were in the file when you opened it. Now the first page of the file is the first page of the index. Press (Command-S)[Control-S] to save index.qxd (see Figure 10.17).

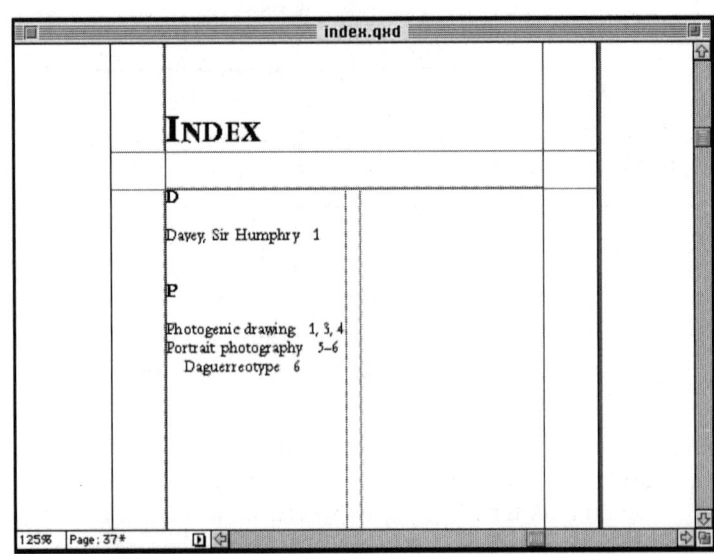

Figure 10.17

If you didn't add any index markers other than the ones listed above, this is what your index should look like.

23. You can update a previously generated index to reflect additional markers, deleted markers, and markers that have moved. To update an index, open the index file and choose Utilities➡Build Index. Make sure the settings are the same as they were the first time the index was generated, click Replace Existing Index, and click OK to update the index.

Planning an Index

Indexing is an editorial function, rather than a layout or design function. That means that layout people creating indexes will need to work closely with a book's editors to decide how the index should be structured and what terms it should include.

Traditionally, a professional indexer reads through a book's page proofs, noting index entries and their page numbers on index cards and then arranging the cards in alphabetical order. If you're using XPress's indexing feature, you won't have to arrange the entries, just mark them in the pages. Here are two techniques you might use to determine what words should be marked:

- Have the book's author or editor supply a list of key words that should appear in the index and use XPress's Find feature to locate these words in the pages.
- Have an indexer mark index entries on page proofs with a highlighter. Different colors can be used for different index levels, and notes about alternate sorting and entry wording can be added in the margins.

After an index has been created, it will need editing. For example, you might end up with separate entries for "photographer" and "photographers." To combine these entries so they both appear under "photographers," use the Index palette to locate entries for "photographer" and edit the markers. That way the index will be correct each time you update it and you won't end up having to make the same edits several times over.

The page numbers given for each index entry are determined by the location of the markers for that entry in the chapter files. In turn, where each index marker begins and ends is determined by the Scope pop-up menu. Different options in the Scope menu provide additional pop-up menus and entry fields. The choices are as follows:

- Selection Start places the marker at the beginning of the current selection.
- Selection Text begins and ends the marker at the beginning and end of the current selection, respectively.

- To Style begins the entry where the selection is and ends it at the next place where the specified paragraph style is used. If this option is chosen, a paragraph style sheet pop-up menu appears next to the Scope menu.
- Specified Number of Paragraphs lets you enter the number of paragraphs included in the marker; a number field appears next to the Scope menu if this option is chosen.
- To End Of ends the index marker at the end of the current document or story; if this option is chosen, you can choose Document or Story from a pop-up menu.
- Suppress Page Number leaves the page number off index entries created from the marker, so the actual location of the marker is irrelevant.
- X-Ref leaves off the page number in the index entry, as well, but adds a cross-reference to another entry. You can choose the wording of the cross-reference: "See," "See also," or "See herein," and then you can type the other entry in the field next to the wording pop-up menu.

You can change the characters XPress uses in the index, as well as the color of index markers, in the Index preferences. By default, XPress uses these separators:

- A space between entries and page numbers
- A comma and a space between multiple page numbers
- A hyphen between a range of pages
- A period and a space between entries and cross-references
- Nothing between entries when the run-in style is used (not even a space—generally, you'll want to set this to something like a semicolon and a space)

For more information on changing the Index preferences, see "Index Preferences" in Day 1, "XPress Basics."

Creating a Table of Contents

Using XPress's Lists feature to create a table of contents is much less time-consuming than building an index. Because lists are based on style sheets, specifying what text to include in them is a fairly simple process that happens in one dialog box.

Tip

The lists feature can also be used to create lists of figure captions, table titles, or any other text that uses consistent style sheets throughout a book. Geometry books could include a list of theorems; computer books could even include a list of Tips!

This example uses the same photography book used above. To create a table of contents:

1. If the photobk Book palette isn't visible, choose File➡Open and navigate to the book file on your hard drive. Click Open to open the book.
2. Click the book button at the top of the Book palette, navigate to /lessons/chap10/TOC.qxd, and click Add to add the table of contents file to the book (see Figure 10.18). Double-click on TOC.qxd in the Book palette to open the file.

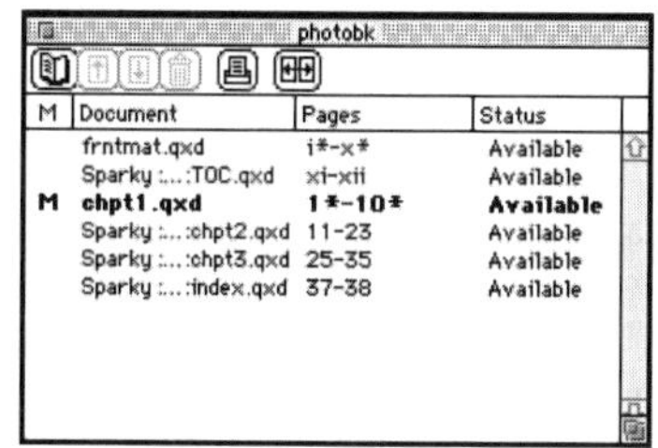

Figure 10.18

The book now contains a file for the table of contents.

This file contains the style sheets and master pages that will be used to format the table of contents. The extra style sheets are as follows:

- TOC 1, for chapter numbers
- TOC 2, for chapter titles
- TOC 3, for first-level headings (the Head 1 style sheet)

The master pages for the table of contents are just like the ones used in the chapter files (see Figure 10.19).

3. Open the master chapter and choose Edit➡Lists to bring up the Lists dialog box (see Figure 10.20).
4. Click New to bring up the Edit List dialog (see Figure 10.21).
5. Type "Table of contents" in the Name field. Then choose the style sheets in the Available Styles list that should be included in the table of contents list: Chapter number, Chapter title, and Head 1. Double-click each style name to move it to the Styles in List side of the dialog box.

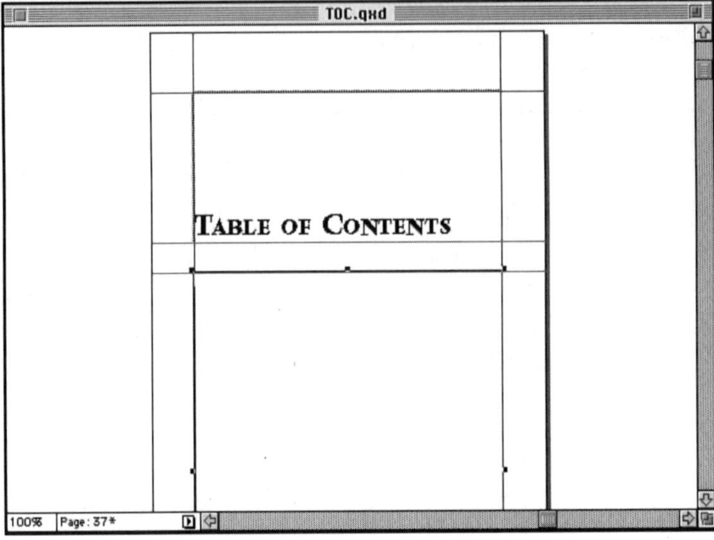

Figure 10.19

The first page of the table of contents file.

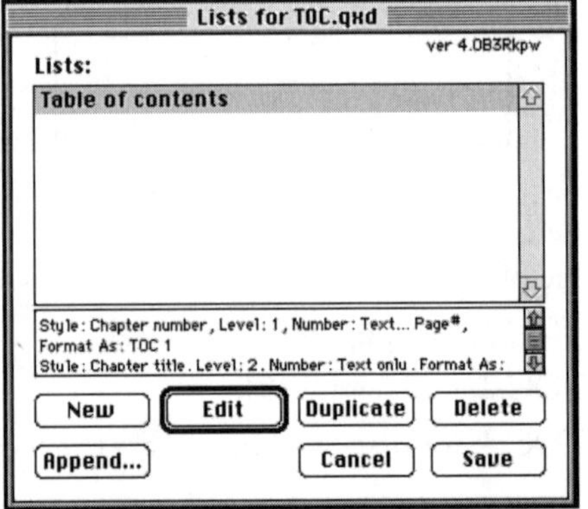

Figure 10.20

Like the Styles dialog box, the Lists dialog box shows the specifications for the selected list.

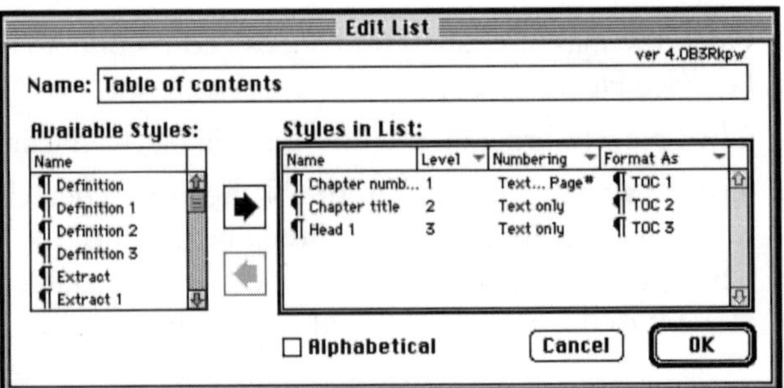

Figure 10.21

The Edit List dialog box.

6. For each style in the list, you'll need to specify a Level, Numbering, and Format. Click Chapter number and choose 1 from the Level pop-up menu at the top of the list. Choose Text...Page # from the Numbering menu and choose TOC 1 from the Format As menu. These choices assign the TOC 1 style sheet to each chapter number in the table of contents and add a page number next to the entry.
7. Click Chapter title and choose 2 from the Level menu, Text only from the Numbering menu, and TOC 2 from the Format As menu. The chapter titles in the table of contents will use the TOC 2 style, and they don't need page numbers because those numbers will be the same as the page numbers for the chapter numbers.
8. Click Head 1 and choose 3 from the Level menu, Text only from the Numbering menu, and TOC 3 from the Format As menu. The chapter titles in the table of contents will use the TOC 3 style, and they will not have page numbers; that's simply a matter of preference. Click OK to complete the list settings.

Note

Some books include two tables of contents, one that lists only chapter numbers, titles, and first-level heads and a more detailed one that lists every heading used in the book. Define a separate list with different settings if you want to include a second table of contents.

9. The Lists dialog box contains several other functions similar to those in the Styles dialog box.
   - Click the name of a list then click Edit to change any of a list's settings, including its name.
   - Click the name of a list and then click Duplicate to make a copy of a list with a different name.
   - Click the name of a list and then click Delete to remove that list from the document.
   - To append lists from another document, click Append to bring up the Append dialog box. Choose a file and click Open to bring up the Append Lists dialog box (see Figure 10.22), which works just like the Append Styles dialog box. Double-click the lists you want to append to move them to the right side of the dialog box, then click OK to append the

lists. If they're duplicated in the file to which you're appending, you'll see a dialog box asking whether you want to rename the duplicate lists, use the old lists, use the new lists, or cancel the operation.

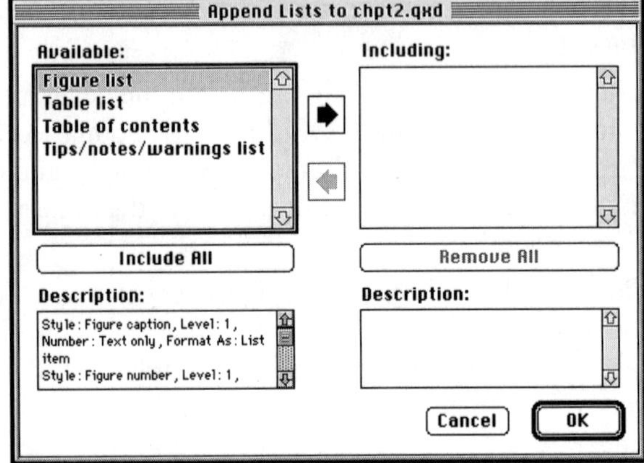

Figure 10.22

The Append Lists dialog box.

When you're done creating and editing lists, click Save to return to the document, then synchronize the book to add this list format to all the book's chapters.

10. Return to TOC.qxd and click in the main text box on the first page of the file with the Content tool. Unlike the Index feature, the List feature inserts the list in the currently selected text box, as long as there's not text already in the box.
11. Choose View➡Show Lists to make the Lists palette visible. The Show List For menu determines whether the palette shows list entries located in the current document or the entire book; choose "photobk" from the menu, and choose Table of contents from the List Name menu.

Tip

If your Table of contents list doesn't show up in the List Name menu, make sure you've synchronized your book.

Tip

Use the Current Document option in the Show List For menu to create a small table of contents at the beginning of each chapter, listing only the headings in that chapter.

12. Click the Update button to display the text of the table of contents list in the palette (see Figure 10.22). You can double-click any entry to open the file in which it's located and see that text.

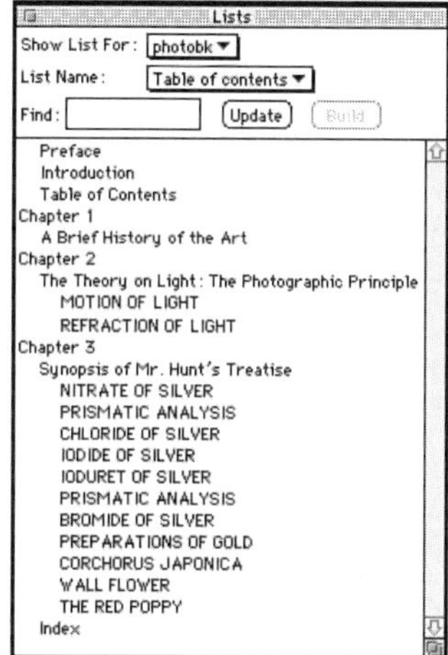

Figure 10.23

The updated Lists palette.

13. Click Build to insert the table of contents text in the empty text box, along with the appropriate page numbers. The three levels of text are formatted with the TOC 1, TOC 2, and TOC 3 style sheets. Each page number is separated from the entry text by a tab, so the TOC 1 style sheet includes a right tab setting at the right margin (see Figure 10.23).

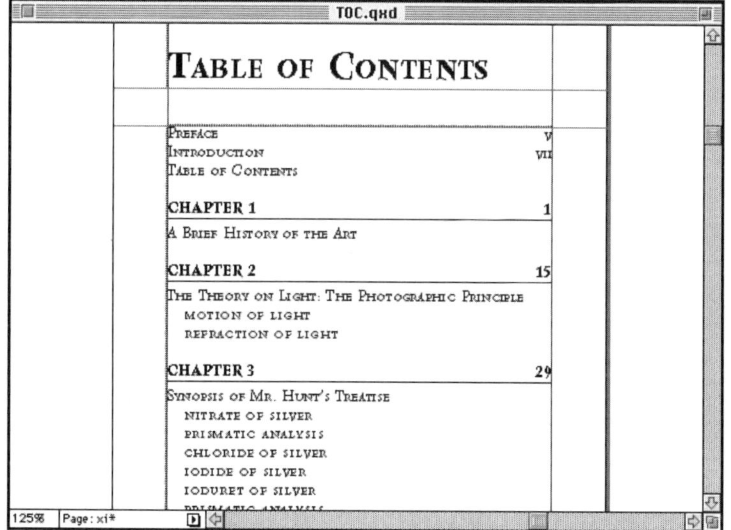

Figure 10.24

The generated table of contents.

14. Now make any formatting tweaks necessary. In this case, click in the Index entry and change its style sheet to TOC 1, then do the same for Preface and Introduction.

    XPress assigned these entries the TOC 2 style because this text appears in the pages using the Chapter title style, but it looks better in the table of contents if it has the same style used for the chapter numbers. Also, delete the entry for Table of Contents; it was included because "Table of Contents" is formatted with the Chapter title style sheet, but it doesn't need to be included here. If you're really annoyed by having to delete it each time, you can create a separate style sheet with the same attributes as Chapter title but a different name and apply that to "Table of Contents" in this chapter only. The final table of contents should match the one shown in Figure 10.24.

Figure 10.25

The final table of contents.

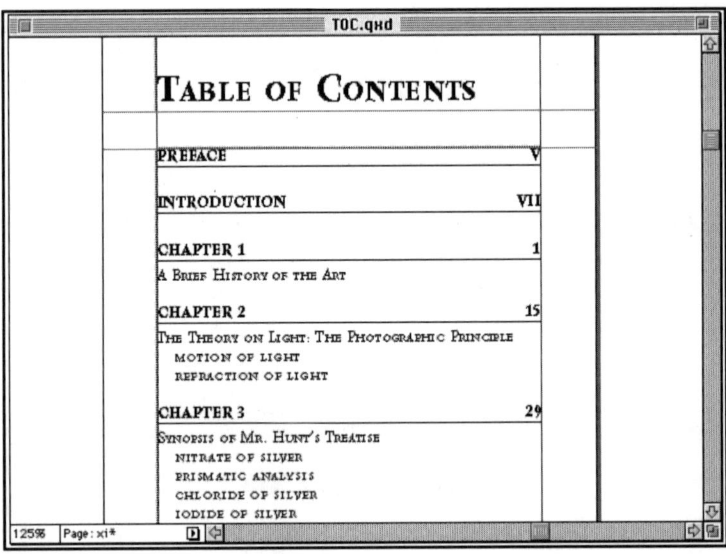

15. You can update the table of contents to account for added text, deleted text, and changed page numbers at any time. Just click in the text box containing the table of contents and click Build on the Lists palette (make sure you have the Table of Contents list chosen in the List Name menu). XPress asks if you want to add the new list to the existing one or replace the existing one; most of the time, you'll click Replace.

Tip

Like style sheets, colors, and custom dashes and stripes, you can create lists that will be added to each new document you create in XPress. This can save a lot of time if you often use the same style sheet names in different projects. Choose Edit➡Lists when no documents are open and create the new lists or append lists from an existing document. It won't matter that the style sheets from different projects use different fonts and formatting, because XPress uses only style sheet names to create lists.

Troubleshooting

No process is ever trouble-free, even in XPress. Here are a few questions you might have as you create and use books, indexes, and tables of contents in QuarkXPress.

Why Don't My Printouts Match My Files?

Because the Book feature makes changes to files without specifically telling you what's changed, you might not notice when it changes page numbering or style sheets, so you might not realize that you'll need to print new page proofs. Always check files for changes after synchronizing a book or making substantial changes to any file contained in a book.

I Changed the Head 1 Style Sheet, But Now My Changes Are Gone

You probably didn't make those changes in the master chapter before synchronizing the book. Always make style sheet, color, and H&J changes to the master chapter (or append them from the chapter you did make them in), or they will be lost when you synchronize the book.

Why Doesn't My Index Have Any Entries?

Make sure Entire Book is checked in the Build Index dialog. If it's off, XPress only looks for index markers in the current document. If that current document is an empty index document, there won't be any index markers, so there won't be any index entries.

Why Does My Table of Contents Have Only One Entry—"Table of Contents"?

Make sure the book file is chosen in the Show List For menu, rather than Current Document. As with the Index feature, you need to make sure XPress knows that you want it to search all the files in the book for the text to include in its list. In this case, Current Document was chosen and the only text found was text in this file.

Summary

The book, lists, and indexing features make managing long documents much easier, but you have to do a little planning before you get started. Know which chapter will be the master chapter, and always update it before you synchronize the book. Make sure the right styles for formatting a table of contents exist before you create the list, and have a logical plan for deciding what terms should have index markers. Don't forget, too, that the lists feature can be used to generate lists other than tables of contents, like figure lists. If you're careful in the way you use them, these features can eliminate a lot of the human errors that usually occur in designing and composing long documents.

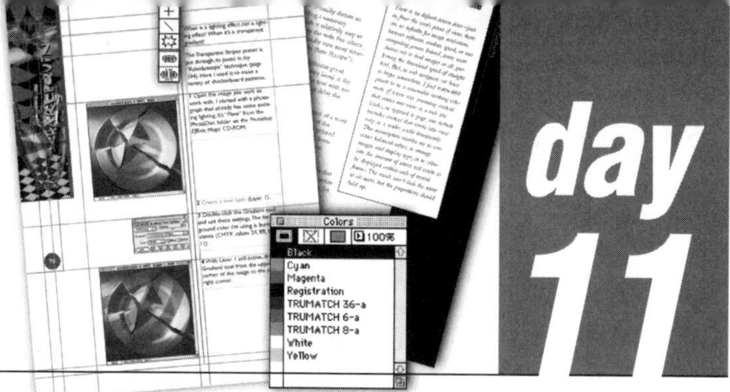

Storing Common Elements in Libraries

- Creating libraries and adding items
- Labeling library items
- Rearranging and deleting library items
- Using library items in documents

Lots of people probably have a glamorous idea of what a graphic designer does all day long—sitting around in a black beret drinking espresso and creating fabulously beautiful and incomprehensible advertising campaigns. As graphic designers themselves know, the truth is that there's a lot of repetition and drudgery involved in creating functional and attractive designs. That's where a category of software features called "productivity tools" comes in—and that's where QuarkXPress's Library feature can help out a lot. In this chapter you learn how to create and best use libraries to save you time and effort in creating designs that use common elements.

Library Logic

Libraries are a way to store frequently used elements so that you can access them quickly and incorporate them into your designs without having to either recreate them or search through piles of documents looking for the last time you used them. Any time you find yourself using the same element over and over—a logo, an **endmark**, a piece of clip art—you can add it to a library so that it will be there when you want it.

Depending on the work you do, there are a number of ways you can organize libraries. If you're a magazine or newspaper designer, you might want to have a library of blank ad size templates, one of house ads, one of department or column standing heads, and one of the publication's different logo versions. A book typesetter might create a library for each book or series of books, containing tip and warning icons, picture box/caption combos, and chapter opener graphics. Anyone running a small business will find it useful to have a library with company logos, a text box containing the company's contact information, and other elements used in correspondence and in designing the company's printed materials.

A few library guidelines:

- It's usually best to have more than one library to contain various kinds of elements. Although libraries can hold more elements than most people are capable of keeping track of, the bigger they get the harder it is to find elements within them.
- When you're putting items in libraries, first make them as generic as possible. If, for example, you're adding a text box containing a letter to subscribers, change the name at the top of the letter to "Dear Subscriber." It's better to forget to re-personalize an item than to use it with the wrong name.
- When you're sending a job out to someone who will work on it and then send it back to you, you can conserve bandwidth or disk space by adding the required graphics to a library and sending just the library. When the job gets back to you, you can relink the graphics used in the document to your original files.

Creating Libraries

Library items can be QuarkXPress graphics (such as colored boxes and rules), text boxes containing styled text, imported graphics, and groups of elements. In this example, we'll open several existing documents and add elements from them to a new library.

1. Open lessons/chap11/ltrhead.qxd on the CD-ROM that came with this book. This is a letterhead design for a company called Analogy Design Associates (see Figure 11.1).
2. Choose File➡New➡Library to bring up the New Library dialog box (or press (Command-Option-N)[Control-Alt-N]) (see Figure 11.2). Enter analogy.qxd in the Library Name field and click Create or press (Return)[Enter] to create the new library.
3. The library is a floating palette labeled "analogy.qxd" at the top. It's empty so far, since no elements have been added to it. In the letterhead document, choose the Item tool and click the box that contains the company's logo—the

two triangles at the top of the page. Drag the box into the library palette. A thumbnail of the picture box and picture appears in the library palette (see Figure 11.3). The Windows version contains an extra pop-up Edit menu with Cut, Copy, Paste, and Delete commands.

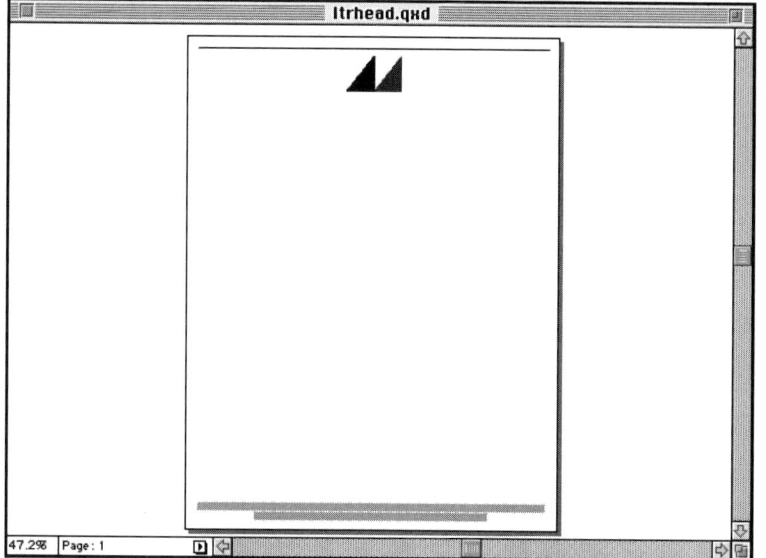

Figure 11.1

Elements from this letterhead design can be saved in a library and reused in other documents.

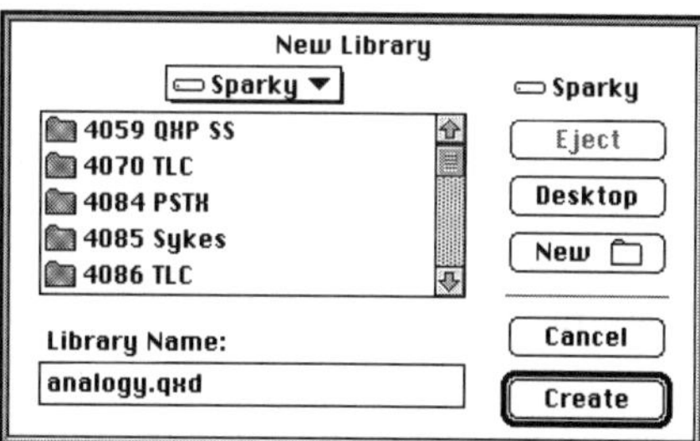

Figure 11.2

The New Library dialog box.

4. Double-click the logo library entry and assign it a label by entering ID in the dialog box (see Figure 11.4), then click OK. Labels enable you to group library items together and view just those items that apply to the job you're doing. In this case, any other items relating to the company's corporate identity materials that you add to the library should also be labeled "ID."

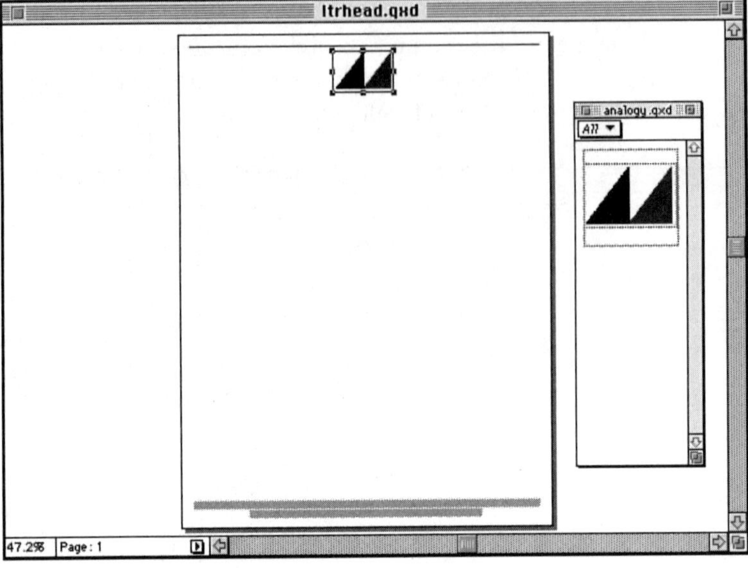

Figure 11.3

The library palette shows a thumbnail of each item in the library.

Figure 11.4

Assigning labels to library items lets you view only the groups of items you need for a given project.

5. Again with the Item tool, click the text box at the bottom of the page that contains the company's address, phone number, and URL. Drag the box into the library palette and a thumbnail of the text box is added to the library palette. Double-click the logo library entry and assign the "ID" label—this time you can choose ID from the menu to the right of the label field—then click OK.

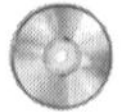

6. Open lessons/chap11/letter.qxd on the CD-ROM that came with this book. This is a note that the company's boss sent to his employees (see Figure 11.5).
7. Again with the Item tool, click the box that contains the signature scan (the boss's signature—always a handy thing to have around). Drag the box into the library palette. A thumbnail of the picture box and picture appears in the library palette.
8. Double-click the signature library entry and assign it the label Jameson in the dialog box, then click OK.

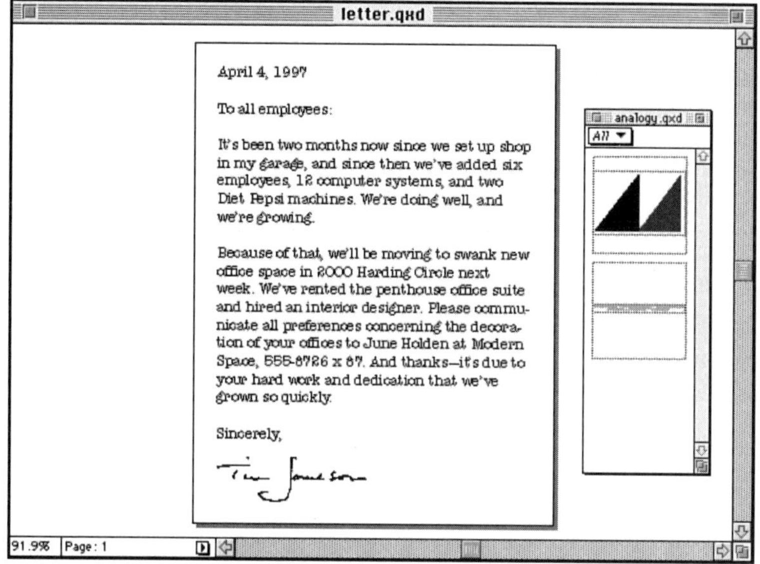

Figure 11.5

This note from the boss includes a scan of his signature.

9. To view just the ID items in the library, choose ID from the Library palette menu (see Figure 11.6). To view just the Jameson items, choose Jameson from the menu, and to see all the items again, choose All. Choose Unlabeled from the menu to see items to which you haven't yet assigned a label. Right now, there are no unlabeled items in the Analogy library, so the palette will be empty if you choose option.

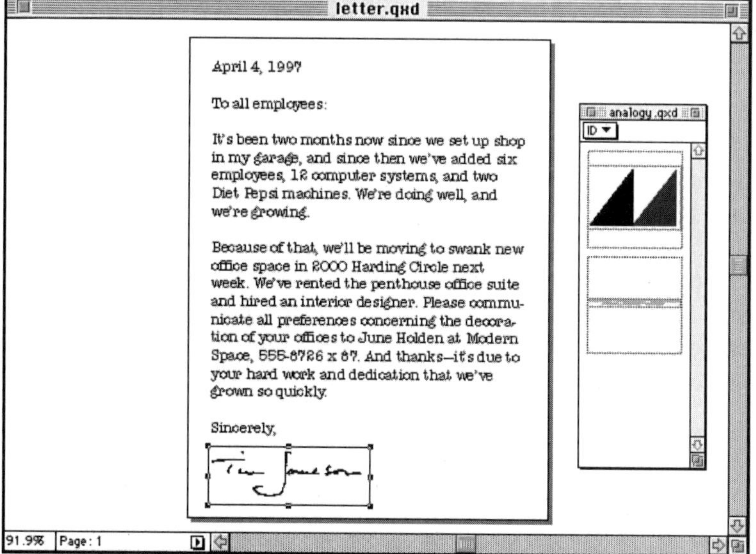

Figure 11.6

The Library palette menu lets you choose the item labels you want to view. Here only the ID items are visible.

Tip

You can display more than one group of library items by choosing the first label in the Library palette menu, then choosing subsequent labels from the menu; the menu changes to say "Mixed labels" if you're showing items with more than one label. To go back to viewing just one group, choose All from the menu, then choose the label you want to view.

10. To save the library, just close it or quit QuarkXPress. If your computer system is prone to crashing, or if you're just generally careful about such things, choose Edit➡Preferences➡Application and click the Save tab, then Auto Library Save. This saves libraries every time you add an item to them.

You can create as many libraries as you need. If you're designing ads in an advertising agency, for example, you'll probably want to have a library for each client, containing all the variations of that client's logos and other identity graphics. Magazine, newspaper, or newsletter designers might have libraries containing their publications' nameplates.

Tip

If you use one library often, don't close it before quitting QuarkXPress. Any open libraries will be reopened when you run XPress the next time.

Opening and Using Libraries

Once you've placed items in libraries, you can drag them into documents any time you want. You can also exchange libraries with other people—just remember the one pitfall: imported graphics.

Imported graphics placed from libraries aren't necessarily linked to the original file—the library retains the pathname of the original file as it was when you added that item to the library, but if you later move the original the link is broken. You can restore the link with Get Picture, then delete the old library item and drag the relinked graphic back into the library. To delete a library item, Mac users click it and press Delete, whereas Windows users click the item and choose Cut or Delete from the Library's Edit menu; in the dialog box, click OK or Cancel (see Figure 11.7).

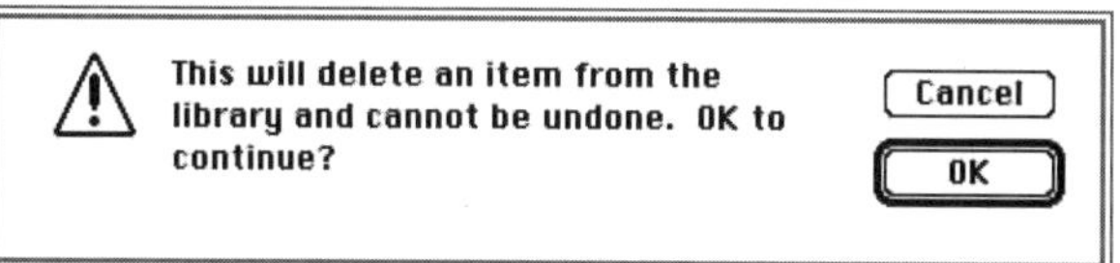

Figure 11.7

Deleting a library item prompts XPress to ask if you're sure you want to get rid of that item.

The solution when you're exchanging libraries is to remember that the original graphics files must go with the library, just as they must when you send QuarkXPress files to be output (see Day 12, "Printing").

In this example, you'll use the library file created in the last example to design some more documents for Analogy Design Associates.

1. Choose File➡New or File➡New➡Document. If you don't make a choice from the New submenu, QuarkXPress assumes you want to create a document rather than a library.
2. In the New Document dialog box (see Figure 11.8), enter 7" in the Width field and 4" in the Height field. Make the top, bottom, left, and right margins all .2", enter 1 in the Columns field, and make sure Automatic Text Box is off.

New Document
Page
Size: Custom
Width: 7"
Height: 4"
Orientation:
Margin Guides
Top: 0.2"
Bottom: 0.2"
Left: 0.2"
Right: 0.2"
Facing Pages
Column Guides
Columns: 1
Gutter Width: 1"
Automatic Text Box
Cancel
OK

Figure 11.8

The New Document dialog box settings to create a four-up business card layout.

3. This document will be a business card laid out four up—in other words, with four copies of the card on a page, which is how the printer will print the card. Press (Command-R)[Control-R] to show the rulers if they're not visible, and press F7 to show guides if they're not visible. Pull down horizontal guides at 1.8" and 2", and pull across vertical guides at 3.3" and 3.5" (see Figure 11.9). This divides the page into four sections, with extra guides .2" in from the outer edge of the upper left section, where you'll build the business card. Make sure Snap to Guides is on (choose the View menu and make sure there's a checkmark next to Snap to Guides).

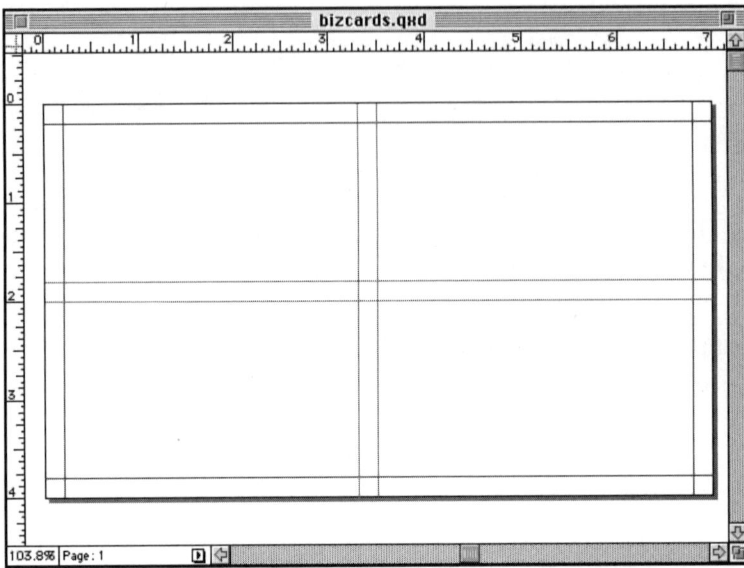

Figure 11.9

Guides create margins for the upper-left card.

Tip

If you have trouble placing the guides exactly where you want them (watch the Measurements palette to monitor their positions as you drag), try zooming in to a higher, even percentage such as 200%, 400%, or even 800%.

4. If the Analogy library isn't still open, choose File➡Open, find the library and click Open to open it. Drag the triangle logo graphic from the library into the business card document (see Figure 11.10).
5. The logo is far too big to fit on a business card. First, double-click in the X and Y picture coordinate fields in the Measurements palette and change both to 0 (zero). Then, to scale the box and picture simultaneously, hold down (Command-Option-Shift)[Control-Alt-Shift] and drag the lower-right corner of the box up and to the left until the X and Y percentage fields on the Measurements palette both show about 28%. Move the box to the upper-left corner of the card, flush with the top and left margin guides (see Figure 11.11).
6. Drag the address text block out of the library and place it flush against the left margin guide in the card area. With the Content tool, press (Command-A)[Control-A] to select all the text and press (Command-Shift-L)[Control-Shift-L] to left-justify the text.

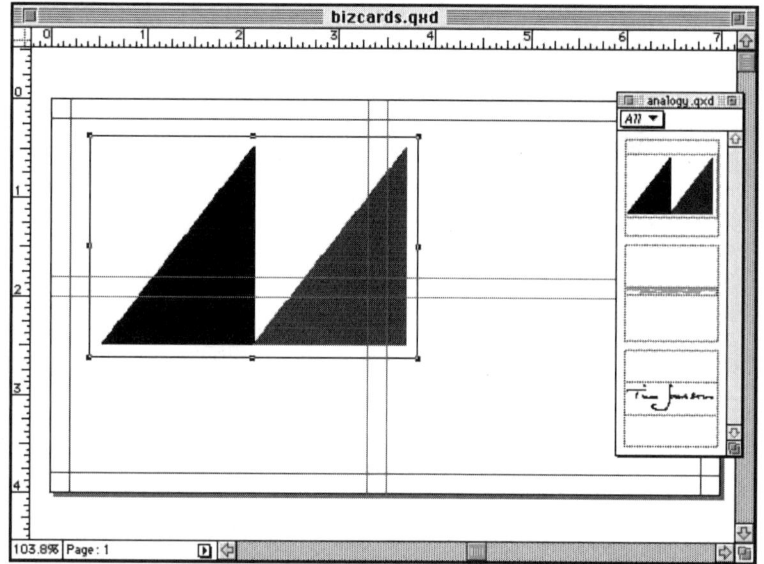

Figure 11.10

Placing library items in a document is a simple matter of dragging them onto the page.

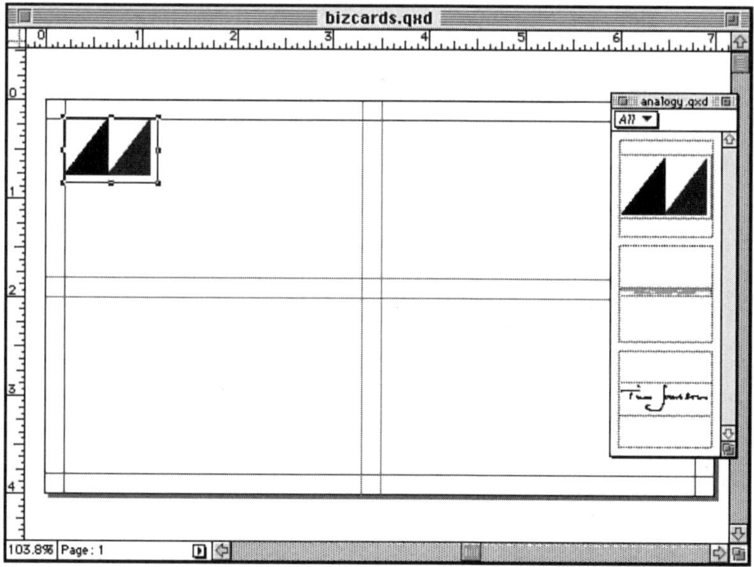

Figure 11.11

The logo is scaled and placed in the corner of the business card.

7. Press F12 to show the Colors palette. Click the middle (text) icon and click Black in the list of colors to make the text black (see Figure 11.12).

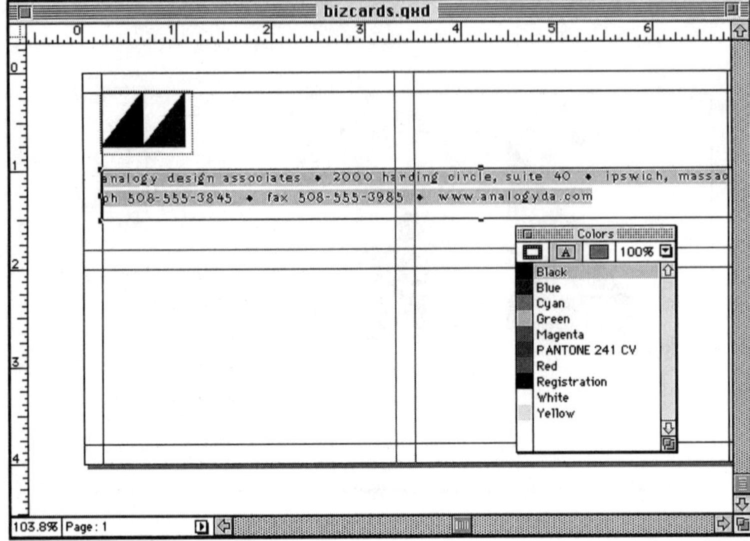

Figure 11.12

The text is changed to black from its original PANTONE purple.

8. The type is too large to fit in the card. Still with all the text selected, double-click in the point size field of the Measurements palette, type 7, and press (Return)[Enter] to apply the change. Double-click in the leading field, type 10, and press (Return)[Enter]. Then remove the tracking by double-clicking in the tracking field on the Measurements palette and typing 0, then (Return)[Enter], to replace the current value of 31.
9. The lines of the address information are separated by bullets instead of carriage returns, since this text block originally ran across the bottom of a piece of letterhead. With the Content tool, select each bullet and the en spaces on either side of it and press (Return)[Enter] to add line breaks. You will probably have to drag the bottom of the box down far enough that you can see all the text.
10. Adjust the size and position of the box so it's about 1.5" wide and about .95" deep. The top of the box should be flush with the bottom of the logo's picture box and the bottom with the horizontal guide at 1.8" (see Figure 11.13).
11. Choose Item➡Modify and click the Text tab. From the Vertical Alignment field, choose Justified and click OK to apply the change. The lines of the address text are spread vertically to fill the space in the box. Choose the Zoom

tool and drag to select a small portion of the last line of the text; the view zooms in to 800%. Pull the bottom of the text box down so that the baseline of the last line of the text is sitting right on the 1.8" guide (see Figure 11.14).

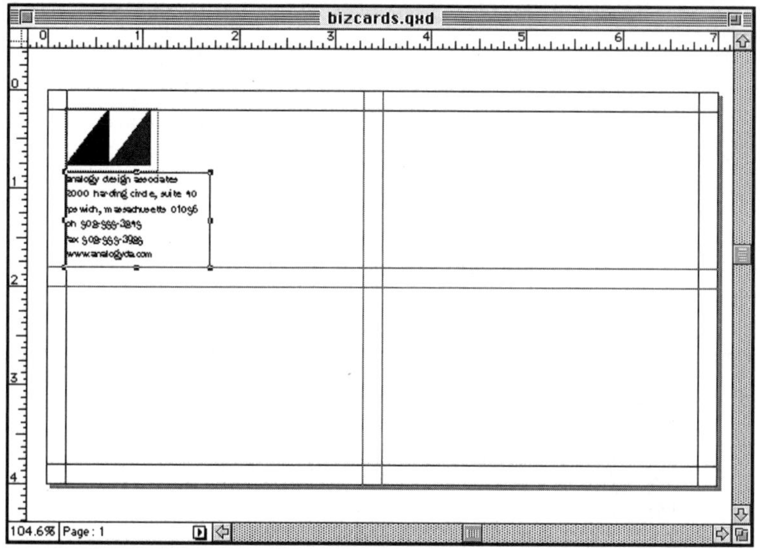

Figure 11.13

The text fits between the logo and the edge of the page.

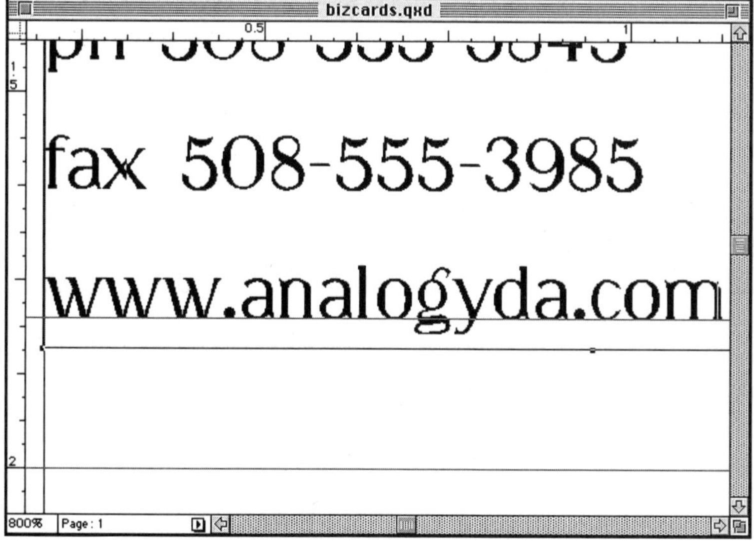

Figure 11.14

Adjusting the bottom of the text box aligns the baseline of the last line of the text with the guide.

12. Press (Command-1)[Control-1] to bring the view back to 100% and draw another text box from the top margin guide down to the 1.8" guide, about 1.25" wide and flush with the 3.3" vertical guide. Press (Command-M)[Control-M] to bring up the Modify dialog box and click the Text tab. From the Vertical Alignment field, choose Centered and click OK to apply the change.
13. The Content tool should be active, so you can start typing in the box right away. Type "Paul Anderson," then press (Return)[Enter] and type "Senior Designer." Press (Command-A)[Control-A] to select all the text and make it 11-point David Farewell on 14-point leading.
14. Triple-click in the first line to select the whole line and press (Command-Shift-B)[Control-Shift-B] to make it bold. Then select all again (Command-A)[Control-A] and press (Command-Shift-R)[Control-Shift-R] to right-justify the text (see Figure 11.15).

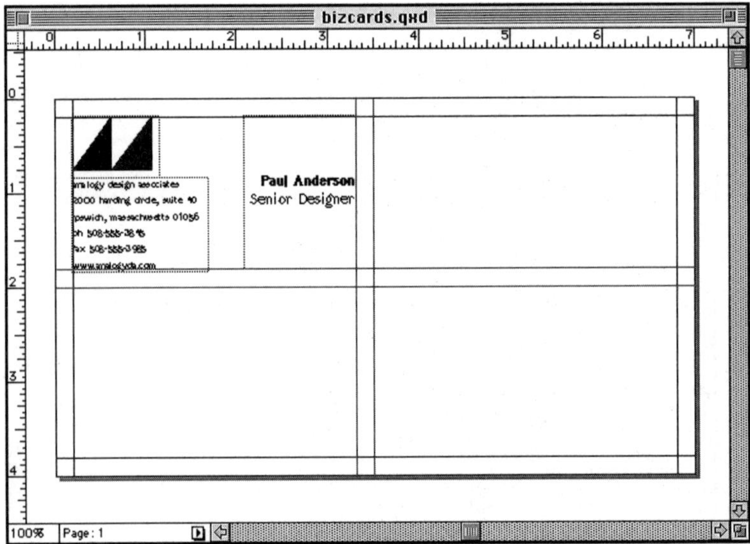

Figure 11.15

The business card's name and title are placed to the right of the logo and address information.

15. The business card is complete. Select the two text boxes and the picture box and press (Command-G)[Control-G] to group them, then press (Command-D)[Control-D] three times to make three copies of the card. Drag one copy to the upper-right corner of the page, then pull down a horizontal guide to 2.2". Align the tops of the other two copies with this guide, and place them flush with the left and right margin guides (see Figure 11.16).

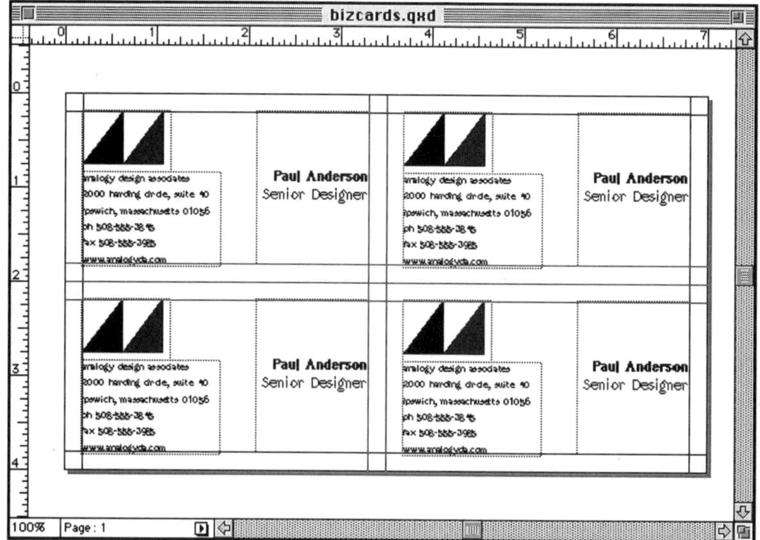

Figure 11.16

The printer will print the business card four copies to a page and then cut the cards apart.

16. Press (Command-N)[Control-N] to bring up the New Document dialog box (see Figure 11.17). Enter 9.5" in the Width field and 4.125" in the Height field and choose Landscape orientation. Make the top, bottom, left, and right margins all .2", enter 1 in the Columns field, and make sure Automatic Text Box and Facing Pages are off.

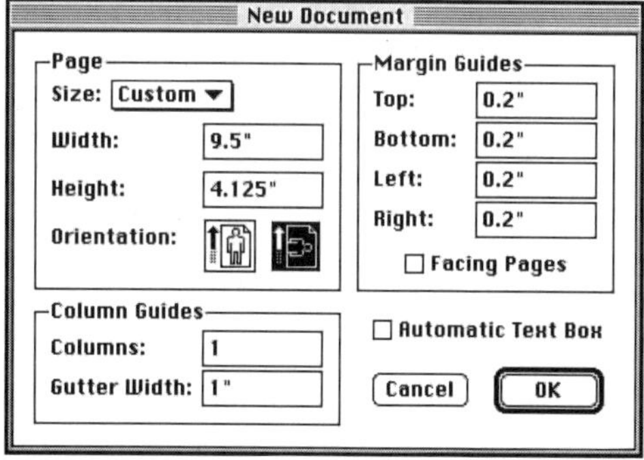

Figure 11.17

The New Document dialog box for a business envelope.

17. This document will be a business envelope to match the Analogy Design Associates letterhead. Drag both the logo and the address text block into the document from the Analogy library.

18. First, format the text. Change the bullets and en spaces to line breaks, as in Step 9, then select all ((Command-A)[Control-A]) and press (Command-Shift-L)[Control-Shift-L] to left-justify the text. Change the point size to 9 and the leading to 12. Make the box narrower and deeper to show all the text.
19. Delete the phone numbers and web address from the text box, leaving only the company's address.
20. Place the text box flush left on the left margin guide and zoom in on the end of the first line of the text by dragging a small marquee with the Zoom tool. Drag a vertical guide across to the end of the line (see Figure 11.18).

Figure 11.18

Most of the same address info used on the letterhead can be used on the envelope as well.

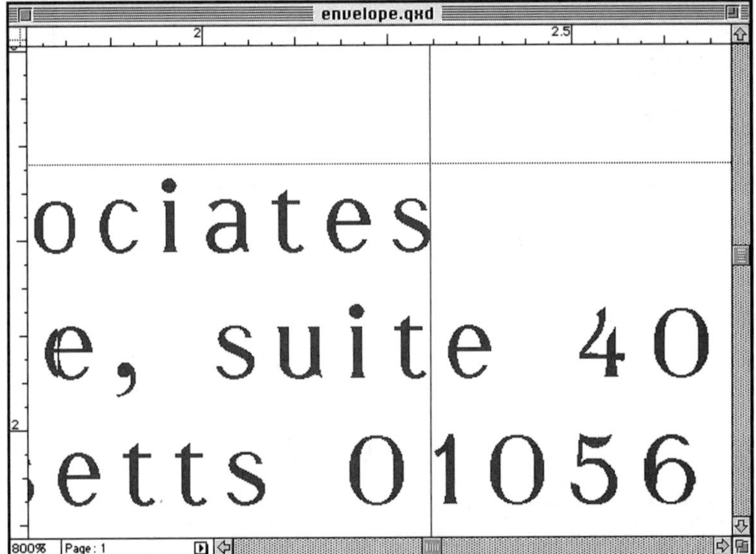

21. Go back to 100% view ((Command-1)[Control-1]. Click the logo picture box, press (Command-T)[Control-T]) to bring up the Runaround tab of the Modify dialog box, and choose None from the Type pop-up menu.
22. Move the logo picture box to the upper-left corner of the envelope, then change the X and Y picture coordinates for the logo picture box to 0 (zero). Scale the box and picture simultaneously by holding down (Command-Option-Shift)[Control-Alt-Shift] and dragging the lower right corner of the box down and to the right until the right edge of the purple triangle is flush with the vertical guide you placed in Step 19 (a reduction percentage for the logo graphic of about 66%).

Tip

At this point, you're probably wishing you'd changed the picture's coordinates before you added it to the library. You can always delete the item from the library and drag a new copy in, modified as you prefer.

23. Move the address text box up or down so that its Y coordinate is 1.6". That completes the envelope (see Figure 11.19).

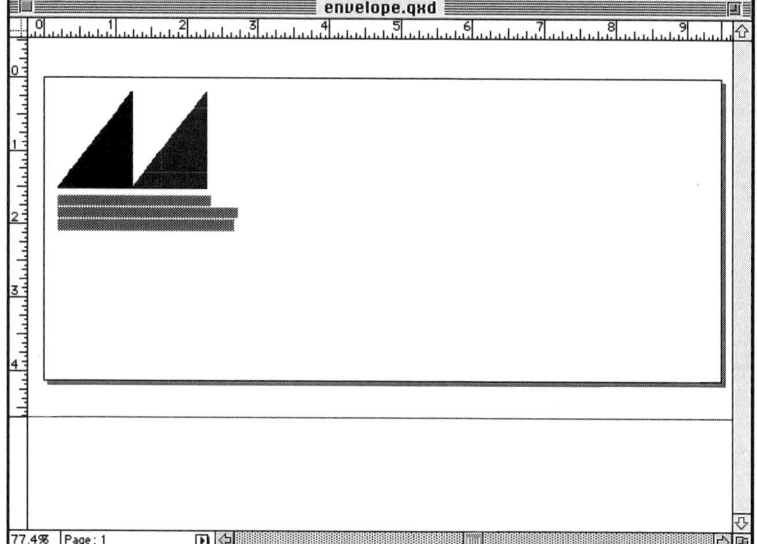

Figure 11.19

The complete envelope.

Summary

Libraries can help you get organized, providing a handy place to store items you use often. Because they're floating palettes, it's easy to keep libraries open and drag items into and out of them as you work on one or many documents at a time. Remember that libraries store only the references to imported graphics, not the files themselves. As you work with libraries, you can use their labeling feature to view only the items you want to work with, and you can arrange library items in whatever order seems most logical to you.

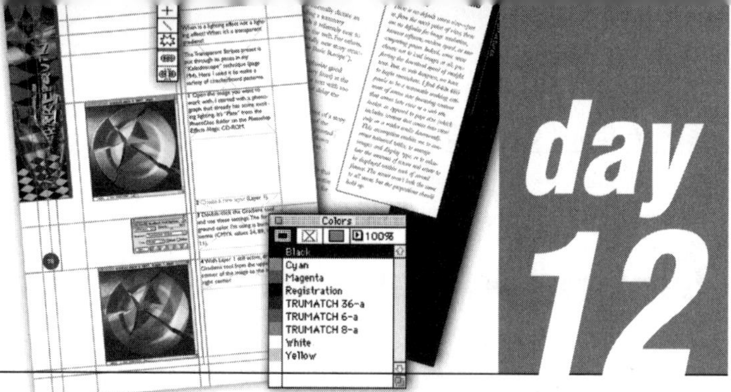

Printing

- Printing hard copies of documents
- Creating PostScript files of documents
- Creating and using print styles
- Trapping
- Collecting files for output
- Managing PPD files
- Troubleshooting printing problems

Eventually, you're going to need to print almost every document you create with QuarkXPress. As with most modern software, printing is easy, provided the printing components of your system software are correctly set up—press (Command-P)[Control-P]. But XPress does provide quite a few options for printing. Some are based on the output medium you'll be using (paper or **film**, for example), whereas others depend on the use to which you'll put a printout—is it for proofing, or is it final output? You can trade printing quality for speed, too. This chapter covers what you need to know to print your documents on a variety of media, using different kinds of printers. You also learn just enough about trapping to show why it's usually left to the professionals, and you learn how to collect files for output at a service bureau.

Tip

If you want something that's not actually located on a page to be included when you print (such as folding directives for the printer), you can group it with a small picture box (make sure the color of the box is None) that *does* extend onto the page. The entire group will be printed, but the box won't show up because it doesn't have a color.

Printing XPress Documents

Printing in QuarkXPress 4.0 is virtually the same whether you're using Windows or a Mac OS system. Steps in the printing process that are different for Mac OS and Windows users are indicated here with a Mac or Windows icon—skip the steps that don't apply to your platform. All the print options are in one dialog box, with tabs for different groups of settings. To print an XPress document, follow these steps:

1. Choose File➡Print or press (Command-P)[Control-P] to bring up the Print dialog box (see Figure 12.1).

Figure 12.1

The Print dialog box.

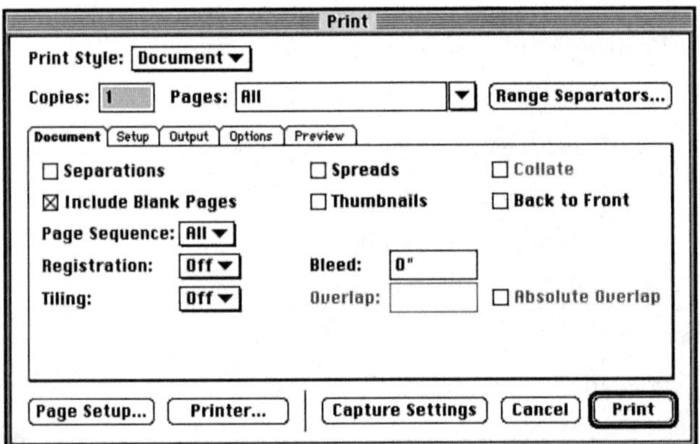

2. For Windows, choose a printer from the Printer pop-up menu, and then click the Properties button to set printer driver options for things such as paper size, graphics, and **PostScript** output. The options you see in the Properties dialog box will vary depending on the **printer driver** you're using. The options shown here are fairly representative; they're what you'll get using the PostScript Printer Driver 4.0 that comes with Windows 95.

   - **Paper:** Here you can choose the paper size, layout, orientation, paper source, and number of copies to be printed. In the Paper Size area, choose the paper size of the paper that is actually in the printer, regardless of the size of the pages in your document. Different layout options enable you to reduce the size of the printed pages and place multiple pages on each sheet of the printout. The Orientation choices are Portrait and Landscape, and Landscape pages can face either way. Paper Source determines which paper tray the printer uses, and the number of copies can be set here as well as in the main Print dialog box. (See Figure 12.2.)

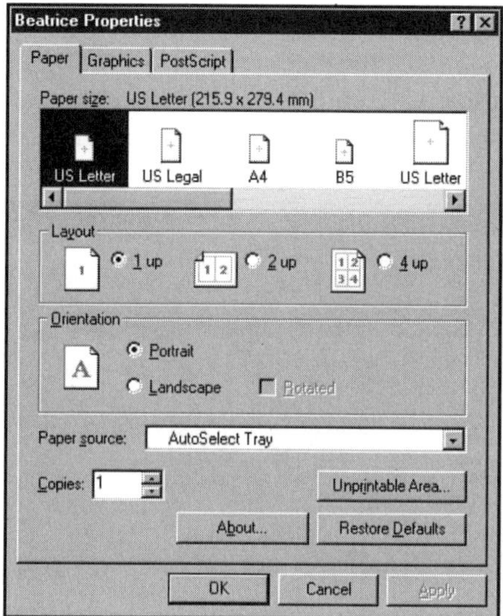

Figure 12.2

The Properties dialog box's Paper tab.

- **Graphics:** If your printer can print at multiple **resolutions**, you can choose a resolution here, as well as determining a **line screen** and **angle** for halftones (the size of the halftone dots and the angle at which rows of dots are placed). You can choose to print a **negative** or flipped image, and you can scale the printout to make it larger or smaller (see Figure 12.3).

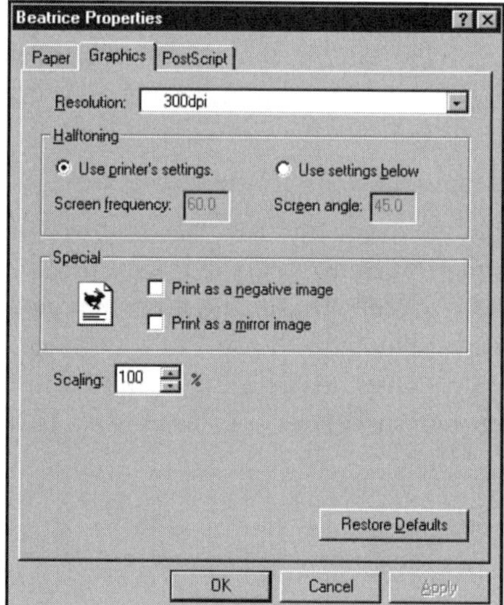

Figure 12.3

The Properties dialog box's Graphics tab.

- PostScript: This particular printer driver can modify the PostScript that's produced when you print a file so that it will work better in various situations. It can also create an EPS file rather than sending the PostScript information to the printer. See Figure 12.4.

Figure 12.4

The Properties dialog box's PostScript tab.

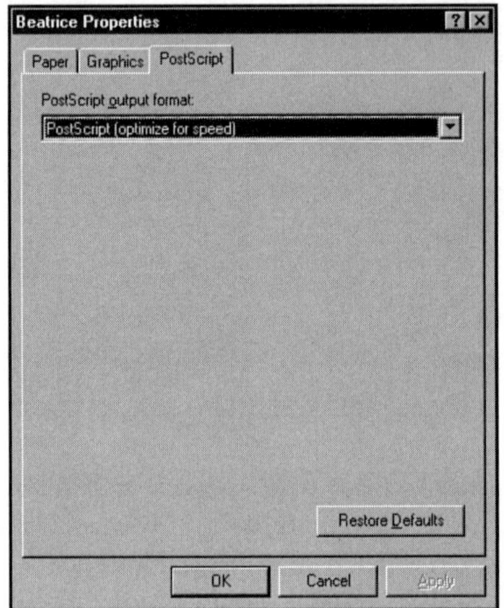

3. If you've created **print styles**, choose one from the Print Style menu. Print styles let you save groups of printing settings that you use often for particular tasks; see "Creating Print Styles" later in this chapter for more information. If you're using a print style, you can skip Steps 6 through 9. If not, leave this menu set at Document.
4. Enter the number of printouts you want in the Copies field.
5. Choose All from the Pages menu or enter the page numbers of the pages you want to print. Type End to print from a specified point to the end of the document—for example, "7, 9-end". By default, a hyphen between two numbers indicates that you want to include all pages in that range, and a comma should be used between non-consecutive pages. Click Range Separators to bring up the Edit Range Separators dialog box (see Figure 12.5), where you can change these settings.

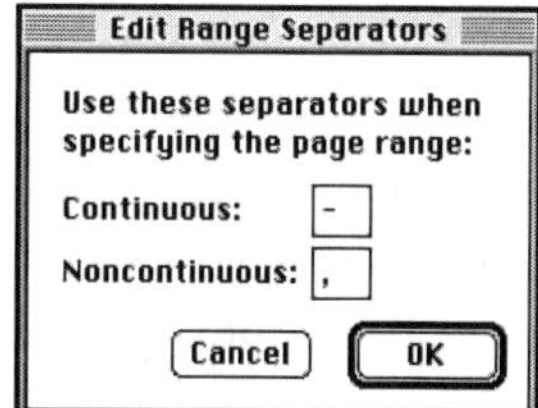

Figure 12.5

The Edit Range Separators dialog box.

Tip

Use a plus sign to enter pages based on their position in the document rather than their page numbers; for example, enter "+1" to print the first page of a file whose numbering starts at page 47.

6. Click the Document tab to view its settings (refer to Figure 12.1).
   - **Separations:** Check **Separations** to print a separate plate for each color; leave it off to print a composite printout.
   - **Include Blank Pages:** Check Include Blank Pages to print all pages, whether they contain any elements.
   - **Page Sequence:** Choose All, Odd, or Even to print all pages, just the odd-numbered ones, or just the even-numbered ones. This setting comes in handy when you're printing on both sides of the paper and don't have a duplexing printer.
   - **Registration and Bleed:** Choose Off, Centered, or Off Center from the **Registration** menu to determine whether registration and crop marks will be placed on the printouts and where they will be. Enter a measurement in the **Bleed** field to determine how much of objects that extend off the edge of the page will show on the printout.
   - **Tiling, Overlap, and Absolute Overlap:** Choose Off, Manual, or Automatic from the **Tiling** menu to determine whether large pages will be printed on multiple sheets. If you choose Manual, the point at which tiling begins is determined by the zero point of the rulers in the document, so be sure it's positioned where you want it before you print. If you choose Automatic, XPress decides how many pages to use when creating the tiles, based on the paper size, and uses the value you enter in the Overlap field to decide how much area between tiles appears on multiple tiles (the default is 3"). Click off or on Absolute Overlap to determine whether the document will be centered on the tile sheets—if Absolute Overlap is off, the document will be centered.

- **Spreads:** Click **Spreads** to print facing pages together on one sheet.
- **Thumbnails:** Click Thumbnails to print small versions of a document's pages on a single page rather than full-sized printouts.
- **Collate:** Click **Collate** when you're printing more than one copy of a document and want the copies to be automatically collated. This is the equivalent of using the Print command multiple times, so collated printouts will take longer to print than uncollated ones.
- **Back to Front:** Click Back to Front when you're printing to a device that stacks pages face-up in the output tray, so that the last page will be printed first and the first page will end up on top of the stack.

7. Click the Setup tab to view its settings (see Figure 12.6). For Mac users, some of these settings are duplicated in the Page Setup dialog box (see Step 12); Windows users will find some of these settings duplicated in the Properties dialog box (see Step 2). You can make the settings in either location, but be aware that having conflicting settings in the two locations can be confusing when you print.

Figure 12.6

The Setup tab.

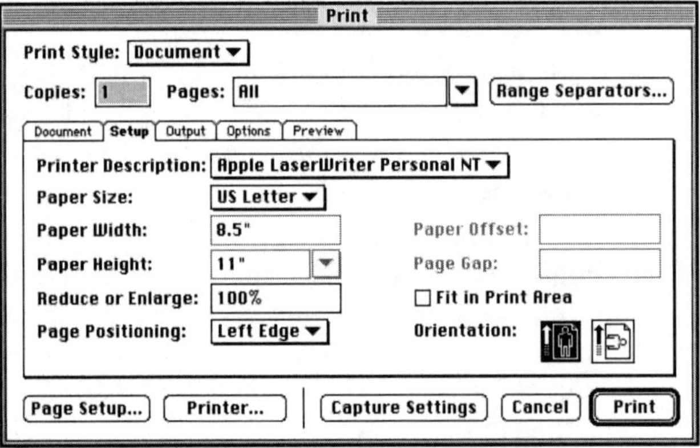

- Printer Description: Choose a PPD for your printer from the Printer Description menu. These are printer descriptions that provide XPress with necessary information about the capabilities of your printer. If you don't have a PPD for the printer you want to use, use a generic one or one for a similar printer model.

Tip

That list of PPDs can get long. Use the PPD Manager to determine which PPDs appear in the menu (see "Using the PPD Manager," later in this chapter).

- Paper Size: Choose a paper size based not on the document's page size but on what size paper is really in the printer.
- Paper Width and Paper Height: If you're using a custom paper size, you can enter its dimensions here.
- Reduce or Enlarge: Enter a scaling percentage to print the document at a larger or smaller size than 100 percent—the available range is 25 percent to 400 percent.
- Page Positioning: Choose Left Edge, Right Edge, Center, Center Horizontal, or Center Vertical from the Page Positioning menu to let the printer know how the paper is positioned in its tray.
- Paper Offset and Page Gap: These settings are available only when you're printing to an **imagesetter** or other device that uses rolls of output media rather than sheets. The Paper Offset measurement lets the printer know how far from the edge of the printer's rollers the paper or film begins, and the Page Gap setting determines how much space should be left between consecutive pages printed on the roll.
- Fit in Print Area: Click Fit in Print Area to have XPress reduce or enlarge the printout so that it will fill the printable area on the paper.
- Orientation: Choose either Portrait or Landscape in the Orientation area.

Tip

Choose File➡Page Setup or press (Command-Option-P)[Control-Alt-P] to open the Print dialog box with the Setup tab active.

8. Click the Output tab to view its settings (see Figure 12.7).
   - **Print Colors/Plates:** If Separations is not checked in the Document tab, choose Black & White, Grayscale, or **Composite Color** from the Print Colors menu to print in black and white, grayscale, or color. If you're printing color separations, the menu is labeled Plates and your choices are

Process & Spot or Convert to Process; the former prints separate plates for each color and the latter converts all spot colors to their process equivalents and prints plates for only the four process colors.

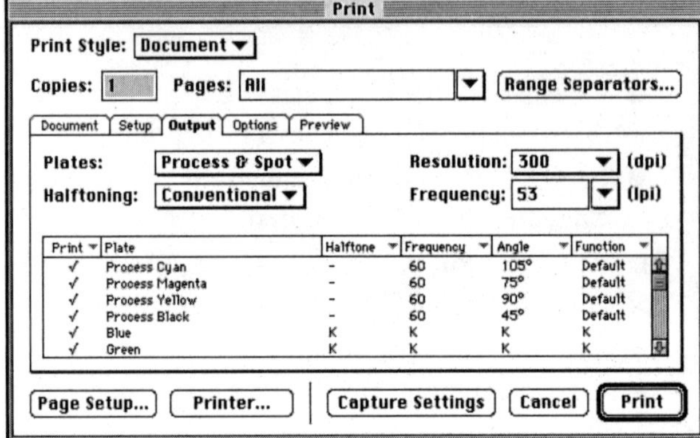

Figure 12.7

The Output tab.

- **Resolution:** If your printer can output at more than one resolution, choose the desired resolution.
- **Halftoning:** Choose Conventional or Printer from the Halftoning menu; the Printer option uses the line screen frequency and angle settings recommended by the printer's manufacturer and stored in its PPD. The Conventional setting lets you determine the screen and angle values for each color; if you choose Conventional, the options below (the **Frequency** field and the **Plates** list) become available. Only Conventional is available if you have checked Separations in the Document tab.
    - **Frequency:** Enter a line screen value to be used for all halftones and screened colors. You can change the frequency for individual colors in the Plates list.
    - **Plates:** The Plates list shows the color plates that will print; you'll see only one plate listed if you haven't checked Separations in the Document tab. Click a color name in the Plates list to change its Halftone, Frequency, Angle, and Function settings, and determine whether it will print. Click the checkmark under the Print column or choose Yes or No from the Print pop-up menu to specify whether a plate should print. For spot colors, choose C, M, Y, or K to assign the same line screen angle used for one of the four process colors to each spot color. Choose Default or Other from the Frequency pop-up menu to specify a line screen; the higher the line screen, the more detail shows in photographs but the muddier the images get.

Choose Default or Other from the Angle pop-up menu to set an angle for the rows of dots that make up a halftone screen; the angles used for the different colors must mesh properly or they'll form an unattractive moiré pattern on the printout. Choose a dot pattern from the Function pop-up menu: Dot, Line, Ellipse, Square, or Tri-Dot, or leave this set at Default, which will use the setting built into your printer.

9. Click the Options tab to view its settings (see Figure 12.8).

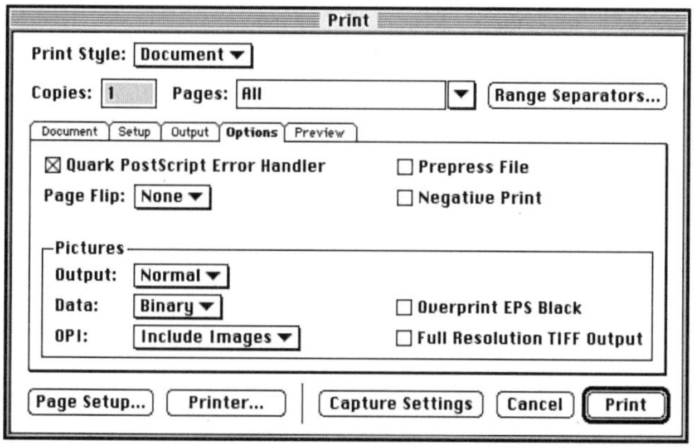

Figure 12.8

The Options tab.

- **Quark PostScript Error Handler:** Click the error handler to activate an XPress utility that helps you track down the causes of **PostScript errors**. If it's on, you'll get a printed report of errors when they happen, and XPress will print as much of the problematical page as it can, with a gray box indicating the specific element causing the error.
- **Page Flip:** Choose None, Horizontal, Vertical, or Horizontal & Vertical to flip the printouts.
- **Prepress File:** Click Prepress File to create a **PostScript file** on disk rather than a physical printout. This option essentially divides the printing process in half, assembling the information needed by a PostScript printer or imagesetter to create a printout but not sending it to the printer. You can use a PostScript utility program to send the file to a printer later.
- **Negative Print:** Click Negative Print to create a negative printout rather than the customary positive.
- **Output:** Choose Normal, Low Resolution, or Rough from the Output pop-up menu. Normal is the default; all imported pictures will print at

their highest possible resolution. Low Resolution prints imported pictures at their screen preview resolution, and Rough doesn't print them at all.

- **Data:** Choose an encoding method for the data that will be sent to the printer. **Binary** is the default and the quickest method; **ASCII** may work better with some printers that have trouble understanding binary encoding. Clean 8-bit is similar to Binary but may work better with printers connected via a parallel port.
- **OPI:** Choose Include Images, Omit TIFF, or Omit TIFF & EPS from the **OPI** menu to control which imported images are printed. Ordinarily, you'll use Include Images to print all imported pictures. If, however, you're using an OPI (Open Prepress Interface) server to substitute high-resolution images as you print documents, you'll need to choose one of the other options. Check the documentation for your OPI system.

Tip

You also can use the OPI settings when you're trying to track down the source of a PostScript error. If the file prints with Omit TIFF chosen but not with Include Images chosen, for example, you know the source of the error is a TIFF file.

- **Overprint EPS Black:** Click Overprint EPS Black to force all black elements in imported EPS image to overprint, regardless of the trapping settings made for them in their originating programs.
- **Full Resolution TIFF Output:** Click Full Resolution TIFF Output to print grayscale TIFF images at the highest possible resolution of the targeted printer. If it's off, then grayscale TIFFs will be printed only at the resolution necessary to achieve the specified line screen setting.

10. If QuarkXPress's color management software is turned on, a Color Management tab appears in the Print dialog box as well. See Day 9, "Using Color," for more information about using color management.
11. Click the Preview tab. No settings are on the Preview tab; it shows you the results of the paper size and other settings you've made (see Figure 12.9). The preview window shows the outline of the page size in blue against a white area that represents the printer's paper size.
12. For Macintosh, click the Printer button to bring up the traditional Page Setup dialog box for the print driver you're using (see Figure 12.10). Some of these settings are duplicated elsewhere in the Print dialog box, but the ones accessible by clicking the Options button are not (see Figure 12.11).

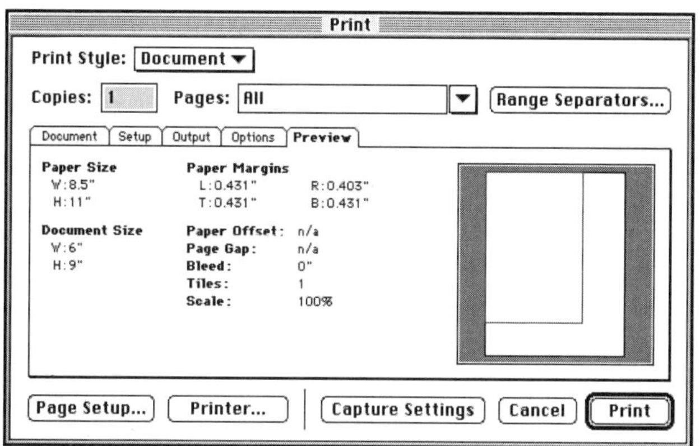

Figure 12.9

The Preview tab.

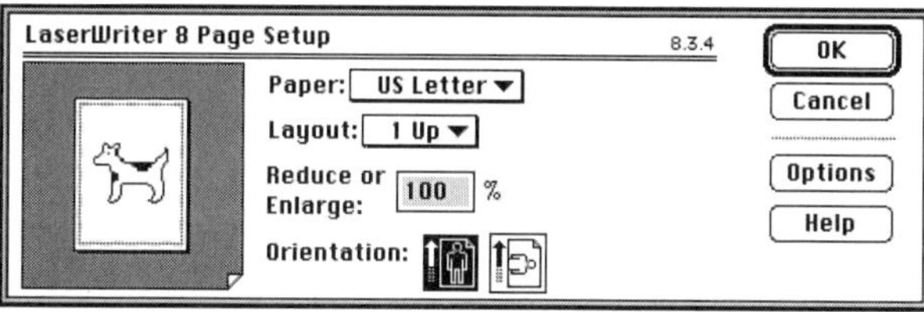

Figure 12.10

These Page Setup settings are found elsewhere in the Print dialog box.

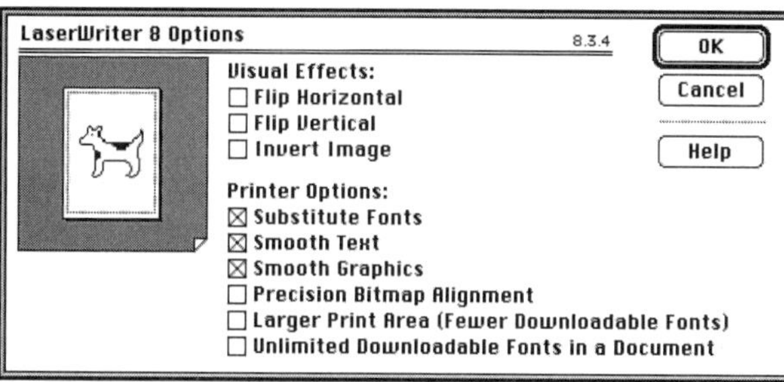

Figure 12.11

These are the Page Setup Options for the Mac OS LaserWriter 8.3.4 driver; they're not found elsewhere.

13. Click the Cancel button to return to the document without saving the settings you've made.
14. Click the Capture Settings button to close the Print dialog box and save the settings for the next time you print.
15. Click the Print button to—hold your breath, now—print the document or the pages you've specified.

You don't have to check every setting each time you print—for example, most times Windows users probably won't have to enter the Properties dialog to change those settings because the default settings are fine.

You can suppress the printout of individual elements in any document by clicking Suppress Printout in the Modify dialog box for each element. Suppress output of imported pictures in the Picture tab of the Usage dialog box by clicking on the checkmark next to the name of each picture.

A similar function is offered by the Halftone command, which lets you control the halftone frequency, angle, and dot pattern for individual imported grayscale images. It doesn't work for color images because they appear on more than one plate and so need to use different angle settings for each color. Select a grayscale picture and press (Command-Shift-H)[Control-Shift-H] to bring up the Picture Halftone Specifications dialog box (see Figure 12.12).

Figure 12.12

The Picture Halftone Specifications dialog box.

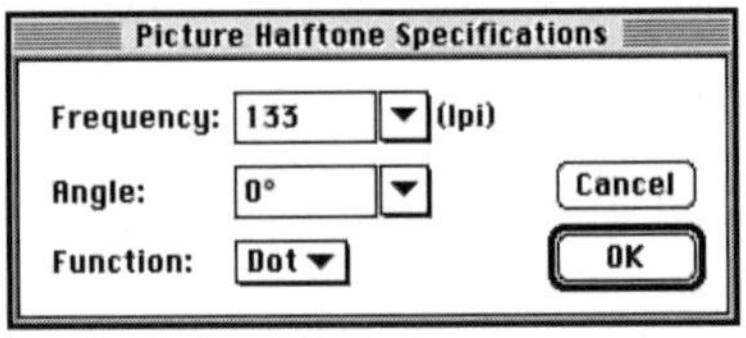

In the dialog box, choose settings from each of the three menus.

- Choose an option from the Frequency pop-up menu or enter a value in lines per inch (lpi). The choices in the menu are commonly used values: 60, 85, 100, 133, and 150, as well as Default. The Default setting uses whatever is specified in the Output tab of the Printer dialog box.
- Choose an option from the Angle pop-up menu or enter a value in degrees. The choices in the menu are commonly used values: 0, 15, 45, 75, 90, and 105, as well as Default. The Default setting uses whatever is specified in the Output tab of the Printer dialog box.
- Choose an option from the Function pop-up menu. The choices in the menu are Dot, Line, Ellipse, Square, and Ordered Dither, as well as Default. The Default setting uses whatever is specified in the Output tab of the Printer dialog box. The Ordered Dither option is designed to provide the best results when printing to laser printers and when making photocopies of your printed output.

Creating Print Styles

If you find yourself switching back and forth between two or more sets of print settings, you can store those settings in print styles and change them all with one menu choice each time you print. You might, for example, create styles for printing to a color printer, a black-and-white laser printer, and an imagesetter. Settings that are included in print styles include those in the Document, Setup, Output, and Options tabs of the Print dialog box. To create a print style, follow these steps:

1. Choose Edit➥Print Styles to bring up the Print Styles dialog box (see Figure 12.13).

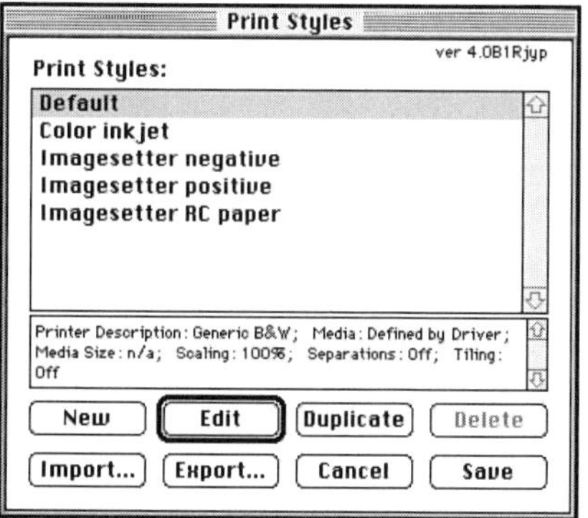

Figure 12.13

The Print Styles dialog box shows a list of the existing print styles, with a description of the selected style below the list area.

2. Click New to bring up the Edit Print Style dialog box (see Figure 12.14).

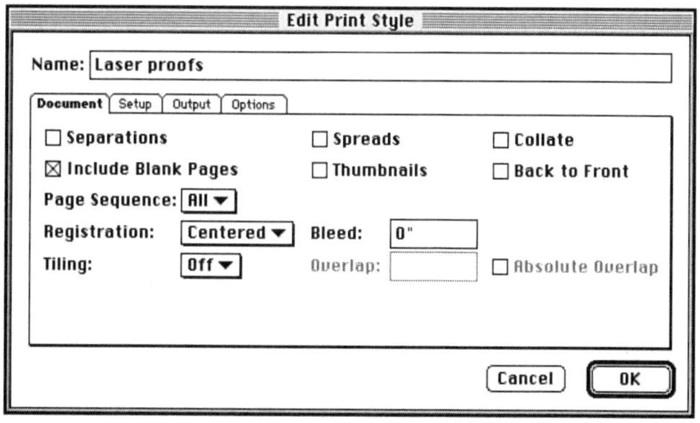

Figure 12.14

The Edit Print Style dialog box contains four of the five tabs in the Print dialog box.

3. Enter a descriptive name for the new print style, such as "Agfa Imagesetter negative."
4. Make settings in the four tabs as you would in the Print dialog box. See Steps 6 through 9 under "Printing XPress Documents," earlier. Then click OK to create the print style and return to the Print Styles dialog box.
5. Click Edit to make changes to an existing print style.
6. Click Duplicate to make a copy of an existing print style.

7. Click Delete to remove a print style.
8. Click Export to save a print style in a file that you can share with others, and click Import to add a print style from a file. The filename extension for print style files is qpi.
9. Click Save to save your changes or Cancel to leave the Print Styles dialog box without creating or modifying any styles.
10. To use a print style, choose it from the Print Styles pop-up menu at the top of the Print dialog box. The settings you made when you created the print style are put in place throughout the Print dialog box, so you don't have to make them again.

Tip

Print styles are saved with the XPress application, rather than with individual documents, so print styles you create will be available to you in any documents you create afterwards.

Trapping

Trapping consists of making sure that different colored elements overlap enough that there won't be gaps between them even if the paper shifts slightly when the document is printed. Traditionally, trapping has been done by hand at the prepress house or printer. More recently, electronic trapping has been done by standalone applications such as TrapWise or Island Trapper, which work with PostScript files generated by any application. QuarkXPress has built-in trapping that's sufficient for many jobs, though not for all. Which trapping method you use needs to be decided by you and the printer who will be handling a given job.

Tip

To turn off XPress's trapping, choose File➡Preferences➡Document and click the Trapping tab. Set the method to Knockout All.

The first thing to do if you're planning on trapping with QuarkXPress is set the trapping preferences (choose File➡Preferences➡Document and click the Trapping tab). For a complete list of the preference settings, see "Setting Document Preferences" in Day 1, "XPress Basics." Here are the highlights:

- The trapping method choices are Absolute and Proportional (Knockout All turns off trapping). The Absolute method applies the same amount of trapping throughout a document, whereas the Proportional method uses less trapping for colors that are similar.
- Process Trapping enables XPress to vary its trapping on the different color plates that make up process color objects. Turning on this feature results in much more attractive and effective traps.
- The Auto Amount and Indeterminate fields are where you determine how much trapping is applied—how much elements will overlap. The Auto Amount value is applied when a color overlaps one other color; the Indeterminate value, which is sometimes lower, is applied when a color overlaps more than one other color. The default value for both fields is .144 point, but many users prefer a slightly higher value, say .25 point.
- The Knockout and Overprint Limit fields determine how dark or light a color needs to be before it's knocked out or overprinted regardless of what XPress would ordinarily do with that color. 95 percent and 0 percent are the default settings and generally work well.
- Leave Ignore White checked on; it makes sure that XPress doesn't try to trap colors to white, which isn't really a color. Because in the real world white is produced by not applying any ink to the paper at all, the color should be ignored when determining traps.

Although you can set the trapping behavior of specific colors in the Colors dialog box (click the Edit Trap button), these settings override your trapping preferences, and you'll have to work with trapping for a while before you can edit them correctly. Consult with an expert before you change these settings.

Using Collect for Output

Because so many files don't stay where they're begun but instead have to be distributed to other users, Quark has included the Collect for Output command in XPress. It copies the document and the graphics files it needs to another location and creates a report listing the information a prepress professional will need to have about the file. To use Collect for Output:

1. Choose Edit➡Collect for Output to bring up the Collect for Output dialog box (see Figure 12.15).
2. Navigate to the disk or folder where you want to save the collected files.

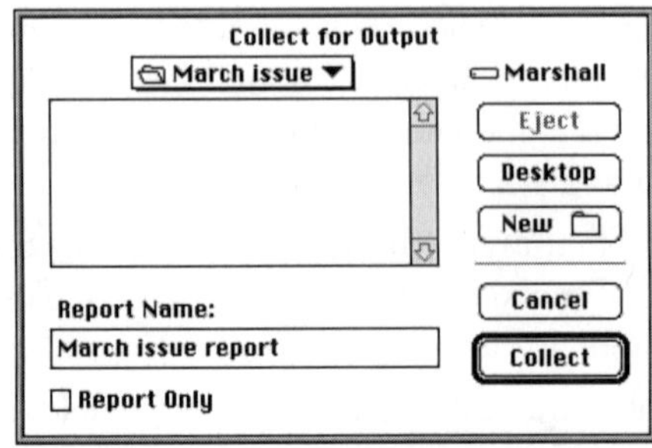

Figure 12.15

The Collect for Output dialog box.

3. Enter a name for the report file that XPress will generate. Mac versions automatically enter the name of the XPress file with the word "report" added to the end, whereas Windows versions use the filename with the extension .xtg because the report is an XPress Tags file. Click Collect to create the report and collect the necessary files. Click Report Only, then click Collect, to generate the report without copying any files.

Note

If you've made changes to the XPress document you're collecting, XPress will ask you to allow it to save the document first.

4. Open the Output Request Template located in your XPress folder, click in the main text box at the bottom of the page, and choose File➡Get Text. Click Include Style Sheets, navigate to the report file created by the Collect for Output command, and click Open to import the text. This template created by Quark includes style sheets that match the coding used in the XPress Tags report file, so the report information is imported with neat formatting already applied.

Tip

Customize the Output Request Template by adding your own company name and any other information you like (such as your name and phone number), then save it as a template file to use for future reports.

5. Print the Output Request Template and fill out the information at the top of the first page.

Using the PPD Manager

As with the XTensions Manager (see "Using XTensions" in Day 13, "XTending XPress's Capabilities"), the PPD Manager determines which PPDs are installed when you start up QuarkXPress. The fewer PPDs you load, the faster XPress starts up, the less RAM it requires, and the fewer choices you'll have to contend with in the Printer Description pop-up menu in the Setup tab of the Print dialog. To use the PPD Manager:

1. Choose Utilities➡PPD Manager to bring up the PPD Manager (see Figure 12.16).

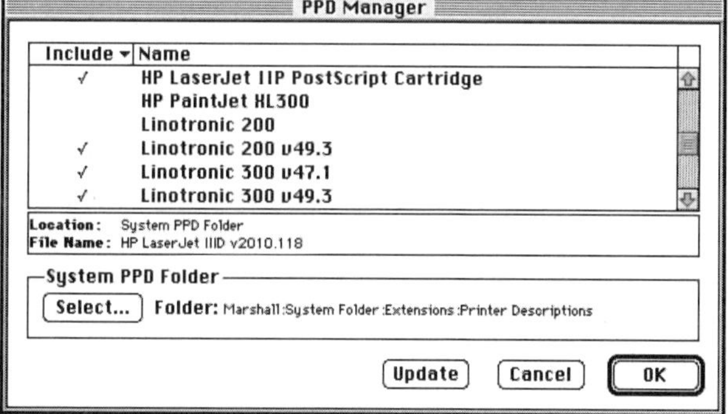

Figure 12.16

Using the PPD Manager, you can control which printer descriptions load when XPress starts up.

2. To turn on or off PPDs, click the name of a PPD and click in the Include column to add or remove a checkmark or choose Yes or No from the Include pop-up menu.
3. To select multiple PPDs, click the first one, then Shift-click the last one in a range, or (Command-click)[Control-click] on non-consecutive PPDs.
4. Click a PPD to display its filename and location below the list of PPDs.

   By default, XPress looks in (\System Folder\Extensions\Printer Descriptions\)[\Windows\System\System PPD Folder\] for PPD files. It also looks in the PPD folder inside your XPress folder, if you have one. To change the default system PPD folder that XPress checks (you might want to store PPDs on a network server, for example), click the (Select)[Browse] button and navigate to the folder you want to use (see Figure 12.17).
5. Click the Update button to revise the list based on any changes made to your PPD collection because you started QuarkXPress.
6. When you're done choosing PPDs, click OK to save the changes. Only the chosen PPDs appear in the Printer Description menu on the Print dialog box's Setup tab; you don't need to restart XPress to see the effects of your changes.

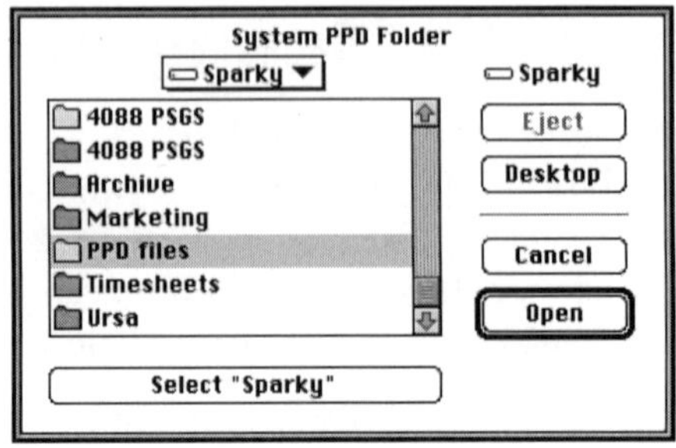

Figure 12.17

You can specify that XPress check for PPDs in any folder accessible to your computer.

Troubleshooting

Printing can be a complicated operation, because it involves all different kinds of hardware and software—printer drivers, printers, XPress itself, system software—trying to work together. Here are a few problems you might run into as you print from QuarkXPress.

Why Won't My Document Print?

If a document doesn't print at all, first check to make sure the printer is powered on and running correctly (no paper jams), and that the physical connection between the printer and your computer is not broken. If the printer's on a network, check to see whether you have access to other printers, servers, and workstations on the network—if not, the problem may be with the network itself or with the system software that gives your computer access to the network.

Look at the Options tab of the Print dialog to make sure that Prepress File isn't checked—if it is, XPress is generating a PostScript file and saving it to the disk rather than sending it to the printer to produce a printout.

Be aware that files containing large imported graphics may take a long time to print—or your printer may not be able to handle them at all, depending on its capabilities. Adding more RAM to a printer can enable it to print larger files and to print faster.

If part of a document prints, the printer is probably encountering a PostScript error. See the next section.

What's a PostScript Error and What Do I Do About It?

PostScript is a computer language used in printers to describe the pages they output. Most professional publishing hardware and software uses PostScript. EPS files are individual PostScript graphics, whereas what many Windows users call ATM (Adobe Type Manager) fonts are actually PostScript **Type 1** fonts.

PostScript errors occur when a printer or piece of software doesn't understand the PostScript code it's trying to read, or when it can't handle it for some other reason. This may happen because the "flavor" of PostScript generated by an application—such as CorelDRAW!—isn't completely pure, or because the printer has PostScript emulation instead of actual PostScript code licensed from Adobe Systems, Inc. PostScript errors may also indicate that a printer is simply overloaded—an EPS graphic contains too many points for a printer to interpret correctly, for example.

To deal with a PostScript error, first you need to determine what's causing it. Here are some techniques that can help you track down the problem and deal with it.

- Try printing one page at a time. First of all, the printer's memory may not have the capacity to handle the entire document at once. Second, if the PostScript error is being caused by a single element, this technique can help you locate the page that element is on.
- Use one of several ways to suppress the printout of graphics. First, try printing with Rough chosen from the Output pop-up menu on the Options tab; this omits all graphics. If the document prints then, try printing with Omit TIFF (if you've only used TIFF and EPS graphics) or Omit TIFF & EPS (if you've used other formats) chosen from the OPI menu in the Options tab to narrow down the type of graphic that's causing the problem. Then go to suppressing individual graphics in the Picture tab of the Usage dialog box.
- If you do determine that an individual graphic is causing the PostScript error, delete it, resave it in its originating application, and reimport it. If that doesn't work, try converting it to another format and then reimporting it—for example, try saving a CorelDRAW! EPS graphic in Illustrator format, then open it in Illustrator and save it as an Illustrator EPS.
- Another remedy for not enough RAM is to reduce the area of each page that the printer must image. Mac users can try unchecking Larger print area in Page Setup Options (refer to Figure 12.11). Windows users should click the Restore Defaults button in the Paper tab of the Properties dialog box (refer to Figure 12.2). Dealing with that extra area around the page's perimeter can be the last straw for a printer without much RAM.

- Reducing the number of fonts in a document is another thing to try. The more fonts a document contains, the likelier it is that you'll have printing problems. Mac users can check Unlimited Downloadable Fonts in the Page Setup dialog box to force the system to download each font every time it's used on a page, rather than once for the entire document. The difference is that if a font is downloaded only once, it has to stay in the printer's memory until the document is entirely printed. Downloading the font again for each occurrence takes longer, but it can save RAM. Windows users, depending on their printer drivers, may have a Clear Memory Per Page option available in the Windows Properties dialog box (click the printer's icon and choose Properties from the File menu).
- If you've used Mac OS PICT graphics in a document, you can run into mysterious output problems with PostScript printers. Stick with TIFF and EPS graphics if you can—they're designed for print work, rather than onscreen work.
- Check vector graphics to make sure their paths are as simple as possible. Vector graphics with too many points can overload printers. You'll run into this problem most often with autotraced graphics and with some clip art, and the only solution is to open the graphics in their originating application and edit the paths.
- Try using different printer drivers: the LaserWriter or PostScript driver that came with your system software, Adobe's drivers (available on the Type on Call CD-ROM), and maybe a proprietary one that came with your printer. In QuarkXPress, make sure you have the correct PPD file selected in the Setup tab of the Print dialog box.

Why Is My Color Document Printing in Black-and-White on a Color Printer?

You probably have the wrong PPD file selected. Choose one for a color printer—otherwise XPress doesn't realize that it needs to send color information to the printer. If you don't have the PPD that came with your printer, try using another one that's similar—use Generic Color, which is built into QuarkXPress, if you don't have any other color PPDs. Then go looking for the printer manufacturer's Web site, where you may be able to download the correct PPD. Or, if you don't have Internet access, try calling the company's customer support phone number.

Summary

Most documents created in QuarkXPress end up being printed, but your results can vary wildly depending on the settings you make in the Print dialog box. When you're printing negatives or creating PostScript files, be sure that the settings are what your prepress house or printer prefers. Printing a document at intervals during its design can help pinpoint when a problem element is introduced, one that will cause problems every time the document is printed. Whatever print settings you use or kind of document you create, print styles can save you time and help you ensure that the right settings are used consistently.

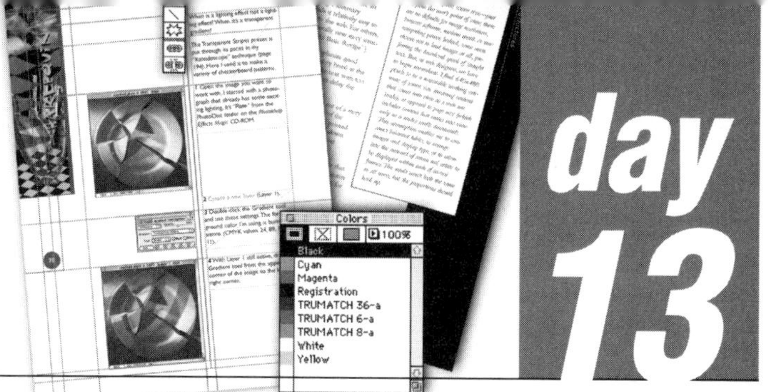

XTending XPress's Capabilities

- Using XTensions
- Buying XTensions

One of the best parts of using QuarkXPress is XTensions. If you need a feature that isn't included in the application, chances are you can get an XTension that will do what you want. This chapter is intended to give an idea of what types of things XTensions do and how you can use them to increase your efficiency and even make your design and production work more fun.

Using XTensions

QuarkXPress comes with several XTensions, such as Cool Blends, which lets you make blends with rectangular or other shapes. Then there are free XTensions, available both from Quark and from other companies. Wherever you get them, odds are that you'll end up with a more-or-less unmanageable collection of XTensions. Because each XTension clutters the interface and makes XPress take longer to load, you won't always want to load every XTension you own. There's also the unfortunate fact that some XTensions conflict with others or cause other types of problems—printing errors or crashes, even. Quark has added the XTension Manager to XPress 4.0 to make it easier to control which XTensions load.

Mac users will find the XTension Manager similar to the Mac OS Extensions Manager or Startup Manager, which control what parts of the system software load on bootup. The XTensions Manager is also somewhat similar to the Usage dialog box (see Figure 13.1).

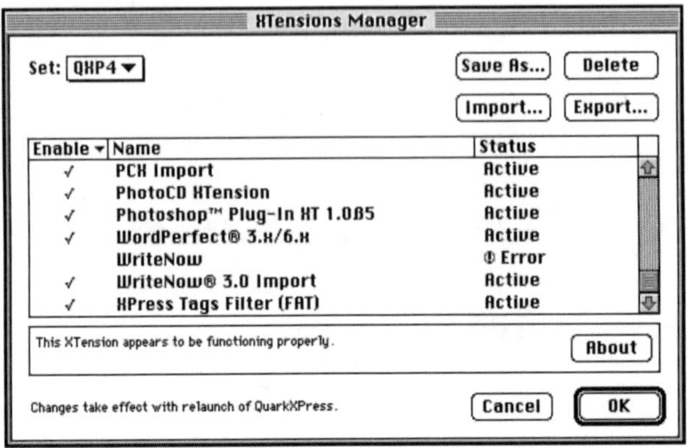

Figure 13.1

You can control which XTensions load when XPress starts with the XTensions Manager.

You can choose to have the XTensions Manager appear every time you start XPress, when you start XPress after changing the XTensions folder, or when XPress encounters an error loading an XTension (see Chapter 1, "XPress Basics"). Other than those occasions, you can view the XTensions Manager any time you want:

1. Choose Utilities➡XTensions Manager to bring up the XTensions Manager.
2. To turn on or off XTensions, click in the Enable column to add or remove a checkmark.
3. To save a set of XTensions for future use, click Save As and assign the set a name. Saved sets appear in the Set pop-up menu, along with the following choices:
   - All XTensions Enabled: Turns on all XTensions.
   - All XTensions Disabled: Turns off all XTensions (including import and export filters).
   - 4.0-Optimized XTensions: Turns on XTensions updated specifically to work well with version 4.0.

   To activate the XTensions in a particular set, choose that set from the Set menu.
4. To delete a set, choose the set you want to delete and click Delete.
5. To save a set to a file that you can share with other users, click Export and assign the file a name; to import a set, click Import and choose the set.
6. Click on an XTension and then click About to see information about the XTension (see Figure 13.2).
7. When you're done choosing XTensions, click OK to save the changes; the chosen XTensions will load after you quit and restart QuarkXPress.

About Cool Blends ver 4.0B1Rjyp

XTension Name:	Cool Blends
Enabled:	Yes
File Path:	:XTension:Cool Blends
4.0 Optimized:	No
FAT:	Yes
PowerPC Enhanced:	Yes
Version:	Cool Blends 2.11
Copyright:	© 1986-1996 Quark, Inc.
Status:	Active. This XTension appears to be functioning properly.

Figure 13.2

The XTensions Manager can display information about an XTension, such as its version and creator.

Active XTensions are stored in the XTension folder; XTensions you disable with the XTensions Manager are stored in the (XTension (Disabled))[XTension.off] folder. In general, to install an XTension, just place it in the XTension folder and start QuarkXPress; if an XTension requires more complex installation, it will come with instructions.

Buying XTensions

The following gives a look at some of the XTensions on the market as this book is written—it's not a list of recommended XTensions, and it doesn't include anywhere near all the XTensions on the market. I've created several rather arbitrary categories, as follows:

- Administration XTensions help you track jobs and administer groups of people working together in XPress.
- Libraries and catalog XTensions let you make collections of documents and document elements.
- Productivity XTensions help you increase your efficiency in a variety of ways.
- Text XTensions add to XPress's text formatting and editing features.
- Graphics XTensions increase XPress's graphics handling capabilities, both with imported graphics and with XPress graphic objects.
- Layout XTensions add features geared toward laying out pages more quickly accurately.
- Color XTensions help you manage colors.
- Printing XTensions help with file preparation and output.
- Specialty XTensions are intended to be used for a range of different kinds of publishing, from foreign-language to crossword puzzles.

For more information about any of the listed XTensions, contact XChange, XTension.com, or the XTension publisher—Appendix B lists contact information for publishers of all the XTensions mentioned here. XChange and XTension.com are the two major resellers of XTensions, and all the XTensions listed in this chapter are available from their catalogs.

- XChange

  XChange Publishing Systems International, Ltd.
  2700 19th Street, 1st Floor
  San Francisco, CA 94110
  Phone: 1-800-788-7557
  Fax: (415) 642-3816
  XChange@slip.net
  ftp.xchangeus.com/pub
  www.xchangeus.com

- XTension.com

  Media-Network
  821 Sansome Street
  San Francisco, CA 94111
  Phone: (415) 283-1811
  Fax: (415) 283-1806
  info@media-network.com
  www.xtension.com

Many free XTensions are also available from Quark's web site: www.quark.com.

Note

Because QuarkXPress 4.0 was released at the same time as this book, some of these XTensions may not yet work with version 4.0. Contact the XTension publisher to find out if an updated version is planned.

Administration XTensions

One of the most common administrative needs is to track the amount of time spent on each part of a job. Job Time (Mac, Techno Design), AdInfo (Mac, Vision's Edge), AdTracker (Mac/Windows, Vision's Edge), JobSlug (Mac/Windows, Vision's Edge), and Time Stamp (Mac/Windows, Vision's Edge) all do this, along with keeping track of various other pieces of information such as which people have worked on a document (see Figure 13.3).

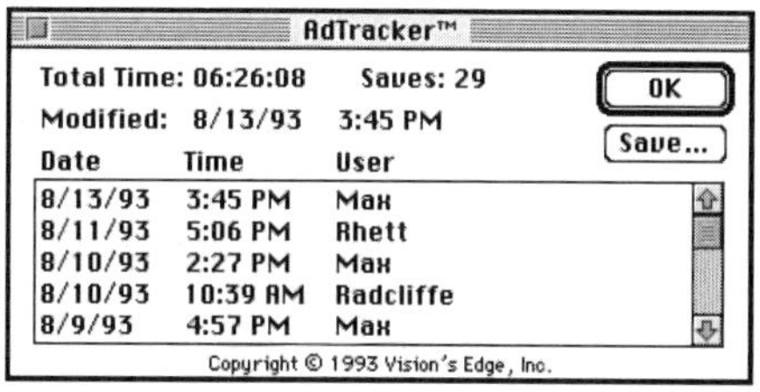

AdTracker™

Total Time: 06:26:08 Saves: 29

Modified: 8/13/93 3:45 PM

OK

Save...

Date	Time	User
8/13/93	3:45 PM	Max
8/11/93	5:06 PM	Rhett
8/10/93	2:27 PM	Max
8/10/93	10:39 AM	Radcliffe
8/9/93	4:57 PM	Max

Copyright © 1993 Vision's Edge, Inc.

Figure 13.3

AdTracker lets you know who's worked on a file, when, and for how long.

The FCSLock (Mac, FCS) XTension enables administrators to disable any menu item, tool, or palette of XPress to keep documents from being modified. LockPrefs (Mac, The NewMedia Workshop Ltd.) lets you create a master preferences file and keep users from modifying those preferences—this cuts down on problems with non-matching preferences when opening documents.

Communication is paramount when you're working with a group of people, and there's a selection of XTensions to keep the lines of communication open. Notes (Mac, freeware) and XNotes (Mac, freeware) enable you to add non-printing notes—like sticky notes—to a document, while SoundMemo (Mac, Imagemakers Software Systems) lets you leave recorded voice messages in documents. And, for those deadline situations when one hand on the mouse just isn't good enough, Press2Go Multi-User (Mac/ Windows, Atex) lets several users work simultaneously on the same page.

Library and Catalog XTensions

AutoLib (Mac, Vision's Edge) automatically creates standard XPress libraries from folders of graphics files, whereas Touch (Mac, Vision's Edge) lets you create special libraries that can contain text, pictures, or entire XPress documents (see Figure 13.4). Another way to catalog XPress documents is to use an image catalog program such as Extensis Fetch, but this software can't actually display documents because XPress documents don't contain a preview; the Preview Editor (Mac, Vision's Edge) XTension attaches a PICT preview to XPress documents to get around this problem.

Finally, you can make printable catalogs of your graphics with the Exposé (Mac/ Windows, Vision's Edge) XTension, which automatically builds catalogs based on a master page you design; it can also scan images directly.

Productivity XTensions

Scripting—creating small programs that automate actions within an application—may be intimidating to some people; after all, it's essentially the same as programming. But the two scripting languages XPress can use (AppleScript and Frontier) are designed to be simpler than programming languages, and there's a range of XTensions that make scripting even easier.

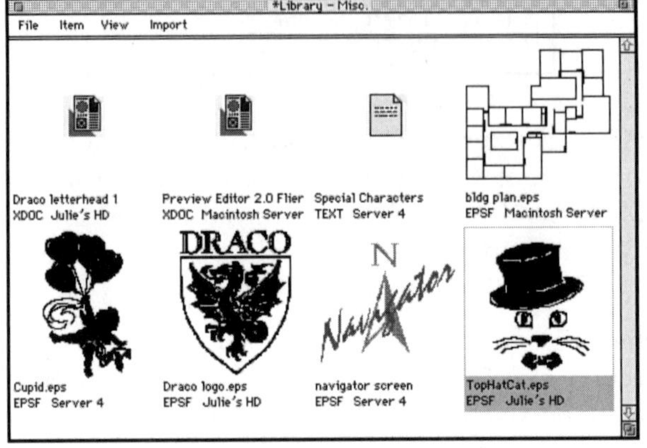

Figure 13.4

Graphics in Touch libraries can be placed in QuarkXPress documents by dragging them into the document window.

DocuScript (Mac, Graphic Arts Technologies) and ScriptIt (Mac, a lowly apprentice production) let you use any OSA (Open Scripting Architecture) scripts within XPress, while ScriptMaster (Mac, Street Logic Software) makes XPress recordable—so you don't need to write scripts. Using ScriptMaster XT, you just perform the actions you want to script and they're recorded into a perfectly formatted script that you can run any time you want. Once you start using scripts, Script Manager (Mac, Vision's Edge) can provide a convenient palette-based interface for launching them with a mouse-click (see Figure 13.5).

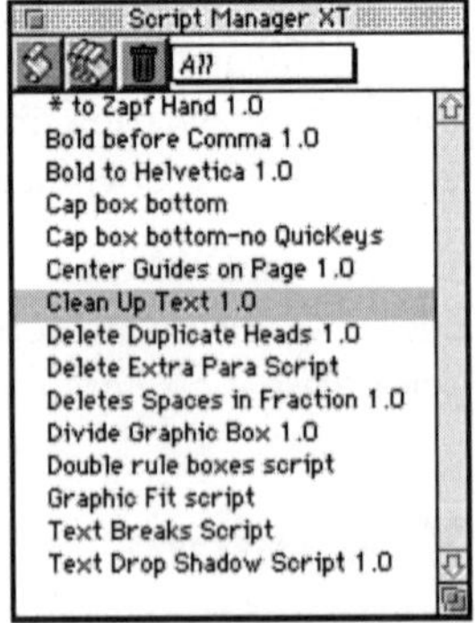

Figure 13.5

Script Manager lets you run scripts with a click.

Two XTensions that aim to improve productivity when opening files are Nouveau II (Mac/Windows, freeware) and QuickOpen (Mac, freeware, a lowly apprentice production). The former adds several features to the New Document dialog box, including the capability to create a document that starts on a specific page and contains a specified number of pages. QuickOpen is simple—it bypasses the conflicting preferences dialog and always opens documents using the document preferences, rather than XPress's preferences.

Collections of miscellaneous productivity XTensions are offered by several XTension publishers. Here's a look at a few:

- Notable because it's targeted at Windows users, the Windows Design ColleXTion (Windows, Vision's Edge) contains seven design-oriented XTensions.
- Extensis, maker of PageTools and PhotoTools, also produces QX-Tools (Mac, Extensis), which contains 15 different XTensions.
- The two volumes of XPert Tools (Mac, a lowly apprentice production) include tools like floating rulers and add extra functions to XPress's graphics greeking, text linking, scripting, text scaling, and other features.
- Ad Creation Toolkit (Mac/Windows, Vision's Edge) includes several utilities for building ads in XPress. It stores frequently used ad sizes and ad information (client name, ad number, and so on) within XPress documents, prints ad information on documents, and tracks user time (see Figure 13.6).

Figure 13.6

The different tools contained in Ad Creation Toolkit range from drop shadow creation commands to the capability to copy and paste character attributes.

- A unique set of features is offered by MarkzTools II (Mac, Markzware), which lets you open higher-version documents and libraries, set a preference for handling preferences conflicts when opening documents, and add color previews and special icons to XPress documents.

Text XTensions

Despite all its graphics capabilities, XPress is, first and foremost, text-handling software. These XTensions are designed to add even more power to XPress's text features.

Importing and Exporting

Perfect XT (Mac, Techno Design) and RFT-to-XPress (Mac, PrimaFont) let you import text in Mac WordPerfect 2.0 and RTF formats, respectively, while maintaining character formatting. The EDGAR Filter (Mac/Windows, Vision's Edge) exports text from XPress in the format used by the Securities and Exchange Commission. Batch text exporting can be accomplished with TeXTractor (Mac/Windows, Vision's Edge) and ArchiverXT (Mac, CSE); Archiver can also move documents to archive storage.

Making changes to both text and graphics can be easier in the original application; CopyFlow (Mac, NAPS) lets you export any or all of the text and graphics, make changes, and then reimport those items automatically. A similar capability is provided by Verbaytum (Mac, Vision's Edge), which can monitor imported text files and let you know if the original files have changed, then reimport the modified text.

It's not exactly a text feature, but PM2Q (Mac, Markzware) is probably one of the most desired XTensions on the market. It lets you open a PageMaker 5.0 document within QuarkXPress—not all elements translate perfectly, but it's a great start to converting a PageMaker document to XPress.

Editing

Although word processors generally are better for editing text, as opposed to formatting, there's still a lot of editing that must be done in XPress for the sake of convenience or a deadline. Quite a few XTensions add some oomph to XPress's text editing features.

You can improve hyphenation with one of these XTensions:

- Add Hyphens (Mac, Techno Design) lets you add hyphenation exceptions by importing a text file.
- Dashes (Mac, Windows, Compusense) and DiHyph XT (Mac, van Gennep) use different—and, theoretically, better—hyphenation algorithms than XPress.
- XTalos (Mac, Media Support & Development) provides foreign-language hyphenation.
- HyphenSet (Mac/Windows, Vision's Edge) shows a palette listing H&J settings, like the Colors and Style Sheets palettes.

Writers need a little help every now and then; that's where Thesaurus reX (Mac, Vision's Edge) comes in. It's a 220,000-word thesaurus that also wins the prize for "Best XTension Name." Taking over for XPress's built-in spellchecker is Spellbound (Mac, Compusense), which lets you use multiple auxiliary dictionaries and an exception dictionary (see Figure 13.7).

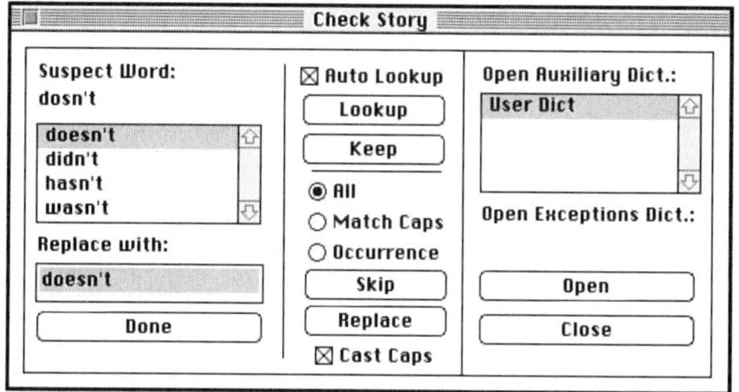

Figure 13.7

Spellbound is a more powerful spellchecker than the one included with QuarkXPress.

HX Glossary (Mac, HanMac) speeds up typing by replacing typed abbreviations with text; it also includes Symbol and Picture Font palettes that lets you quickly enter special symbols and dingbats. Sometimes it's the smallest features that save us the most frustration. Two small Xtensions in this category are ex Double Space (Mac/Windows, CoDesCo) and ChangeCase (Mac, freeware), which prevent you from typing double spaces and let you change the case of upper- or lowercase characters without retyping them, respectively.

Another word processor feature that XPress users covet is the ability to sort text in alphabetical order; this capability is offered by Exchange & Sort (Mac, The Last Word).

Before you can edit text, though, you have to be able to select it. Text Grabber (Mac, Meadows Information Systems) allows you to select text with a marquee rather than the text cursor (see Figure 13.8); HX PowerSelect (Mac, HanMac) and PowerEdit (Mac, Elex Computer) both let you select non-contiguous areas of text.

For editors who work in XPress, there are XTensions to replace that proverbial blue pencil. The Redlining (Mac, The Last Word) XTension, for example, lets you mark text as redlined text, which can be hidden and later deleted.

PageMaker aficionados will appreciate the StoryEditor (Mac, The Last Word) and Press2Go Editor (Mac/Windows, Atex) XTensions; they provide a separate, word processor-like window for editing text. Overset text (text that has overflowed its box and does not show) can be dealt with using the OverMatter (Mac, The Last Word) and

Overset Alert (Mac, freeware) XTensions that let you see the overflow text without affecting your layout. PowerBalance (Mac/Windows, Miles 33) is a related XTension that fits text within a box by slightly altering its formatting.

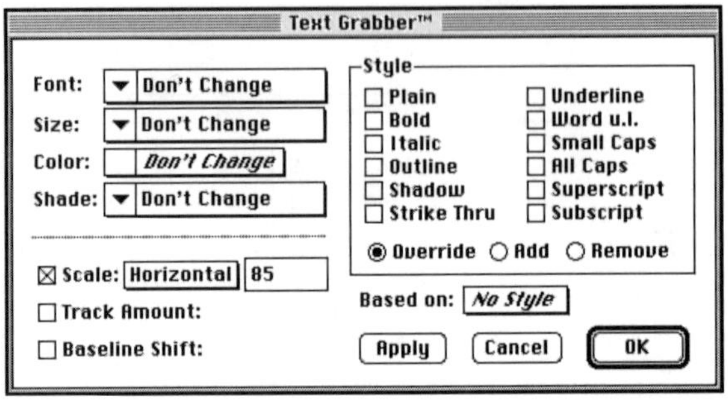

Figure 13.8

Once you've dragged a marquee to select text with Text Grabber, this dialog box lets you change its format.

If you prefer to edit by the numbers, ex Galley (Mac/Windows, CoDesCo) places an extra text box next to your text showing line numbers, whereas ex Counter (Mac/Windows, CoDesCo) provides character, word, and line counts. Press2Go Line Count (Mac/Windows, Atex), which counts words and lines and measures the amount of text that's over- or underset. LineCount (Mac, The Last Word) estimates how many words and lines of text will fill the space available in a document (see Figure 13.9).

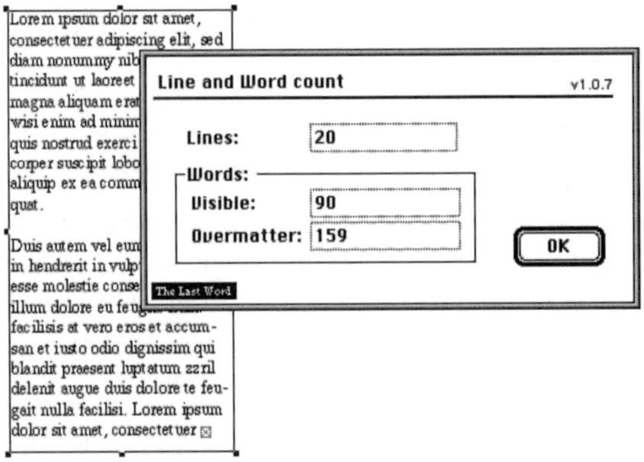

Figure 13.9

LineCount can count the lines and words in a text box, as well as tell you how much overset text there is.

If you're dissatisfied with XPress's Find/Change command, you're not the only one. Alias Pro (Mac, Patrick Perroud) lets you search for all special characters and replace with wildcard characters; it can save searches so that you can use them repeatedly. HX PowerSearch (Mac, HanMac) enables you to search and replace style sheets, box attributes, or line attributes. MAX (Mac, Vision's Edge) can search and change for more text formatting attributes than XPress's built-in Find command.

Formatting

Text formatting XTensions can speed up everything from formatting tabs to choosing a point size for text.

Several XTensions add to XPress's tab features. Super Tabs (Mac, Techno Design) displays tab settings in an editable list on a floating palette. Copy Grabber (Mac, Meadows Information Systems) lets you cut, copy, and paste a column of tabular copy in two easy steps by dragging a marquee around the area. And Tab Grabber (Mac, Meadows Information Systems) allows tab settings to be edited by dragging columns of text.

To speed up application of style sheets, StyleWorks (Mac, Media Support & Development) gives you an expandable palette with all the style sheet controls on it.

Anyone who's composed books that have to cross-align (the baseline at the foot of each page must be at the same depth as that of the facing page) will appreciate XTensions like ex Vertical Space (Mac/Windows, CoDesCo), which helps you align pages by applying specific amounts of extra space before and after paragraphs based on their style sheet; VJXT (Mac, KyTek) provides a similar function.

Finally, XPress Tags is great, but Xtags (Mac/Windows, Em Software) is a more powerful filter that supports XPress Tags plus other tags.

Graphics XTensions

XTensions such as MatchPrints (Mac,Vision's Edge) and Live Picture XT (Mac, Live Picture) enhance XPress's graphics capabilities in a number of ways. MatchPrints places text labels near imported pictures in XPress documents, so you can tell instantly which graphics files are used in the file, while Live Picture XT brings some of the functions of the Live Picture image editor to QuarkXPress, including the ability to crop, rotate, and resize original graphics files.

Special graphics effects are not just the province of Photoshop and Illustrator—they're attainable within XPress. 3d XT (Mac, Strata) lets you bend, stretch, and extrude type and boxes; I Shadow (Mac/Windows, Vision's Edge) and ShadowCaster (Mac, a lowly apprentice production) create soft drop shadows for any objects (see Figure 13.10); and Punch (Mac, Globimage Software) can create both outline and drop shadow effects for text.

Getting pictures in and out of XPress is a vital function that gets a lot of help from XTensions like Assassin (Mac/Windows, Vision's Edge), which can immediately delete some or all imported pictures in a document, and Batch Update (Mac, Meadows Information Systems), which can update all modified and missing pictures in multiple documents at the same time. Picture Dæmon (Mac/Vision's Edge) searches for and imports graphics by name and type. And Photoshop users usually have to save images in a format like TIFF or EPS before XPress can import them, but Photoshop Import (Mac/Windows, Techno Design) enables you to import layered Photoshop images directly into XPress.

ShadowCaster

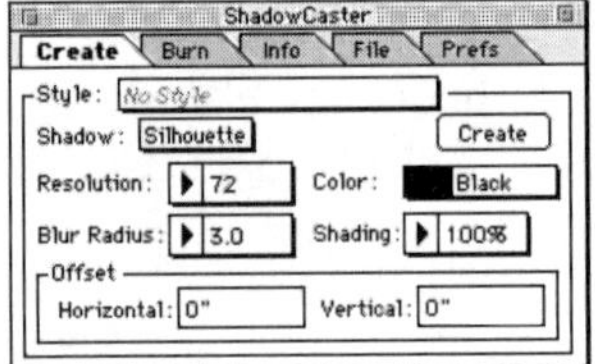

Figure 13.10

Create soft-edged TIFF shadows for any XPress text or shape with ShadowCaster.

Ordinarily, importing a new picture into a picture box that already contains a picture resets the picture position, scaling, and rotation settings to their defaults; Scitex TwoPoint (Mac, Scitex) retains all that information.

XPress lets you save pages in a document as EPS file, but you can expand on that capability. PageShot (Mac/Windows, Vision's Edge) lets you designate a certain area of the page to be saved as an EPS, or even just a single text or picture box. PICTmaker (Mac, Hologramophone Research) lets you export pages to PICT files—convenient for both multimedia use and because you can then batch convert the PICT files into any other raster format, such as TIFF or GIF. Or go directly to TIFF with the TIFF Export (Mac/Windows, Vision's Edge) XTension; you can specify the DPI and scale of the resulting image (see Figure 13.11).

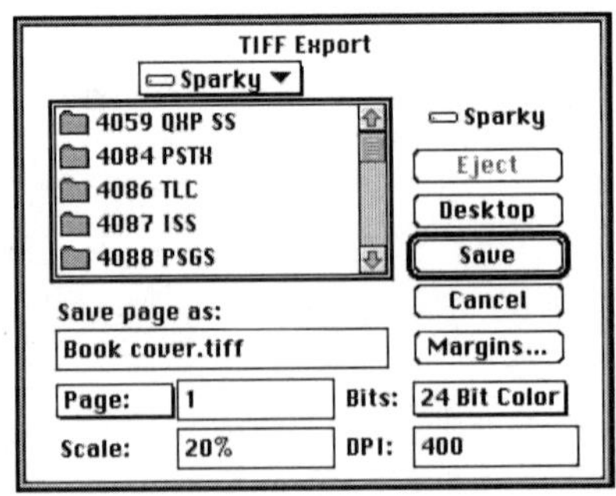

Figure 13.11

For those times when exporting pages as EPS won't do the job, TIFF Export lets you create TIFF files from XPress pages.

Layout XTensions

Basic layout functions—creating and arranging elements on the page—can be enhanced in myriad ways with XTensions, from the Pasteboard (Mac, Markzware) and CursorPos (Mac, KyTek) or CaretPos (Windows, freeware) XTensions, which let you respectively increase the vertical size of the pasteboard and display the cursor's position in a floating palette, to Pianzhang (Mac/Windows, Miles 33) and AutoPage (KyTek), which automatically paginate a document based on rules you define. XFlow (Mac, Vision's Edge) is a similar but less expensive product that imports text and graphics into template files but doesn't refine the layout (see Figure 13.12).

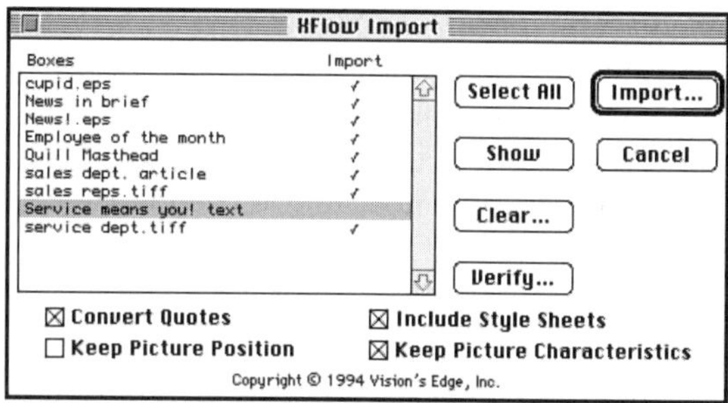

Figure 13.12

XFlow batch-imports text and images into named text and picture boxes.

XPress's Step and Repeat command is the basis for creating multiple, regularly spaced elements; Clone (Mac, Second Glance Software) and StepIt (Mac, XTend, Inc.) build on that capability. Clone lets you create templates and lay out multiple duplicates with one command, whereas with StepIt you can offset items accurately without having to do any math.

Box attributes can be modified in a number of ways. ex Inset (Mac/Windows, CoDesCo), MeasurementsPlus (Mac, The Last Word), and SetInset II (Mac, XTend, Inc.) let you define separate text inset values for different sides of text boxes, and ex ColumnBalance (Mac/Windows, CoDesCo) automatically resizes text boxes to fit the text they contain. Place Modify settings in a floating palette with HX BoxTool (Mac, HanMac), which also has a search command for boxes and remembers which box was active the last time you worked on a document.

Altering XPress items is even easier when you can make style sheets for them as you can for text. BoxStyles (Mac/Windows, Vision's Edge), ItemMaster (Mac, a lowly apprentice production), and ItemStyles (Mac, The Last Word) all enable you to create item styles that work like XPress's paragraph and character styles (see Figure 13.13). Taking a slightly different approach, HX Shortcut (Mac, HanMac) enables you to use keyboard shortcuts to apply predefined sets of attributes to items or text.

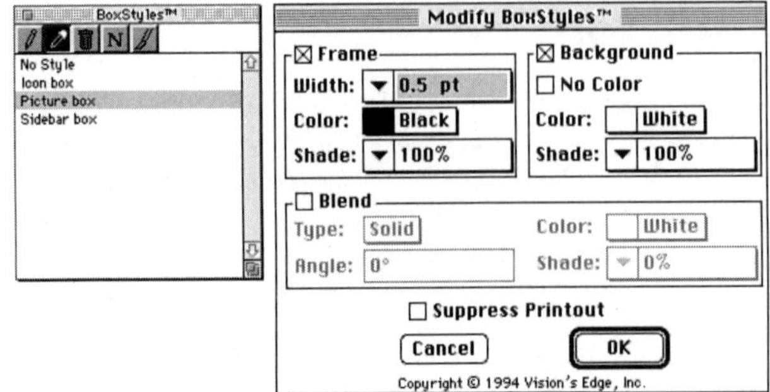

Figure 13.13

BoxStyles lets you create style sheets for boxes, just as you can for text.

Anyone who creates documents of more than one page has spent a lot of time linking and unlinking text boxes. The Missing Link (Mac/Windows, Vision's Edge) lets you link text boxes that both already contain text and duplicate boxes that are part of the text flow, with the copy containing only the text from the original box instead of the entire text flow. Unlinker (Mac, Hologramophone Research) unlinks text boxes while leaving the text in place.

You can combine rules and text in new ways with XTensions like ex Lines & Frames (Mac/Windows, CoDesCo), and PowerRules (Mac/Windows, Miles 33), all of which add column rules in text column gutters. EXPRESSWAY Rules (Mac, John Juliano) lets you paste rules into the text flow, as you can with boxes.

There are several XTensions that facilitate the creation of guides and grids in XPress documents, such as Guide Master (Mac/Windows, Vision's Edge) and GridLock II (Mac, Automatic Software). Another XTension, Scitex Grids & Guides (Mac, Scitex), lets you specify guides' numerical coordinates, color, and the view percentage at which they show.

One feature long wished-for in XPress is layers that would work like those in Illustrator so that specific objects could be shown or hidden, printed or not printed as desired. Two XTensions that provide this capability are Scitex Layers (Mac, Scitex) and Layer It! (Mac/Windows, Vision's Edge).

Other layout XTensions include Perfect Template (Mac, Adept Solutions), which creates documents whose margin guides exactly match your printer's printable area; Resize XT (Mac/Windows, Vision's Edge), which lets you resize groups of elements (see Figure 13.14); and UngroupIt (Mac, a lowly apprentice production), which ungroups multiple groups with one command.

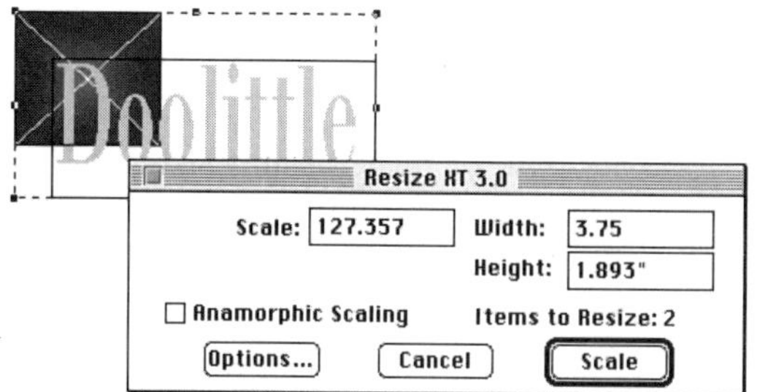

Figure 13.14

Resize multiple objects with Resize XT.

Color XTensions

Although XPress's Edit Colors dialog box and Colors palette work better than the color features in a lot of programs, XTensions can add features that make managing colors even easier.

Using ColorChange (Mac/Windows, Vision's Edge) and ColorManager (Mac/Windows, Compusense), you can search and replace colors and shades; ColorManager can also toggle whether colors are set to print as CMYK separations or spot colors (see Figure 13.15). PickUpSpot (Mac, Adept Solutions) lets you add spot colors that exactly match colors in imported images.

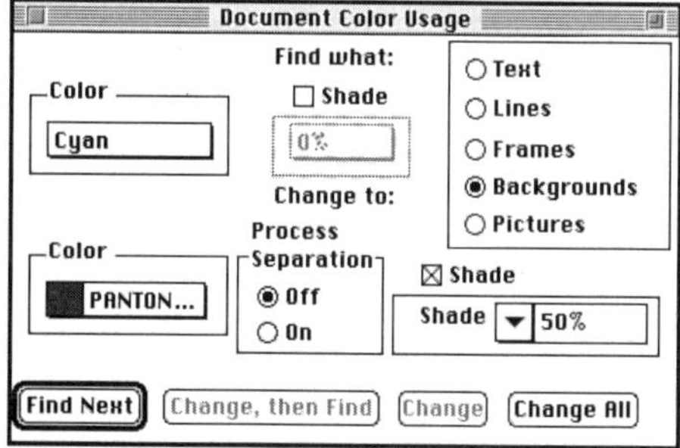

Figure 13.15

ColorManager's Color Usage dialog box lets you search and replace colors within a document.

Preparing a color document for output by a service bureau or prepress shop requires supplying a color proof with "color breaks"—written notes indicating the color composition of each color element. ColorBreaker (Mac, Hologramophone Research) automates that process, printing the XPress color information on or next to each element. Also helpful in film output is No-Trap (Mac, Focoltone), which uses the Focoltone color system to eliminate the need for trapping.

Printing XTensions

XTensions abound to improve the speed, efficiency, and quality of printing, whether you're printing laser proofs on your desk or running imposed negatives from a giant imagesetter. The place to start is with batch printing; Batch Print (Mac, Meadows Information Systems) lets you print as many as hundreds of XPress documents unattended, updating modified pictures and keeping a log of its activities.

PS Utilities (Mac, freeware) adds a PostScript error handler and other useful features, while FCSPrint (Mac, FCS) changes the Page Setup and Print dialog box settings to save as much film as possible and avoid common printing problems. You can compensate for dot gain using the Printer Calibration (Mac, freeware) XTension, which compensates for the spreading of halftone dots.

Imposition—rearranging pages for correct positioning on a printing plate—is often handled by a stand-alone application, but several XTensions can tackle the job. Bookletizer (Mac/Windows, Vision's Edge) and Signatures LT (Mac, Hologramophone Research) work for smaller documents, rearranging reader's spreads into printer's spreads (see Figure 13.16). Imposer (Mac, a lowly apprentice production) rearranges pages only as they're sent to the printer so that the source document isn't affected. For more heavy-duty imposition, INposition (Mac/Windows, DK&A) comes in two versions—regular and Lite; the regular version can handle any imposition job, while the Lite version can use up to 4-up plates and 32-page signatures.

Figure 13.16

Quick-and-easy printer's spreads are within reach with Bookletizer.

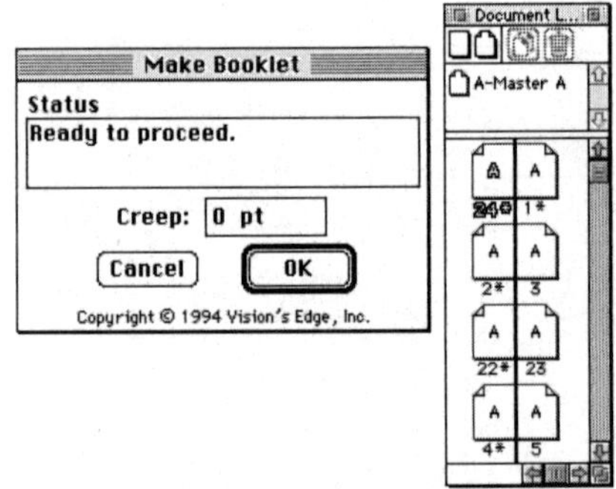

Printing color documents in black and white often results in muddy-looking or even illegible pages. Proofer (Mac, Hologramophone Research) and ReproTime (Mac, Hologramophone Research) both convert color documents to high-quality black and white, although the former is targeted to proofreaders (who sometimes can't read grayscale printouts of color documents) and the latter is targeted to those who need to create a repro paste-up version of a color job.

It can be difficult to be sure you're including all the files necessary for a service bureau to output your documents. XTensions intended to allay your fears include Bundler (Mac, Compusense), which creates a self-extracting archive of the document and supplemental files, and Batch Collect (Mac, Meadows Information Systems), which works like the Collect for Output command, only in batch mode with groups of documents.

When XPress's built-in crop marks don't do the trick, you can try any of several XTensions. ArtSlugger (Mac, Hologramophone Research) places the filename and path, as well as registration and crop marks, next to any graphic. PressMarks (Mac, Vision's Edge) uses custom PostScript registration marks and document information that you create. Crops XT (Mac/Windows, Vision's Edge) adds crop and registration marks, as well as color and grayscale bars, to any item or group on a page. MarkIt (Mac, a lowly apprentice production) lets you create crop and registration mark styles that you can save and use again.

Sometimes you don't want to print a whole page; PartialPrints (Mac/Windows,Vision's Edge) and Print Grabber (Mac, Meadows Information Systems) will print or save as an EPS file any part of an XPress page. In a similar vein, Selector (Mac, Media Support & Development) and SpotLite (Mac, Media Support & Development) let you print only selected color plates of a document, in your preferred order—a particularly useful feature when you have a feisty EPS graphic that thinks it's CMYK when it's not.

Other printing XTensions include FlexScale (Mac/Windows, Vision's Edge), which lets you scale printouts' horizontal and vertical dimensions independently, and PageBorder (Mac, freeware), which lets you add a border to a page or spread when you print it (see Figure 13.17).

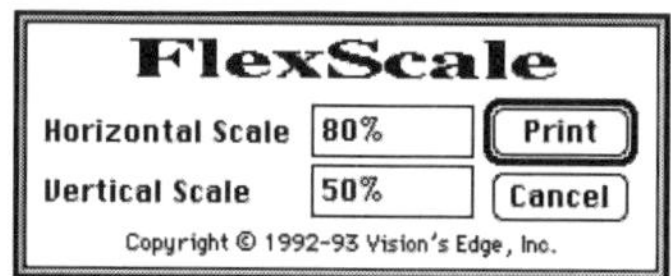

Figure 13.17

FlexScale's one function is to scale items disproportionately.

Specialty Publishing XTensions

Every publishing project has its own quirks—but some types of publishing are quirkier than others.

- Math: Most of us have had occasion to create an equation or two, but composing an entire math book is another story. Scitex Fractions (Mac, Scitex) lets you fine-tune fractions, specifying numerators and denominators of up to three characters, and adjusting the size and position of the fraction's numerator, denominator, and divisor. XMath (Mac/Windows, York) (York) can create equations from XPress elements, and Mathable (Mac/Windows, York) is a combo XTension that adds York's XTable to XMath. PowerMath (Mac, PowerHouse Software) can build extremely complex equations using specialized math fonts.

- Tables: Table-making XTensions use XPress's tab features to build tables much more quickly than you could by formatting each line separately. They include FCS TableMaker (Mac, FCS), TableMaker (Mac, Hologramophone Research), TableWorks Plus (Mac/Windows, Npath Software), and XTable (Mac/Windows, York) (see Figure 13.18).

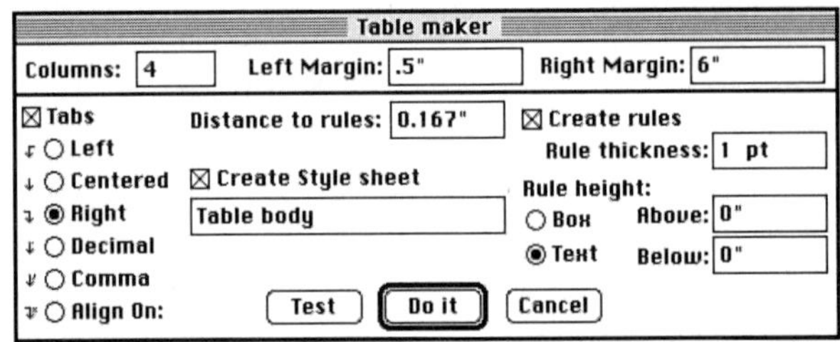

Figure 13.18

FCS TableMaker is part of FCS's utility collection.

- Database publishing: More and more XPress users are finding that repetitive documents like catalogs can be more easily created by combining the information-handling capacity of a database with the formatting power of XPress. XTensions that take this approach to publishing include AutoPrice (Mac, Meadows Information Systems), which can link XPress documents to any database where each record contains a numerical "key value"; DTP603 (Mac, System Clinic), which includes its own relational database application, and Xcatalog (Mac/Windows, Em Software), which can link to any database.
- Bar codes: Bar Code Pro (Mac/Windows, Synex) and UPC-EAN (Mac/Windows, Azalea Software) (Azalea) create bar codes in several flavors (see Figure 13.19).
- Web publishing: Everyone's got to get on the World Wide Web these days; PDF Design (Mac, Techno Design) lets you create hyperlinks and bookmarks within QuarkXPress that translate when you create Acrobat PDF documents, and HexWeb (Mac, HexMac International), BeyondPress (Mac, Astrobyte), HTML XPort (Mac, shareware), and CyberPress (Mac, Extensis) all provide variously sophisticated levels of HTML export.

Figure 13.19

UPC codes, saved in EPS format, can be created within XPress using UPC-EAN.

- Long-document features: Although QuarkXPress 4.0 now includes indexing and table of contents features, XTensions are still available that help with other long-document features; fXT (Mac, KyTek) automates the placement and numbering of footnotes within XPress documents using markup codes and a floating palette, and Headers XTn (Mac, ESS) places the correct heading text in the running header or footer on each page.

Creating Internet and Multimedia Documents

- Converting QuarkXPress documents to HTML
- Converting QuarkXPress documents to Acrobat
- Converting QuarkXPress documents to Immedia

An increasing number of design projects have nothing at all to do with paper, and many paper-based designs—for brochures, reports, even résumés—are turning out to have a second life in the form of electronic presentations. In this chapter you'll learn about three methods you can use to take documents from print to the Internet, or to other electronic media; each has both drawbacks and advantages.

Exporting HTML Documents

HTML can be considered the lowest common denominator of electronic publishing. It's a text-based coding system that can be interpreted by web browser applications and turned into formatted text with links to pictures.

The advantages of using HTML for electronic publishing include:

- The HTML text files and **GIF** and **JPEG** graphics involved are usually small and easy to handle. They're quick for you to upload to a web server, and they're quick to download so that the end user can view them.
- With existing utilities, the HTML code is quick and easy to generate from scratch or from existing QuarkXPress documents.
- Consistent coding can be generated by scripts and databases, so you can automate the HTML conversion of large batches of documents, or even generate both XPress Tags text and HTML text from the same database and publish in both print and web forms with the same information base.

- HTML is the universally accepted format of the World Wide Web, although you can use it in other contexts, and it's accessible to anyone with Internet access. It can even be used on a command-line operating system that doesn't display graphics.

HTML has disadvantages, too:

- HTML offers little control over how a document looks onscreen. It uses only the fonts installed in the end-user's system (although that restriction may disappear soon), and it has a limited number of styles that you can assign to text. Although it's becoming more customizable, it's not there yet—what you see on your design workstation is *not* what you get on the user's end most of the time.

Note

Web designers would really like to be able to send the necessary fonts along with their HTML documents so that users could see the designs as they were created. That ability is on its way, with technology such as Bitstream's TrueDoc system. TrueDoc lets you include fonts in web pages, position type with greater accuracy, and anti-alias type so that it looks smoother onscreen.

- HTML code can be esoteric and difficult to learn. Although HTML export tools and design applications can insulate you from the actual HTML code most of the time, the best web designers are those who can hammer out the code by hand when it's necessary.
- Although basic HTML is supported by all browsers, some features added by third parties are not supported by some browsers. That's why you see those "Best viewed with Netscape Navigator" and "Optimized for Internet Explorer" icons on the splashier web pages. To be sure that everyone can read all your web pages, you have to stick with the lowest common denominator of HTML coding.
- To use the cool multimedia effects that attract attention on the web, extra software has to be installed on both your end and the user's end. Whether it's Shockwave, Java, or RealAudio, you'll have to tell each new user where and how to download the appropriate software before he or she can view your pages, and then you'll have to hope those users come back after they've upgraded.

Despite its drawbacks, HTML is the appropriate choice for documents with lots of text that don't depend on their design to carry the message. It has the added advantage of being searchable so that HTML pages appear in Internet search engines while other documents may not. And it's even easier to include HTML documents and a browser application on a CD-ROM as software documentation or even as a presentation.

Converting QuarkXPress documents to HTML can be accomplished in a number of ways. First, you can simply export a document's text in ASCII format and add the HTML coding by hand. Or you can export the text in XPress Tags format and use scripting or macros to replace the XPress Tags coding with HTML coding. A free Perl script called Quark to HTML, created by the publishers of MIT's student newspaper, *The Tech*, can convert XPress Tags to HTML; download it from `tech.mit.edu/~jeremy/qt2www.html`. You'll also need Perl, a Unix scripting language that's been ported to the Mac OS and to DOS; the Quark to HTML page tells where to get Perl, as well.

Two XTensions that can export XPress documents to HTML format are BeyondPress (Mac OS/Windows, Astrobyte) and HexWeb (Mac OS/Windows, HexMac), along with CyberPress (Mac OS, Extensis), a "lite" version of BeyondPress. Each converts and exports graphics to web formats, and CyberPress and BeyondPress let users map QuarkXPress styles to HTML styles. HexWeb can build an entire hierarchical web site, and its HexScape XT lets you use Netscape plug-ins as you create pages.

Using Adobe Acrobat

You can create **Acrobat PDF** (portable document format) files from almost any application that can print, including QuarkXPress. These files can be viewed and printed by anyone who has the free Acrobat Reader software, and a plug-in lets you view PDF files in Navigator or Internet Explorer. Acrobat PDF files look and print just like the original documents, without the need for the end user to have the original application, fonts, or graphics. They're one way to preserve the look of a document and still distribute it widely, whether it's by handing a floppy disk to a potential employer or by uploading the file to a web site.

There are two ways to create a PDF file from QuarkXPress:

- PDF Writer is a printer driver; if it's active, you can create PDF files by using XPress's Print command (see Figure 14.1). Mac OS users choose PDF Writer in the Chooser; Windows users choose PDF Writer from the Printer pop-up menu in the Print dialog box. PDF Writer can't handle EPS artwork or other PostScript-only features, so it's best for those who aren't working in a PostScript environment.
- Acrobat Distiller offers better results and more control than PDF Writer (see Figure 14.2). To use Distiller, you first create a PostScript file by printing to a disk file instead of to a printer; then you open the PostScript file in Distiller, which converts it to a PDF file (see Figure 14.3).

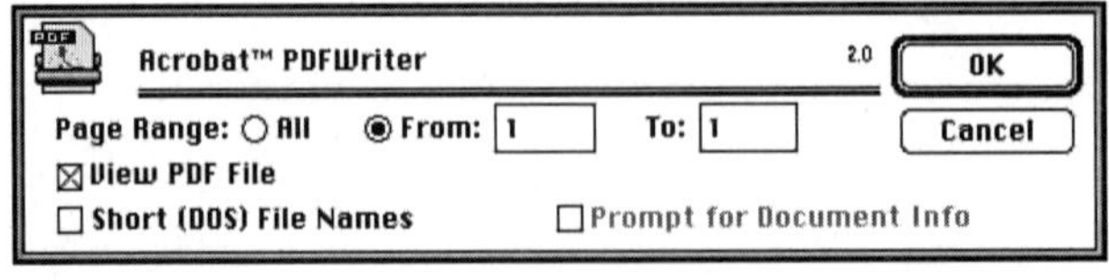

Figure 14.1

PDF Writer changes your Print command into a "create PDF" command.

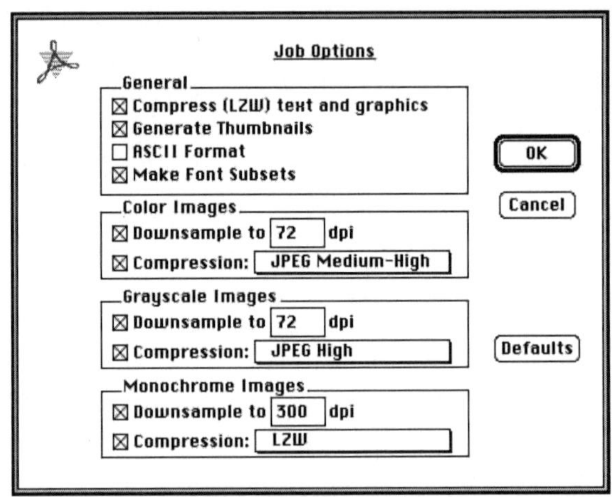

Figure 14.2

Distiller's Job Options dialog box lets you specify how PDF files are created.

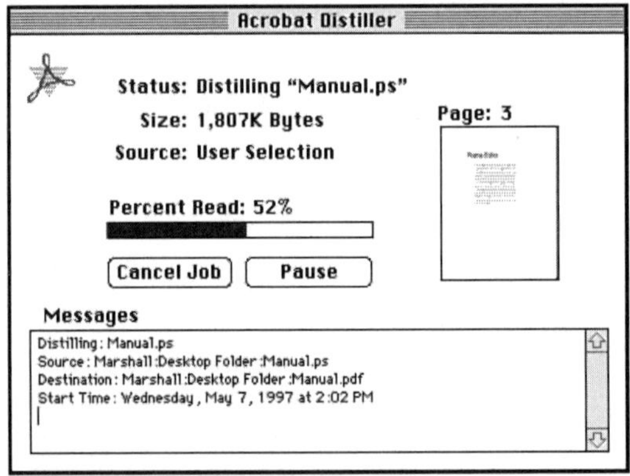

Figure 14.3

Creating PDF files with Distiller is a one-step process.

After you've created a PDF file using PDF Writer or Distiller, you can add notes, hyperlinks, and other features to it using Acrobat Exchange (see Figure 14.4).

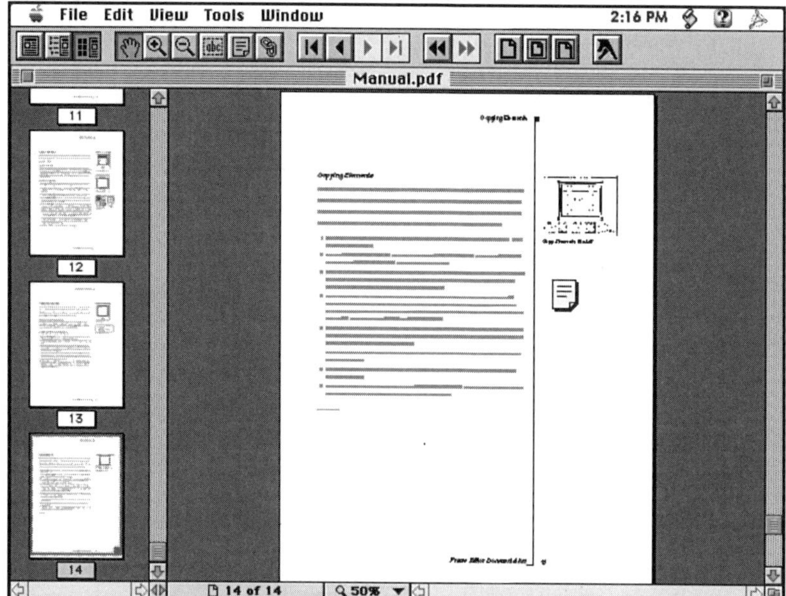

Figure 14.4

Exchange lets you fine-tune PDF documents.

Using QuarkImmedia

Immedia is a QuarkXTension that you use within QuarkXPress to create multimedia presentations that can be distributed as standalone documents or viewed on the Internet. Using Immedia, you can create new multimedia documents or start with an existing XPress document and add to it. Immedia projects can include sound, video, interactive buttons, hyperlinked text, and animations.

If you're used to QuarkXPress, you'll find Immedia easier to learn than most multimedia design applications. After you've created a new Immedia project (see Figure 14.5), you edit using XPress tools and Immedia functions, most of which are contained in one floating palette with six tabs:

- The Page tab (see Figure 14.6) lets you name pages in the **project**, assign actions to them, and control **transitions** between pages. You can choose actions, such as playing a sound, to be performed when the viewer reaches a page and when moving to another page, and you can choose to move on to a new page after a specified amount of time.

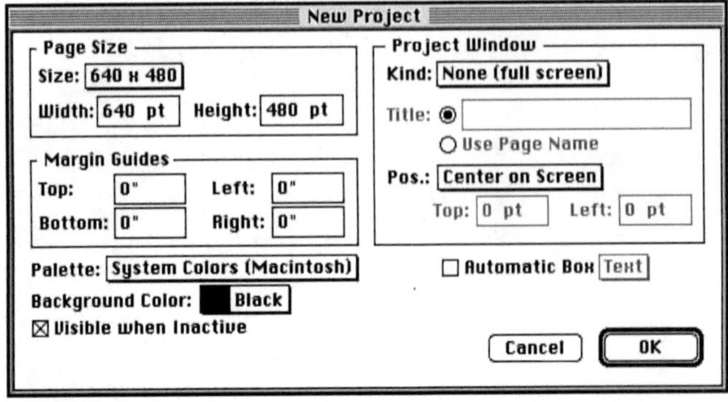

Figure 14.5

Immedia's New Project dialog box is equivalent to XPress's New Document dialog.

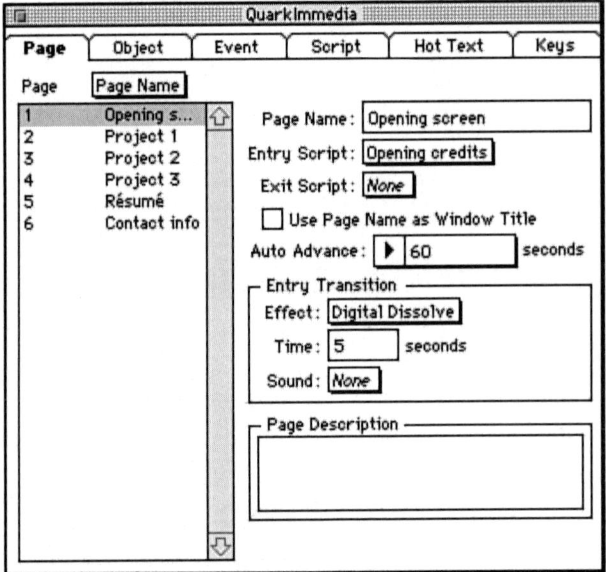

Figure 14.6

The Page tab of the Immedia palette.

- The Object tab (see Figure 14.7) lets you specify objects on the pages as Immedia objects so that you can use Immedia's features with them. For example, you can specify that a picture box is actually a movie box, then import a QuickTime movie into the box.
- The Event tab (see Figure 14.8) lets you determine what happens to objects when users click them. You can assign any of dozens of responses to an object, from printing to opening the **URL** for a web page. You can also assign sounds and special cursors to be displayed when an object is clicked.

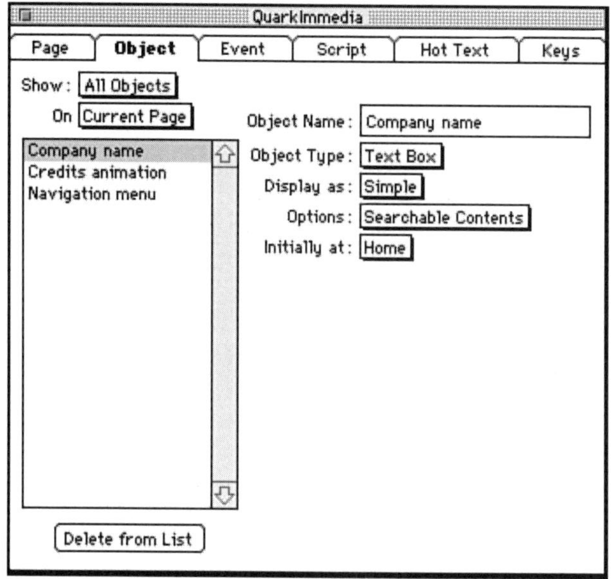

Figure 14.7

The Object tab of the Immedia palette.

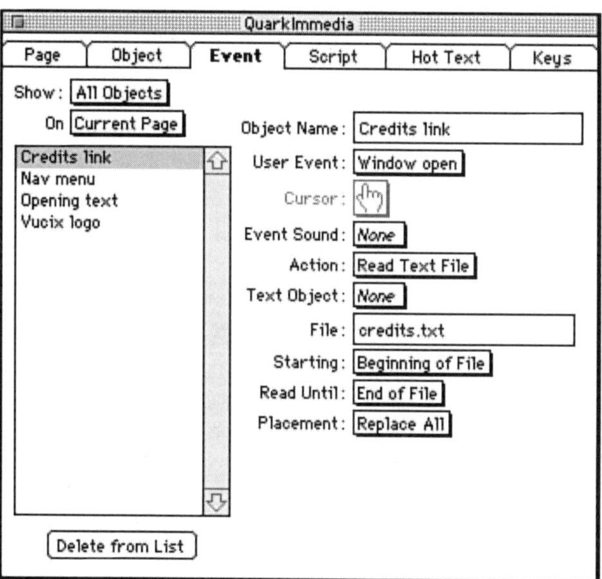

Figure 14.8

The Event tab of the Immedia palette.

- The Script tab (see Figure 14.9) lets you string series of actions together to make **scripts** that can be assigned to objects or pages so that multiple actions take place when the viewer enters a page or clicks on an object. Script actions are chosen from a menu and can be reordered by dragging.

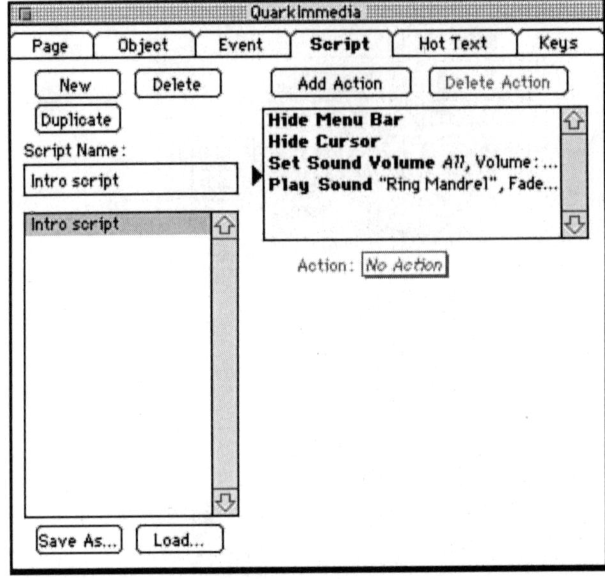

Figure 14.9

The Script tab of the Immedia palette.

- The Hot Text tab (see Figure 14.10) lets you assign similar actions to text so that when the viewer clicks on **hot text** the page changes, a sound plays, or a URL is opened. You can control factors associated with each type of action, such as transitions and which page is opened.

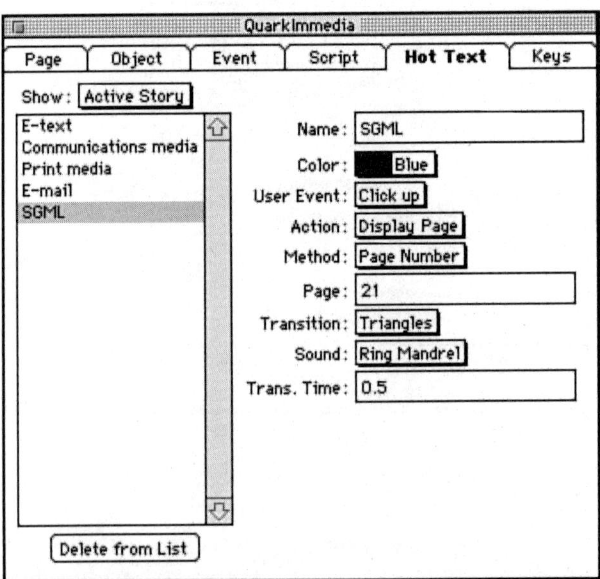

Figure 14.10

The Hot Text tab of the Immedia palette.

- The Keys tab (see Figure 14.11) lets you assign keyboard shortcuts to actions.

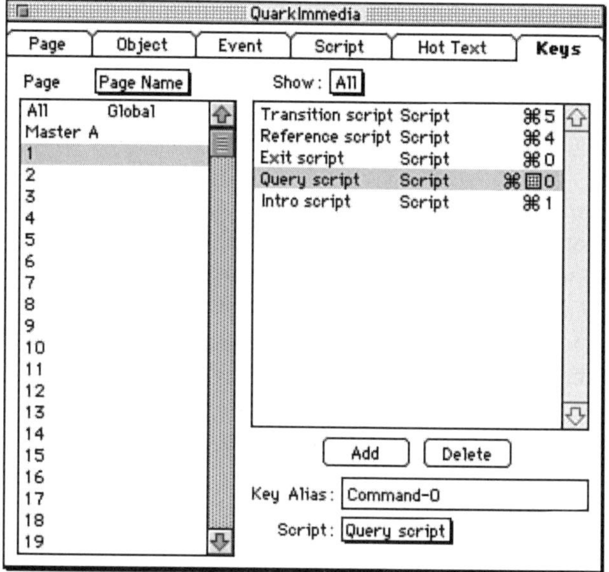

Figure 14.11

The Keys tab of the Immedia palette.

The rest of Immedia's functions appear in the QuarkImmedia menu to the right of XPress's Utilities menu. These commands let you convert XPress documents to Immedia projects and vice versa, play a project while you're designing it, add menus to a project, and create custom transitions. The Make Index command lets you create HTML index files that contain all the text in a project so that projects can be included in Internet search engines.

Once you've created an Immedia project, you have two choices. You can export it as a standalone file, with an embedded copy of the Immedia Viewer application; this file can be viewed by anyone. Or you can distribute the project without the embedded viewer—this is what you'd do if you were adding the project to your web site—and require users to download the free Immedia Viewer application. The viewer is a standalone application that needs to be specified as the helper application for Immedia files before you can view Immedia projects on the web.

Immedia costs more than QuarkXPress, but you can try a free demo version before buying. Download the demo at `www.quark.com/demo002.htm`.

For more information about Immedia, check out these web sites:

- Quark's Immedia home page is at `www.quark.com/qim001.htm`.

- For Immedia tips and links to other Immedia sites, try Peter Togel's The Immedia Place at `members.aol.com/immediapt`.
- Even more Immedia sites are listed at `www.desktoppublishing.com/quarkimm.html`, part of the huge desktopPublishing.com jumplist.

Summary

Moving documents from print format to an electronic format is certainly possible, and often even easy. It's important to determine the right format first, though. For documents in which the text is very important and the design not particularly vital, use HTML. For documents in which the design is the biggest concern, and that don't need multimedia bells and whistles, use Acrobat. For documents that you want to enhance with sound, scripting, video, and other "extras," use Immedia.

appendix A

Cross-Platform Use

It's increasingly a cross-platform world. These days, Mac OS systems and Windows systems can talk to each other more easily than ever before, and collaboration is becoming the norm rather than the exception. QuarkXPress is one of the most cross-platform applications out there—its Mac OS and Windows versions can open each other's files without a hitch. On the other hand, there are a few factors involved in using cross-platform files that XPress can't control—that's where the information here will come in handy.

Getting Files to Your Computer

The first issue you'll have to deal with in moving QuarkXPress files from one platform to another is the actual file transfer. One of the easiest ways to move files across platforms is via a network, whether it's a corporate LAN or WAN or the mother of all networks, the Internet. Just place your files on a server and then retrieve them from the destination platform. Essentially the same operation can take place using direct modem-to-modem transfers or by attaching the file to an email message. For best results, compress the file first; Mac OS software like StuffIt Expander and ZipIt can read PC zip archives, so that compression format is your best bet.

If electronic file transfer is not an option for you, try good old floppy disks. Both Mac OS systems and Windows systems can read DOS-formatted floppies, so that's the lowest common denominator for "sneaker-net" transfers. Most other removable media formatted on a Windows system can be used on a Mac OS system, too, including Zip and SyQuest disks. To convince a Windows system to read Mac-formatted disks, you'll need a third-party software package like Mac-in-DOS (Pacific Microelectronics).

Opening Files

Although Windows 95 and NT can use long filenames, that doesn't mean you should go crazy. Windows 95 files appear to have long filenames, but underneath they're still using eight-letter versions of those names, and that's what you'll see if you transfer a Windows 95 file to a Mac OS system on a floppy disk. To be on the safe side, stick with the eight-three naming convention on both platforms, using the appropriate filename extensions (see Table A.1). In that same safety-conscious vein, don't use punctuation (other than hyphens and periods) or spaces in filenames.

Table A.1 QuarkXPress filename extensions.

File type	Extension
Documents	QXD
Libraries	QXL
Templates	QXT
XPress Tags	XTG
Dictionaries	QDT
Encapsulated PostScript file	EPS

You can always open a QuarkXPress file using File➡Open. Windows will let you open a QuarkXPress file, whether it came from a Mac OS or a Windows system, by double-clicking if it has a QXD filename extension and if QXD is registered with Windows as representing an XPress file. To open a PC XPress file by double-clicking in the Mac OS Finder, you'll need to map the filename extension in the PC Exchange control panel.

When you open a cross-platform file in XPress, you'll first see a dialog indicating that XPress is converting the file (see Figure A.1). Then you may see the non-matching preferences dialog; treat it as you would with any other document—in other words, most of the time you'll want to use document preferences. Then you may need to deal with fonts. Even if you have the appropriate fonts loaded on your system (see "Dealing with Fonts" later in this appendix), you may need to tell XPress which fonts to substitute for the fonts used on the other platform; it will substitute the new fonts in the document's existing text and in its style sheets. Finally, the file opens with the same name it had on the other platform. The first thing you should do is save it, since the conversion process does make changes to the file.

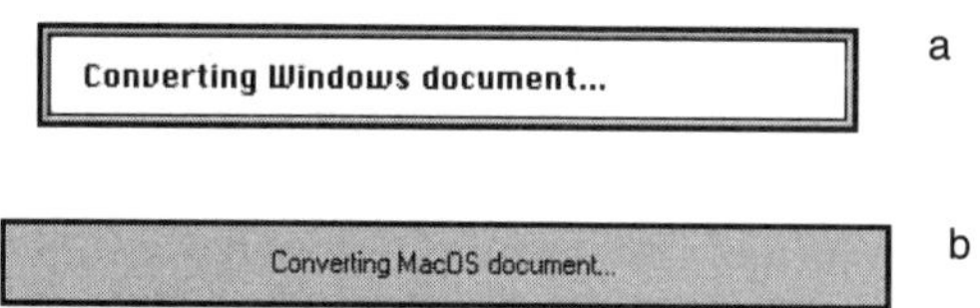

Figure A.1

The (a) Mac and (b) Windows versions of this dialog appear onscreen while XPress converts cross-platform documents.

Dealing with Fonts

Fonts probably cause the most problems in transferring XPress files across platforms. The key to eliminating as many problems as possible is using high-quality PostScript or TrueType (but not both) fonts from the same vendor on both platforms. In other words, don't use the Adobe version of Caslon on the Mac, substitute the Monotype version of Caslon on the PC, and then expect the text to look just the same. Differences in font metrics (character widths) may occur even in fonts from the same vendor, causing some text reflow, but this will be kept to a minimum if you can bring yourself to lay out the money for the right cross-platform versions of the fonts you're using.

If you can, avoid custom fonts, and don't use fonts that are specific to one platform or the other. While many fonts that used to be Windows-only, like Arial and Wingdings, are now available in Mac versions, the same isn't true for the famous Mac city fonts: Geneva, New York, Monaco, and so on. Mac OS users should stay away from these fonts if their documents are destined to move to Windows. Fonts can be converted, but they won't necessarily work right, especially with regard to printing and using special characters. Make this a last resort.

Even if you've got the same fonts on both sides of the translation, some characters may not translate. Special characters like the Mac ligatures and Windows fractions don't exist on the other side, so other characters will be substituted for them. You'll need to use Find/Change to restore these characters to what they should be.

Because Windows fonts don't have ligature characters, the Auto Ligatures feature doesn't exist in the Windows versions of QuarkXPress. Mac OS documents that use automatic ligatures will translate correctly, with the individual letters used instead of ligatures.

Dealing with Graphics

The best form of protection when working with cross-platform graphics is to use cross-platform formats like TIFF and EPS.

Mac OS EPS files present two problems for Windows users; first, the preview image that's shown onscreen is usually in PICT format, and second, it's stored in a separate part of the file called the resource fork. Because PCs can't read Mac files' resource forks, Mac EPS files appear to have no preview image. That means they can be imported into a document and printed, but you'll see a gray box (see Figure A.2) on the screen instead of a low-resolution preview of the EPS file's actual contents. To get around this, you'll need to save EPS images with a TIFF preview that's intended for use on PCs. Some Mac OS programs can do this, and others can't. QuarkXPress 4.0 can save an EPS file with a color TIFF preview, for example, but while FreeHand 7 can give an EPS file a TIFF preview, it's black-and-white only. Also, if you encounter printing problems on the Windows side, try saving the EPS file using ASCII encoding rather than binary; ASCII is slower but binary may confound older PC printers.

Figure A.2

If XPress can't find a preview in an EPS image, this is what it displays.

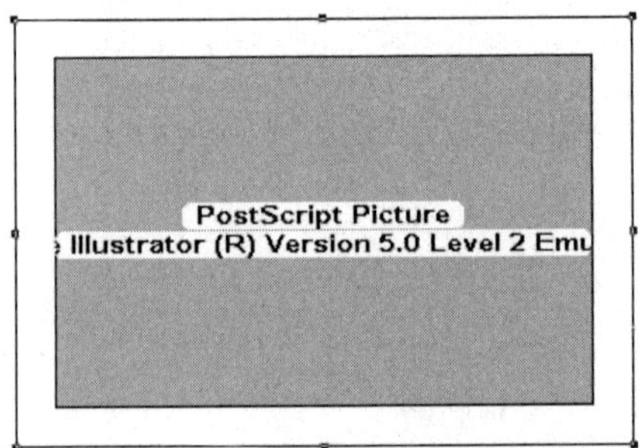

Avoid CorelDraw EPS files—they use nonstandard PostScript and often cause printing problems. They also can't be converted to another PostScript application format like Illustrator, as most other PostScript graphics can.

Tip

You can, however, convert a standard CorelDRAW! file to an Illustrator file by saving it from CorelDRAW! in Illustrator format. Then open the file in Illustrator and resave it as Illustrator EPS.

TIFF files are usually easier to deal with, especially since Photoshop is so popular on both platforms. While there are dozens of TIFF "flavors," the more oddball ones are being slowly pushed out of the way by standardized versions—it's fairly rare these days to find a TIFF file that you can't read. When saving TIFF files intended for cross-platform use, use PC encoding—Mac OS systems won't care.

Graphics file formats to avoid include Windows- or Mac-only formats like WMF and PICT. If you've got graphics in an undesirable format, you can convert them to another format using either an image editor like Photoshop or graphics conversion software such as DeBabelizer (Equilibrium Software). As with XPress document filenames, stick to the eight-three conventions for graphics filenames, and use the right filename extension for the format (TIF for TIFF files, EPS for EPS files).

If you're sending files to another user, include the original graphics files, rather than just the resulting files. That generally means including the original files from applications like FreeHand and CorelDRAW!, both of which allow you to export separate EPS files. With the original files, a user who's having trouble printing the EPS files can open the originals and save them in a different format that might work better, or edit them to remove the elements that are causing trouble.

Depending on your folder organization, you may need to relink graphics after opening a cross-platform document. Windows users need to be aware that the Mac OS version of XPress will not be able to maintain links with graphics inserted via OLE—don't use this method if your files must be cross-platform. Mac OS users should follow the same rule with regard to Publish and Subscribe. These two features are specific to their respective operating systems, and they just don't work both ways.

XTension Buyer's Guide

a lowly apprentice production, inc.

5963 La Place Court

Suite 206

Carlsbad, CA 92008-8823

Phone: (619) 438-5790

Fax: (619) 438-5791

support@alap.com

www.alap.com

Adept Solutions

7314 Creekwood Place NE

Bremerton, WA 98311

Phone: (360) 308-9831

Fax: (360) 308-9832

info@adeptsolutions.com

Astrobyte USA

625 16th Avenue

Denver, CO 80203

Phone: (303) 861-4861

Fax: (303) 861-4876

info@astrobyte.com

`www.astrobyte.com`

Atex Media Solutions, Inc.

15 Crosby Drive

Bedford, MA 01730

Phone: 1-800-433-ATEX

info@atex.com

`www.atex.com`

Automatic Software Ltd.

1-2 Bromley Place

London W1P 5HB

U.K.

Phone: 0171 636 6809

Fax: 0171 580 1243

info@automatic.com

`www.automatic.com`

Azalea Software, Inc.

P.O. Box 16745

Seattle, WA 98116-0745

Phone: (206) 932-6028

azalea@azalea.com

www.azalea.com

CoDesCo GmbH (Extended Technologies)

Im Hegen 11

D-22113 Oststeinbek

Germany

Phone: 49 40 71300130

Fax: 49 40 71300160

sales@codesco.com

www.codesco.com

Compatible Systems Engineering, Inc.

7630 Little River Turnpike

Suite 216

Annandale, VA 22003

Phone: (703) 941-0917

Fax: (703) 941-0924

cse@compatsys.com

www.compatsys.com

CompuSenseLtd.

Avondale House

The Square, Ballincollig

Cork

Ireland

Phone: 353 21 871394

Fax: 353 21 874513

compusen@indigo.ie

DK&A, Inc.

1010 Turquoise Street

Suite 300

San Diego, CA 92109

Phone: (619) 488-8118

Fax: (619) 488-4021

sales@dka.com

`www.dka.com`

Elex Computer, Inc.

Phone: 02 709 8000

Fax: 02 709 8452

`www.elex.co.kr`

Em Software, Inc.

503 Belleview Boulevard

Steubenville, OH 43952

Phone: (614) 284-1010

Fax: (614) 284-1210

info@emsoftware.com

www.emsoftware.com

ESS Hard- & Software GmbH

Liborius-Wagner-Straße 15

97096 Würzburg

Germany

Phone: 49 0 931 27795

Fax: 49 0 931 277 90

info@ess-gmbh.de

www.ess-gmbh.de

Extensis

1800 SW 1st Avenue

Suite 500

Portland, OR 97201-5322

Phone: 1-800-796-9798

Fax: (503) 274-0539

info@extensis.com

www.extensis.com

FCS, S.L.

Gremio Tejedores 22, 1º

07009 Palma de Mallorca

Spain

Phone: 34 71 43 12 77

Fax: 34 71 43 08 18

ckefauver@ibacom.es

`www.ibacom.es/fcs/DefaultEng.html`

Focoltone Ltd.

Springwater House

Taffs Well, Cardiff CF4 7QR

Wales

UK

Phone: 44 22 281 0940

Fax: 44 22 281 0962

Globimage, Inc.

7070, Beaubien Est

Anjou, Quebec H1M 1B2

Canada

Phone: (514) 353-9447

Fax: (514) 353-9550

groupimage@zercom.net

Graphic Arts Technologies

1373 Indian Creek Drive

Wynnewood, PA 19096-3321

zvigat@fast.net

HanMac

DongWoo Building 4F

#784-13 Yeoksam-dong

Kangnam-ku, Seoul

Korea

Phone: 82 2 3452 7235

Fax: 82 2 3452 7238

hanmacsw@nuri.net

www.hanmac.com

HexMac Software Systems

Postfach 100310

70747 Leinfelden-Echterdingen

Germany

Phone: 49 711 9754961

Fax: 49 711 9754962

info@hexmac.com

www.hexmac.com

Hologramophone Research, Inc. (Gluon)

108 E 4th Street, #23

New York, NY 10003

Phone: (212) 529-8845

Fax: (212) 529-2565

ptm@pixound.com

www.hologramophone.com

Imagemakers Software Systems, Inc.

XChange

2700 19th St.

San Francisco, CA 94110

Phone: 1-800-788-7557

info@xchanges.com

www.xchanges.com

John Juliano Computer Services Company

215 Church Street

Suite 205

Decatur, GA 30030

Phone: (404) 377-9450

Fax: (404) 377-9931

jjcs@jjcs.com

www.jjcs.com/~jjcs

KyTek, Inc.

P.O. Box 338

Weare, NH 03281

Phone: (603) 529-2512

Fax: (603) 529-2015

sales@kytek.com

www.mv.com/ipusers/kytek

Live Picture, Inc.

5617 Scotts Valley Drive

Suite 180

Scotts Valley, CA 95066

Phone: (408) 438-9610

Fax: (408) 438-9604

info@livepicture.com

www.livepicture.com

Markzware

1805 E. Dyer Road

Suite 101

Santa Ana, CA 92705

Phone: 1-800-300-3532

Fax: (714) 756-5108

info@markzware.com

www.markzware.com

Meadows Information Systems, Inc.

1305 Reminton Road

Suite G

Schaumburg, IL 60173

Phone: 1-888-XTENSION

meadows@meadowsinfo.com

www.meadowsinfo.com

Media Support & Development

Box 6088

S-600 06 Norrköping

Sweden

Phone: 46 11126600

Fax: 46 11126605

www.msd.se/MSD/Text/Page_1.html

Miles 33 Ltd.

Miles House

Old Bracknell Lane West

Bracknell

Berkshire RG12 7AE

U.K.

Phone: 44 1344 861133

Fax: 44 1344 860224

NAPS (North Atlantic Publishing Systems, Inc.)

9 Acton Road

Suite 13

Chelmsford, MA 01824

Phone: (508) 250-8080

Fax: (508) 250-8179

naps@napsys.com

`www.napsys.com`

Npath Software, Inc.

P.O. Box 523

Issaquah, WA 98027

Phone: (206) 392-7745

Fax: (206) 392-7816

info@npath.com

`www.npath.com`

Patrick Perroud SARL

208, rue de la Convention

MBE 253

75015 Paris

France

Phone: 33 01 45 42 66 23

Fax: 33 01 44 19 60 29

pperroud@speedy.grolier.fr

`www.grolier.fr/pperroud`

PowerHouse Software

P.O. Box 860

Barbara Road

Phillipsport, NY 12769

mike@phsoftware.com

`www.phsoftware.com`

PrimaFont Software

P.O. Box 2123

D-61470 Kronberg

Germany

Scitex America Corp.

Eight Oak Park Drive

Bedford, MA 01730

Phone: (617) 275-5150

Fax: (617) 275-3430

`www.scitex.com`

Second Glance Software

25381-G Alicia Parkway

Suite 357

Laguna Hills, CA 92653

Phone: (360) 692-3694

Fax: (714) 586-0930

info@secondglance.com

`www.secondglance.com`

Strata, Inc.

2nd West St. George Blvd.

St. George, UT 84770

Phone: 1-800-STRATA3D

Fax: (801) 628-9756

sales@strata3d.com

www.strata3d.com

Street Logic Software

11895 River Rim Road

San Diego, CA 92126-1150

Phone: (619) 689-4037

Fax: (619) 586-7875

stlogic@connectnet.com

www.street-logic.com

SYNEX

692 10th Street

Brooklyn, NY 11215-4502

Phone: 1-800-447-9639

synex@snx.com

www.snx.com

System Clinic

8-11-2 Mikagehonmati

Higasinada-ku

Kobe 658

Japan

Phone: 81 78 811 2318

Fax: 81 78 841 1032

Techno Design

jeroen@techno.nl

`www.techno-design.com`

The Last Word Systems PLC

Kiln House

210 New Kings Road

London SW6 4NZ

U.K.

Phone: 44 171 736 7656

Fax: 44 171 731 7655

sales@lastword.demon.co.uk

The NewMedia Workshop Ltd.

15 Hillfoot Road

Shillington

Nr. Hitchin

Hertfordshire SG5 3NH

U.K.

Phone: 01462 712947

info@newmedia-works.co.uk

`www.newmedia-works.co.uk`

Van Gennep Media Automation Consulting BV

Burg. Stramanweg 105

1101 AA Amsterdam

The Netherlands

Phone: 31 20 697 6029

Fax: 31 20 697 2249

info@vangennep.nl

`www.vangennep.nl`

Vision's Edge

3491-11 Thomasville Road

Suite 177

Tallahassee, FL 32308

Phone: 1-800-XTENDER

info@xtender.com

`www.xtender.com`

XTend, Inc.

XChange

2700 19th St.

San Francisco, CA 94110

Phone: 1-800-788-7557

info@xchanges.com

`www.xchanges.com`

York Graphic Services, Inc.

3600 West Market Street

York, PA 17404

Glossary

8-bit color: Color mode in which a computer monitor can display 256 different colors at one time.

16-bit color: Color mode in which a computer monitor can display 32,768 different colors at one time.

24-bit color: Color mode in which a computer monitor can display more than 16 million different colors at one time.

A

Acrobat: A technology from Adobe Systems, Inc., that enables documents to be displayed and printed by anyone with the free Acrobat Reader software, regardless of the documents' originating application.

alignment: Manner in which lines of text are lined up—flush with the left, right, center, or both sides of a text box.

alpha channel: An extra channel in a raster image containing image data that can be used to mask parts of the image.

angle: In printing, refers to the angle of the dot rows in a line screen; each color of ink in color printing needs to be printed at a different angle.

ascender: The part of a letter that extends above the letter's main body; the vertical stroke of a lowercase "d," for example.

ASCII: A data-encoding format that can represent most alphanumeric characters; ASCII files are often called "plain text" files because they don't contain formatting information, just text.

auto leading: An amount of leading determined by a page layout program based on a percentage of the text point size.

Auto Save: QuarkXPress feature that automatically saves documents at a specified time interval.

automatic text box: Text box on a master page that is linked to the Automatic Text Link icon so that when the text in the corresponding box on a document page overflows, a new page is added to the document.

auxiliary dictionary: Spell-checking dictionary containing terms not found in the main dictionary.

B

background color: The color within a box.

baseline: The imaginary line along which the bases of letters rest.

baseline grid: A set of non-printing horizontal guides at a specified distance interval, usually set to match the leading amount that will be used in a document.

baseline shift: To move characters up or down so that their bases no longer rest on the baseline.

Bézier curve: A curve defined by the location of two endpoints and four points whose distance and angle from the endpoints determine the shape of the curve.

Binary: A data encoding format that is more compact than ASCII encoding but sometimes less comprehensible to older hardware and software.

bleed: To extend off the edge of a page.

blend: A gradient created by the combination of two or more colors.

blend color: The color that is combined with a box's background color to create a blend.

book file: QuarkXPress file that contains information about a group of QuarkXPress documents that together make up a larger document such as a book.

border: A frame around the edge of a box.

C

center-aligned: Centered with respect to the center of a text box.

character attributes: Text formatting attributes (such as font and point size) that can be applied on a character level, rather than to an entire paragraph.

clipping path: A path defined within a raster image that determines the image's silhouette; parts of the image outside the clipping path are not displayed or printed from within QuarkXPress.

CMS: Color management system.

collate: To print each of a set of copies as a whole before printing the remaining copies.

color depth: The number of colors contained in an image (see 8-bit color, 16-bit color, 24-bit color).

color management software: Software designed to make color reproduction more accurate in scanning, onscreen, and in color printouts.

color picker: A dialog box that shows the available color choices in one or more color space.

color separation: Printout of a document in which a separate page is made for each ink color that will be used on press when the document is printed.

color space: A model representing the colors that can be described by a particular method of quantifying color, such as RGB or CMYK.

complex box: A box made up of smaller boxes combined into one shape; the component boxes may or may not touch each other.

composite color printer: A device that produces color proofs rather than color-separated film or printing plates.

constrain: To restrict the movement and size of one XPress element by placing it within another element.

Content tool: Tool that enables you to edit the contents of a box, such as text or a picture, rather than the box itself.

copyfitting: Adjusting text formatting and editing text to make text fit in a certain space.

corner point: Point on a Bézier curve whose adjacent curve segments extend at different angles.

corner radius: Measurement determining how round corners of a box are; the number represents the radius of the largest circle that fits neatly into the rounded corner.

D

descender: The part of a letter that extends below the letter's main body; the vertical stroke of a lowercase "p," for example.

device profile: Part of a color management system that describes the color reproduction characteristics of a particular hardware device, such as a scanner, monitor, or color printer.

diacritical marks: Accents and other characters that indicate how a letter is pronounced.

display ad: Advertisement purchased on the basis of the space it will occupy, rather than how many words or letters its text contains.

document page: The basic unit of a QuarkXPress document, as opposed to a master page.

E

em space: Traditionally, a space as wide as the point size of the font in which it's used; in modern usage, a space as wide as two zero characters in the font in which it's used.

embedded graphic: Image that is copied into a document rather than referenced; once the image is copied, the application never again refers to the original image file.

empty boxes: Boxes that cannot contain text or images.

en space: Traditionally, a space half as wide as the point size of the font in which it's used; in modern usage, a space as wide as a zero character in the font in which it's used.

endcap: Arrowhead or other graphic attached to the end of a line.

endmark: Graphic placed at the end of an article in a magazine or other publication.

F

facing pages: Pages designated as "left" or "right" and defined by the elements placed on the left and right pages of their corresponding master page spreads.

fill: The color inside a box; background color.

film: The material used to make traditional metal printing plates.

flex space: A space whose width can be defined by the user's preference.

folio: Page number.

frequency: In printing, the number of rows of dots per inch in a line screen.

G

generic master pages: Non-editable master pages that can be applied to a document page to remove all master page elements.

GIF: Graphic Interchange Format, a graphic file format commonly used on the Internet for flat-colored graphics like logos.

Grabber Hand: Tool that enables you to drag the page around onscreen just as you would move a piece of paper on your desktop with your hand.

grayscale: Refers to an image containing only white, black, and shades of gray.

greeked: Traditionally, greek text was nonsense text used to create a design layout before the actual text was available; in page layout applications, greeked text is displayed as gray bars and greeked graphics as gray boxes.

group: A set of elements "fastened" together such that they can't be moved or resized individually with the Item tool.

guides: Non-printing colored lines onscreen that help in positioning elements.

gutter: Space between columns of text.

H

hairline rule: The finest rule a particular printer or imagesetter can generate; usually .25 points or thinner.

halftone: A photograph converted to small dots of varying sizes that give the appearance of different shades and/or colors to areas of the image. All the black or gray areas of an image will be printed with black ink, for example, but the dots of ink will be smaller in the lighter gray areas.

Hexachrome: A six-color hi-fi printing system created by Pantone; it adds orange and green inks to Pantone's enhanced versions of cyan, magenta, yellow, and black ink.

hi-fi color: Short for high-fidelity color; a variety of methods, including six-color printing and stochastic screening, that achieve premium results in printing.

horizontal scaling: Stretching letters horizontally so that they're wider than the normal width of the characters.

hot text: Text in an Immedia project that acts as a hyperlink, displaying another page, linking the viewer to a Web site, or performing another action when clicked.

HTML: HyperText Markup Language, the coding language used on the World Wide Web and interpreted by Web browsers to display text in different sizes and styles.

hyphenation: The process of inserting hyphens between syllables in words to make text fit better in its specified column width.

I

ICC: International Color Consortium, the organization that established the standard format for device profiles.

imagesetter: High-resolution printing device that can produce paper or film output.

imported graphic: A graphic file whose location is referenced in a page layout document, rather than the entire image's being stored as part of the page layout file; also called a referenced graphic.

indention: The correct term for what most people call indentation, the space between the text margin and the point at which the text actually begins.

index markers: Invisible indicators used to mark text referenced in an index.

inline box: A box pasted into a text flow so that it flows with the text as though it were a text character.

inside margin: The inner margin on one of a pair of facing pages—the right margin on a left page and the left margin on a right page.

Item tool: Tool that enables you to edit a box itself rather than its contents, such as text or a picture.

J

JPEG: Joint Photographic Experts Group format, a graphic file format commonly used on the Internet for graphics that contain gradients, like photographs.

justification: The process of inserting or removing space between words and letters so that text fits within its allotted column width.

K

kerning: Adding or removing space between individual pairs of letters to improve the appearance of text.

knockout: In printing, forcing all color behind an element not to print, so that the element itself is the only color at that point on the page; see overprint.

L

landscape: Horizontal (wide) page orientation; see portrait.

leading: Vertical space from the baseline of a line of text to the baseline of the following line; measured in points.

left-aligned: Placed along the left edge of a text box.

letterspacing: Spacing applied between each pair of letters in a range of text; also called tracking.

library: QuarkXPress file used to store elements that can be placed in a document by dragging them out of the library onto the document's pages.

ligatures: Special, "streamlined" characters used to replace particular letter combinations such as "ff" and "fi."

line screen: Pattern of dots necessary to reproduce shaded graphics and photographs.

M

master page: Non-printing page in a document that can be used as a template for creating and editing document pages.

moiré: Pattern resulting from the intersection of rows of dots in a line screen.

monospaced: Refers to a typeface in which each letter is the same width.

N

negative: Printout in which all color values are reversed—black is printed as white (or clear, in the case of film) and so on.

O

OLE: Object Linking and Embedding, a Windows feature that enables for automatic updating of modified text or graphics files.

OPI: Open Prepress Interface, a software system that enables designers to work with low-resolution image files for the sake of speed and then substitute the high-resolution versions automatically when final output is done.

orthogonal line: A straight horizontal or vertical line.

outside margin: The outer margin on one of a pair of facing pages—the left margin on a left page and the right margin on a right page.

overprint: In printing, forcing all colors behind an element to print, so that the color produced by the printing is a combination of all the element colors at that point on the page; see knockout.

overset text: Text at the end of a flow for which there's no room in the text box or boxes containing the flow; it remains stored at the end of the flow but is not visible.

P

PANTONE: Color reference system containing a large selection of colors available by mixing Pantone colored inks (as opposed to mixing process inks).

paragraph attributes: Text formatting attributes (such as leading and indents) that are applied on a paragraph-wide level, rather than to individual characters within a paragraph.

pasteboard: The area around the page in a QuarkXPress document; objects on the pasteboard won't be printed but will be saved with the document for future use.

PDF: Portable Document Format, the format in which Acrobat documents are saved; see Acrobat.

picture box: Box that can contain an imported graphic.

plates: Pieces of film or metal representing the parts of a document page that will be printed in a particular ink; while the term properly refers to the printing plates, it's also sometimes used to refer to the pieces of color-separated film that are used to make printing plates.

point size: Text size measured in points (72 points = 1 inch). Traditionally, point size referred to the size of the piece of metal type rather than the letter itself, so it's somewhat larger than the height of the characters.

portrait: Vertical (tall) page orientation.

PostScript: Graphics language that uses mathematics to define graphics and text in terms of objects and their positions on a page.

PostScript error: A printing error that results when a printer or other output device doesn't properly comprehend the PostScript code that's sent to it.

PostScript file: A file containing a document translated into PostScript from its original format (such as a QuarkXPress document); PostScript files can be printed by downloading them to a PostScript printer, without the need to use the document's originating application.

preferences: User-customizable software settings.

preview: Part of an image file that contains a low-resolution version of the image that can be stored in a QuarkXPress file that uses the image.

print styles: Print setting configurations that can be saved and assigned names.

printer driver: System software that allows applications to communicate with printers and take advantage of each printer's special features.

process ink colors: Cyan, magenta, yellow, and black, the four colors used in traditional full-color printing.

project: QuarkImmedia multimedia document.

Publish and Subscribe: Mac OS feature that enables automatic updating of modified text or graphics files.

R

raster image: Image defined in terms of pixels rather than one created in PostScript or another graphics language that defines images in terms of points, lines, strokes, and fills.

recto: Right page.

referenced graphic: A graphic file whose location is referenced in a page layout document, rather than the entire image's being stored as part of the page layout file; also called an imported graphic.

registration: Proper alignment of printing plates so that each color prints in the correct position with regard to the other colors.

resolution: The number of pixels per inch in a raster image.

right-aligned: Placed along the right edge of a text box.

rulers: Areas along the top and left sides of a document window marked in user-definable measurement units.

running head: Text along the top of a page, usually containing information about the document such as its title, the author's name, and the current page number.

S

scripting: Creating simple "programs" that automate tasks in QuarkXPress or another program; the Mac OS's built-in scripting language is called AppleScript.

selection handle: Point along the edge of a box that can be dragged to resize the box.

separation characters: Characters used in index entries to separate text from page numbers and in ranges of page numbers.

separation: Color separations.

skew: To angle an XPress element by moving its top without moving its base.

small caps: Characters shaped like uppercase letters but sized like lowercase letters.

Smart Quotes: QuarkXPress feature that substitutes typographer's (or curly) quotation marks and apostrophes for straight ones as the user types.

smooth point: Point on a Bézier curve whose adjacent curve segments connect smoothly through the point.

spot color: Color that will be reproduced by a specific ink color instead of a combination of process ink colors.

spread: Two facing pages.

stacking order: The back-to-front order in which elements are placed on a page.

stochastic screening: Screening method in which dots are placed randomly instead of in lines (see line screen); this screening method eliminates moiré patterns.

style sheets: User-specified groups of paragraph and/or character attributes that can be named and applied to text all at once.

subscript: Small character placed below the baseline.

substrate: Printing medium, such as paper or plastic.

superior: Small character whose top is vertically aligned with the top of full-size characters in the same font and size.

superscript: Small character placed above the baseline.

swatchbook: Printed booklet of color samples.

symmetrical point: Point on a Bézier curve whose adjacent curve segments extend at the same angle.

T

tab leader: Characters, such as periods, placed in the area defined by a tab character; for example, in a table of contents there is often a tab leader between each chapter title on the left and the page number on the right.

template: A QuarkXPress document file that, when opened, actually opens an untitled document identical to itself.

text box: A box that can contain text.

text cursor: The blinking vertical line that indicates where the next character to be typed will appear.

text inset: The amount of space between the inner edge of a text box and the point at which the text begins on all sides.

text path: Straight or curved line with text attached to it and running along it.

thumbnail: Small representation of a page that's not intended to be readable but to give a general idea of the page's appearance.

TIFF: Tag Image File Format, a raster image format used for print publishing.

tile: Print in several pieces, or tiles, that are then manually reattached; used for documents too large to fit on one piece of paper.

tracking: Spacing applied between each pair of letters in a range of text; also called letterspacing.

transitions: Special visual effects used when moving from one page to another in an Immedia project.

trapping: Adjusting the size and shape of colored elements on a page to allow for possible misregistration on press.

TruMatch: Color reference system containing a large selection of colors available in four-color process printing.

Type 1 font: PostScript font in the most common format; generally considered more reliable than TrueType fonts, the most common alternative.

U

URL: Uniform Resource Locator, the "address" of a Web page or other file on the Internet (such as `http://www.quark.com`).

V

vector image: Image created in PostScript or another graphics language that defines images in terms of points, lines, strokes, and fills rather than in terms of pixels.

verso: Left page.

X

X and Y coordinates: Numbers that define the position of an element with respect to the upper-left corner of a page or spread.

XPress Tags: Coding language that adds formatting information to plain text.

XTensions: Add-on software, both from Quark and from third parties, that expands QuarkXPress's feature set.

Z

Zoom tool: Tool that enables you to change the view magnification of a document.

Index

Symbols

A

B

C

E

I

N

O

P

Q

R

S

T

X

Y - Z

JUST TYPE

The No-Hype Type CD contains 500 original fonts for either Macintosh or Windows 95 computers. All typefaces are in both Apple's TrueType and Adobe's PostScript 1 formats. There are no unlocking fees or shareware fonts. Fonts come with the accented characters and punctuation of Western European languages.

The CD contains an assortment of faces you will find nowhere else, ranging from the Elegant to the Mundane, from the ornate to the Plain, from the Irritating to the insane, even a font for THE RAIN!

For more information, e-mail <bobs@kagi.edu> and a message.

Special offer (expires June 30, 1998)
Send this form and payment of $25 to receive a copy of the No-Hype Type CD (Mac and Windows 95 only)

Name:______________________
Address:______________________
____
City:______________________
State:______________________
ZIP:______________________
e-mail:______________________

Complete and mail to:

Ingrimayne Type
PO Box 404
Rensselaer, IN 47978-0404

<http://homepage.usr.com/b/bobs>

Technical Support:

If you need assistance with the information in this book or with a CD/Disk accompanying the book, please access the Knowledge Base on our Web site at **http://www.superlibrary.com/general/support**. Our most Frequently Asked Questions are answered there. If you do not find the answer to your questions on our Web site, you may contact Macmillan Technical Support **(317) 581-3833** or e-mail us at **support@mcp.com**.